Democracy and Markets

A volume in the series

Cornell Studies in Political Economy

EDITED BY PETER J. KATZENSTEIN

A full list of titles in the series appears at the end of the book

Democracy and Markets

The Politics of Mixed Economies

John R. Freeman

Cornell University Press

Ithaca and London

First published 1989 by Cornell University Press.

International Standard Book Number (cloth) 0-8014-2326-0
International Standard Book Number (paper) 0-8014-9601-2
Library of Congress Catalog Card Number 89-869
Printed in the United States of America
Librarians: Library of Congress cataloging information
appears on the last page of the book.

The paper in this book is acid-free and meets the guidelines for permanence
and durability of the Committee on Production Guidelines
for Book Longevity of the Council on Library Resources.

For Barbara

Contents

Preface   ix

PART ONE INTRODUCTION

1. Which Political-Economic System Is Most Desirable?   3
2. Theoretical Perspectives   21

PART TWO THEORY

3. Private Enterprise and Mixed Economies Compared   57
4. Democratic Polities Compared   82
5. The Politics of Mixed Economies   97

PART THREE EVIDENCE

6. Welfare Outcomes: Cross-national Evidence   137
7. A Tale of Two Political Economies   149
8. The Italian and Swedish Experiences   203

PART FOUR EXTENSIONS AND IMPLICATIONS

9. The Politics of Openness and Foreign Public Enterprise   227
10. The Tale of Two Political Economies Revisited   252
11. Democracy and Capitalism   273

References   287
Index   305

Preface

Studies of political economy range from liberal analyses of the rationale for and consequences of government intervention in markets to radical critiques of the privileged position of business in market-oriented systems and the threat this position poses for democracy. Their epistemological underpinnings also vary tremendously, from thick descriptions and qualitative studies of the political and economic institutions of particular countries to mathematical and statistical analyses of various political-economic relationships, such as that between voting and economic policy.

This book emphasizes the threads common to all these works. What ties these studies together, I argue, is a concern with fundamental questions. Are some forms of democratic capitalism more desirable than others? Is some alternative political-economic system more desirable than *any* form of democratic capitalism? These questions motivate most of the work done in political economy and, in turn, define it as a field of study.

Existing work provides some answers to these fundamental questions, but in at least two respects these answers are not satisfying. First, they are based on a poor understanding of public ownership rights and of the workings of economies where such rights are prevalent—that is, *mixed economies*. Mixed economies are those in which governments own and operate a substantial number of firms and in which a large number of investment decisions are in public hands. In *private enterprise economies*, in contrast, most or all firms are owned privately and most investment decisions are in private hands. Political economists do not understand how these two kinds of economy differ, let alone how their logics are interconnected with the logics of such democratic institutions as electoral systems and modes of interest intermediation. These logics and interconnections are the primary focus of this book.

Second, modern political economy suffers from the use of an underdeveloped or incomplete set of welfare criteria. One set of studies emphasizes the relative efficiency of political-economic systems and the resulting collective welfare gains or the intergenerational distribution of wealth. Another emphasizes the intragenerational distribution of wealth that is achieved within different political-economic systems. In effect, these two bodies of literature talk past one another; the possibility that one form of democratic capitalism might satisfy both welfare criteria is not seriously considered. Here I apply a more complete set of welfare criteria—a framework that incorporates both collective gain or loss and distributional equity.

This book analyzes the workings and welfare consequences of four basic types of political-economic systems: pluralist–private enterprise, corporatist–private enterprise, pluralist–mixed, and corporatist–mixed. The result is a welfare taxonomy for these four basic systems, that is, a characterization of the *blends* of collective gain and distributional equity that can be achieved in them. This taxonomy implies that, in terms of societal consumption, corporatist–private enterprise political economies produce the highest and that pluralist–mixed political economies produce the lowest levels and rates. It also implies that pluralist–private enterprise systems have the greatest and corporatist–mixed systems the least potential for producing maldistributions of wealth between private asset holders and wage earners. How pronounced are the differences in the performance of the four political economies? The answer is determined by the character of state administration, the development and workings of capital markets, the degree of societal dissensus over the ends and means of government market intervention, and the citizens' willingness and ability to exercise public ownership rights through certain political institutions. Several meso-level propositions also emerge from the analysis of the four systems. For example, political business cycles in public investment, if they exist at all, are more prevalent in pluralist–mixed than in corporatist–mixed systems. Finally, the analysis is extended to incorporate the politics of openness and of foreign public enterprise. In this context I derive some additional propositions about such things as the relative power of private enterprise and state enterprise workers in closed and in open systems.

The validity of the welfare taxonomy and the analysis on which it is based is demonstrated through a brief examination of the performance of countries with different kinds of political-economic systems and through studies of the workings of four particular national systems. The countries I examine are Britain (pluralist–private enterprise), Sweden (corporatist–private enterprise), Italy (pluralist–mixed), and Austria (corporatist–mixed). The analysis is qualitative rather than quantitative, because the quasi-experimental setting does not allow meaningful statistical tests of the theory developed here (see Freeman and Wilson 1986; Freeman and Job 1979). The quasi-experimental setting does allow for meaningful statistical tests of some meso-level propositions, and these tests are reported elsewhere (Freeman 1988; Freeman and Alt 1987).

Regarding the two basic concerns that define the field of political economy, this book explains why democratic mixed systems might be preferable to democratic private enterprise systems. Both public enterprise and private enterprise are, in some senses, incompatible with democracy. Under certain conditions a pluralist–private enterprise system would be more compatible with democracy than a pluralist–mixed political economy; under other conditions the opposite would be true. These conditions relate to factors already mentioned: citizens' willingness and ability to exercise their public ownership rights through certain political institutions (citizens' sense of "collective ownership efficacy"), and other factors such as the size of public and private firms. Under *prevailing* political and economic conditions, I conclude, the corporatist–mixed system produces a relatively high degree of collective gain and a modicum of distributional equity while, at the same time, preserving important democratic norms and procedures.

As one trained to focus on meso-level propositions that could be formalized and tested with quantitative techniques, I found the writing of this book a challenge. Many people helped me meet this challenge. Foremost was my wife, Barbara, who, over the years, gave me countless hours to work on the book and, despite repeated changes in the completion date, never doubted my ability to finish it. Here, too, the patience of my sons, Bryan and Thomas, should be acknowledged. I thank them for the many nights they waited patiently for their bedtime stories and for the many afternoons they waited patiently for me to come home and play with them. Without the support of Barbara, Bryan, and Thomas I would not have finished this book.

Two other people should be thanked in this context. The first is the late Ithiel de Sola Pool, who taught me the importance of the larger questions that motivate the study of political economy and how my early work helped answer these questions. Peter Katzenstein is the second. He convinced me to contribute to the series Cornell Studies in Political Economy. Through his prompt and constructive feedback, he taught me a lot not only about how to write a book but also about what I wanted to say.

Numerous other people and agencies supported this project. I have benefited greatly from comments received from my colleagues Ernest J. Wilson, Raymond Duvall, Walter Dean Burnham, Raymond Duch, Richard Samuels, Kaare Strom, Dennis Quinn, and Michael Wallerstein. An anonymous reviewer also made several useful suggestions about how to structure the book. Able research assistance was provided by Kevin Brown, Tse-min Lin, Karilyn Komp, Mary Sexton, and Jutta Weldes. They performed statistical analyses for me and also helped translate German documents into English. Valuable information about contacts in Britain and Austria were secured through the good offices of the British Nationalised Industries Chairmen's Group, Oesterreichische Industrieverwaltungs-Aktiengesellschaft, Sozialwissenschaftliche Studiengesellschaft, and Austrian Press and Information Service. These contacts and others were the bases of interviews I conducted in London in October 1984 and in Vienna and Linz in October 1984 and November 1986. I thank all the people who were willing to meet with me in both countries. I am especially grateful for the help and advice I received from three individuals: Erich Andrlik, James Driscoll, and Ewald Nowotny.

The main financial support for the project came from the National Science Foundation under Grant Number NSF8318887. Additional support was provided by the Department of Political Science, Center for Western European Studies, Center for Austrian Studies, Office of International Programs, and College of Liberal Arts, all at the University of Minnesota. Of course, none of these individuals or agencies is responsible for the contents of this book or other publications that have emerged from my project.

Last and by no means least I thank the people who helped produce this book. Foremost among these are Roger Haydon of Cornell University Press and Mary Ellen Otis of the University of Minnesota. Roger's editorial advice proved invaluable in the closing stages of the project. Mary Ellen helped copyedit the manuscript, and she also handled all the word-processing. How she remained so pleasant and helpful over the years—especially on those days I had exceeded my coffee limit—I will never know. But I do know that without her help the book would have been many more months in the making. Thanks, "MEO."

JOHN R. FREEMAN

Minneapolis, Minnesota

PART ONE

INTRODUCTION

CHAPTER ONE

Which Political-Economic System
Is Most Desirable?

The events of the 1970s and 1980s spawned much debate in the United States and other countries about the desirability of existing political and economic institutions. Citizens and policy makers questioned the effectiveness of their political-economic systems. They asked whether their institutions ought to be restructured to make them more like institutions in countries that seemed to be performing so much better.[1]

This interest in alternative ways of organizing politics and economics has abated somewhat in more recent years. Many Americans believe that their country performs as well as many other Western countries, or that the crises of the 1970s and 1980s have ended. But it is not clear that the performance of the United States matches that of other countries. A massive national debt and an increasing gap between rich and poor suggest that serious distributional inequities have arisen in recent years.[2] In addition, it is likely that the 1990s will bring new economic crises comparable to those we witnessed in the 1970s and 1980s, as once again we will be forced to cope with major changes in the terms of world trade. For these reasons, the issue of institutional reform continues to capture the imagination of citizens and policy makers.

This book locates that interest in alternative political-economic systems in larger debates about democracy and markets. The basic issue underlying our interest in institutional reform, I argue, is the ques-

1. For the United States, illustrative works include Rohatyn (1983), Bluestone and Harrison (1982), Dahl (1982, 1985), and Lindblom (1977).
2. For instance, the much-heralded increase in the number of jobs in the United States in recent years may in some part be a "feminization of poverty"; see, for instance, Wilensky and Turner (1987: 80–84).

tion whether some forms of democratic capitalism are preferable to others. Is mixed ownership preferable to private ownership? And is a pluralist type of democratic politics preferable to a corporatist type of democratic politics? A related, if secondary, issue is whether there is a feasible, democratic socialist alternative to democratic capitalism. Is there, for instance, a viable way of organizing the polity and economy such that politics is democratic but no large-scale enterprises are privately owned? These deeper questions motivate the recent comparisons of political-economic systems. They are questions this book seeks to answer.

This opening chapter is an overview of my argument. I begin with a brief summary of the answers other theorists have produced over the last fifteen years and a critique of the analyses from which those answers derive.[3] Our understanding of democratic capitalism rests on weak empirical footings; it is based on an inadequate set of welfare criteria; and it fails to appreciate important differences in the workings of certain economic and political institutions. The keys to deciding which form of democratic capitalism is preferable—and to gaining some insight about whether there is a feasible, democratic socialist alternative—lie in the comparison of (1) the logics of private enterprise and mixed economies, (2) the logics of pluralist and corporatist forms of democracy, and (3) the ways the *interconnection* of these economic and political logics produce fundamentally different opportunities for realizing both collective gains for and distributional equity among living and future generations.

THE DEBATE

The Case for Particular Forms of Democratic Capitalism

The major schools of political economy make fundamentally different claims about the most desirable form of democratic capitalism. Liberals either stress the virtues of certain forms of democracy and ignore ownership structures altogether or stress the value of combining certain types of democracy with private enterprise. The former line of thought holds that some political institutions enhance the workings of markets and, in turn, improve the collective welfare of the citizens more than other political institutions do.

The case for democratic corporatism illustrates this first strain of liberal thought, which holds that corporatist types of interest intermediation together with proportional types of electoral systems yield

3. Chapter 2 contains a more thorough review of the literature.

welfare outcomes superior to pluralist types of interest intermediation and electoral systems with single-member districts. In particular, democratic corporatist political systems exploit the "logics" of domestic and international markets in ways that yield higher growth rates and lower unemployment and inflation rates than do democratic pluralist political systems. Democratic pluralist political systems, according to this view, make labor and other markets inflexible and hence comparatively less efficient. The superior performance of small West European countries relative to large West European and North American countries is presumed to demonstrate the validity of this thesis, since the former countries have democratic corporatist systems and the latter have democratic pluralist systems.[4]

A related strain of liberal thinking argues that consensual democracy and private enterprise combine to produce the most desirable kind of political economy.[5] Defenders of this view argue that *all* forms of interest-group and party politics are socially harmful because they produce arbitrary or unjust distributions of wealth together with collective welfare losses. Interest-group politics produces uncertainty about the course of fiscal policy, for example, and so discourages long-term investment. These liberal thinkers hold that distributional issues should be resolved consensually or "naturally" by the market. Macroeconomic policies should also be made consensually, on the basis of some mutual understanding of the workings of domestic and international markets or on the basis of some mutual deference to technocratic authority.

This body of work maintains that state-owned enterprise is incompatible with democracy. In democracies, state-owned enterprise is manipulated by self-interested politicians or bureaucrats, whereas private enterprise is subject to impersonal market forces, including the shareholding transactions of private property owners. Market forces yield welfare outcomes more just and efficient than do nonmarket forces such as those that arise from electoral competition. Electoral competition and other facets of democratic politics presumably produce arbitrary distributions of wealth and inefficient market out-

4. The case for democratic corporatism is exemplified by Katzenstein (1984, 1985). He defines democratic corporatism in terms of an ideology of social partnership expressed at the national level; a relatively centralized and concentrated system of interest groups; and voluntary and informal coordination of conflicting objectives through continuous political bargaining among interest groups, state bureaucracies, and political parties (1985:32). Pluralism differs in all these respects but especially in its embracing multiple decentralized, nonofficial interest groups that espouse no such ideology. See Schmitter (1979, 1981).

5. The distinction between majoritarian and consensual democracy is made by Lijphart (1984). Simply put, the latter system restrains majority rule and promotes more dispersal and sharing of political power than the former.

comes. These harmful effects are most prevalent in mixed economies, where segments of the workforce and some managers use state-owned enterprise to capture an unfair share of wealth as well as to prevent adjustments that would augment collective consumption.

Commentaries on the "British Sickness" illustrate this line of thought. Britain's economic performance in the 1970s and early 1980s, comparatively poor in terms of growth and employment, is traced by this group of liberal thinkers to the deleterious effects interest-group and electoral competition have had on the macroeconomic policies of government and on the behavior of the country's nationalized industries. Commentators call for a new British consensus on macroeconomic policy and support privatization of British public enterprise.[6]

Radical political economists, by contrast, hold that all forms of democratic capitalism are undesirable because they all produce distributional inequity between capitalists and wage earners. As they see it, privately owned enterprise is incompatible with democracy. According to radical thought, the distributional inequities that markets produce are neither natural nor just. Rather, inequities are outgrowths of exploitation—exploitation that derives from the way property rights are distributed in capitalist society. Private property confers investment rights. The welfare of wage earners depends on how these private investment rights are executed; if private owners refuse to invest or disinvest, wage earners' current and future welfare suffers. It follows that wage earners are constrained in their ability to tax and to regulate private enterprise by private owners' threats of disinvestment. Electoral and other forms of democratic politics therefore have little or no impact on the distribution of wealth in Western societies. All parties, including workers' parties, are "structurally dependent" on private owners and privately owned enterprise. Wage earners cannot adopt redistributive policies without provoking private disinvestment and hence harming the welfare of their constituents and of future generations of citizens. Radicals point to the enduring gap between the income levels of rich and poor in all Western societies and the minimal impact elections have on various indicators of social equality in Western democracies as evidence of the "structural depen-

6. This is the strain of liberal theory associated with the "ungovernability thesis." Reviews of this segment of the literature include Birch (1984). The proposition that state enterprise is incompatible with democracy—that a drift to bureaucratic socialism inevitably results—is advanced by Dahl (1982, 1985). The conventional wisdom that democracy renders state enterprise inefficient is presented by Monsen and Walters (1979). Applications of both ideas to the British case include Birch (1984), Brittan (1984), Corti (1976), and Redwood and Hatch (1982); see also Zysman (1983:229–32).

6

dency" of the corresponding governments on privately owned enterprise.[7]

Interestingly, one strain of radical theory argues that democratic corporatism constitutes the least undesirable form of democratic capitalism. These radicals contend that wage earners' power is greatest where politics is corporatist. However, they are quick to point out that even in such cases the distribution of social power is still skewed toward the owners of private enterprises because these private owners continue to make investment decisions and hence to determine the future flow of wages and consumption. It is in this vein some radicals suggest that workers in some Scandinavian countries are less exploited than workers in other Western countries.[8]

The Case for Democratic Socialism

Radicals contend that there is an alternative to democratic capitalism: democratic socialism. They suggest that all forms of democratic socialism are preferable to all forms of democratic capitalism. Democratic socialism will supposedly meet more of the basic needs of *all* of a country's citizens than will democratic capitalism. Radicals' visions of democratic socialism differ. As regards the economy, some advocate the virtual elimination of private enterprise and the creation of self-governed or public enterprises. Others propose *mixed* economies composed of state-owned firms, cooperatives, small-scale private firms, and "freelancers" (e.g., journalists and artists).[9] Almost all radicals provide for some form of democratic planning or for what one theorist refers to as "[popularly] articulated self-management, based on deliberate and free cooperation." In this context the advocates of democratic socialism propose that citizens rely on a wide range of electoral processes and majority rule to make economic and political decisions.[10] Radicals readily admit that their preferred system is more

7. The works of Lindblom (1977, 1980), Offe (1983), and Wright (1984) are illustrative. See also Dahl's critique of corporate capitalism (1985). Evidence that elections and worker party incumbency have little impact on various facets of social equality is reviewed by Jackman (1980, 1986).

8. See, for example, Przeworski (1980c); see also the review in Jackman (1986).

9. Mandel (1986) advocates the elimination of private enterprise and of all forms of market competition; the same position is taken by radical groups such as those that publish the *New Unionist* in the United States. Nove (1983:227–28) proposes a democratic socialist system with a *mixed* ownership structure and certain other features, including conscious planning by an authority responsible to an elected assembly for major investments of "structural significance."

10. The quotation is from Mandel (1986:25). Mandel stresses (p. 50) that Nove's plan (1983) rests on a foundation of multiparty democracy with periodic elections to a parliament; see Nove (1986:50, 91, 121, 208, 210, 216). Mandel also advocates majori-

hypothetical than real. In making their case for democratic socialism, they therefore refer to but do not attach a great deal of importance to the actual experiences of Eastern countries and various socialistic communities in different parts of the world. Frequently, for instance, radicals refer to the experiences of Hungary and Yugoslavia.[11]

THE WEAK UNDERPINNINGS OF THE DEBATE

Evidence and Welfare Criteria

This debate rests on shaky empirical footings. For example, much evidence suggests that, in democratic countries, the *financial* performance of state-owned enterprise is indeed inferior to the *financial* performance of privately owned enterprise. However, the liberals' claim that democratic countries with private enterprise economies outperform those with mixed economies is difficult to prove. Rather, data such as those depicted in Figure 1 show no simple relationship between scope of state-owned enterprise investment and growth rate in democratic countries. One reason is that Austria and France have high rates of growth (and productivity) despite large numbers of state-owned enterprises and substantial amounts of public investment. In the United States, on the other hand, there is little state-owned enterprise activity and comparatively little public investment, yet growth (and productivity) rates are relatively low.[12]

Nor is it clear that state-owned enterprise promotes an egalitarian distribution of income or subverts democratic institutions. Anecdotes about wage earners and public managers benefiting from state-owned enterprise are easy to find. But scatterplots of the investment shares of state-owned enterprise on various measures of social equality fail to reveal any systematic differences between countries with private enterprise economies and those with mixed economies (Figure 2). Some countries with mixed economies, such as Italy, have comparatively inegalitarian income distributions. Others, like Sweden, which with the exception of a few years has had a high concentration of private investment, have a relatively egalitarian income distribution.[13]

---

tarian democracy, for firms and for the state (1986:27, 31). Other advocates of democratic socialism do the same. See, for instance, Brus (1985:52) and Dahl (1985:118).

11. Dahl admits that the virtues of his plan are essentially hypothetical (1985:118). Most of his evidence is drawn from the Yugoslavian experience and from accounts of the Mondragon cooperatives of Spain.

12. For more information on the financial performance of European state-owned enterprises in the 1960s and 1970s see Monsen and Walters (1983).

13. There is no simple relationship between the employment share of state-owned enterprises and the distribution of income. Brooks's (1983) analysis of social equality

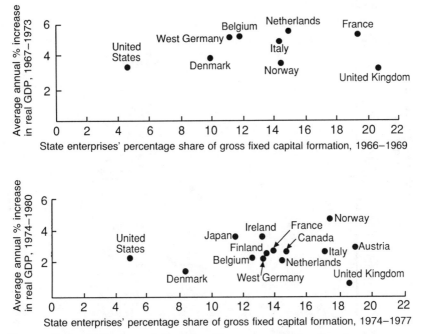

Figure 1. Real growth rates and the scope of state enterprise investment

Notes. Growth rate data are from OECD (1982); state enterprise data from Short (1983: Table 1). For Figure a, state enterprise data for the following countries are from slightly different periods: United States (1967–69), Denmark (the average of 1965 and 1974), Netherlands (1968–70), and Italy (1967–70); for Figure b, state enterprise data are also from slightly different periods for Austria (1976–77), France (1974), Finland (1974–75), and Denmark (1974).

As regards the presumed threat to democracy posed by state-owned enterprise, the French and Austrian election systems rank in some comparative analyses among the four Western systems that afford citizens the *highest* degree of popular control over government decision making. This fact is hard to reconcile with liberal claims that state-owned enterprise, which is so prevalent in these two countries, represents a threat to democracy.[14]

Radical thought rests on weak empirical footings as well. Radicals assume that all democratic countries have private enterprise econo-

---

indicates that although Austria has a highly mixed economy, income distribution there became more *inegalitarian in the period* 1950–1970.

14. For instance, Powell (1986) compares electoral systems in terms of their clarity of responsibility, opportunity for desirable choice, decisiveness, and effectiveness of representation. He finds that among Western democracies only the Austrian, French, West German, and British systems have most of these desiderata.

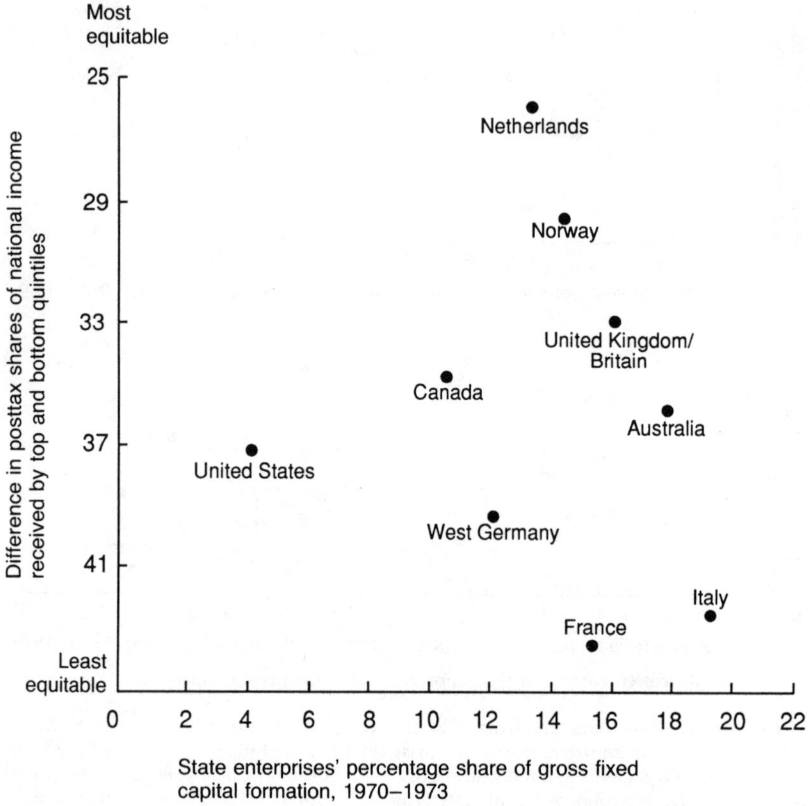

Most
equitable

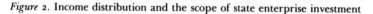

Figure 2. Income distribution and the scope of state enterprise investment

Notes. The source of income distribution data is OECD (1976a); state enterprise data from Short (1983: Table 1). The state enterprise figure for the Netherlands is for the period 1971–73. Income distribution data for Britain and state enterprise data for the United Kingdom are reported. Short does not give data for Sweden in the period 1970–1973. According to the *Statistisk årbok för Sverige* (1971, 1974, 1975) the ratio of state capital investments by state businesses to gross national fixed capital formation was about 5 percent during these years. The ratio of the sum of state capital investments by state businesses and investments by state joint stock companies to gross national fixed capital formation was about 8 percent. Sweden would be located directly to the left of the Netherlands and midway above the United States and Canada in Figure 2.

mies. However, numerous state-owned enterprises operate in national and international markets, and many firms in such industries as autos, steel, energy, and transporation are owned and operated by governments. Even some high-technology sectors have substantial numbers of state-owned businesses operating in them. The economies of Austria and Italy, in fact, are highly mixed. In Austria, for instance, the state owns about two-thirds of the largest fifty firms. Transportation, communications, steel, banking, and other industries are wholly or largely owned by the Austrian state. Together, the nationalized industries and all government bodies account for roughly half of the investment decisions in the Austrian economy.[15]

State-owned enterprises survive and some economies remain mixed despite the so-called privatization wave that has hit Western Europe and other parts of the world. Many recent episodes of privatization are actually attempts at "rationalization" or efforts to reduce the size of government holdings in certain firms, for example, efforts to form joint ventures with privately owned firms. In one Western country, Great Britain, more than twenty public holdings have since been sold off, and more of its public holdings are for sale. In another, France, the government plans to privatize more than sixty publicly owned businesses. However, the British and French cases are unusual.[16] Austria and Italy have sold only a few public holdings, and only a few more are for sale. In Sweden and France the state business sector actually expanded in the late 1970s and early 1980s. The Swedes have not privatized or closed all of these public enterprises; rather, they have attempted to improve their financial performance. It is therefore inaccurate to characterize the economies of several democratic capitalist countries as being of the private enterprise variety. These countries' economies are composed of a genuine *mix* of privately owned and publicly owned enterprise.[17]

More important, there is evidence that state enterprises in some countries behave in ways fundamentally different from private enterprises. The behavior of the Austrian nationalized industries is illustrative. During the recession of the late 1970s the Austrian nationalized industries wholly or partly owned by the government-owned holding company, Oesterreichische Industrieverwaltungsgesellschaft (OeIAG), maintained employment and reduced output and productivity while both total Austrian industry and German industry were maintaining productivity and production and reducing employment (Figure 3). This observation suggests that radicals are correct to assume that state enterprise can have substantially different welfare consequences. However, radicals are incorrect to assume that these

15. On the scope of state enterprise activity in Western Europe and the world in general see Aharoni (1986) and Monsen and Walters (1983). Data on the structure of the Austrian economy are presented in Chapter 7.

16. On privatization see Hemming and Mansoor (1988) and Laux and Molot (1987); *The Economist*, December 21, 1985, and December 20, 1986; and Vernon (1985).

17. These facts clearly indicate that Dahl's (1982:115) and Lindblom's (1977:100) classifications of the world's economies are not only crude but also, for Austria and Italy, incorrect.

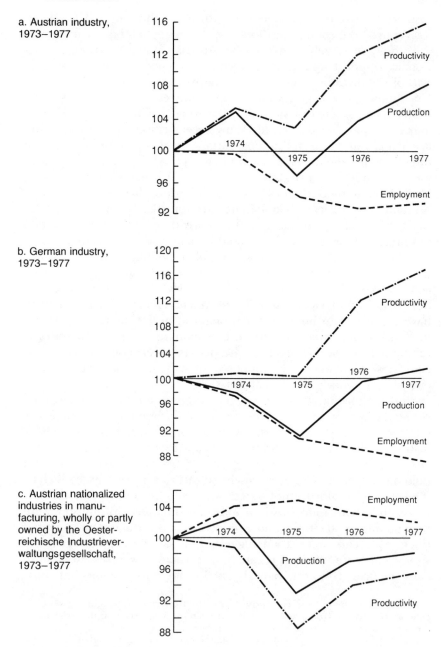

a. Austrian industry, 1973–1977

b. German industry, 1973–1977

c. Austrian nationalized industries in manufacturing, wholly or partly owned by the Oester-reichische Industrieverwaltungsgesellschaft, 1973–1977

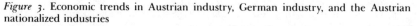

Figure 3. Economic trends in Austrian industry, German industry, and the Austrian nationalized industries

Source: Nowotny (1978), reprinted by permission of the author.

different welfare consequences are not realized in any democratic countries.[18]

The structures of some Western economies and the behavior of the state-owned enterprises that do business in them thus are much more complicated than most theorists realize. Some Western economies are highly mixed; some state-owned enterprises behave in ways that produce welfare outcomes different from those in privately owned enterprises. The theoretical points at issue are why these structural and behavioral differences occur and how they are related to the workings of democratic institutions. Under what conditions do the two types of enterprises produce similar or different blends of output, employment, and income? How do these conditions reflect and affect democratic politics, both pluralist and corporatist? Our interest here is in the *blends* of social welfare that can be achieved in private enterprise economies and mixed economies. We are interested in both collective and distributional consequences of privately owned and state owned enterprise, not in one of these dimensions of social welfare alone. Most liberal theorists emphasize the former welfare criterion whereas radical theorists emphasize the latter. As a result, the two groups talk past each other. We can best speak to our concerns if we evaluate alternative political-economic systems in terms of their ability to promote *both* collective gain *and* distributional equity simultaneously.

The empirical issue is how the experiences of countries with mixed economies and democratic polities differ from those with private enterprise economies and democratic polities. For example, how do the workings and welfare consequences of Austria's corporatist–mixed system differ from the workings and welfare consequences of Britain's new, pluralist–private enterprise system?

Austria is especially important because it has a democratic corporatist political system, which both liberals and radicals agree enhances the relative power and welfare of wage earners, and an economy that ostensibly gives the government a great capacity to redistribute wealth. In fact, Austria may be the best setting in which to study the potential virtues of democratic socialism. Austria more than other parts of the old Austrian-Hungarian empire has a polity and economy that together better approximate the democratic socialist ideal than either Hungary or Yugoslavia. The larger significance of the Austrian experience needs to be more fully appreciated.[19]

18. For parallel discussions of the countercyclical behavior of Italian and French public enterprises see Fausto (1982) and Stoffaes and Gadonneix (1980).

19. Przeworski (1980b:53) and others tend to relegate the Austrian and Italian experiences to the realm of historical accident. Brooks (1983:412) cites Przeworski's work and fails to consider the greater capacity for redistribution in Austria and Italy. Katzenstein (1984, 1985) has produced extensive analyses of the Austrian experience, and his

The British experience also is of much interest, not only because of the British government's recent effort to construct a private enterprise economy but also because in the 1960s and 1970s Britain had a democratic–mixed system. At the end of the 1960s more than 40 percent of gross fixed capital formation in Britain was accounted for by public corporations and other government authorities. And Britain has a highly pluralist polity. So for some part of its recent history Britain is a case of a pluralist–mixed system and as such can tell us something about the potential performance of such systems.[20] Both the Austrian and the British cases are studied in detail in the second half of this book.

Political-Economic Analysis

Neither school of political economy has produced an adequate political-economic analysis of democratic capitalism or of democratic socialism. The case for democratic corporatism rests on claims about the salutary effects of "economic flexibility" and the accommodation of an essentially undefined "market logic." Proponents never fully explain the connections between market processes, market accommodation, and economic performance. For instance, they provide little analysis of the role that capital markets play in promoting or inhibiting economic change—change that promotes productivity and growth in small European countries. We are simply told that wise investments are made in these countries; the wisdom of the investments is inferred ad hoc, with little in-depth analysis of the way capital markets encourage or evaluate the investments of the respective states.[21]

research figures prominently in this book. Katzenstein does address, indirectly, the question of whether ownership structure affects states' capacities to compensate workers for economic change. However, he does not systematically compare the capacity to redistribute wealth of the Austrian government with that of states with private enterprise economies, especially states in pluralist–private enterprise systems such as the United States. Nor does he consider the lessons of the Austrian experience for studies of democratic socialism. Nove, Dahl, and other students of democratic socialism fail to exploit the substantial similarities between the systems they propose and those which exist in Austria and Italy. Nove, for example, draws few lessons from the experiences of these *democratic* capitalist countries. The same is true (surprisingly) of Dahl, who focuses almost exclusively on the Yugoslavian experience.

20. Data on the mixed nature of the British economy of the late 1960s and early 1970s are given in Chapter 7. Interestingly, the history of the United States also provides a laboratory in which to study the politics of mixed economies. See, for example, Hartz (1948), Calendar (1902), and Million (1896). See also accounts of North Dakota's experience with state-owned enterprise, in *Forbes*, January 15, 1975, pp. 38–39.

21. Katzenstein emphasizes the ability of the Austrian state to influence investment decisions (1984:159). But he does not tell us much about how Austrian capital markets affect the state's activities in this regard. Contrast Katzenstein's analysis with Hankel's call to create a regional capital market in Austria (1981:112).

14

Liberal thought generally does not address the effects of disinvest-ment and capital mobility on government capacity to redistribute wealth. Most liberals simply assume that fiscal policy can be used for this purpose (see Chapter 2). Yet radical theory argues, somewhat convincingly, that private investment rights render fiscal policy inef-fective for redistribution, that public ownership is at least a *necessary* condition for governmental redistribution of wealth. The two schools of thought need to confront each other on this issue. As we shall see, in Chapter 3, it is clear that under some conditions, government ca-pacity to redistribute wealth is substantially greater in mixed than in private enterprise economies.

Both liberals and radicals generally ignore the problem of manage-rial control. Liberals assume that private managers respond to market signals in efficient ways whereas state managers ignore these signals. State managers either are willing and able to pursue their own selfish interests or are consistently forced to serve the selfish interests of elected politicians. Radicals, on the other hand, assume that state managers can and will serve some democratically articulated public interest, efficiently and with due concern for the basic needs of all citizens. Radicals downplay or ignore altogether the potential for skill-based exploitation or malevolent behavior on the part of state man-agers. Yet the problem of managerial control exists in all economies. It becomes more pronounced when firms, private and public, expand into world markets and national economies become more open to in-ternational trade and financial flows. Deeper, comparative analysis of the severity of the problem of managerial control in private enter-prise and mixed economies is therefore called for.[22]

Political analyses of democratic capitalism and democratic socialism are seriously incomplete. The reality of societal dissensus over eco-nomic and other policy questions—the widespread disagreements among informed citizens—must be more fully addressed by liberal theorists. The case for democratic corporatism downplays the possi-bility that the social partners regularly harm the interests of certain groups of citizens or that these same citizens are unable to voice their concerns about government policies through corporatist or parlia-mentary channels. Thus, for example, proponents of democratic cor-poratism contend that trade union leaders have put aside the issue of income redistribution for the sake of increases in societal consump-

22. See Chapter 3 below. European political economists such as Edmond Langer (1964) have for years stressed that the problem of managerial control is present in *both* privately owned and publicly owned enterprise. Illustrative of radicals' insensitivity to this fact is Mandel's willingness (1986:25–27) to rely on the benign experts and benign inventors of new technologies. A more reflective, radical treatment of this problem can be found in Wright (1984).

tion and other forms of collective gain and intergenerational equity. Yet they do not supply survey and other kinds of information showing that the rank and file or general citizenry supports leaders' decisions in this regard. Nor do they adequately analyze dissent within producer groups and political parties. In fact, they point out that parliamentary and, by implication, electoral politics are comparatively less important in the small European states that have this kind of political system. But if they are right, then in exactly what sense are these countries "democratic"?[23]

Other liberals presume that citizens have no real conflicts of interest and that democratic institutions can articulate a well-defined popular will. If adequately informed, that is, all citizens would choose a private enterprise economy since they would know that this economic structure makes them all better off.

Consider the popular opinion data in Figure 4. These time series show there has been a marked degree of dissensus in Britain over nationalization. Liberals would have us assume that more than two-thirds of the British citizenry is consistently mis- or uninformed about a issue of tremendous importance. If this is the case, why should we believe citizens will ever be sufficiently informed to make less important decisions about fiscal and monetary policy? Perhaps recent events in Britain show that citizens have learned something about the virtues of privately owned enterprise and, through the electoral process, they have elected a political party that understands these lessons. Then majoritarian politics is desirable since it lets the informed citizenry make decisions that benefit all citizens, including the ignorant ones. Wouldn't any attempt to forge a real societal consensus give these supposedly ignorant citizens too much say in public decisions?

But there is another possibility. It may be that British citizens, unlike citizens in other countries such as the United States, have genuinely conflicting opinions about the best way to structure an economy and, more generally, about what ends government should pursue. If this is the case—and much writing on the British case suggests that it is—then no single popular will or single public interest exists. There

23. See Katzenstein's passing references to (1) trade unions' indifference to questions of income distribution (1984:36), and (2) the lesser importance of parliamentary politics in small European states (1985:209). Moreover, though Katzenstein stresses that democratic corporatism compensates citizens who suffer from the economic dislocation that market accommodation produces (1985:118–19, 132), he provides no survey evidence that citizens are pleased with the compensation they receive, or socioeconomic data on the welfare of citizens in different regions of small states. Nor does he examine, in any depth, controversies within corporatist countries about the adequacy of this compensation.

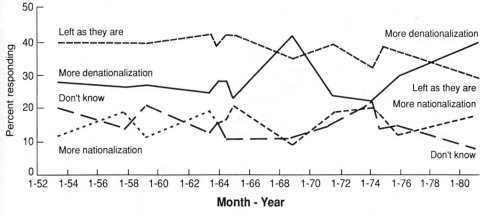

Figure 4. British public opinion about the scope of nationalization between 1953 and 1981

Notes. For 1953–1971, the response to the question "What are your views on nationalization? Do you think there should be more nationalization, more denationalization, or should things be left as they are?"; for 1971–1981, the response to the question "Which of these statements comes closest to what you, yourself, feel about nationalization? A lot more industries should be nationalized / Only a few more industries should be nationalized / No more industries should be nationalized but the industries that are nationalized should stay nationalized / Some of the industries that are nationalized now should be denationalized / Don't know." (The category "more nationalization" is defined as the sum of the first two responses to the question used in the period 1971–1981.)

Sources. Gallup International Opinion Polls, Britain 1937–1975; Index to International Public Opinion, 1981–82.

is no basis for societal consensus. There are competing conceptions of the public interest and, concomitantly, of how best to structure the economy. Majoritarian democracy might be preferable in these circumstances because it allows each faction of the British public to rule some of the time, or because it allows each conception of the public interest to be represented over the medium or long term.

Liberal theory does not offer satisfying answers to these questions or adequate solutions to these dilemmas. Rather, liberals are too quick to presume that they alone understand the workings of private enterprise and mixed economies. And they are too quick to assert the primacy of collective welfare criteria—especially Pareto optimality—over distributional concerns and the idea of a hierarchy of human needs. The possibility that democratic politics, with its provisions for popular elections and majority rule, is the best means of adjudicating genuine disagreements about the appropriate means and ends of public policy is not seriously entertained by many of the liberals who favor private enterprise economies. But this possibility must be entertained if we are to understand which form of democratic capitalism is most desirable.[24]

Radicals realize that societal dissensus often is real, and generally they are committed to democratic politics as the best means of coping with it. The weakness in radical theory lies in its failure to appreciate fully, or at least to address, the problems inherent in democratic decision making. At times, some radicals assume, like some liberals, that citizens can be perfectly informed and rational in voting and other kinds of political behavior. Yet they also warn that socially harmful, electorally motivated cycles in public policy can occur; that is, radicals suggest that the "legislators" (in firms and in the government at large) may be able to buy the votes of citizens. This position is inconsistent.[25]

In addition, some radicals ignore the problems of majority tyranny, assuming that if a majority of workers enacts a policy, then the majority alone bears the costs of policy errors. Others recognize the problem and advocate the creation of institutions that resemble those associated with consensual conceptions of democracy. But these same radicals do not then consider the potentially greater prevalence of state managerial control in consensual democratic systems, in spite of the fact that they issue warnings about the abuse of managerial power and privilege.[26]

Finally, radicals draw few explicit lessons from the experiences of democratic corporatist countries. Although many of them see corporatist forms of interest intermediation as meaningful channels for articulating and serving some wage earner interests, they equate democratic politics with pluralism. Radicals make few provisions for any particular mode of interest intermediation in their plans for democratic socialism.[27] These inconsistencies must be eliminated and these problems more adequately addressed if the virtues of democratic socialism are to be understood.

24. The idea that democratic institutions provide fair representation of competing interests *over time* is advanced by Miller (1983); see also Manley (1983).

25. For instance, Brus (1985:55) and Nove (1983:173–74) both fear that electorally motivated investment and employment cycles will occur in democratic socialist societies. Yet both advocate extensive popular supervision of planners; cf. the ninth feature of Nove's plan (1983).

26. Mandel's inadequate treatment of majority tyranny is evident in his recent essay. Nove fails to explore adequately the tension between centrally directed investment planning and the operation of democratic political institutions.

27. For example, Brus (1984:52) does not base his strong commitment to pluralism on any systematic comparison of democratic pluralism and democratic corporatism.

The issue is how these variables differ in democratic pluralist and democratic corporatist systems. How do pluralist and corporatist forms of democracy cope with dissensus? How does each system translate dissensus into public policies? How does each system cope with the problem of managerial control? Chapter 4 analyzes the workings of electoral systems, modes of interest intermediation, and styles of state administration. It shows how these three political institutions affect the stability, temporal orientation, and content of public policy; for instance, how pluralism promotes societal dissensus and imparts a short-term orientation to policy making whereas corporatism promotes consensus and a long-term orientation.

This analysis leads, in Chapter 5, to a study of the interconnections between the logics of different economic and political systems and, in turn, to the possibilities of achieving different blends of collective gain and distributional equity. That is, Chapter 5 fuses the analyses in chapters 3 and 4 to produce a fuller evaluation of the four basic political economies: pluralist–private enterprise, corporatist–private enterprise, pluralist mixed, and corporatist mixed. The result is a taxomony of welfare outcomes, a characterization of the *blends* of collective gain and distributional equity that can be achieved in the four types. The taxonomy implies that (1) the level and rate of societal consumption and wealth of future generations is greatest in corporatist–private enterprise political economies and lowest in pluralist–mixed political economies; and (2) the potential for maldistribution of wealth between private asset holders and wage earners is greatest in pluralist–private enterprise political economies and lowest in corporatist–mixed political economies. These differences are most pronounced when certain conditions hold, conditions pertaining to the character of state administration, nature of capital markets, degree of societal dissensus, and citizens' sense of "collective ownership efficacy" (with regard to public assets).

The validity of this taxonomy and the analysis on which it is based is demonstrated in the next three chapters. Chapter 6 shows that measures of social welfare for democratic capitalist countries are generally consistent with the typology. Chapter 7 shows that welfare outcomes in two countries with pluralist–private enterprise and corporatist mixed political economies—Britain and Austria, respectively—derive from the interrelated workings of political and economic institutions in ways predicted in the fifth chapter. The workings of the Italian and Swedish political economies—systems of the pluralist mixed and corporatist–private enterprise types, respectively—are shown in Chapter 8 to conform to my theoretical expectations.

The analysis is extended and its larger implications spelled out in the concluding chapters. The openness of all four kinds of political economies is explicitly considered in Chapter 9, which leads to a refined set of results regarding the welfare consequences of the four systems. The validity of this revised welfare taxonomy is demonstrated in Chapter 10, which reexamines the British, Austrian, Italian, and Swedish cases. Certain anomalies in the performance of the four countries, noted in Chapter 6, are explained in Chapter 9 on the basis of this revised analysis.

The final chapter returns to the debates between liberal and radical theorists. The virtues of democratic mixed economies are examined relative to those of democratic private enterprise and (hypothetical) democratic socialist political economies. In this context I explore the sense in which democracy is compatible with state-owned and privately owned enterprise. In particular, I show that under certain conditions a pluralist–private enterprise political economy will be more compatible with democracy than a pluralist–mixed political economy; under alternative conditions, however, the opposite will be true. Finally, the relative virtues of corporatist mixed systems are examined. I argue that this particular type of political economy produces a socially desirable blend of welfare outcomes; under prevailing political and economic conditions, moreover, it best approximates the democratic ideal.

CHAPTER TWO

Theoretical Perspectives

There are two major schools of political economy, each offering its own theoretical account of mixed economies. The liberal school emphasizes the self-regulating virtues of markets and the virtues of societal consensus. The radical school stresses the conflictual nature of class relations in capitalist society and markets prevent the democratic state from creating socially preferred distributions of wealth. The two schools may be subdivided into classical liberalism and neoliberalism, on the one hand, and instrumental, functionalist, and class compromise forms of radicalism, on the other.

This chapter evaluates liberal and radical analyses of mixed economies. Although both schools offer us useful insights about the politics of mixed economies, neither provides a satisfactory treatment of the subject. Our understanding of the workings and welfare consequences of democratic mixed economies is seriously deficient.

The discussion is divided into reviews of the liberal and the radical perspectives. In each section, I first summarize defining features. I then examine the different branches of the school of thought, offering some illustrations of each approach to the study of mixed economies. At the end of each section I identify the strengths and weakness of those approaches. In the conclusion of the chapter, I call for particular kinds of analyses—analyses that must be completed before we can decide if democratic mixed economies are or are not preferable to democratic private enterprise economies.[1]

---

1. This chapter illuminates the basic differences in the two perspectives and illustrates them. A more comprehensive review would include, among other things, an examination of Second and Third World thinking on this subject, including a review of nondemocratic mixed economies.

THE LIBERAL PERSPECTIVE

The liberal school holds that the workings of markets are socially benign, or that markets resolve the diverse goals and aspirations of individual citizens in mutually beneficial ways. At the same time, it recognizes the need for state intervention in markets. The state must perform certain duties if markets are to realize their potential for enhancing social welfare. For example, the state must provide national defense and protect and enforce property rights. More generally, the state, in Adam Smith's words, has the "duty . . . of erecting and maintaining those public institutions and those public works, which, though they may be in the highest degree advantageous to a great society, are, however, of such a nature, that the profit could never repay the expence to any individual or small number of individuals, and which it therefore cannot be expected that any individual or small number of individuals should erect or maintain."[2] Because markets are in certain respects imperfect—they contain the possibility of suboptimal production of certain goods and the likelihood of socially deleterious behavior on the part of large (monopolistic) producers—there is a need for state-owned enterprise. The state must launch ventures that are designed to eliminate market imperfections. These public undertakings will make some or all members of society better off than they would have been had the production of the respective goods and services been left in private hands.

Liberal theories differ in the importance they attach to politics and, more specifically, in the way they treat the process whereby society decides that government should assume a commercial presence in the economy. This difference distinguishes two strains of liberal theory.

Classical Liberal Analyses of Mixed Economies

Classical liberals argue it is through collective enlightenment that economies become mixed. The wisdom of state business ventures is essentially discovered by citizens; mixed economies are created and operated in ways that reflect the harmony within and the collective rationality of society. Democratic politics should be a means of articulating this harmony.[3] That state-owned enterprise may alter the distribution of wealth within society is less important than the fact that some or all citizens benefit from the elimination of certain market imperfections. And imperfections will be eliminated by the adaption

2. Smith 1920, 2:214. See also Okun 1975:32ff.
3. See, for instance, Barry's review of the "Virginia" strain of classical liberalism (1983:101–5).

of the collectively preferred scope of public ownership and operational guidelines for state-owned enterprises.

Perhaps no work in this strain of liberal theory is better known than that of Jan Tinbergen. Tinbergen (1959, 1963) studies the mutually beneficial mix of public and private enterprise as one aspect of his Theory of the Optimum Regime. Public authority, as he sees it, is constituted in "bundles" of institutions that control public spending, raise taxes, regulate commerce, and, most important for our purposes, produce goods and services for sale in the market place. Tinbergen argues that decisions concerning the government business sector are among the "main choices" facing a community because markets invariably display two imperfections: external effects and increasing returns. In the former, the productivity of one industry depends on the volume of output in another industry so that competitive pricing behavior by private producers leads to suboptimal welfare outcomes. More socially beneficial transactions can be achieved if the pivotal industry is operated in a way that explicitly recognizes the profit rate in industries it supplies. This, according to Tinbergen, is the rationale behind governmental provision of such services as defense and education as well as public undertakings in transportation and energy.

With the phenomenon of increasing returns we recognize that in some industries the costs of production decline with the level of output. In such a circumstance, marginal cost pricing—the kind of behavior that implies welfare optimization in a perfectly competitive market (with no external effects or increasing returns)—leads to permanent losses for private producers. This difficulty can be at least partially circumvented through such means as non-flat rate structures and monopoly. But the first option is difficult to implement in a competitive economic system, and the second often threatens the "general interest." So, once more, there are reasons for the state to undertake the production of goods and services. Supposedly this consideration explains why some governments, substantially own and operate heavy industries.[4]

The optimal regimes for two different countries need not be identical in every respect, according to Tinbergen. Even if the societies in the two countries have the same preferences, the best schemes of economic organization may vary because of contrasts in the technical features of the countries' markets, differences in resource endowment, and so on. However, the *range* of possible regimes is relatively

---

4. Tinbergen is careful to note the tradeoffs between regulating privately owned monopolies and creating or operating public monopolies (1959:297). I return to this distinction below.

uniform across societies; more specifically, the common features of modern economic processes rule out some extreme forms of organization. Not surprisingly, the possibility of a purely private, competitive market with no state enterprise is one of the excluded extremes. Also ruled out are certain paths of adjustment; as Tinbergen (1959:301) argues, "the optimal regime will as a rule shift only slowly and . . . sudden changes in regime are indicative of a deviation between the actual and the optimum regime either before the change, or after it, or in both cases. Sudden changes anyhow should be avoided under the present conditions of a complicated and very sensitive system of production and exchange." Tinbergen therefore predicts that large-scale reprivatization of state-owned firms should occur infrequently, if at all.

For Tinbergen, politics serves only to impede or undo the work of those who are striving to install the optimum regime. The ideological dispositions of politicians—especially elected politicians—often produce "doctrinaire deviations" from the socially preferred scheme of organization. In other cases, it is the short-sightedness of politicians that prevents societies from realizing mutually beneficial market outcomes. Consensus over state business ventures and other forms of state activity is always possible, if only politicians would rely on the "less emotional," informed judgment of economic thinkers. Because he was confident that eventually such reason would prevail, and because he believed that only a limited range of regimes is possible, Tinbergen predicted that the structures of modern economies would become more and more alike in the latter half of the twentieth century.[5]

Over the years refinements have been made in Tinbergen's Theory of the Optimum Regime. For example, Kenneth Arrow and Mordecai Kurz (1970) spell out the dynamic implications of the "special nature of social investment." More specifically, they show how the application of specialized criteria for public investment decisions together with an appreciation for the interrelationships among consumption, private investment, and public investment can produce deep insights about government's role as an investing agent.

Arrow and Kurz assume that government is essentially an altruistic entity that applies certain economic instruments in an attempt to enhance citizens' welfare. Government's social welfare function is defined in terms of a sum of discounted flows of utility or felicity adjusted for population growth. The government's decision problem then can be conceived as a dynamic analogue to the one Tinbergen

5. See Tinbergen (1959:301–2). On the convergence thesis see such works as Ellman (1980).

studied: the public authority chooses *time paths* for the mix of public and private investment in an attempt to maximize the welfare criterion described above. Arrow and Kurz consider the possibility that the most socially beneficial policy could not be realized and what in these circumstances the second-best policy would be. They demonstrate that an optimal accumulation policy depends on the relation between the marginal product of capital and the consumption rate of interest; and they show that the interest rate for optimal public investment can be determined only in relation to this appropriate level of aggregate investment activity.[6]

These and other classical liberals give us some insights into why some economies are more mixed than others and, to some extent, how the welfare consequences of mixed economies differ from those of private enterprise economies. They offer us an explanation as to why citizens agree to create state-owned enterprise: mixed schemes of economic organization are adopted because citizens anticipate or experience certain forms of market failures; citizens believe state-owned enterprise can ameliorate these failures and, in turn, make some or all of them better off.

A rationale for the direct involvement of governments in investment decisions is also provided by classical liberalism. Government coordination of the mix of public and private investment is shown to produce a socially preferred time path for aggregate consumption. Our understanding of the workings of mixed economies in this respect is enhanced by Arrow and Kurz's analysis. They alert us to the pitfalls of using the same standards to evaluate private and public investment, for example, and to the mistake of assuming that the prices charged for publicly produced goods and services should or will bear any direct relation to the marginal value of those goods to society.

To the extent that external effects and increasing returns prevail and citizens realize the potential benefits of government management of certain investment decisions, then, we should expect consensus about the need to construct a mixed economy. Moreover, we should expect citizens' evaluations of public investment to display an appreciation for its special "nature," that is, mutual recognition that the financial profits and losses of state-owned enterprises in any given year may bear little relation to future effects on aggregate consumption.

What these works fail to explain is the dissensus that exists within societies, both over the appropriate mix of private and public enterprise and over the operations of publicly owned firms. Citizens have demonstrably different preferences on these issues. Contrary to

6. Subsequent developments in the study of optimal investment are reviewed in Von Furstenberg and Malkiel (1977) and Lintner (1981).

what Tinbergen suggests, changes in government sometimes result in major alterations in the scope of public ownership as well as in the pricing and investment policies of public enterprises. More generally, evidence shows that state-owned enterprises serve some citizens' equity claims; public firms alter the distribution of wealth within society. The activity of state-owned enterprises is an outgrowth of compromises between groups with genuinely conflicting interests and is explicitly designed to serve the interests of some groups at the expense of other groups.

Classical liberalism either claims this dissensus is not real or ignores it. Classical liberals contend that mixed economies can embody the harmony of collective interests, that mixed economies can be created through collective enlightenment. In so doing they assume that citizens have identical tastes and aspirations. They assert the existence of a consistent set of social preferences regarding the costs and benefits of alternative economic "regimes," and they assume that government is simply a device through which *the* collectively preferred regime is realized. In general, classical liberals ignore the reality of societal conflict over the creation and operation of state-owned enterprise.

The classical liberal account of mixed economies would be more useful if it were based on a careful analysis of the distributional consequences of economic regimes; for example, if equity criteria were explicitly incorporated in the social welfare functions these theorists use. But the fact is that classical liberals consistently ignore distributional issues. Their analyses tell us little about the way competing, possibly irreconcilable, equity claims are resolved in the optimum regime, let alone about the role that democratic institutions play in this process.

Consider Tinbergen's work. Tinbergen's social welfare function is constructed from "ethical principles" whose legitimacy is a matter of assumption rather than debate. His notion of "least differences" holds that citizens have utility functions not only of essentially the same shape but also with roughly identical coefficients. In addition, Tinbergen assumes that his social welfare function can be formed as a sum of individual utilities; distributional matters pose no difficulties for his analysis. These conventions are unreasonable.[7]

---

7. For instance, Tinbergen ignores the fact that social preferences can be intransitive and suboptimal (see Frohlich and Oppenheimer 1978). Arrow and Kurz acknowledge but do not explore the relevance of distributional issues (1970:xxiii). They incorporate intergenerational equity concerns in their analysis. More specifically, they assume that government maximizes aggregate consumption over time subject to uniform preferences among citizens regarding the consumption rate of interest and an even spread of social risk across citizens. The intragenerational distribution of income is posited to be egalitarian, the result of policies other than those pertaining to the mix

In sum, classical liberalism is not satisfactory because it offers us few insights about how to resolve competing equity claims or about how democratic politics reflects and shapes the distributional consequences of state-owned enterprise. The scope of these analyses must be broadened to allow for the possibility of genuine societal conflict over the creation and operation of public firms. Collective choice must be conceived as an aggregation of possibly diverse preferences of individuals or groups—preferences that may be, in some respects, irreconcilable but that nonetheless are aggregated and enforced by democratic institutions.

Neoliberal Analyses of Mixed Economies

Neoliberalism differs from classical liberalism in that it focuses more on the distributional consequences of state-owned enterprise and mixed economies. Neoliberals do not assume that all citizens necessarily benefit from the elimination of market imperfections, or that society necessarily prefers a single mix of private and public investment. Rather, they stress the gains that accrue to certain groups of citizens within and between countries. The workings of mixed economies are explained in terms of political competition between groups, each of which has somewhat different interests and possesses unequal shares of power and wealth. The scope of public ownership and the operation of state-owned firms reflect the terms of political compromises that are forged among competing groups. Whether ultimately the distributional consequences of these compromises are fair is thought to hinge on such things as whether (or how) democratic procedures are adhered to in negotiations over the mix of private and public enterprise. For instance, do all groups participate in decisions to create and operate publicly owned business ventures? But neoliberals do not assume that the democratic process necessarily should yield a consistent set of social preferences regarding the structure of the economy or the content of government policies.[8]

In their writings on mixed economies, neoliberals emphasize several kinds of political cooperation and political conflict. In the first case, mixed economies are explained in terms of some mutually perceived need to defend national interests against threats posed by foreign investment and in terms of the political cooperation that this mutual perception spawns. In particular, direct foreign investment is

---

of investment (1970:13). Von Furstenberg and Malkiel (1977) are among those who criticize students of public investment for not having incorporated distributional concerns in their analyses.

8. See, for example, Vernon (1981).

shown to produce consensus among local business people, labor unions, and public administrators about the need for national ownership of those industries threatened with foreign takeover. Or consensus forms about the need to create state-owned firms in certain industries rather than recruit foreign-owned firms because native groups agree that foreign-owned firms are likely to be insensitive to local concerns for growth and equity within the domestic economy. Differences in the ownership structures of industrialized and industrializing countries are also attributed to such structural factors as the global competitiveness of local firms at particular phases of the product cycle or the ability of local firms to initiate new industrial ventures. Contextual factors such as the intensity of nationalist reactions to foreign investors are sometimes stressed as well. Stuart Holland (1974) exemplifies such neoliberal accounts in arguing that the second wave of European state-owned enterprise was the result of a wide political consensus having formed in opposition to the postwar expansion of American multinationals.[9]

Another strand of neoliberal theory focuses on the political conflicts surrounding state-owned enterprises. These works attribute the distributional consequences of mixed economies to the relative power of political parties and party coalitions or, more generally, to the power of particular alliances of societal groups. One popular explanation for mixed economies, for example, suggests they are the result of political victories of the Left. Proponents of this view downplay the Keynesian practices of social democratic parties; they emphasize the socialist doctrines of Left parties, especially these parties' (long-term) plans for worker control of the means of production. Changes in patterns of government commercial activity are traced to the electoral fortunes of Leftist parties. In Britain, for instance, changes are traced to the defeat of the Labour party by Conservatives with programs for denationalizing the steel industry, dismantling the Industrial Reorganization Corporation, and, recently, imposing cash limits, efficiency audits, and privatization on the nationalized industries. In France, the explanation stresses the electoral success in the early 1980s of the Socialists with a program for government takeover of certain industries.

The fact that the immediate financial returns from public investments are often inferior to those from private investment is cited as

9. See Holland (1974:27ff.). That the threat of foreign takeover produces partisan consensus about the need for government commercial activity is stressed in neoliberal accounts of the Austrian nationalizations (Langer 1964:116–17; Lacina 1977; van der Bellen 1981), the Italian state undertakings (Holland 1972; Prodi 1974; Martinelli 1981; Grassini 1981), the creation of the Irish state-sponsored bodies (Lemass 1969; Bristow 1966; Coyle 1973; Jacobsen 1980:136ff.), and the Canadian Crown corporations (Laux and Molot 1987).

evidence that Leftist parties attempt to maximize electoral support by appealing to the short-term interests of their supporters. More specifically, decisions to maintain jobs in state-owned industries and to set low prices for certain publicly produced goods and services are attributed to the influence that Leftist parties wield and the ability of politicians to use state-owned enterprise to enhance the welfare of working-class voters at the expense of the constituents of other parties. Contrasts in the ownership structure of industrialized countries supposedly are also an outgrowth of the relative influence of social democratic parties within national political systems.[10]

Neoliberals agree that political institutions have much to do with the ways negotiations unfold over the mix of private and public enterprise. Institutionalized forms of bargaining such as corporatism are held not only to promote cooperation between competing interest groups but also to limit the *range* of changes that conceivably can be made in the structures of economies.[11] Another line of neoliberal argument attempts to demonstrate that democratic supervision of public enterprise is responsible for distinctive types of (state) managerial behavior. More specifically, it argues that because of the way public business ventures are created—through a voting mechanism rather than through a market mechanism—and the fact that there is no direct relationship between citizens' ownership shares and the returns they accrue from government business ventures, the managers of public firms behave in a fundamentally different manner from their counterparts in private enterprises. As Henry Tulkens (1976:30) argues,

> as an alternative behavioral hypothesis of profit maximization, public enterprises might be considered as striving at achieving those specific programs which obtain a majority vote in the public body on which they institutionally depend, given the financial implications of such programs for these same voters. Financial performance thus appears as a constraint in the analysis, not as an objective, and the physical production mix itself (including the specification of both inputs and outputs) becomes the objective . . . [and therefore] just like the private manager who is assumed by the neoclassical economist to be hunting for all profit-promising opportunities, motivated by maximization, a "public manager" might reasonably be assumed, by the "public economist", to be

10. For example, see Monsen and Walters (1983). Evidence of differences in parties' conceptions of the purpose of state-owned enterprise includes for Austria, Lacina (1977), Andrlik (1983), and Katzenstein (1984); for Britain, Beesley and Evans (1981), Heald and Steel (1982); and for France, Kuisel (1981: chap. 3) and Holton (1986). See also Przeworski (1980a).

11. See, for instance, Andrlik (1983) and Katzenstein (1984, 1985).

hunting for all majority-promising ventures, on the basis of a "votes maximization" hypothesis.

It follows that to understand the operation of state-owned firms, one must incorporate a theory of voting into the study of what amounts to a "new public economics."[12]

Illustrative of this approach is Sam Peltzman's (1971) analysis of the pricing policies of public and private utilities. Peltzman explores the incentives of managers in state-owned firms, especially the incentives that derive from the limited possibilities for "reshuffling" the ownership of government businesses. He argues that "with the higher costs of reshuffling ownership in government enterprise . . . the management of government enterprise will be enabled to trade more of the owner's wealth for objects of utility to the managers than will the managers of private enterprises." At the same time, state managers usually are more closely supervised or regulated than their private counterparts: "The government manager is likely to be encumbered by various rules or procedures which are designed to attenuate (or amplify) the incentive to trade owner wealth" (Peltzman 1971:111). The challenge, then, is to determine whether contrasting sets of incentives and constraints induce behavioral differences among managers of public and private firms.

For the problem of price determination, Peltzman argues from assumptions regarding the economic and political motivations of state managers and the electoral behavior of consumers-voters-owners to show that government firms will set prices in a way that maximizes support from groups of citizens within incumbent coalitions. This practice, in turn, will produce greater price homogeneity and less product variety than would occur if the firms were privately owned and operated. For example, the structure of incentives and constraints is such that if the cost of supplying one group within the incumbent coalition suddenly rises while the costs of serving other groups within the coalition remain fixed, state managers will raise the price for *all* groups and thereby reduce the overall purchase of votes (rather than pass on the costs to the affected group, as a private firm supposedly would).

Arguments such as Peltzman's have spawned disagreements among neoliberals about whether democracy undermines the potential for equitable growth which mixed economies offer. Some writers contend that state managers are able to conceive and to implement efficient

12. The quotation is from Tulkens (1976:111), who with others has attempted to recast structural and behavioral assumptions of the theory of competitive markets to allow for the existence of a substantial public enterprise sector. See also Arrow (1981), Lintner (1981), and Raiffa (1981).

and just corporate policies. But "democratic interference" continually prevents them from doing so. Elections, for example, allow all politicians—regardless of their ideological disposition—to advocate and support state business ventures or policies that serve only the short-term interests of their constituents at the expense of other citizens, including the unborn.[13] What is needed, these theorists argue, is a better balance between democratic and managerial control. The democratic process should help state managers decide how mixed the economy should be, what social objectives state-owned firms should pursue, and what range of policies managers should adopt. But once these decisions have been made, state managers should be allowed to carry out their democratically mandated program of public profit accumulation.[14]

Other neoliberals take the opposite view. They argue that the inequities in mixed economies are the result of the absence or inadequacies of democratic control. The distributional consequences of prevailing mixes of private and public enterprise are inequitable because the managers of publicly owned firms have captured a disproportionate share of political power. Episodes in which state managers resist parliamentary supervision, attempt to buy the votes of legislators, and force private enterprises out of business give evidence of the lack of democratic control over the state business sector and of the danger of allowing state managers to impose their own notions of the public interest on society.[15]

In this vein, neoliberals warn of the dangers of creating a mixed economy. Writers such as George Corti (1976:75)argue that Britain's adoption of Italy's mix of public and private enterprise would mean the end of its democracy. Students of European industrial policy, such as Victoria Curzon Price (1981:129–30), contend that state-owned enterprise threatens citizens' liberty and freedom. Others, Arrow (1981) among them, recommend *more* public interference in public enterprise decision making, including government encouragement of risk taking by public enterprises. Still others advocate combining a decentralized form of public ownership with a pluralist style of politics. As these last theorists see it, the potential for the abuse of power by state managers should be combatted with restrictions on the size of

13. For instance, see Schloss (1977) and Mazzolini (1979a, 1979b). For related commentaries on the politics of Italian state enterprise see Fausto (1977), Stefani (1981), Price (1981: chap. 3), and Grassini (1981).

14. See Holland (1972: chap. 1), especially his summary of the views of the founder of the Italian state holding companies.

15. The problems posed by the bureaucratization and "autonomization" of the state business are discussed by such authors as Chubb (1970), Prodi (1974), Mazzolini (1979a), and Cassesse (1981).

publicly owned firms and a commitment to a more competitive and open political system. This kind of system would, they suppose, ensure that the distributional consequences of mixed economies would be "humane."[16]

Neoliberal theorists have made important refinements in the classical liberal account of mixed economies. Indeed, in some respects they have constructed a more satisfying and compelling explanation for the existence of different mixes of private and public enterprise. Neoliberals help us understand how a consensus might form about the need to create state-owned enterprises. They suggest that mutual appreciation for the problems of increasing returns and external effects depends, in some part, on the *identity* of the firms involved, that is, on whether the firms are owned by foreigners or by native citizens. The threat of disinvestment is perceived to be greater when firms are foreign-owned, which leads groups to coalesce in support of state-owned business ventures in the affected industries.

An explanation for societal dissensus over the need to eliminate market imperfections is also provided by neoliberal theorists. Conflict over the mix of private and public enterprise is a product of competing equity claims among particular groups of citizens rather than an outgrowth of the ignorance or malevolence of citizens and governments. Contrasts in the scope of public ownership are related to real differences in configurations of power and interest across countries instead of deficiencies in the cognitive capabilities of societies.

Neoliberal theorists help us decide if mixed economies have a greater potential than private enterprise economies for achieving certain distributions of wealth. In so doing, they build on Arrow and Kurz's demonstration of the general irrelevance of the price mechanism in evaluating the performance of state-owned firms. In particular, the workings of a *nonmarket* mechanism for evaluation—popular elections—are linked to distinctive kinds of (state) managerial behavior; and the impossibility of disinvestment is shown to create somewhat different expectations among citizens, as public owners, about the goals state-owned firms should pursue.[17] In turn, additional insights are gained into the ways public enterprise affects the distribution of wealth across groups at particular points in time.

What is lacking in neoliberal theory—and liberal theory in general—is an analysis of the similarities and differences in the configu-

16. Recall that many socialists advocate a decentralized system of publicly owned but relatively autonomous enterprises, presumably because large-scale enterprise has proved to be inhumane and undemocratic (Dahl 1982:28–29). See also Tilton's (1979, 1987) summary of Wigforss' rationale for the creation of "public enterprises without owners."

17. See, for instance, Posner (1981:19) and Price (1981:34).

ration of interests that mixed economies serve. This body of work does yield useful insights into how the distributional consequences of market imperfections spawn political coalitions in certain places at particular points in time. But it does not explain, in any systematic way, how or why these coalitions are similar or different. For example, it is useful to know that, in democracies, state managers may adopt homogeneous pricing policies in order to maximize electoral support. But to explain similarities in the ownership structure of industries in different economies, we must know whether such pricing policies preserve or transform existing distributions of wealth and power, whether this result is anticipated by groups that benefit from price homogeneity, and whether these same groups engineer state takeovers of the respective industries in order to bring the redistribution about. Then we must try to show that similarities in ownership structures across countries are the result of the implied series of political events, with like consequences for distribution and collective welfare. Assessments of the prospects for convergence in the ownership structures of industries and countries should be based on an analysis of the likelihood of similar coalitions being forged in them in the future, coalitions that use a particular mix of public and private enterprise to achieve essentially the same ends.

Neoliberals have made strides in distinguishing private from public investment and in demonstrating the need to employ different performance criteria in evaluating private and public enterprise, but they have yet to provide meaningful standards against which to compare the workings of private enterprise and mixed economies. Two important questions remain to be answered: How should equity consequences of state-owned enterprise be incorporated in these evaluations? How is the welfare of citizen-owners and citizen-workers affected by the impossibility of "reshuffling public shareholdings," that is, by the much lower likelihood and high cost of disinvestment from state-owned enterprise? The liberal view holds that all citizens gain, or at least are made no worse off, when market imperfections are eliminated. And *conceivably* a country's share of global wealth and power may be preserved or enlarged by the substitution of state-owned for foreign-owned enterprise. But the creation of a mixed economy also affects the distribution of wealth within a country; not all citizens benefit equally from the elimination of market imperfections or from defense of the national interest by state-owned enterprises.

It is not clear how we should incorporate these distributional consequences into comparisons of the welfare consequences of mixed versus private enterprise economies. One might argue that if the in-

33

OKUN

come effects of a particular state-owned firm are regressive, they render desirable a combination of private ownership and transfer payments to lower-income groups (in that under certain conditions, such a combination would lead to greater output over the long term while not threatening the ability of lower-income groups to consume the respective good or service).[18] However, such an argument assumes that, under private ownership, authorities would agree to make the transfer payments required to maintain consumption levels regardless of the price charged for the good or service.[19] Moreover, it ignores the gains that might accrue to future generations from the provision of low-cost goods to local industries that eventually might provide employment opportunities and additional goods and services to the unborn. The survival of local industries might be substantially less likely if the firm were privately owned and the economy more open to foreign investment.

Closely related is the question of how to incorporate the gains and losses that accrue to state enterprise workers and to public owners (citizens) in an evaluation of mixed economies. One must consider, on the one hand, the psychological benefits that accrue to employees from the knowledge that their jobs are more secure than those of their fellow workers in private industry. At the same time, one must take into account the substantial costs that citizens, as public owners, must bear if they are to divest themselves from or organize a collective decision to privatize public enterprises. The benefits that citizens acquire from their greater ability to prevent closure of state-owned firms and to avoid the substantial costs associated with disinvestment must be considered along with the losses that unborn generations must bear if the operation of state-owned firms is partially financed by borrowing against future national income.

Neoliberal evaluations of mixed economies do not adequately incorporate these equity and security concerns. Their attacks on the myth of benign socialism are based on an examination of after-tax, nominal income distribution statistics and the assumption that the operating deficits of state-owned firms always indicate net losses in social welfare. That a more just set of welfare outcomes could be achieved in the absence of state-owned enterprise is often assumed or asserted rather than demonstrated. Nor do neoliberals fully appreciate the role that democratic institutions play in articulating and pro-

18. See Jones's (1981b) discussion of "opportunity costs" and "opportunity subsidies" in the context of a more general treatment of the "perverse" distributional consequences of state-owned enterprise.

19. See, for instance, Baer and Figueroa's (1981:81) comments about the likelihood that the same distributional outcomes would occur in a private enterprise–oriented economy in Brazil.

34

moting citizens' equity and security concerns through state-owned enterprise. It is clear that the welfare consequences of public enterprise reflect and are reflected in the workings of democratic institutions. How particular institutions produce differences in these welfare consequences is not explained by neoliberal theory.[20]

Until improvements are made in neoliberal theory, it will be difficult to decide whether state managers or any other group of citizens have imposed an unjust distribution of wealth on society. It will also be difficult to resolve the controversy over whether democracy prevents mixed economies from realizing their potential for improving social welfare. More generally, it will be difficult to decide whether democratic mixed economies are more desirable than democratic private enterprise economies.

Before laying out a strategy for making these improvements in neoliberal theory, I acknowledge that another school of political economy claims to have found similarities in the political coalitions that form on behalf of mixed economies. It also claims to have made a more complete accounting of the welfare consequences of democratic mixed and democratic private enterprise systems.

THE RADICAL PERSPECTIVE

According to radical political economists, Western economies are mixed because they are capitalist economies. Capitalism spawns class conflict between the owners of private enterprise and workers (wage earners). The politics of mixed economies is an expression of this class struggle, and the outcome is the same in that the scope and operations of state-owned enterprise always preserve the greater power and wealth of the owners of private enterprise. Thus the radical school sees mixed economies as an expression more of societal conflict and political domination than of societal consensus and political compromise.

Radicals disagree about how the need for mixed economies is realized and then met. State-owned enterprise is, for some, an instrument with which a unified and far-sighted capitalist class furthers its own special interests; for others, a means by which a relatively auton-

20. Dahl's brief discussion of mixed economies (1982: chap. 8) suffers from the application of a crude and ill-defined set of welfare criteria together with a failure to consider how some democratic institutions are better suited than others to the management of mixed economies. Heurtibise's discussion (1978) is much more useful. He argues that democratic control is incompatible with public enterprise efficiency, that is, continuity in the management of the public sector is essential for efficiency but electoral institutions are *designed* to prevent such continuity.

omous state seeks to fulfill the needs of a divided, myopic group of capitalists; and for a third group, a tool of a class coalition between wage earners and capitalists. Let us examine the second and third branches of radical theory more closely.

Functionalist Accounts of Mixed Economies

Functionalists argue that the key to understanding the politics of mixed economies lies in the "objective relation" between the state and the capitalist class, specifically the way the state stabilizes and reproduces the capitalist system of production. The mix of private and public enterprise is not a tool of an all-powerful capitalist class but rather a functional requisite of capitalism, discovered and enforced by a relatively autonomous state. The *state* realizes that capitalist economic activity cannot be sustained and the class struggle cannot be managed effectively unless publicly owned business ventures are undertaken. It therefore builds societal consensus for a mixed economy. It convinces capitalists who might otherwise oppose state-owned enterprise that they ought to join with other members of their class in supporting the state's plans to launch and manage publicly owned business ventures. The state may even persuade capitalists to take a direct financial interest in such ventures. Once commercial activity has been reorganized, the state stands watch over the mix of private and public enterprise, making sure that most investment decisions remain in private hands, no financial surpluses are reaped from public investments, and workers are satisfied. The shift from a private enterprise to a mixed economy thus leaves the state dependent on and excluded from the process of accumulation. The social privilege and disproportionate wealth of the capitalist class are preserved.

A functionalist account of the politics of mixed economies can be found in the writings of the German capital school. These theorists argue that the capitalist state is engaged in two basic kinds of activity.[21] The first is allocative in nature: the state imposes order on an area of economic or social activity by dispersing (that is, using) some of its own resources. Criteria for evaluating allocative intervention are based on the self-interest of decision makers together with their legal or political power; in fact, allocative policies are "congruent with politics." Keynesian demand management exemplifies this form of intervention.

Productive activity is the second basic kind of intervention. The state promotes capital accumulation by providing inputs to produc-

21. The following is a brief summary of Offe (1975).

36

tion—inputs that, for various reasons, private enterprise is unwilling or unable to produce on its own. Claus Offe (1975:132) states the position well:

> In state productive activity the state fulfills its function as a capitalist state (to create and maintain the conditions of accumulation) not only on a broader scope, but in a *new way*. By such activity the state responds to situations in which labor and(or) capital fail to operate in the accumulation process by producing material conditions that allow the continuation of accumulation. By its material production the state creates conditions that are essential for the accumulating units that cannot be achieved by their own activity. Such productive state activity is initiated by the actual or anticipated, sectoral or general absence of accumulation (or disturbances in the accumulation process). The rationale is to restore accumulation or to avoid or eliminate perceived threats to accumulation.

State-owned enterprise thus involves a wide range of activities, including the generation of electricity, transportation, education, and technology, all of which are intended to ensure orderly continuation of the accumulation process.

Members of the German capital school, like other functionalists, recognize definite limits on the ways and extent to which the state can promote accumulation. They argue that "the state cannot *initiate* production within private enterprises that is thought to be *not* accumulative by the private accumulating unit, and it cannot, conversely, *stop* production that *is* considered accumulative (profitable) by the accumulating unit. The state is no capitalist itself; accumulation takes place only in private accumulating units."[22] They also stress that when the state "owns" the resources it disperses and where demands for intervention are positive and specific, productive activity usually is motivated by *perceived* threats to accumulation and by demands for intervention that the capitalist class articulates poorly. Finally, because of the fundamental weakness of the capitalist class—its lack of class consciousness—the state supposedly must decide *for itself* how best to institutionalize productive activity.

Three options are available to the state in this regard: bureaucracy, purposive action or planning, and consensus. None of these "logics of

22. This is Offe's (1975) first property of the capitalist state. The other three hold that the capitalist state (i) has a mandate to create and sustain the conditions of accumulation; (ii) depends for its decision-making power on the presence and continuity of the accumulation process; and (iii) continues to exist as a capitalist state only as long as it conceals its nature as a capitalist state. See also Poulantzas's discussion of the difference between state intermediation in Britain and France and his evaluation of the implications of nationalization in these and other industrialized countries (1973:172ff., 271ff.).

policy production" is adequate for performing the productive functions of the capitalist state, however. The bureaucratic mode of decision making is inefficient and ineffective, but it challenges the prerogatives of private accumulation; the consensus mode allows the working class to participate in decision making, thereby undermining long-range planning and overburdening the state with too many demands for the production of goods and services. In the final analysis, then, the very need to engage in productive activity makes it impossible for the capitalist state to fulfill its functions. Hence "the reality of the capitalist state can . . . be described as the reality and dominance of an unrealistic attempt" (Offe 1975:144).

A more concrete functionalist analysis of mixed economies can be found in Alex Dupuy and Barry Truchil (1979). Briefly, Dupuy and Truchil trace the rise of European state enterprise to the transition from competitive to monopoly capitalism, particularly the political implications of (1) the concentration of capital in key sectors of developed economies; (2) the higher organic composition of capital (capital-intensive nature of production) in those sectors; (3) the increasing export of capital; and (4) the dominance of monopoly sectors over competitive sectors. The new problems of capitalist reproduction that these developments present—especially those of overproduction and overaccumulation—require the state to become much more deeply involved in providing investment opportunities, and producing infrastructure. More generally, Dupuy and Truchil (1979:18) argue, the state "assumes most of the costs and risks of an increasing number of productive processes and through various projects directly contributes to a more rapid rate of turnover of capital, and provides the impetus for technological innovation through the funding of research and development programs, and the subsidization of energy and transportation industries."

Dupuy and Truchil argue that in Italy, France, and other European countries, the operation of state-owned firms and joint state–private business ventures supports the accumulation process and the hegemony it affords to the capitalist class. Nothing in the politics of mixed economies, including efforts to manage such economies through state planning, embodies a transformation of a capitalist system of production into a system of state as opposed to private monopoly capitalism.[23]

The functionalist branch of radical theory offers a relatively simple political explanation for mixed economies. Functionalists claim that

23. "The introduction of state economic planning in the advanced capitalist countries . . . neither displaces the dominance of private capitalism nor subordinates the operation of the market (of the law of value) within those countries" (1979:21–22).

the welfare consequences of mixed economies are in essence no different from those of private enterprise economies. They attribute variations in the scope of public enterprise to differences in states' capacities for anticipating and solving problems that arise in the development of capitalism. Similar mixes of private and public enterprise are observed in some countries because the respective *states* have discovered that a particular scheme of economic organization will ameliorate what are common threats to the power and privilege of the capitalist class. Differences in the severity and timing of crises in capitalist economic development are responsible for any contrasts we observe in mixes of private and public enterprise. Although some functionalists (including Offe) argue that the hegemony of the capitalist class ultimately cannot be sustained because of the need for state productive activity for which no fully functional policy-making logic exists, few of these theorists see any difference in the welfare consequences of private enterprise and mixed economies. Rather, the distribution of wealth is always inequitable in capitalist society, however extensive state-owned enterprise may be.

Some evidence supports the functionalist account. Commentaries on the politics of the Italian and other mixed economies often note that governments have made substantial concessions to private business in order to enlist their support for public enterprise.[24] This and other state activities can be interpreted as an attempt to unify the capitalist class behind a reorganization of Italy's economy—a reorganization that presumably will preserve the power and privilege of a certain group of Italian businesspeople. Government attempts to build consensus for the "rationalization" of various industries might be explained in the same way. The takeover of ailing firms by the state can be seen as part of an effort to resolve a crisis of overproduction in a way that benefits businesspeople and momentarily pacifies affected workers.[25]

Although such interpretations are possible, they are generally implausible or at least incomplete, because there is much evidence that states are often unable or unwilling to reorganize economies in ways that serve the interests of a capitalist class. To begin with, many states lack the centralized, administrative apparatus needed either to reorganize commercial activity or to operate publicly owned firms in the service of the capitalist class.[26] As a consequence, capitalists some-

24. See, for instance, Martinelli (1981). Also, it is interesting that the Italian fascists' Charter of Work provided for "intervention of the state in production . . . only when private initiative is absent" (Sachs 1964:61).
25. See, for instance, Miliband (1969) and O'Connor (1973).
26. On this general point see Skocpol (1980:173).

times suffer from the poor quality of goods and services produced by public firms as well as from relatively low rates of financial return on investment in joint ventures with state-owned enterprises. Capitalists conceivably may also suffer from their failure to back state plans for taking over certain kinds of production.

The U.S. experience is illustrative. The weak nature of American states was, in part, responsible for the widespread failure of publicly owned firms in the 1830s and 1840s. Some of these firms were eventually purchased at low cost by private business, but not before members of the capitalist class, especially British investors, had borne substantial costs.[27] During the Depression, bureaucrats attempted to organize certain kinds of production under the Reconstruction Finance Corporation. However, business strenuously opposed the reorganization of commercial activity, charging among other things that the RFC posed a threat to democracy. Bureaucrats were unable to overcome this opposition. Their efforts to have government corporations treated as autonomous legal entities were thwarted by various administrative and legal decisions. Shortly after the war, most of the RFC's holdings were reprivatized. Today, most problems of over production are handled privately, without the benefits that state takeover of the affected industries would supposedly provide. Moreover, American business remains opposed to nationalization, and the government bureaucracy shows no signs of being able to unify the capitalist class behind an expansion of state-owned enterprise or to prevent administrations from reprivatizing those public corporations which do exist.[28] Functionalist theory does not adequately explain these facts. It relies on tautologies about the severity of crises and the true role of the state in trying to account for the experiences of the United States and other countries.

Evidence also suggests that states are unwilling to serve the interests of the capitalist class, even that public enterprises directly challenge private interests. Governments have prevented privatization of public firms when they feared the result might be takeovers by for-

27. Million (1896:230) is among the authors who attribute the failure of the American states' enterprises to the absence of an administratively centralized state; see also Hartz (1948). The losses (and gains) to private business from the operation of these same public firms are discussed in the same works and also in Calendar (1902), Violette (1918), and Shonfield (1965).

28. Business opposition to the RFC is discussed in Shonfield (1965) and in National Academy of Public Administration (1981:12). The Truman administration opposed attempts to treat government corporations as government agencies rather than autonomous corporations, but individuals advocated strengthening the administrative apparatus of the federal government to allow for a more active role for the RFC and the TVA. See Shonfield (1965:307ff.) and Moe (1982) for a discussion of the thinking of these individuals.

eigners or concentration of ownership in private hands. And in some countries, worker management of publicly owned firms has been encouraged by state bureaucrats and elected officials.[29] Both practices undermine capitalists' privilege and power. Neither practice is adequately explained by functionalist theory.

Functionalist evaluations of the welfare consequences of mixed economies are suspect. Functionalists apply the same criteria in judging the performance of privately owned and state-owned firms. As a consequence, they fail to see why citizens might prefer government takeover of an ailing firm to either bankruptcy or state-financed continuation of private ownership. The substantial gains that accrue to workers in these and other state-owned industries are either ignored or attributed to the need to keep workers disorganized. But as we have seen, under certain conditions all citizens may have reasons to advocate state-owned enterprise as well as to subsidize the operation of the same firms. Functionalists have not seriously considered the possibility that these conditions exist in some Western countries.

To put it simply, functionalists underestimate the state's potential for serving both private and public interests. The architects of mixed economies often espouse a philosophy of state entrepreneurship—a belief in the need for state supervision and management of the economy for the sake of achieving some mutually preferred pattern of equitable growth. These individuals, some of whom are state bureaucrats, claim that the gains some citizens acquire from state-owned enterprise, for example, the benefits from regional development and countercyclical investment and employment policies—could not be realized in private enterprise economies, where private owners would be unwilling or unable to protect citizens' current and future interests.[30] If we accept the functionalist view we must conclude that either these claims are unfounded or they are intended to conceal the states' attempts to manage the class struggle; we must conclude that the welfare of certain citizens is enhanced in order to create dissension within the working class. In view of the inadequate welfare crite-

29. See the discussion of labor and state managerial opposition to the idea of People's Shares in Austria, in Langer (1964:127). In Ireland workers are represented on the boards of such state-sponsored bodies as Aer Lingus, Bord na Mona, British and Irish Steampacket Co., Irish Sugar Co., Coras Iompair Eireann, Electrical Supply Board, and Nitrigin Eureann Teoranta. Government support for workplace democracy in the context of the nationalizations of the early 1980s in France is discussed by Holton (1986).

30. Despicht (1972:155) and Martinelli (1981:94) both argue that the behavior of Italian state managers is guided by the basic tenets of Catholic social philosophy. Prodi (1974) also stressed the "social consciousness" of these state managers. Functionalist theory fails to refute these authors' claims.

41

ria functionalists apply in their study of mixed economies, neither conclusion is warranted.

The functionalist account of mixed economies is in need of substantial revision. In particular, it must make allowance for the possibility that elements of the state can, by advocating certain mixes of private and public enterprise, realize real collective gains and alter the distribution of power and wealth within capitalist society. Admitting this possibility would necessitate closer examination of the bargains that elements of the state strike with business over the organization of commercial activity, as well as those it strikes with labor over the same issue. In this context it is important, as Offe suggests, to consider the institutional framework in which such negotiations take place. The welfare consequences of mixed economies vary with the relative importance of planning and "politics." Finally, it is conceivable that some compromises over the organization of commercial activity could produce a set of welfare outcomes that most citizens genuinely prefer. Hence the capitalist state need not necessarily fail to reproduce itself.

Class Compromise Accounts of Mixed Economies

A second branch of radical theory explicitly recognizes the power wielded by workers. It explains mixed economies in terms of a compromise forged between the classes, a compromise enforced by the state. A mixed economy exists either because the bargain between capitalists and workers provides for state operation of those (unprofitable) industries which support private enterprise, or because workers lack an effective strategy for nationalizing the entire means of production.

Such an account of mixed economies is contained in class compromise analyses of democratic capitalism. These works are motivated by the question of how and why capitalism has survived despite the crises that exist in that system of production and despite the rise of democratic politics. The answer, these radicals argue, is that, under certain conditions, class conflict is reconcilable; capitalists and workers can agree to a compromise. Adam Przeworski and Michael Wallerstein (1982a:54) express it thus: "Those who do not own the instruments of production consent to the institution of the private ownership of capital stock while those who own productive instruments consent to [democratic] political institutions that permit other groups to effectively press their claims to the allocation of resources and the distribution of output." The basis for the compromise is, on the one hand, workers' belief that capitalists will use part of the current product to increase future output and that some of that output will benefit them; and, on the other, capitalists' belief that they will be able to retain control over investment decisions or to choose what portion of net earnings they will save and what portion they will consume.

If workers are excessively militant or if capitalists decide to disinvest, there is no basis for a compromise. Worker militancy—claims on most or all of the existing capital stock through plans for nationalization—threatens future returns to the owners of private enterprise; it causes capitalists to rapidly disinvest rather than seek an agreement with workers. Similarly, capitalists' refusal to save and invest means output will diminish, sharply reducing the wages and transfer payments that accrue to workers. Disinvestment therefore causes workers to become increasingly militant, again providing no basis for a compromise.

Przeworski and Wallerstein (1982a) have conducted a rigorous analysis of the conditions under which a class compromise is possible, that is, the circumstances in which workers do not become highly militant and capitalists do not rapidly disinvest.[31] Working within a mathematical model of the capitalist system of production in which each class chooses optimal strategies—best levels of militancy and savings rates—in anticipation of the optimal response by its adversary, they show exactly how prospects for compromise vary with the relation between the prevailing capital output ratio in the economy and workers' and capitalists' discount rates for future wages and consumption. Although their analysis does not presuppose the existence of any particular institutions under which negotiations take place, they note that workers and capitalists might be better off if they agreed to install "corporatist arrangements" as a part of the compromise (1982a:231–32).

Przeworski and Wallerstein claim their analysis yields valuable insights into why and when workers might decide to attempt a transition to socialism. To this end they present a brief extension of their investigation, in which the gains to workers are disaggregated into a discounted flow of earnings up to the instant the capital stock is nationalized and a discounted flow of earnings workers expect to receive in the period after nationalization. In including the latter component of workers' wages they incorporate the possibility that a capitalist dictatorship rather than socialism may be imposed on society and hence substantially less in benefits may actually accrue to workers after the transition is attempted. It is less important to take

31. See also Bowles and Gintes (1982).

the possibility of capitalist dictatorship into account "the greater the proportion of capital stock [that] is already publicly owned and the greater the strength of socialist parties" (235–36).

It follows from the work of class compromise theorists that the state and its policies are essentially instruments of a class coalition: "The organization of the state as an institution and the policies pursued by this institution constitute an expression of the class compromise." In particular, it is up to the state to enforce the terms of the compromise, seeing to it that "segments of each class that enter into the compromise are protected from non-cooperative behavior by their fellow class members." In addition, the state must make sure that the class coalition is successful at the polls (236).

The state's role is embodied in the Keynesian policies of Western governments. Class compromise theorists interpret Keynes as saying that public ownership of the means of production was unnecessary, that the objectives of workers could be achieved through demand management and the state regulation of and support for private enterprise. In the context of the crisis of the 1930s, then, Keynesianism promised workers higher earnings together with various forms of social security. In doing so it provided an escape for social democrats who were unwilling to carry out nationalization programs. By embracing Keynesianism, social democrats could avoid charges of reformism yet still claim to promote the welfare of their constituents. Finally, Keynesianism assured capitalists that governments would continue to support them at home and abroad, and that their "investment prerogatives" would remain intact.[32]

Seen in this light, the mixed character of economies is an outgrowth of a bargain which stipulates that state productive activities will not challenge the privileged position of private business. The state assumes responsibility for those commercial activities which are supposedly unprofitable as private enterprises but still "necessary" for the operation of the economy as a whole. In this way, state-owned enterprise assists the private sector in producing the output on which the income of workers and capitalists depends.[33]

Beyond this, mixed economies have no special theoretical significance. The extensive scope of state ownership and the relative importance of public investment in Austria, Italy, and other countries do

32. For an extended discussion of how these and other aspects of Keynesianism were well-suited to the needs of the class coalition of the 1930s, see Przeworski (1980b), Przeworski and Wallerstein (1982a), and Offe (1983). See also Tilton (1979), who argues that, in some respects, Swedish Social Democratic policies anticipated Keynesianism.

33. See Przeworski (1980b).

not indicate class compromises significantly different from those which exist in private enterprise economies. Rather, these mixed economies can be explained in terms of "special historical circumstances" or simply in terms of a more massive effort, on the part of the class coalition, to support the private sector.[34]

Class compromise theory offers for mixed economies a more complete political explanation than either of its radical counterparts. It avoids the pitfalls of assuming that the scope and character of state-owned enterprise always serve the interests of a single omnipotent class. Rather, like liberal theory, it recognizes that markets serve the material interests of several social actors, not only capitalists. Like classical liberalism, it incorporates intergenerational concerns.[35] Like neoliberal theory, it views mixed economies as outcomes of both societal conflict and societal cooperation; mixes of private and public enterprise are understood to serve interests that are in part complementary and in part competing. In addition, class compromise theory shares with neoliberal theory an appreciation for the ways political institutions shape negotiations over the organization and operation of commercial activity. It explicitly recognizes the intervening effects that corporatism and other forms of interest intermediation have on the welfare consequences of mixed economies. The idea that political institutions are designed to rationalize capitalists' control over the organization of commercial activity or to conceal states' attempts to use public enterprise to serve the interests of the capitalist class is rejected by both class compromise and neoliberal theorists.

What distinguishes class compromise theory from liberal theory is its attempt to demonstrate that the same political coalition creates both private enterprise and mixed economies, and further, that for a given set of democratic political institutions the distributional consequences of both economies are essentially identical. Class compromise theory holds that the same coalition always decides how the economy is structured. The same two classes use state-owned enterprise to create the conditions under which essentially the same Keynesian compromise is agreed to and maintained. Differences that exist in the scope of public ownership in the industrial democracies merely reflect the special needs that capitalists had at the time the class compromise was forged; for instance, how many unprofitable private firms the coalition had to turn over to the state.

34. Przeworski (1980b:53) dismisses the large government business sectors of Austria as an outcome of "confiscation." He sees the mixed economic structure of Italy as a "fascist legacy."

35. For example, Przeworski and Wallerstein (1982a:219) suggest that nonmilitant workers would be best off materially after about a generation.

Unlike liberals, class compromise theorists argue that the distributional consequences of private enterprise and mixed economies are essentially uniform. Both economies afford capitalists a privileged position relative to workers. Capitalists enjoy an inequitable share of power and wealth because, under the compromise that prevails in all the industrial democracies, they control most of the investment decisions on which output and hence workers' material well-being depend. By threatening to disinvest or to withdraw their consent to democratic institutions, capitalists therefore can extract an excessive share of current product. This outcome is no different in mixed economies, because supposedly capitalists still control most investment decisions and presumably state-owned enterprises do not significantly enhance workers' welfare. Hence even in the mixed economy the working class remains structurally dependent for its welfare on private owners of production. Finally, the fact that a large share of investment decisions remains in private hands in all economies makes a transition to socialism no more likely in one Western country than in another.[36]

The class compromise account of mixed economies is superior to both the instrumentalist and the functionalist accounts, and it provides definitive answers to questions which neoliberal theory often leaves unanswered. It is nonetheless seriously flawed. To begin with, it rests on weak empirical foundations. Major shares of investment decisions—as much as half—are or have been in public hands in several Western countries. Moreover, there is much evidence that workers in Austria and other countries benefit substantially from the distinctive behavior of state-owned enterprises.

From a theoretical standpoint, class compromise theory—indeed, the entire radical perspective—suffers from an inaccurate conception of the democratic state. The state is not necessarily an instrument of a coalition of capitalists and workers. The state has the potential to join or even forge coalitions with certain *segments* of the capitalist and working classes. These alternative coalitions can organize commercial activity in such a way that state-owned enterprises serve the material (and nonmaterial) interests of state bureaucrats and certain workers as well as the interests of some private owners of production. For these coalitions, mixed economies appear to be more than transitory schemes of economic organization or half-way stops between capi-

36. Class compromise theorists contend that, if any major change occurs in the 1980s and 1990s, it will be in Western *polities*. See especially Przeworski's concluding remarks (1980a). See also the comments he and Wallerstein make about the possibility of the "Chileanization" of the industrial democracies (1982b).

talism and socialism; such coalitions appear to *prefer* mixes of public and private enterprise both to private enterprise capitalism and to socialism.[37]

Class compromise theorists do not appreciate how coalitions use state-owned enterprise to undermine the investment prerogatives of certain segments of the capitalist class. These radicals focus on the ways states' productive activities support private enterprise *within* national economies. Their class coalition is composed of capitalists, some of whom depend on the state to secure inputs to production, market their products overseas, and also protect and promote their foreign investments. The first and second kinds of support pose no serious problem for class compromise theory. In fact, state demand for and supply of military goods and services is recognized as having solidified the Keynesian class compromise at a critical juncture in its early development.[38] To the extent that the erection of an open world trading order made possible greater output, from which both capitalists and workers then gained, the postwar foreign economic policies of Western states—especially the American state—may conceivably have strengthened the compromise.

State protection and promotion of direct foreign investment is less easily incorporated within class compromise theory, however. This kind of activity makes it substantially easier for capitalists to shift investment out of the native economy into foreign economies. In turn, workers become more and more uncertain about their ability to maintain, let alone augment, their share of the future product. But the state is supposedly an instrument of *both* classes. So either workers fail to anticipate the long-term effects of the states' foreign economic and military policies on their bargaining position, or, from the outset, part of the capitalist class demands and receives an agreement to use the state to undermine the very conditions that made the compromise possible. Both eventualities have yet to be explored by class compromise theorists.[39]

The problems posed by state promotion of direct foreign investment are even more serious. This facet of states' activities forces us to assume that the *identity* of capitalists is of no political significance in countries where foreign investment occurs, that foreign ownership of

37. See, for example, Austrian political economist Ewald Nowotny (1982b); see also Lemass's case for the creation of the Irish state-sponsored bodies (1969:287).

38. See, for instance, Block (1977) and Skocpol (1980:183).

39. Note that as earlier (1982a), in most of their more recent work Przeworski and Wallerstein (1985, 1986) ignore the constraints imposed by capital mobility. They assume there is a *single* governmental jurisdiction in which workers and capitalists negotiate the compromise.

firms and industries can be substituted for native ownership without any substantial alteration in the terms of the compromise or in the uses to which state-owned enterprise is put. Yet as I pointed out in reviewing neoliberal theory, there is much evidence that these assumptions are unreasonable. In the eyes of workers, as well as some local capitalists and some elements of the state, foreign ownership often is *not* a perfect substitute for native ownership. Workers are frequently uncertain about the durability of agreements forged with foreign investors; they judge the threat of disinvestment to be more pronounced if firms are foreign-owned. But workers do not then proceed to nationalize the entire means of production. Nor do foreigners always install capitalist dictatorships in countries where workers oppose their investments. In such circumstances, rather, workers often ally with local capitalists and elements of the state to ensure native ownership of the affected firms or industries. The corresponding investment decisions are placed in public hands, and the respective enterprises are operated by the state, because a coalition of native groups decides its mutual interests are served better by a mix of private and public enterprise than by either some combination of foreign-private and local-private enterprise or socialism. And this coalition *is* powerful enough to defeat the advocates of those alternative schemes of economic organization.[40]

Why might elements of the state join coalitions that oppose direct foreign investment? For one reason, some politicians and bureaucrats believe foreign-owned enterprise undermines their ability to manage the national economy; for instance, their ability to insulate certain (native) groups from international market fluctuations. To this end, even the first Thatcher administration placed some restrictions on foreign purchases of British nationalized industries.[41] More significantly, the desire to maintain native control over the national economy has led elements of states to reject or to interpret differently Keynes's position on public ownership. Politicians and especially some state bureaucrats contend that privately owned enterprise is unfit or unable to make certain investments; the investment prerogatives of certain capitalists must be sacrificed so that the state and its allies can, through the installation and management of a mix of private and public enterprise, meet their "obligations" to the citizenry. The mixed

40. In his article on possibilities for a transition to socialism (1980c:142), Przeworski argues that "economic militancy not backed by political power opens the threat of political reaction." My point is that, in the face of direct foreign investment, workers sometimes join alliances that are powerful enough to greatly reduce the likelihood of such a "reaction."

41. See Heald and Steel (1982:336).

character of the economies of Austria, France, and Italy appears to be, in part, an outgrowth of such elements of the state having allied with other groups to transfer control over critical investment decisions from private to public hands. In this way the failure to consider the effects of states' foreign economic policies leads class compromise theorists to overlook the possibility that mixed economies may be created by coalitions in which the state is an ally, not a tool, of some capitalists and some workers.[42]

Class compromise theorists fail to recognize the existence of this alternative kind of coalition because they inaccurately assess the welfare consequences of state-owned enterprise. Like other branches of radical theory, the class compromise school focuses almost exclusively on the material gains and losses from, and the financial results of, state-owned enterprise; it uses the same criterion to evaluate the performance of both privately owned and publicly owned firms.[43] But the price system is, I repeat, not operative for public investments. Hence the fact that public enterprises sometimes do not yield financial dividends does not mean that capitalists benefit disproportionately from state productive activity. Nor should we conclude, on the basis of the financial performance of publicly owned firms, that the state depends on capitalists for the benefits it bestows on workers. By providing job security, promoting regional development, and implementing various other policies designed to satisfy the equity claims of certain workers, the state, through its enterprises, serves the interests of noncapitalists as well as capitalists. Desire for nonmaterial gain and trust in the benevolence of those state bureaucrats who reject or interpret differently Keynes's position on state ownership could easily lead workers to join an alternative coalition.

But workers might support state takeovers of ailing firms and industries even if the price system were operative for public investments. Workers might be willing to mortgage part of the future earnings and revenue of public-owned firms in return for greater

42. Evidence of state bureaucrats who rejected or reinterpreted Keynesianism are easy to find in histories of industrialized and, especially, industrializing mixed economies. On Italy see Holland (1972: chap. 2) and Prodi (1974:56ff.); on France see Zysman (1977:6–7) and Kuisel (1981:213, 215); and on Austria see Langer (1964) and Hankel (1981:34). The implications of the more general behavioral problems surrounding ownership and control for this and other class-based theories have been stressed by such writers as Dahrendorf (1959:136).

43. Przeworski is aware (1980c) of the need to take nonmaterial gains into account in any comparison of private enterprise and socialist economies. However, his and Wallerstein's work focuses almost exclusively on the material basis for a compromise between workers and capitalists.

control over investment decisions or because they judge gains from a continuation of private ownership to be less than those which accrue to them from subsidizing the operation of state-owned firms.[44]

Peltzman's work suggests still another interpretation. Some segments of the working class may intend to nationalize and then reorganize existing firms on behalf of certain collective interests. But nationalization creates incentives for segments of this and other classes to press their short-term claims on publicly owned firms; hence an unintended but still real mortgaging of future earnings takes place. Workers in state-owned enterprises have such incentives, and according to some observers, their demands may result in policies that produce such a mortgaging of future earnings.[45] In such circumstances, elections do not necessarily serve to endorse and maintain the Keynesian practices of social democrats. Rather, elections alter the way coalitions of groups use state-owned enterprise to serve a competing set of interests, some of which may be intergenerational in nature. This, of course, is the basis for neoliberal attacks on democratic supervision of mixed economies: the idea that elections and other democratic institutions allow certain groups or coalitions of groups to use state-owned enterprise to serve their own self-interests at the expense of the interests of other groups, including the unborn. Because of its deficiencies, class compromise theory provides little defense against this attack.

In sum, the class compromise account advances our understanding of mixed economies but does not eliminate some of the major flaws in neoliberal theory. Class compromise theory itself is based on an inaccurate conception of the state, an excessively aggregated conception of social actors, and an inaccurate evaluation of the welfare consequences of state-owned enterprise.

Understanding the Politics of Mixed Economies

This review demonstrates the need for three kinds of analysis. First, we need a deeper investigation of the workings and potential welfare

44. In this sense, Przeworski and Wallerstein's analysis of the transition to socialism (1982a:233ff.) suffers from the failure to consider the possibility that some workers are willing to mortgage their own future earnings and those of other noncapitalists. See Alt's summary of the reasons members of the British Labour party give for supporting and opposing nationalization (1979:10–11). The same author provides evidence that these partisans' commitment to nationalization was relatively insensitive to economic decline (pp. 250ff.).

45. See the review of the Wellington-Winter hypothesis in Hamermesh (1975), for example.

consequences of mixed economies, especially in relation to private enterprise economies. Liberal theory gives us the most valuable insights about the institutions that promote or undermine market efficiency in the two types of economies; and in this context, it illuminates important differences in the character of private and public investment. It thus helps us understand the collective and intergenerational welfare outcomes that can be achieved in each type of economy. We need to delve deeper into this body of work in order to clarify the similarities and differences of mixed and private enterprise economies.

Neoliberal and radical theories give us some useful insights into distributional matters. Radical theory makes an important contribution in pointing out that capital mobility is a structural barrier to government taxation and transfer of societal wealth. What we need to know is how or if capital mobility and related facets of market processes simultaneously promote Pareto gains and intergenerational equity, that is, whether there is a tradeoff between collective and distributional outcomes, and if so, how this tradeoff differs in private enterprise and mixed economies. For example, does the greater control public enterprise affords over local capital allocation make a large segment of the workforce—state enterprise workers—substantially better off in a mixed economy but only at the expense of future generations? Neoliberals and radicals offer different answers to this question. We need to go deeper into the workings of the two economies—particularly their international dimensions—before we can resolve this dispute.

Neither perspective adequately incorporates behavioral factors. Classical liberal and some neoliberal accounts of mixed economies are too quick to assume that state managers and planners will necessarily pursue some benign conception of the public interest. Liberals and radicals generally fail to scrutinize the assumption that private owners control private managers and hence the behavior of private firms. We need a deeper analysis of the behavioral features of both economies, especially of the behavior that limits the two economies' potential for promoting collective gain and distributional equity.

Second, neoliberal and class compromise theories show that the workings and welfare consequences of both types of economies depend, to some degree, on the workings of certain political institutions. We need a more precise statement of the relevant structural and behavioral characteristics of these institutions. Three institutions appear to be especially important: elections and electoral systems, modes of interest intermediation, and styles of state administration. Neoliberal theory illuminates the importance of the first of these institutions. It suggests that elections and electoral systems play an important role in articulating and enforcing citizens' conceptions of the means and ends of government activity, including the ends of state-owned enterprise. In this context, neoliberal theory argues that elections create behavioral incentives for state managers to emphasize short-term, distributional objectives over long-term, collective objectives. We need to better understand how elections perform this role, especially in the context of dissensus about state-owned enterprise.

Neoliberal theory and class compromise theory both alert us to the importance of producer group relations and the mode of interest intermediation. In particular, they suggest that the workings and welfare consequences of political economies differ depending on whether societal conflict is negotiated by several official producer groups (corporatism) or a multiplicity of nonofficial interest groups (pluralism). This body of theory gives good reason to believe that any tradeoff between collective and distributional outcomes will be negotiated differently under different modes of interest intermediation, for instance, that corporatism may be more conducive than pluralism to the pursuit of capital and labor's long-term interests. We need to better understand the behavioral features of the two modes of interest intermediation, for example, the incentives of producer group leaders relative to the incentives of interest group leaders to pursue long-term mutual interests. Class compromise theory offers us few insights in this regard. New developments in neoliberal theory offer us such insights; they need to be more closely examined.

Liberal theory also illuminates the important role of state administrators in designing the amount and pattern of public investment. We need to know more about how much influence state administrators actually exercise over public investment decisions, or alternatively, when various groups in society defer to these individuals to make public investment decisions. As it stands, liberal theory assumes, erroneously, that all societies are equally prone to defer to the authority of state administrators. This simply is not the case.[46]

Third, and most important, we need a deeper and more complete analysis of the *interconnections* between the logics of the two economies and the logics of the three political institutions. We need to better understand how the workings of different constellations of political institutions interact with the workings of each type of economy to produce potentially different levels and distributions of wealth across time. As we have seen, classical liberal and functionalist radical theo-

46. See, for instance, Shonfield (1965), Suleiman (1974), Zysman (1977, 1983), and Véliz (1980).

ries are inadequate for this purpose, because these perspectives attribute too much power to a single social actor and employ only one welfare criterion.

Class compromise theory and neoliberal theory are more complete, and they yield insights about both the collective and the distributional dimensions of social welfare. But the former perspective fails to recognize both the structural (and behavioral) distinctiveness of mixed economies and the possibility that compromises are forged between *segments* of capital and labor. The latter perspective is not flawed in these ways, but neoliberalism generally offers us few generalizations about what *set* of coalitions might form in each economy or about how the possible *range* of welfare outcomes might differ in alternative political-economic systems.

These three kinds of analysis are needed to advance our understanding of the politics of mixed economies. They are the subject of the next part of this book.[47]

47. The next section of the book does not consider the historical forces that shape the structural and behavioral features of the four systems. See Freeman (1987), where I show how mixed and private enterprise economies emerged over time from a distinct series of compromises between four social actors: native–private business, foreign–private business, agencies of the state, and wage earners. Out of this investigation emerges a theoretical proposition about the origins of mixed economies, namely, the more delayed industrialization is relative to the English case and the more centralist the administrative tradition is in a particular country, the more mixed the (market-oriented) economy will be. The proposition is defended with case study material from the experiences of Britain, Austria, and Ireland and with some simple analyses of cross-sectional data on the scope of state-owned enterprise in fifty-nine countries.

PART TWO

THEORY

CHAPTER THREE

Private Enterprise and
Mixed Economies Compared

Private enterprise and mixed economies are similar in that each economy is, in essence, "market-oriented." Prices, in large part, are determined by domestic and international supply and demand. And the performance of firms in each economy is an outgrowth, to some extent, of their abilities to compete in local and in global markets. More generally, in private enterprise and in mixed economies alike the withholding from current consumption on which future material well-being depends results from investment out of profits—either out of the earnings of private enterprises or out of the earnings of a mix of private and public enterprises.[1]

Private enterprise and mixed economies are, in other respects, quite different. Each has distinctive structural and behavioral characteristics. The separation between ownership and control is less pronounced in most private enterprise economies than in most mixed economies. Different economic institutions exist in each economy for the purpose of ameliorating this and other problems. These institutions and the more general contrasts between the two economies are summarized in Table 1.

This chapter explores the workings of private enterprise and mixed economies in relation to our two welfare criteria. It shows that, under certain conditions, the two economies can produce fundamentally different levels and distributions of wealth. Foremost among these conditions are capital market development and the degree of capital mobility. Capital markets and capital mobility enhance the efficiency of both kinds of economies and thus help realize collective gains and

1. Market-oriented economic systems are distinguished from systems with a central economic authority and from preceptoral systems by such authors as Lindblom (1977). See also Przeworski and Wallerstein (1982a:216).

Table 1. The workings and welfare bases of private enterprise and mixed economies

	Private enterprise economies	Mixed economies
Welfare bases	Pareto gains in consumption and in earnings of current generation Intergenerational equity through optimization of societal consumption over time Intragenerational equity through governmental redistribution of societal wealth	Pareto gains in consumption and in earnings of current generation Intergenerational equity through optimization of societal consumption over time Intragenerational equity through governmental supply of employment, government production of goods and services, and government redistribution of societal wealth
Mechanisms	Productive efficiency in competitive markets (marginal cost pricing, etc.) Fiscal policy (taxation and transfer)	Productive efficiency in private sector Public monopoly where there are increasing returns to scale Public production where there are certain external effects Government design and implementation of optimal fiscal and (public) investment policies
Structural problems	Market failure—shortfalls in or absence of production of certain goods and services Market imperfections—rigidities in and underdeveloped nature of capital markets Mobility of firms—constraints on amount of wealth that can be redistributed by governments (within a particular jurisdiction)	Market imperfections—rigidities and underdeveloped nature of capital markets (inaccurate benchmark for calculation of social discount rate) Mobility of private firms in parts of jurisdiction (sectors) where public firms are not located Disproportionate bargaining power of state enterprise managers and workers

Behavioral problems	Bounded rationality of firms and investors Managerial control of large firms Government inability to design "neutral" fiscal policies (fiscal policies that do not undermine productive efficiency)	Bounded rationality of private firms and private investors Bounded rationality of government—inability to operate monopolies in ways that achieve productive and social efficiency or to identify optimal fiscal and investment policies Managerial control of state enterprise and of large private firms Government inability to design "neutral" fiscal policies
Institutions that ameliorate structural and behavioral problems	Governmental regulation (regulated private monopoly, etc.) Stockholders' meetings Capital market transactions Labor market processes Company law	For private business sector: Stockholders' meetings Capital market transactions Labor market processes Company law For public business sector: Public audits Reprivatization threats

intergenerational equity. At the same time capital markets and capital mobility undermine governments' capacities to redistribute wealth among citizens. To the extent they allow relatively fewer capital market transactions and less capital mobility than private enterprise economies do, mixed economies are more inefficient and hence produce comparatively smaller collective welfare gains; but they also give the respective governments greater capacity to redistribute wealth. To the extent the same private enterprise economies are open to highly mobile, foreign-private capital, this contrast in the potential performance of the two economies will be even more pronounced. Finally, the relative power of certain groups varies within and across the two economies. The owners of private firms have, in some respects, more control over private managers than the (collective) owners of public firms have over state managers; the owners of private firms also can thwart governments' efforts to redistribute wealth in private enterprise economies. Managers and workers in public firms are in certain respects more powerful than managers and workers of private firms in either kind of economy. These power differences translate into potentially different distributions of wealth in the two economies.

This discussion is divided into examinations of the workings of each economy. These examinations are further subdivided into two parts: a brief explanation of how, in theory, each economy satisfies certain of our welfare criteria and government's role in this process, and a discussion of how, in practice, certain structural and behavioral problems produce inefficiencies and collective welfare losses on the one hand and distributional inequities on the other. The chapter concludes with the critical role that political institutions play in shaping government preferences and behavior and, more specifically, the role that political institutions play in translating distributions of power into specific policies.

PRIVATE ENTERPRISE ECONOMIES

Private enterprise economies are thought to be desirable because they produce efficient market outcomes. And efficient market outcomes yield Pareto gains to society—that is, they enhance the welfare of at least some current and future members of society while leaving other members of society no worse off than they were before efficient outcomes were achieved. Market processes determine a societal distribution of wealth. In private enterprise economies, disagreements about the fairness of this distribution presumably can be resolved through the creation or improvement of various submarkets and through government reallocation of output and earnings.

Efficiency means several things about the workings of private enterprise systems.[2] As regards production, for example, it means that inputs and outputs cannot be shifted from one firm to another in order to raise the level of production of any good without, in the process, lowering the level of production of another good. Productive efficiency also implies that, for a given pattern of output, it is impossible to use less of any one productive input without increasing the use of other productive inputs. Productive efficiency therefore implies that the marginal product of any two inputs is the same for each firm that produces the same kind of good, and that the ratio of marginal products of two inputs is the same for firms producing the same good. (The reason is that if the ratio of the marginal products were not identical, a reallocation of inputs could raise the output of one firm without decreasing that of another and thus produce a more efficient market outcome.)

From a behavioral standpoint, productive efficiency implies that each firm in a private enterprise economy chooses a combination of inputs such that the marginal rate of technical substitution—the ratio of the marginal products of two inputs—is equal to the (common) relative prices they must pay for these inputs. Also, as long as there are constant returns to scale, each firm expands output until the point where price equals marginal cost.

The benefits from productive efficiency supposedly accrue in the form of Pareto gains—more specifically, in the form of higher levels of consumption and investment earnings for at least some citizens and, at the same time, no diminution of the consumption and earnings levels other citizens enjoyed prior to the achievement of market efficiency. This welfare outcome is optimal in the sense that any departure from the conditions for productive efficiency—any reduction in the level of output, for instance—would translate into lesser gains for those whose welfare has been enhanced or into harm to the welfare of those members of society whose welfare was otherwise unaffected by the achievement of productive efficiency.

Private enterprise economies have the potential to enhance the welfare of some citizens and of future generations over time. In an intertemporal or dynamic sense, efficiency means that the price of capital is equal to the present value of its future returns and that, at the same time, producers continually attempt to maximize the value of net per capita output subject to constraints, namely, the condition

2. This summary of the nature of productive efficiency and the welfare outcomes it produces follows Millward and Parker (1983:201–203).

that the sum of consumption per worker and investment per worker equals the difference between output per worker and the combined cost of depreciation and equipping new workers. Efficiency also means that the returns from owning or investing in any one capital good equal the returns from any other and, again, the rate at which individuals presently value the future returns from holding that asset. When these and some related conditions are met, a private enterprise economy is in dynamic, competitive equilibrium; the economy yields an optimal time path of consumption and earnings so that at least some individuals—born and unborn—consume more and earn more while other individuals consume and earn no less than they did before this equilibrium was achieved. A desirable history of societal consumption and capital accumulation supposedly is possible in a private enterprise system, then, through the achievement of a dynamic, competitive equilibrium.

What role does government play in bringing about this welfare outcome? Is there a need to create an omniscient and benign governmental authority that can ascertain and implement an optimal set of economic policies, in particular an authority that ascertains and implements the optimal savings rate for the private enterprise economy? In its purest form, the case for the private enterprise economy does not require any public intervention of this kind. When private enterprise economies are in a state of competitive equilibrium, their internal logic is essentially the same as that employed by a central planner; the perfectly competitive market and the individually rational private enterprises and consumers of which it is composed produce the identical, welfare-enhancing outcome that an omniscient and benign central planner would produce.[3] In principle, then, private enterprise systems allow citizens to forgo the costs of governmental decision making yet also realize the Pareto gains that central decision making (if it were fully rational and interested in enhancing the welfare of some citizens and not harming the welfare of others) would produce.

The case for private enterprise economies can be challenged on several grounds. To begin with, private enterprise systems are normally plagued by structural deficiencies that prevent Pareto gains from being realized; private enterprise economies rarely satisfy the

3. Thus Burmeister and Dobell write, "In a complete system of perfect markets, therefore, the planning agency becomes otiose . . . the maximum principle of Pontryagin is seen to be the culmination of the logical sequence originating in the maximum principle of Adam Smith." Quoted in Wallerstein (1982:15). The same source provides a useful summary of the theory of optimal growth.

condition that at least some citizens are made better off while no citizens are made worse off in terms of consumption and earnings. Recall, for example, that to achieve productive efficiency firms must apply a marginal cost-pricing rule in each and every sector of the economy. If there is an uncontrolled sector in which prices are not set equal to marginal cost—as where there are increasing returns to scale so that natural monopolies exist—private production will fall short of the optimal level, and the maximum gains will not be realized by society. Nor is it the case that a combination of marginal cost-pricing and private monopolistic revenue-maximizing behavior will necessarily lead to welfare outcomes superior to those outcomes which obtain when alternative combinations of pricing behavior are adopted by firms in a private enterprise system.[4] In principle, problems of this kind can be solved through price regulation and government monitoring of private monopolistic production. However, it is questionable whether governments are willing and able to regulate private pricing and production decisions in a way that restores efficiency. Among other things, it is difficult for public authorities to determine the appropriate price for the goods produced by the monopolist when consumer demand for those goods always falls short of average cost. In such a situation, it is difficult for public authorities to decide what kind of fiscal incentive will make the market behave efficiently.[5]

Similarly, there is no reason to assume that capital markets satisfy the conditions for competitive equilibrium or that asset holders' behavior is consistent with the conditions for optimization of social welfare over time. For dynamic, competitive equilibrium to be achieved, asset markets must link short-term with long-run economic process; for example, they must link the short-run prices at which reproducible assets sell and the long-run average cost of producing those assets. In many countries, unfortunately, capital markets are underdeveloped. Capital markets are plagued by a wide range of imperfections that mean, among other things, the price of capital is not equal to the present value of its future returns.

This problem is not necessarily the result of government intervention. In some countries governments have actively sought to create efficient asset markets. But these efforts have failed to bear fruit, in part because investors apparently are not interested in being able to insure themselves against risk (through capital market transactions).[6]

4. See Millward and Parker (1983:203). The Theorem of the Second Best indicates that if any one of the necessary conditions for perfectly competitive market equilibrium is not met, no rigorous basis exists for presuming that the second-best solution is to maintain competitive market conditions (see Wallerstein 1982:50–51).

5. See Millward and Parker (1983:208).

6. See, for example, Hankel's (1981) analysis of the problems posed by the disequi-

Also, there is much evidence that the conditions for allocative efficiency are not met because investors are not fully informed; investors
are unable to estimate accurately the future stream of earnings from
different assets.[7]

Private enterprise economies are also plagued by behavior problems, especially by the separation of ownership and control of private
firms. Analyses of the welfare outcomes of private enterprise economies normally assume that firms are unitary actors who pursue material gain in a self-interested, rational fashion. Such behavior leads
inadvertently, in the context of perfect market equilibrium, to an outcome in which at least some groups of citizens and generations are
better off in terms of consumption and accumulated earnings from
investments. But in reality, firms are collections of contracts between
self-interested individuals, individuals who may not act in either a
unitary or a rational manner.

Consider the managers of private firms. They forge agreements
with workers for a certain amount and kind of work at a particular
wage. They also contract with suppliers for inputs that are used in
production. When, as in small—especially family-owned—firms,
managers and owners are the same people, managers often tend to
forge these contracts in an efficient manner, because the return to
these owner-managers varies directly with the efficiency with which
they use material and labor inputs in the production process. Inefficiencies such as wage agreements that pay workers more than the
prevailing price of labor directly reduce owner-managers' residual income and hence also their rate of earnings or profit. Accordingly, the
owner-managers of small-scale firms tend to behave in ways that promote efficiency and, in turn, tend to bring about a competitive market equilibrium.

Now, if private enterprise economies were composed mainly of
small, family-owned firms, there would be good reason to assume
that managerial behavior promotes the collective welfare of society.
However, most private enterprise economies are actually made up of
a collection of small, family-owned and large, shareholder-owned
firms. And in the latter firms, owners are not the people who make
pricing and other kinds of decisions; rather, ownership is divorced
from managerial control. In large, shareholder-owned firms, managers therefore may pursue goals that are inconsistent with those of the

librium in and underdeveloped character of Austria's capital market. It should be acknowledged that in the course of his analysis Hankel holds the Austrian government's
fiscal policies partly responsible for the state of that country's capital market (see
Chapter 7 below). The broader relevance of the structure of financial markets is explored in Zysman (1983).

7. See Wallerstein (1982:15–21).

owners. The managers of large firms may attempt to maximize sales rather than profits in order to augment their salaries; they may also fail to seek out the least costly suppliers of inputs or fail to negotiate efficient labor contracts.[8]

Unchecked, such behavior has at least two important welfare implications. First, it prevents owners from earning the maximum rate of return on their investments; it fosters a maldistribution of wealth insofar as managers use their positions of authority to augment their own income at the expense of owners. Second, the divorce of ownership and control in large firms undermines the efficiency of the private enterprise system and therefore prevents society from realizing Pareto gains in consumption.

The divorce of ownership and control is not complete, however. The structure of private enterprise economies usually is such that the shareholders of large firms have opportunities to encourage behavior that is more consistent with conditions for a competitive market equilibrium, realize a greater rate and share of return on their investments, and, in turn, promote the realization of socially desirable (Pareto) welfare outcomes. To begin with, private enterprise economies normally allow stockholders to meet with management on a regular basis. This institution provides owners with an opportunity to hold managers accountable for their decisions. It allows owners to question managers about the rationale behind their decisions and, if necessary, vote sanctions on and rewards to them. Capital markets also offer owners a direct means of influencing managerial behavior. The purchase and sale of shares in firms signal owners' evaluations of managerial performance. Owners can also communicate these evaluations by threatening to sell their shares to other firms that are contemplating a takeover; takeovers may result in managers being dismissed or demoted. The labor market serves as an evaluator of managerial behavior. It provides managers with incentives to forge efficient contracts with laborers and with suppliers. A manager who earns handsome returns for the shareholders of her or his firm may be lured away by the offer of a larger salary, more attractive benefits, and more authority from owners of another firm who seek to increase their rate of return. Managers' awareness of this possibility and their desire for increased wealth and status may therefore lead them to make efficient decisions in order to enhance their personal (labor) market value. In turn, the rate of return to their present owners will

---

8. As regards the British economy, Millward and Parker (1983:214) point out that the shareholdings of company directors usually constitute only a small share of total shareholdings. See also Thonet and Poensgen's (1979) study of ownership and control in the United States and West Germany.

be more in keeping with the rate that obtains when the market is in competitive equilibrium. Finally, in most private enterprise systems a corpus of "company law" requires firms to make public disclosures of their earnings and financial condition at regular intervals. Dissemination of this and related kinds of information pertaining to firms' performance enhances owners' abilities to evaluate and discipline managers.

Opinions differ about how effective these institutions are. Company law is not always enforced, and managers can sometimes evade it. The managerial segment of the labor market is plagued by imperfections that sometimes reward managers who have adopted inefficient policies. And it is not clear that all managers, or even a substantial proportion, are concerned with enhancing their (labor) market value. Large firms—especially in industries with natural monopolies—can be safe havens for inefficient managers. Stockholder meetings are usually held annually, and so short-term adjustments in managerial behavior are difficult to accomplish through this institution. More important, managers usually control the agenda of such meetings. And since in large firms shareholding is widely dispersed, individual owners may have to form coalitions with other owners if they are going to pass any motion disciplining managers for inefficient behavior. This means of asserting control therefore imposes substantial collective action costs on owners.[9]

In contrast, capital market transactions—selling or purchasing shares in firms--can often be accomplished quickly at comparatively much less cost to the individual investor. In addition, the information in company reports and in the materials produced by various other sources allows owners to make these shareholding decisions more wisely than if they had to rely solely on the information managers choose to supply at stockholder meetings. For these and other reasons, capital market transactions are considered the most effective way in which owners can achieve some degree of control over managerial behavior. The existence of a capital market, and the investment opportunities it provides, counterbalances the incentives for inefficiency that exist in large firms. Capital markets—to the extent they themselves are developed and efficient—apparently do most to guarantee that asset holders earn a fair rate of return and, at the same time, that society realizes Pareto gains in consumption and in earnings.[10]

9. On the nature and effectiveness of stockholder meetings see Cubbin and Leach (1983).

10. See the comments of Millward and Parker (1983:214). See also Thonet and Poensgen (1979:36).

But what of the distribution of wealth between owners and those nonowners who are not managers? How is an equitable distribution of wealth achieved between wage earners and asset holders in private enterprise economies? Unfortunately, there are few satisfactory answers to these questions. The case for competitive market equilibrium rests primarily on the possibility of realizing Pareto gains in societal consumption. The theory implies that at least some individuals will be better off in terms of consumption and earnings if competitive equilibrium is achieved. Further, it tells us that overall distribution of income depends on the pattern of production in the economy—the rental unit cost of capital and the wage rate—and that this pattern is determined by the nature of consumer tastes, distribution of asset holdings and of income among consumers, and an economy's stocks of assets. That is, in competitive equilibrium it is the structure of property ownership, preference for leisure versus consumption, and the stock of capital (e.g., talent) that determine how the market distributes wealth intragenerationally. The theory tells us little about who should be better off or how much the welfare of a particular individual or set of individuals should be improved relative to that of other individuals or groups.[11]

The problems with competitive equilibrium theory are more serious. If how individuals value their own income depends on how their descendants and other people value their income (that is, if individual valuations are interdependent), then there is no reason to believe that competitive markets yield either efficient or equitable allocations of resources.[12] Moreover, if owners and wage earners are organized into two groups that bargain over the mix of investment—savings out of profits—and the negotiated wage level represents any positive share of production, then owners consistently underinvest and hence the socially desirable outcomes associated with competitive market equilibrium are not realized; in private enterprise systems, negotiations of this kind will always produce capital accumulation that is less than the social optimum.[13]

In the face of such difficulties, the defenders of private enterprise systems often suggest that redistribution can be handled by govern-

11. See, for instance, Millward and Parker (1983:203). Note that the emphasis is on the "equality of condition" within living generations, particularly on the intragenerational distribution of income. There also are meritocratic, welfarist and emancipatory dimensions of intragenerational equity. See Rae (1979) and Brooks (1983).

12. This point was demonstrated by Sen (1961, 1967) and Marglin (1963). For a discussion of recent work on this so-called isolation paradox see Wallerstein (1982:28–31).

13. See Lancaster (1973) for a demonstration of this "dynamic inefficiency of capitalism."

ments. Governments supposedly can redistribute wealth through their fiscal policies, more specifically, through taxation of the earnings of owners and nonowners and subsequent transfer of this revenue to deserving individuals and groups. All that is required, supposedly, is that fiscal policy not affect the value or volume of production, that the link between marginal cost-pricing and marginal valuation of output be preserved so that market outcomes remain Pareto-opitmal.[14] In a dynamic sense, governments redistribute wealth in response to changes in citizens' social rate of time preferences; changes in citizens' social rate of time preferences occur as a cause and a consequence of "long swings" in economic growth.[15]

This line of argument assumes not only that governments have the ability to redistribute wealth but also that just distributions of wealth—within and between generations—can be ascertained through the political process, that owners and wage earners can always negotiate a just resolution of competing equity claims. Both assumptions are problematic. First, governments' fiscal policies directly affect market efficiency in that they create disincentives for owners to invest and for managers to earn higher salaries. Government attempts to redistribute wealth may therefore undermine the effectiveness of those features of private enterprise economies which would otherwise contribute to the realization of Pareto gains to current and future generations. Thus, for example, some analysts have argued that the creation and financing of social security systems has resulted in underinvestment in Western economies and, in turn, delimited the consumption possibilities for current and future generations in these countries.[16]

But there are deeper problems with the assumption that government has the ability to redistribute income and other forms of wealth. For a variety of reasons, governmental authority exists in numerous geographic locations, each containing somewhat different groups of citizens with partially different conceptions of distributional justice. If these different governmental units attempt to alter existing distributions of wealth through taxes on the earnings of owners and managers who do business in their jurisdictions, those owners and managers will have an incentive to relocate their firms in other jurisdictions that promise to redistribute less of their earnings (either because the groups in these other jurisdictions value distributional equity less and Pareto gains in consumption more, or because they have different conceptions of distributional equity). In private enterprise systems,

14. See Millward and Parker (1983:203).
15. See Neuman (1985).
16. See the discussion in Von Furstenberg and Malkiel (1977:844–847).

therefore, governments compete for firms; or wage earners, to some extent, are in competition with one another for the benefits that private enterprise systems yield. Owners and managers—who have some but obviously not complete freedom to relocate their investments—can frustrate governments' attempts to promote collective gains and distributional equity. The mobility of firms and their investments, in private enterprise economies, limits the range of possible welfare outcomes that government can achieve through taxation and transfer. These are the "unique power resources" embodied in the ownership or control of private firms.[17]

At this point, the importance of the identity of owners becomes clear. For, at the national level, governments must cope with the fact that if they adopt fiscal policies that reduce the earnings of the owners and managers of foreign firms, those individuals may relocate their operations in other countries and thus eliminate opportunities to achieve national Pareto gains in consumption. The owners and managers of native firms will generally have much more difficulty avoiding government's efforts to redistribute their earnings; native owners and managers are often easier to tax, and hence nationally directed redistribution is relatively easier to accomplish if a private enterprise economy is composed primarily of locally owned and operated firms. Of course, if these firms are less efficient than their foreign counterparts, there may be lower earnings to redistribute. In fact, governments may face a tradeoff between foreign ownership and collective gains and intergenerational equity in consumption, on the one hand, and native ownership and intragenerational equity in consumption, on the other.[18]

MIXED ECONOMIES

In principle, mixed economies are more efficient than private enterprise economies, because state-owned enterprise ameliorates the

17. See Korpi (1978: chap. 1), who stresses the importance of the structure of ownership and control in relation to government's capacity to promote all the facets of distributional equity mentioned above (fn.11). See also the discussions in Heidenheimer, Heclo, and Adams (1983:277, 300) and Zysman (1983: chap. 2). Other students of Western political economies, such as Bowler (1986), stress that capital mobility is a matter of degree. We return to this point in Chapter 5.

18. As Sandmo and Dreze (1971:406, fn. 1) have pointed out, countries that use tax rates as a means of competing for internationally mobile investment are in a game-theoretic situation with other countries and with the firms themselves. If we think of the problem in these terms, the possibility of relocation shapes the core (and other) solutions of this n-person game in such a way as to rule out some distributions of wealth within and between countries.

problems caused by increasing returns and external effects. When created in industries plagued by these market imperfections, state-owned enterprise yields a more optimal pattern and level of output than privately owned enterprise does. It is in mixed economies, then, that current—and future—generations can fully realize the Pareto gains associated with productive efficiency. In addition, such economies provide more possibilities for governmental redistribution of societal wealth, because state-owned enterprises are usually less mobile than private enterprises; a larger number of firms can be taxed than in private enterprise economies. Hence in mixed economies, all things being equal, more revenue can be transferred to deserving individuals and groups.

Consider the problem posed by increasing returns to scale or by natural monopolies. Mixed economies are more efficient than private enterprise economies to the extent that state-owned enterprise eliminates the shortfalls in production caused by these market imperfections. By serving as a public monopoly expressly concerned with promoting market efficiency, state-owned firms can make adjustments for the relation between average and marginal costs so as to apply marginal cost pricing in all sectors of the economy. If they adopt a marginal cost-pricing rule and charge consumers a uniform price per unit output, for example, publicly owned firms can cover the costs they incur in producing the optimal level of output either by imposing a lump-sum charge on consumers (a charge unrelated to the size of consumers' purchases) or by obtaining a government subsidy. In this way, market efficiency can be more fully realized in mixed economies.[19]

The case for mixed economies is also based on intertemporal considerations, including concerns for intergenerational equity. Defenders of mixed economies argue that current, and especially future, generations of citizens have an opportunity to consume and earn more over time when an economy is composed of a mix of privately and publicly owned firms that together choose an optimal pattern of private and public investment. The creation and proper operation of a collection of publicly owned firms in combination with appropriate behavior on the part of privately owned firms yields a superior history of societal consumption than is possible in a pure private enterprise system.

Government presumably is responsible for discovering and creating the optimal stream of public and private investment. In doing this, public authorities act in part on behalf of unrepresented, future gen-

19. See Millward and Parker (1983:208).

erations, deciding how large their rate of consumption should be relative to that of current generations.[20] In effect, they decide what discount rate should be applied to future returns from public investments or how society should presently value these future returns. Some liberal theorists hold that this discount rate should be an average of society and market rates of time preference; for example, the average of the social rate of time preference and the opportunity cost of capital,[21] or the average of the discount rate facing consumers and the tax-distorted discount rate facing privately-owned firms.[22] Thus the case for mixed economies explicitly provides for government investment planning as the means to realize Pareto gains in consumption for current generations and an equitable distribution of consumption across generations.

In practice, however, mixed economies may not be preferable to private enterprise economies. First, it is difficult to operate state-owned enterprises in a way that achieves productive efficiency. The problem of determining an appropriate fixed charge on output or an appropriate subsidy for production by state-owned enterprise is not easily solved. Nor is it obvious that public monopolies always perform better than regulated private monopolies; the latter may be more socially efficient and hence contribute more to the achievement of Pareto-optimal outcomes. In a larger sense, then, the problem of increasing returns poses a choice between private enterprise, regulated private enterprise, and public enterprise.[23]

It is also difficult to determine the appropriate "social discount rate" for public investment. Knowing the range in which this rate lies is useful if that range is defined in terms of meaningful benchmarks, more specifically, if the market rate of interest or some variant thereof is an accurate indicator of social opportunity cost. But as capital markets are imperfect, there is much reason to doubt whether individuals can calculate the present value of alternative investments, insure themselves against all types of risk, and so on. Underdeveloped and imperfect capital markets may give governments poor information about the range in which the appropriate social discount

20. For instance, see Arrow and Kurz (1970:6).

21. See the summary in ibid. and von Furstenberg and Malkiel (1977).

22. The idea that the discount rate on public investment should be the average of the discount rate facing consumers and the tax-distorted rate facing private firms is the result of Sandmo and Dreze's analysis of government decision making in a simple closed economy (1971:401). They proceed to show how the possibility of foreign borrowing and foreign direct investment affects the optimal discount rate for public investment. See also Lintner (1981).

23. See Millward and Parker (1983: 200–208), and Hemming and Mansoor (1988: 12–16).

rate is located.[24] As a consequence, decisions to shift resources out of consumption into public investment may fail to enhance societal welfare in the way and to the extent public authorities intend.

The absence of perfect capital markets complicates the decision whether to create a state-owned enterprise. Theory tells us that state-owned enterprise should be created when markets fail to supply certain public goods and that the respective output should be valued at "publicly relevant prices."[25] Now, consider the fact that capital markets are often unable to finance long-term, risky investments.[26] Does this mean that expected returns to society from such investments are relatively low and hence that current and future generations are or would be better off if the state does not invest? Will citizens be better off if markets are allowed to channel savings to alternative private, or even public, investments? Or does the inability of capital markets to finance large, risky investments simply indicate that private investors do not appreciate the potential social gains from these investments? Before governments undertake public investments and create state-owned enterprises, they must answer these questions. Governments must assess the quality and the nature of the information capital markets provide. And, once more, if they decide to create state-owned enterprises, governments must settle on an appropriate social discount rate and an appropriate schedule of user charges and subsidies for those enterprises.

Assume, for the moment, that these problems can be solved, that government can ascertain the appropriate social discount rate, determine the optimal streams of private and public investment, and devise the fiscal policies needed to induce optimal private investment. The separation between public ownership and control over the actual decisions of state-owned enterprises may *still* prevent governments from implementing the optimal set of policies. The managers of state and large private firms may be willing and able to adopt policies inconsistent with those government has mandated—policies that are socially inefficient and socially inequitable in that they serve managers' own personal interests at the expense of other members of society. Then, in turn, the superior welfare outcomes associated with mixed economies may not be realized.[27]

24. In this sense Sandmo and Dreze's incorporation of the tax-distorted discount rate faced by firms is only one possible modification that must be made in the market rate of interest.

25. Arrow and Kurz (1970); see also Gray (1983).

26. See the discussion of the inability of local capital markets to finance the investments that Italian public enterprises undertake, in Fausto (1982:17).

27. Recall that mixed economies are often composed of large public and large private enterprises. So the relationship between ownership and control remains problem-

In private enterprise economies four institutions exist to diminish managerial control and the inefficiencies it produces. These institutions take different forms in mixed economies. First, since for state-owned enterprise ownership is in a sense completely dispersed—the citizens in a governmental jurisdiction collectively own its public firms—participation in annual "stockholder" meetings is necessarily more costly than in private enterprise systems. Usually there is no opportunity for individuals to control blocks of shares and so exert a disproportionately large amount of influence in stockholder meetings. Participating as an owner of a public enterprise is in many respects as costly as participating as a consumer advocate in private enterprise systems, because coalitions must be constructed out of purely individual agreements with other citizens. Indeed, as we shall soon see, participation in annual meetings of the stockholders of publicly owned firms is equivalent, in some respects, to political participation. In the state business sector of mixed economies, in sum, stockholder meetings are ineffective means of holding managers accountable for their performance.[28]

Second, the shares in state enterprises are normally not tradable. Opportunities for divesting oneself of shares in public firms are usually, but not always, quite limited.[29] A citizen can signal his disapproval or approval of managerial performance by migrating into or out of a government jurisdiction; by continuing to reside in a particular jurisdiction a citizen can, in principle, bequeath his or her share of public firms to his or her descendants. In comparison with the sale of shares in a capital market, however, decisions about where to reside are less likely to have an impact on managerial performance. Decisions about where to reside, after all, are not made solely or even primarily on the basis of one's evaluation of state managerial performance. Hence the signal managers receive from migration rates is

atic in the economy as a whole. Indeed, Shonfield (1965:378–379) and Langer (1964:145) have argued that this issue is endemic to the current stage of industrialization of Western countries, regardless of how mixed their economies might be.

28. Some authors do consider the influence of consumer councils on the behavior of public enterprises (Redwood and Hatch 1982: chap. 3). Also, state managers mention this institution in discussing the mechanisms through which they are held accountable by the public (interview with Electricity Supply Council official, London, October 1984).

29. In the course of examining the actual workings and welfare consequences of selected European mixed economies (Chapter 7 below), I examine the manner in which state-owned firms have been and are being privatized. Suffice it to say, at this point, that the British privatizations of the last thirty years have resulted from government decisions to sell public firms rather than from any decentralized sale of (collectively) owned stock by individual British citizens. In Austria, proposals for People's Shares were not fully implemented, and so Austrian citizens have had only limited opportunities to trade shares in certain public enterprises.

much less clear than signals they receive from capital market transactions. Moreover, this means of investing or disinvesting in state-owned enterprise poses much greater costs to citizens-owners than the act of individually selling or buying shares in large private firms. According to some observers, the greater costs of disinvesting translate into a smaller incentive to monitor state managerial performance:

> There is a difference between joint stock companies and public enterprises from an agency and property rights perspective. Whereas in joint stock companies the residual [earnings from shareholding] may act as a direct incentive for shareholders to monitor management and in the extreme shareholders may terminate their property rights by selling shares, in the case of public ownership, the public, the "principals," find the monitoring of their "agents" more costly. Each owner, that is each member of the public, will normally find that the cost of influencing the policy of the enterprise or government policy will considerably outweigh any benefits that he or she will gain from a change in policy. Unlike shareholders in joint stock companies who can sell their shares, their property rights, the cost of terminating ownership rights in public industries is much greater since these ownership rights are compulsory by virtue of residence.[30]

In addition, the threat of takeover of state-owned enterprises is usually minimal. This is in some part a consequence of the fact that publicly owned firms often exist in industries where there are few competitors and in countries where few private firms are willing or able to operate them. But even if privately owned firms are interested in taking over a publicly owned firm, the transfer of ownership normally would not be accomplished through capital market transactions. The decision to privatize the public firm first must be made within governmental institutions; individual citizens would not be approached directly by the private firm contemplating the takeover, and hence those public shareholders would not be able to use the threat to sell their individual shares to directly influence the corresponding group of state managers. The threat of demotion or dismissal of managers must therefore emanate more from the workings of political institutions, such as popular elections, than from the workings of capital markets.

Third, the labor market for state enterprise managers does not necessarily produce the same incentives for efficiency as exist in pri-

30. Millward and Parker (1983:217). Recall Peltzman's (1971) demonstration that the impossibility of "reshuffling" the shares in public enterprises creates incentives for managers to adopt uniform pricing policies and to restrict product variety in order to maximize votes rather than maximize profits. See also the discussion in Aharoni (1986: chap. 4).

vate enterprise systems. The managers of some publicly owned firms have skills that other public enterprises or private enterprises do not always demand. Consequently, even if they perform well, state managers may not be able to sell their services for a higher rate of pay and benefits.[31] In addition, just as goods markets are unable to produce and accurately price the public goods in which state-owned enterprises so often specialize, labor markets are unable to assess accurately the performance of state managers. Potential employers face many of the same problems that governments face in assessing the performance of state managers. For example, a state manager who expands the size of his workforce may be operating on the belief that increases in employment—especially employment in certain regions of a jurisdiction—are socially efficient both over the short term and over the long term. The same manager might justify a large wage increase for public employees on the same grounds or on the grounds that increased labor costs actually bring the rate of social return on his particular public investment back into line with the appropriate rate (that is, wage increases are justified in view of the "social productivity" of the public workforce). Potential employers will have difficulty deciding whether these rationales are justified and hence how well these state managers have performed. Accordingly, there may be little relation between a state manager's value in the labor market and the returns he or she generates for public owners. Mixed economies provide fewer guarantees that the conditions for productive efficiency are being achieved. Rather, they may hold more potential than large private firms do for a maldistribution of wealth between state managers and public owners and for suboptimal levels of societal consumption.

In the application of company law, state-owned enterprises are often subject to many of the same legal constraints that apply to large private enterprises. Indeed, state-owned enterprises frequently are given the status of companies in an attempt to ensure they have a commercial nature. Publicly owned firms are audited at regular intervals, and these audits provide citizens with information about the financial condition of their enterprises. But such information is more difficult to evaluate than the results of the audits of large private firms (in terms of efficiency criteria). Evidence of financial losses— even if accurately compiled—does not necessarily signal that the publicly owned firm has performed inefficiently in a social sense.

31. For instance, the technical skills of the managers of certain British nationalized industries do not appear to be widely marketable (interview, Oxford Management Centre, October 1984). For a discussion of the different incentive structures—especially in regard to risk sharing—in state enterprises, see Adar and Aharoni (1980).

Such losses could yield current and future generations benefits they deserve or desire.[32]

In sum, we have no reason to assume that, even if governments can determine the mix of public and private investment that restores productive efficiency, they can implement this optimal policy. The institutions that promote managerial efficiency in private enterprise systems are less effective in mixed economies. Stockholder meetings, capital market transactions, labor market factors, and company law together do not ensure that state-owned enterprise will be operated in a socially efficient manner. Perhaps the most important distinction between the two types of economies is the fact that it is so much more costly for individuals to threaten state managers with disinvestment and takeover. Such threats, when state-owned enterprise is involved, must be made primarily through political institutions.[33]

When we turn to examine the criterion of intragenerational equity, theory provides some insights into how we should adjust the present value of public investments to account for the distribution of risk bearing within society, for example, for the fact that the costs of public investments are usually shared by the members of society while the benefits of those investments accrue to particular groups of individuals. In such situations, government presumably should use the actuarial, risk-neutral value of the costs and the individual time-risk preferences of the beneficiaries in evaluating the social returns from public investment. It will thereby qualify fewer projects than it would by applying the same discount rate to both costs and benefits.[34] Un-

32. Aharoni (1983) makes the case for ex post, external (third-party, private) audits of state-owned enterprises. Redwood and Hatch (1982) discuss the feasibility of implementing "value for money audits" of the British nationalized industries; they also describe the auditing functions of the Comptroller and Auditor General of the United Kingdom. Other descriptions of and proposals for auditing schemes include Gray (1983), Mallon (1981), Jones (1981a), Stefani (1981), and Van der Bellen (1981).

33. Millward and Parker (1983) review attempts to demonstrate, empirically, differences in the efficiency of publicly owned and privately owned firms. They stress that most authors fail to take into account cost and various other factors, which leads them to make mistaken inferences about the inefficiency of public enterprise. Millward and Parker conclude that the empirical evidence supports the view that "(a) prices are lower and output higher in public firms than in private firms, (b) for different types of production and consumers, relative prices are not as closely geared to relative marginal costs in public firms as they are in private firms, and (c) one or both of the above two factors have contributed to the lower profit rates sometimes found in public firms" (252).

34. This is one of the results of Arrow and Lind's analysis (1970). Their central theme is that one cannot decide whether to undertake an investment solely on the basis of the magnitude of expected returns. Rather, the distribution of risk-bearing is of utmost importance: "When risks are publicly borne, the costs of risk-bearing are negligible; therefore public investment with an expected return which is less than that of a given private investment may nevertheless be superior to the private alternative" (p. 375). Adar and Aharoni (1980) explore the virtues of various internal procedures

fortunately, these and related results tell us little about which group of individuals should or actually will benefit from public investment. Once more, if we incorporate the fact that individuals' valuation of the returns from public and private investment hinges, in part, on the returns that accrue to other individuals, including their descendants and the descendants of other citizens, we cannot deduce the optimal mix of private and public investment that government ought to implement. Rather, we must assume, once again, that government is willing and able to resolve competing equity claims in a just fashion.[35]

What makes mixed economies different from private enterprise economies in this respect is that government has greater capacity to redistribute income in the former type of economy than in the latter. In private enterprise economies, government capacity to redistribute income is limited by the need to compete for private firms; the fact that private owners can relocate to other jurisdictions limits how much revenue public authorities can collect and transfer to deserving citizens. In mixed economies, a substantial number of firms are public property. Hence, if behavioral constraints—the problem of managerial control—can be overcome, the amount of revenue that can be redistributed at any point in time is potentially larger: a greater number of firms are unable to evade taxation by relocating out of the government's jurisdiction. This is especially true in comparison to private enterprise economies that are heavily populated with foreign private enterprises.[36] Finally, the fact that state-owned firms are public property makes it more legitimate for public authorities to demand they pursue social ends. Such demands are more difficult to enforce in private enterprise economies since the property rights of owners usually entitle them to earn purely individual benefits.[37]

This is not to say that governments in mixed economies can create any intragenerational distribution of wealth. Governments are constrained by the size of the product of the state business sector and also by the fact that since their economies are mixed, some constituents may not be served by publicly owned firms—for instance, a particular region may be populated only by privately owned firms that

for ensuring risk-neutral behavior by public firms.

35. Sandmo and Dreze (1971) show in an appendix that their results do not depend on the way in which individual consumption is aggregated. But they do not consider the possibility that individual valuation of consumption is contingent on the consumption rate of others. Recall also the Sen and Marglin criticism of optimal growth theory (fn. 12 above).

36. Various authors stress the value of state-owned enterprise as a means of asserting national control over the economy, for instance, Langer (1964:116–117). Moreover, state-owned enterprise is often used to combat plant closures, including closures by multinationals (Holland 1972:28–31).

37. See Posner (1981:19).

can relocate rather than pay taxes or that can adopt policies inconsistent with governments' ends. But, with respect to the general problem posed by the mobility of firms in private enterprise economies, governments in mixed economies have a greater capacity to redistribute wealth intragenerationally.[38]

The fact that governments in mixed economies have a greater capacity to redistribute wealth does not mean that social welfare is more equitably distributed in mixed economies than in private enterprise economies, either in an intragenerational or in a collective/intergenerational sense. The greater potential for managerial control and the difficulties involved in identifying the conditions that restore efficiency may make mixed economies inherently less productive than private enterprise economies. In terms of productive efficiency, mixed economies may be a third-best alternative. From a behavioral standpoint, for example, the use of publicly owned firms to promote intragenerational equity greatly complicates the problem of monitoring the state business sector. Government concern with intragenerational equity means that evaluations of social rates of return must incorporate the effects of public investment on the *relative* income of different individuals and groups and, conceivably, on the *relative* income of their descendants. Needless to say, both public authorities and citizens (public owners) find it difficult to determine how well managers perform on this count. More generally, managerial claims of having behaved in a "socially responsible" manner—of having accumulated genuine "public profits" for society—are more difficult to evaluate than the claims private managers make about having enhanced the wealth of (private) property owners.[39] For these and other reasons state managers fail to promote productive efficiency and wealth is maldistributed within and across generations in mixed economies.[40]

38. That state-owned enterprise facilitates redistribution of wealth intragenerationally is stressed by such authors as Breton (1964) and Jones (1981b).

39. For example, the law that created the Endowment Fund for Italian state-owned enterprise allows for continued, unprofitable operation if it can be demonstrated that "social ends" are served in the course of loss-making. According to Fausto (1982:20), the wording of the statute has been interpreted to mean that the government invests in an attempt to maximize profits subject to the constraint of maximizing social ends simultaneously. See also Holland (1972), Despicht (1972), and Prodi (1974).

40. Eltis (1979) is among those who argue that state-owned enterprise does not produce sufficient output to finance the welfare programs that the Left political parties hold so dear. See Vallet (1983) for an analysis of how private firms' abilities to choose an alternative partner for a joint venture constrains the policies a state can pursue in such a venture. In Vallet's analysis, the state's desire to promote employment—especially employment in certain locations—leads it to (rationally) choose an amount of subsidy per unit of output from its joint ventures with private firms.

Managerial control is not the only potential source of maldistribution, however. Workers in state-owned enterprises, by virtue of the sometimes monopolistic nature of the firms in which they are employed, have more ability than private enterprise workers to increase their share of intragenerational wealth. The bargaining power of workers in a private firm—unless that private firm also is a monopoly—depends, in part, on their past and potential productivity relative to other workers in the labor market and, concomitantly, on their ability to strike and so capture a larger share of the earnings of their employers. If firms are mobile, workers' bargaining power is diminished, since managers and owners can move their operations to a location where individuals are willing to work for a lower wage; in other words, private firms' ability to relocate diminishes workers' ability to negotiate more favorable contracts with managers. State-owned enterprises sometimes relocate their operations outside their government's jurisdiction, and occasionally, publicly owned firms are privatized and their employees face the prospect of dismissal or demotion. But state-owned enterprises are often located in a single jurisdiction, and they are responsible for most or all of certain kinds of production. Also, the collective nature of decisions to privatize publicly owned firms makes the possibility that public enterprise workers will face dismissal or demotion from a change of ownership, over the short term, comparatively slim.[41] Public enterprise employees face less competition from workers seeking employment in other jurisdictions (for example, other countries), and by striking they can often cause their public owners to incur significant costs as well as lower rates of public return. The bargaining power of public enterprise workers is thus greater than that of workers in most private enterprises.[42] Governments in mixed economies are to some degree constrained in their ability to reduce the share of wealth held by one segment of the labor force. In fact, according to some observers, employment in state-owned enterprise poses more than a constraint; it represents a breeding ground for worker challenges to government authority—challenges designed to bring about a complete overhaul of the distribution of wealth in market economies.[43]

41. Of course, state-owned enterprises operate in foreign markets, and they launch joint ventures with local and foreign multinationals. See Pryke (1981: chap. 7) and Hart (1986). My point here is merely that, in comparison to the situation in private enterprise economies, there is less likelihood of relocation in the face of wage demands.

42. This is known as the "Wellington-Winter effect." For a summary and a test in the American transportation and construction industries, see Hamermesh (1975); see also Price (1981:64) and Lacina (1977).

43. Illustrative is the case that the Sinn Fein Workers Party (1975) makes for strengthening the state-owned enterprise sector in Ireland. See also Kuisel's description of the French CGT's conception of nationalization and his summary of Jouhaux's

The welfare outcomes that can be achieved in mixed economies are thus potentially different from those which can be achieved in private enterprise economies. The main reason is relative immobility, which renders state-owned enterprise more vulnerable than privately owned enterprise to government efforts to redistribute wealth. But at the same time, state-owned enterprise poses problems for government insofar as the task of controlling state managers is more difficult than private owners' control of private managers. Mixed economies are likely to be more inefficient than private enterprise economies as a result. Finally, because state managers and their employees enjoy significantly more bargaining power than their private enterprise counterparts, they may be able to capture a relatively greater share of wealth in mixed economies.

GOVERNMENT AND POLITICS

Many theoretical analyses of the two economies assume that government is willing and able to promote a single, socially preferred blend of welfare outcomes. Government, they assume, knows *who* deserves to receive income transfers in both economies. In mixed economies, government presumably also knows how to define socially desirable objectives for state managers.

These assumptions are unreasonable. Governments are not omniscient. They have difficulty determining what society prefers; indeed, society's preferences are often ill-conditioned. Society's preferences with regard to distribution may be intransitive, for instance. In the case of mixed economies, it is unreasonable to assume government knows how future generations will value public investments and especially to assume it knows how distant generations will value these investments.[44]

Moreover, governments are not unitary actors. Governments are composed of administrators, elected officials, and representatives of interest and producer groups. These individuals almost always have some conflicting interests, and so they are likely to disagree about how fiscal policy ought to be designed and about how publicly owned firms should be operated. And, as we learned in the previous chap-

---

belief in that scheme's potentiality for achieving an "ultimate transformation of society" (1981:79–82).

44. Recall the discussion of popular preferences with regard to nationalized industry in Britain, in Chapter 1 above. On the problem of determining the preferences of future generations see Ball (1985).

ter, they are likely to create and exploit the workings of political institutions that promote their particular interests at the expense of the interests of other citizens. As a consequence, fiscal policies and the ways in which public ownership rights are executed differ, depending on the outcome of elections, producer group negotiations, and other political processes.

In sum, we cannot evaluate the two types of economies in isolation from the politics with which they are combined. Whether or how potential differences in the welfare consequences of the two economies are realized depends, in some substantial part, on the manner in which citizen preferences are articulated, aggregated, and expressed through political institutions.

CHAPTER FOUR

Democratic Polities Compared

Political institutions translate citizens' preferences about the ends and means of government, and distributions of power among those citizens, into specific public policies. These policies are designed, in part, to serve the interests of certain groups of citizens. Theory tells us that three political institutions are particularly important: electoral systems, modes of interest intermediation, and state administration. More specifically, policy choice differs depending on whether electoral systems are majoritarian or consensual, modes of interest intermediation are pluralist or corporatist, and administrative style is centralist or noncentralist. Private enterprise and mixed economies can exist in combination with any constellation of these institutions (Table 2).

This chapter examines the workings of these three important political institutions. It shows that the institutions affect the stability, temporal orientation, and content of public policy. In the face of societal dissensus about the ends and means of government, majoritarian electoral systems produce more unstable policies than consensual systems do. To some extent all electoral systems impart a short-term orientation to public policy making. Pluralism promotes societal dissensus and a short-term orientation in public policy making, whereas corporatism manufactures consensus and imparts a long-term orientation. Centralist administrative style also imparts a longer-term orientation relative to noncentralist administrative style.

Political institutions affect the content of policy as well. Majoritarian electoral systems and pluralist modes of interest intermediation promote the immediate interests of coalitions of groups and, by implication, living generations of citizens. Corporatist modes promote the mutual, aggregate interest of producer groups and future gener-

Table 2. Alternative constellations of political institutions through which public policies are made, and structural and behavioral problems associated with each constellation

PLURALISTIC MODE OF INTEREST INTERMEDIATION

Noncentralist state administrative style

Institutions through which public policies are made

Voting as expression of individuals' preferences for the ends and means of government activity.

Parties and interest groups as articulators and aggregators of individuals' preferences.

Party and interest group competition as the primary way public choices about the ends and means of government activity are made; public policy is more stable the more societal consensus there is and the more consensual the character of the electoral system.

Structural and behavioral problems

Lack of technical expertise among party leaders and appointees means government activity does not promote productive efficiency and Pareto improvements in social welfare.

Instability of public policy and consequent welfare loss under conditions of marked societal dissensus over the ends and means of government activity and/or the presence of a majoritarian electoral system, e.g., frequent changes in fiscal policy cause investor uncertainty and, in turn, retard level and rate of societal consumption.

Politicans' emphasis on short-term welfare gains under conditions of myopic voting and strong partisanship translates into short-term temporal orientation in public policy making.

Centralist state administrative style

Institutions through which public policies are made

State administrators willing and able to promote their conception of the most desirable ends and best means of government activity.

Same as for noncentralist system except that state administrators are potential allies or opponents of political parties and interest groups.

Structural and behavioral problems

Same as for noncentralist system with addition of dangers associated with administrative monopoly over certain kinds of public decisions, e.g., administrators not accountable to voters for promotion of particular distributions of wealth, as through administrative rationing of credit.

CORPORATIST MODE OF INTEREST INTERMEDIATION

Noncentralist state administrative style

Institutions through which public policies are made

Voting in popular elections as expression of individuals' preferences for the ends and means of government activity; parties and interest groups as articulators and aggregators of individuals' preferences.

Voting in producer group elections as expression of individual preferences for the ends of producer group negotiations; producer groups as articulators and aggregators of the preferences of the members of producer groups.

83

Table 2 (continued)

Party and interest group competition as one way in which public choices about the ends and means of government activity are made.

Producer group negotiation as a means of managing capital-labor relations and of distributing the output of firms; relatively long-term temporal orientation in policy making.

Structural and behavioral problems

Same as for pluralistic political systems but with dilemma of achieving and maintaining organizational strength of producer groups while at the same time keeping leadership accountable to group members.

Problems of simultaneously maintaining good relations between and within producer groups, e.g., the difficulty of maintaining support of union rank and file while not alienating leaders of business producer groups.

Centralist state administrative style

Institutions through which public policies are made

State administrators willing and able to promote their conception of the most desirable ends and best means of government activity.

Same as for noncentralist systems with state administrators potential allies or opponents of parties, interest groups, and producer groups.

Structural and behavioral problems

Same as for noncentralist systems but with danger of excessive administrative influence over some sets of public decisions.

---

ations. Centralist administrative styles promote the interests of future generations.

I divide the discussion into analyses of the workings of each of the three institutions; structural and behavioral problems with these institutions are considered in each subsection, and the interconnections between institutions are discussed in the conclusion. This analysis suggests that policy making will be most oriented toward the welfare of current generations and particular groups of citizens in majoritarian pluralist systems with noncentralist administrative styles. In consensual, corporatist systems with centralist administrative styles, policy will be oriented more toward the collective interests of labor and capital and that of future generations.

ELECTORAL SYSTEMS

Citizens have both material and nonmaterial goals. They are concerned about their own material and nonmaterial well-being and about the well-being of other citizens, including their descendants.[1]

1. For an economic treatment of intergenerational equity see Stern (1987). Political

There are differences in the importance various groups and generations attach to material and nonmaterial goals, as well as differences in how citizens view their own welfare relative to the welfare of the public at large.[2] Finally, both across countries and across groups within countries, citizens evaluate privately owned and state-owned enterprise in different ways. In the United States, for instance, we find widespread support for private ownership as the best means of promoting personal and public welfare. In Austria, on the other hand, we find much support for public ownership and a mixed economic structure. Britain and other European countries exhibit much disagreement about the virtues of private and public enterprise, if not outright conflict over how economies ought to be structured.[3] In general, then, societies differ in terms of how much consensus exists about what ends government should pursue and how it should pursue them.

Citizens take various forms of political action in order to promote their views about the ends and means of government. Citizens support governments that enhance their personal economic fortunes as well as the fortunes of their local community and country, for instance, governments that in their minds have augmented real disposable income or the country's consumption level. Citizens also support governments that have promoted the interests of the groups to which they belong, governments that have augmented the income and economic security of the members of their occupation relative to the income and economic security of the members of other occupations.[4] Citizen's desire to bring about these kinds of welfare outcomes leads them to vote for candidates who promise to enact or continue certain public policies and to lobby other elected officials to endorse the same policies. In this vein, citizens sometimes support governments who promise to create or dismantle state-owned enterprises, or operate publicly owned firms in ways that serve their particular interests. In fact, many citizens expect publicly owned firms to

---

analyses of this concept include Ball (1985), who stresses, among other things, our moral obligation to act justly toward those generations with whom we share a common moral language and with whom we have the capacity to communicate. A concrete example of concern for intergenerational justice is legislation in Canada that created the Albertan Heritage Fund out of government oil revenues. See Laux and Molot (1987).

2. On generational differences and trends in material and "postmaterial" values see the works of Inglehart (1977, 1981, 1985). Lafferty and Knutsen (1985) are among those who have studied the relation between personal and public postmaterialism.

3. On the American case see Chong, McCloskey, and Zaller (1983); see also Lane (1986). Public opinion data for Austria are supplied in Chapter 7. Data for Britain were presented in Chapter 1.

4. See, for instance, Hibbs (1982a).

serve their interests in ways and to an extent they do not expect from privately owned firms.[5]

This political behavior is manifest in party politics. Parties are collections of groups that not only have similar views about what material and nonmaterial goals are desirable but also basically agree about the best means to achieve these goals. For example, as noted in Chapter 2, the members and leaders of many European social democratic parties have for several decades been committed to increasing consumption and providing employment security through fiscal and labor market intervention alone rather than through a combination of these policies and state enterprise. Until recently, many European social democrats agreed that state-owned enterprise is not needed to realize their vision of a collectively and distributively just blend of welfare outcomes: their welfare objectives could be achieved through fiscal management of what are, in essence, private enterprise economies.[6]

This is not to say that social democracy, or any other political philosophy, always involves the same set of values or the same set of beliefs about how best to achieve those values. Nor is it true that party members always share identical conceptions of distributional equity or agree that public ownership is an effective or ineffective means of promoting that conception. In Austria, as noted earlier, social democrats have long been committed to a *mix* of private and public enterprise as the best means of achieving their party's goals. In working-class parties, members have sometimes disagreed about the appropriate scope of and policies for state-owned enterprise—so much so that, in the case of the British Labour party, some members eventually left the party and created a social democratic alternative committed to achieving a somewhat different set of welfare objectives through a much smaller state-owned business sector.[7] Nevertheless, to some substantial extent the supporters, members, and leaders of political parties agree about the welfare objectives government ought to promote and about what role, if any, state-owned enterprise should play in this regard.[8]

5. On different expectations for public enterprise see Posner (1981) and Aharoni (1986:158, 271). On citizens' preferences about the content of fiscal policy see Kristensen (1982).
6. Again, see Przeworski (1980a, b, c); also Korpi (1978: chaps. 4 and 8).
7. Since World War II there has been much debate within the British Labour party about its commitment to nationalization. For the competing views of the party rank and file and party activists see Turner (1978). Disagreements within the French Left about the aims of nationalization are discussed in Holton (1986).
8. See, for instance, Alt (1979), Hibbs (1977, 1979), and Esping-Anderson (1985). On the relation between value change and partisanship see Lafferty and Knutsen (1985).

Elections translate citizens' competing preferences, by authorizing one party or a coalition of parties to promote its welfare objectives through its policy programs, into a single public choice, a choice that in some respects represents the preferences of only a segment of the citizenry. The type of electoral system determines how representative are government's policies and welfare objectives. In particular, the more majoritarian or less consensual the electoral system is, the smaller the number of citizens whose preferences are represented in their government's policies and welfare objectives. The less majoritarian or more consensual the system is, the greater the number of citizens whose preferences are represented.[9]

Whether elections yield stable public choices—a relatively unchanging policy program and set of welfare objectives—depends on two related political factors. The first is the degree of societal dissensus over the means and ends of governmental activity. The more dissensus there is about societal welfare objectives, the need for and operation of state-owned enterprise, and the content of fiscal policy, the more likely it is that elections will produce substantial changes in public policy. In this circumstance, elections are likely to translate the dissensus into frequent changes in the partisan composition of government and, in turn, into new fiscal or public enterprise policies. Elections may even produce repeated efforts to alter the structure of the economy, that is, to alter the size and character of the state business sector.[10]

The nature of the electoral system is the second factor that affects the stability of public policy. In general, consensual electoral systems stabilize public choice, because consensual systems provide for the dispersal of and limits on power. They allow minorities to veto collective decisions, for example. In the face of societal consensus, majoritarian systems can also yield a stable sequence of public choices, but in the presence of societal dissensus, such systems are likely to authorize changes from one party's preferences to another's. In this way, a majoritarian system is likely to yield an unstable sequence of public policies.[11]

---

9. Majoritarian and consensual models of democracy are described by Lijphart (1984). Briefly, the former provides for such things as one-party and bare-majority cabinets, the fusion of executive and legislative power, first-past-the-post (plurality) voting schemes, and an unwritten constitution. The latter provides for coalition government, the separation of power, proportional voting schemes, and a written constitution with a minority veto. I emphasize the electoral dimension rather than the intergovernmental or federalist dimensions of Lijphart's models (see ibid., esp. chap. 13).

10. See Zysman (1983:229–232).

11. See Lijphart (1984:30). The status quo orientation or comparatively conservative nature of consensual systems is stressed by Jackman (1986).

This observation brings us to an important behavioral feature of electoral systems. Electoral systems—especially majoritarian systems—create incentives for politicians to manipulate public policies in ways that regularly transfer wealth from future to current generations or from the constituents of nonincumbent politicians to their own constituents. Because of their desire to maintain their positions of authority—to win elections—politicians may favor policies, including policies relating to the structure and operation of the state business sector, that yield short-term gains to their own constituents. Incumbent politicians may believe that in return for short-term material and nonmaterial gains from fiscal policies and public enterprise operations, constituents will reward them with their votes. In such circumstances, politicians can be expected, in Renato Mazzolini's words, to "impose a high discount rate on expected outcomes—that is, they [will] have a short-term time horizon in terms of the results they are sensitive to; they [will] seek visible results—that is, they [will] give highest priority to results which can be readily pointed to and exploited politically and electorally; and they [will] take an often partisan view of things—that is, . . . they [will] reflect biases stemming from factional struggles."[12]

If citizens actually reward their representatives for this kind of behavior, elections may produce frequent attempts to redistribute wealth to the constituents of incumbent politicians. There may even be "political business cycles" in fiscal policy and the policies of state-owned enterprises as politicians repeatedly try to buy votes in the run-ups to elections. Electorally motivated transfers of wealth may retard market efficiency and therefore may produce Pareto losses in societal consumption.[13]

In sum, electoral systems are one important institution through which citizens' competing preferences are translated into public policy. Depending on the degree of societal dissensus about the ends and means of government activity and on the character of the electoral system, elections may produce frequent changes in government policies and welfare objectives, changes that may affect the level and distribution of societal wealth. In particular, in the face of societal dissensus, majoritarian electoral systems will produce more unstable policies than consensual systems do. All electoral systems will impart

12. This is Mazzolini's (1979b:49–50) assessment of the way Italian politicians treat state-owned enterprise. A similar, more general characterization of elections can be found in Brittan (1984).

13. For a review of the political business cycle literature see Alt and Chrystal (1983: chap. 5). The idea of a political business cycle in public investment and/or state-owned enterprise behavior is implicit in the investigations of Frey and Schneider (1978) and Mazzolini (1979a).

a short-term orientation to public policy, and hence an orientation to serve the interests of current generations of citizens at the expense of future generations.

MODES OF INTEREST INTERMEDIATION

Citizens' preferences about the ends and means of public policy are also expressed through interest groups and producer groups. Employer and labor organizations, for example, articulate and promote competing policies and welfare aims. The owners of private firms are often more willing than wage earners to tolerate social inequalities. These owners generally place greater importance on collective gains and intergenerational equity than on intragenerational equity. The owners of private firms often, but not always, see state-owned enterprise as an instrument through which governments transfer their wealth and that of their offspring to segments of the workforce. They feel that state-owned enterprise deprives them of investment opportunities, or that state-owned enterprise is inherently inefficient and hence a source of collective welfare loss.[14]

Labor groups' preferences are somewhat different from those of employer groups. Labor groups are generally more concerned than employer groups about social equality. Labor groups are also more prone to stress short-term, intragenerational welfare issues. But it would be a mistake to assume that labor's preferences are fundamentally different from those of employers in this regard. Labor groups' commitment to collective gain and intergenerational justice is well-documented. Also well-documented are some labor groups' beliefs in the value of state-owned enterprise as a means of promoting both collective gain and distributive justice.[15]

14. See Kuisel's discussion of business opposition to postwar nationalizations in France (1981:209, 258). See also Salvati's analysis (1981) of the political estrangement of business produced by the Italian nationalizations of the 1960s.

15. For a general discussion of producer group preferences with regard to social equality see Esping-Andersen (1985). As regards the temporal orientation of labor, Mazzolini (1979b:54) is among those who argue that union leaders are inherently myopic in policy making and, by implication, that workers impose a high discount rate on future welfare outcomes. For a criticism of this and other aspects of the conventional wisdom about labor unions, see Panitch (1981). A more general review of trade union behavior can be found in Katzenstein (1984, 1985). As for the importance unions attach to public investment and investment planning, see Sinn Fein Workers Party (1975). See also Jacobsen's discussion of the deliberations of the 1973 Conference of Irish Trade Unions (1980:268), and the analysis of Italian metalworkers' attempts to link reductions in workforce levels to worker participation in investment decisions cited in (Cox 1984: fn. 32). The instrumental value Austrian labor leaders attach to state enterprise is revealed in Benya (1975).

Members of producer groups, like members of political parties and of interest groups, do not always agree among themselves about what ends government should pursue or what means government should use to achieve those ends. The interests of small employers frequently conflict with those of large employers. The former, for example, sometimes have an incentive to oppose state support for the modernization of certain kinds of production.[16] Also, as I showed in Chapter 2, international economic relations create splits in employer groups because trade and foreign investment harm some firms and benefit others. Consequently, some local employers may support public policies such as protectionism that are aimed at achieving a particular international distribution of wealth or ally themselves with local labor groups on behalf of a particular internal (that is, national) distribution of wealth. Some local labor groups may agree to such an alliance because of the differential wage gains they stand to realize and because of the economic security they will enjoy relative to other workers as a consequence of public policy.[17] Furthermore, labor groups often disagree about what constitutes a socially preferable level and distribution of wealth and about whether state-owned enterprise is necessary to bring about such welfare outcomes.

Modes of interest intermediation affect the course and outcomes of interest and producer group negotiations. In turn, modes of interest intermediation affect the content and stability of government policies and state business operations. There are two basic modes of interest intermediation: corporatist and pluralist.[18]

Public choice is more stable and long-term in its orientation where the corporatist mode applies. Corporatism unifies producer groups behind a particular set of policies and welfare objectives. This form of interest intermediation manufactures and enforces consensus about what welfare outcomes government ought to promote and about how government ought to promote them. This consensus is created and nurtured on the basis of the mutual gains that producer groups realize from the corporatist bargain. In particular, employer groups benefit from the fact that corporatism ensures reduced labor militancy and greater certainty about the relative size of the private and social

16. For example, see Berger's analysis (1981) of the origins of the Royer Law, which armed small French businesses against interests in the modern sector of that country's economy.

17. Kuisel (1981:20–21) points out that French employer associations had their origins, in part, in the threat posed by competition from foreign producers. See Wallerstein (1987) for an in-depth analysis of the distributional origins and implications of protectionism versus welfare state policies.

18. See Chapter 1, fn. 4, above. Note that here "pluralist" refers to the institutional character of the polity rather than to the character of societal preferences. Cf. Lijphart (1984).

wage bills. Because they are more certain about the cost of these bills, employers invest more than they would in pluralist systems, where they face more instability in the ends and means of government activity. A greater rate of investment yields labor groups a higher level of aggregate income, not only through higher wages but also through the redistribution of a larger amount of societal wealth by government. To the extent that one or both producer groups believe that state-owned enterprise is necessary to realize these benefits, corporatism sanctions the creation of publicly owned firms and ensures those firms are operated in a fashion that conforms to the terms of the bargain producer groups have struck. In these ways, then, corporatism presumably leaves both employer and labor groups better off.

In contrast, the pluralist form of interest intermediation produces dissensus and instability. Pluralism encourages interest groups to pursue their own particular interests in coalitions with other groups that are pursuing their particular interests. Such coalitions generally adopt policies that are concerned more with existing distributional inequities than with long-term collective gain. The makeup of coalitions often changes, and new policies that serve the interests of the new coalition are adopted.

This instability creates uncertainty about fiscal and other kinds of policy, an uncertainty that undermines the willingness of private business to undertake long-term investments. In failing to produce policies that promote labor's collective interest, pluralism encourages labor militancy. This militancy also discourages business investment. For these and other reasons, pluralism is associated with lower productivity and growth rates than corporatism.[19]

Corporatism, however, is not necessarily a socially preferred form of interest intermediation. Corporatism is plagued by serious problems. For example, labor has great difficulty forging and maintaining a corporatist bargain. Unlike private owners, who can exert power individually by refusing to invest, labor can exert power only through collective action; and collective action is difficult to accomplish. In an attempt to promote collective action, labor leaders have often discouraged dissent within their organization. They sometimes enact undemocratic rules and regulations, such as multilayered, indirect procedures for the election of leaders. While these actions promote unity within the organization, they may alienate workers and thereby delegitimize leaders' positions of authority. In turn, labor will find it difficult to forge a corporatist bargain with employers because the latter will question the former's ability to enforce such agreements.[20]

19. See Hibbs (1978) and Pelinka (1987); also Schmitter (1981) and Olson (1982).
20. On the structural problem labor faces in exerting social power, see Offe and

The problem with corporatism goes even deeper. In general, the leaders of producer groups must maintain good relations both with each other and with their members, otherwise the compromise over the ends and means of governmental intervention will break down. According to some analysts, this is an impossible task. Over the long term the leaders of producer groups simply cannot square this political and organizational circle, because it is in the interest of employer and labor leaders to change the negotiating process in a way that serves their own personal advantage. At the same time, mutual recognition of this temptation undermines the leaders' ability to design a self-perpetuating system of bargaining. In their relations with the rank and file of each group, for example, leaders must constantly foment intergroup antagonism in order to keep their own group together. But this need makes it increasingly difficult to negotiate mutually agreeable compromises over the ends and means of government intervention. Fomenting intergroup antagonism also serves to radicalize producer groups and, in turn, to spawn opposition to leaders' authority. Supposedly, therefore, corporatist institutions must eventually break down into essentially the same kind of pluralist institutions that breed and reflect societal dissensus.[21]

In sum, corporatist forms of interest intermediation render public choice more consensual and stable than pluralist forms. Corporatism also promotes labor's collective interest more than pluralism does. Whether this distinction applies over the long term depends on how well producer group leaders cope with the problems outlined above, and especially how effective labor leaders are in maintaining unity among the rank and file.

STATE ADMINISTRATIVE STYLE

Governments are populated by professional administrators. These administrators, some of whom may operate state-owned enterprises, often have well-developed ideas about what welfare objectives government ought to promote and how it ought to promote them.[22] What

Wiesenthal (1980). As regards the concrete problems labor leaders face in promoting collective action, see Korpi (1978: chap. 8). That producer group electoral systems insulate leaders from the rank and file is stressed by Flanagan, Soskice, and Ulman (1983). But see also Lange (1984), who shows that in terms of opportunities for dissent and leader responsiveness, some centralized Scandinavian labor organizations are as democratic as Britain's decentralized labor organizations.

21. See, for instance, Sabel (1981).

22. I conceive of *state administration* as a conglomeration of the executive, civil service, and managers of publicly owned businesses. Salvati (1981:359) refers to a similar notion in a discussion of the differences between the French and Italian "political-

sets state administrators apart from party officials and interest and producer group representatives are their claims of technical competence and their commitment to promoting the interests of future generations of citizens.

State administrators often claim that they know better than any other group how best to promote the public interest. Presumably they have a technical understanding of markets, an understanding that parties, interest groups, and producer groups do not possess. Put another way, parties, interest groups, and producer groups simply do not understand how best to serve their own interests. They are therefore best off delegating authority to state administrators who possess the requisite technical expertise to make fiscal policy and to operate publicly owned firms.[23]

State administrators often see themselves as guardians of the interests of future generations. They frequently believe that they alone know the preferences of the unborn and how to weigh those preferences against the preferences of living citizens. As they see it, parties, interest groups, and producer groups fail to take into account the interests of future generations when they make policy; or these other actors simply do not know how to incorporate intergenerational equity concerns into policy choices, for example, how to calculate an appropriate discount rate for public investment. State administration of public policy solves both problems: it prevents living citizens from harming the welfare of future generations, and it applies technical expertise to the problem of achieving intergenerational equity.[24]

Like other social actors, state administrators do not always share the same views. Technical treatments of social problems often do not suggest a single, preferred solution; technical analysis may merely demonstrate the equivalence of policies or show the impossibility of coming up with a preferred policy.[25] Also, the members of different adminstrative agencies may disagree about what constitutes a just distribution of wealth intragenerationally or intergenerationally; for example, they may disagree about how large the income of future generations ought to be relative to that of current generations and, in such circumstances, what social discount rate should be applied to public investment. State administrators may also disagree about the need for state-owned enterprise; some may prefer to dismantle the

---

administrative complexes."
23. See Aberbach et al. (1981), Lindblom (1980), and Karl (1976). For the technocratic basis of French state administration see Suleiman (1974: chap. 14), Kuisel (1981: chap 3), and Zysman (1977).
24. See, for instance, Pizzorno (1981:266–67).
25. See Lindblom (1980) and also Behn (1981), Cochran (1980), and Karl (1976).

public business sector altogether whereas others prefer to enlarge it.[26] In brief, state administrators have preferences about the ends and means of government activity, and they promote these preferences in negotiations with other social actors.

State administrative style determines how much influence state administrators wield in these negotiations. In centralist systems the manner in which administrators are trained and bureaucratically organized encourages consensus and self-confidence. The centralist style also implies a history of deference to these administrators on the part of various social groups. In these systems, state administrators can be expected to wield a comparatively large amount of influence over public policy. In turn, governmental activity will be relatively stable and relatively long-term in its orientation.

The opposite will be true in noncentralist systems. There, training and organization will produce more dissensus among administrators; administrators will be less confident about their conception of and ability to promote the public interest. And most social actors will not tend to defer to state administrators in making public policy.[27]

A centralist administrative style does not necessarily achieve preferable welfare outcomes. State administration of public policy is plagued by several problems. From a behavioral standpoint, we note that many social problems are difficult to solve; the technical basis for the choice of various public policies, including policies relating to the operation of state-owned enterprise, is quite weak and underdeveloped.[28] From a structural standpoint, it is not clear how or even if state administrators are to be held accountable for their actions, especially if one assumes that only administrators have the technical competence to evaluate public policies and the performance of public enterprise. State administration appears to provide a select group of individuals with opportunities to enhance their own welfare at the expense of the welfare of many living citizens and future generations.

Nevertheless, public policy will be more stable and long-term in its orientation in systems with a centralist form of state administration.

26. Kuisel (1981: chap. 9) describes the splits that developed in the French technocracy in the 1950s, one faction favoring the notion that the state should only arbitrate conflicts between competing societal interests and another believing that the state was the "carrier of progress . . . the agent of material and cultural uplift [which] when necessary might tear the citizenry away from old habits" (p. 256).

27. See Freeman (1987) for an analysis of the role state administrative style plays in the historical evolution of mixed economies. See Zysman (1983) for an analysis of how state administrative style affects the formulation and implementation of industrial policy.

28. Recall, for example, the discussion of the difficulties state managers face in pricing the output of state-owned firms and in calculating an appropriate discount rate for public investments.

In turn, the content of policy in such systems will be oriented more toward the interests of future generations (as conceived, in part, by state administrators).

THE ALTERNATIVE FORMS OF DEMOCRATIC CAPITALISM

Democratic polities have different electoral systems, modes of interest intermediation, and state administrative styles. Depending on the constellation of institutions that exists in a given political jurisdiction, democracy can take one of eight different forms. The effects of these institutions vary with how they are combined with other institutions. For example, majoritarian electoral systems have a greater impact on the stability and temporal orientation of public policy in pluralist systems with noncentralist administrative styles than in corporatist systems with centralist administrative styles, because in the former system elected officials and interest group leaders are freer to pursue the short-term interests of their particular constituents. The mutual interests of producer groups as a whole and of future generations will tend to be emphasized more in the latter political system.[29] The most stable and long-term oriented public policies will be found in democracies with consensual electoral systems, corporatist modes of interest intermediation, and centralist administrative styles; the least stable and more short-term oriented policies will be found in democracies with majoritarian electoral systems, pluralist modes of interest intermediation, and noncentralist administrative styles.

Armed with this knowledge about how political institutions shape public policy, we are ready to return to our basic question: Which form of democratic capitalism is most desirable? The answer entails our joining the analysis in this chapter with that in the previous chapter, that is, studying how the workings of two economies affect and are affected by the workings of alternative constellations of political institutions. The next chapter shows that the mode of interest intermediation is the most important political institution in this regard; pluralism and corporatism have the greatest effects on the efficiency of the two economies and on the distributions of wealth those economies produce. I therefore subsume the analysis of elections and

29. Katzenstein (1985:209) is among those who stress the lesser importance of parliamentary and, by implication, electoral politics in corporatist as opposed to pluralist systems. The minimal impact of consensual electoral systems, and of electoral systems in general, on certain kinds of social inequality is stressed by Jackman (1986) and Brooks (1983).

state administrative style in the discussion of the consequences of pluralism and corporatism. For convenience, I also assume that the two kinds of economies are essentially closed to foreign trade and investment, especially insofar as the activity of public enterprises is concerned. Later, in Chapter 9, I relax this assumption.

CHAPTER FIVE

The Politics of Mixed Economies

Democratic capitalism can take several basic forms: pluralist–private enterprise, corporatist–private enterprise, pluralist–mixed, or corporatist–mixed. As we have seen, the institutional characteristics and workings of these four systems are quite different; the relative power of particular groups varies in them as well (Table 3). The key to deciding which form of democratic capitalism is most desirable lies in understanding how and when these differences translate into different welfare outcomes and what blends of collective gain and distributional equity can be achieved in the four systems.

This chapter is divided into five parts. Parts 1–4 examine the workings and potential welfare consequences of the four individual systems; part 5 compares these workings and welfare consequences. The analysis shows that in comparison to corporatism, pluralism undermines the efficiency of both kinds of economies. Hence pluralist systems produce a more inequitable intergenerational distribution of wealth than corporatist systems do. In addition, pluralism has a greater impact on the intragenerational distribution of wealth in mixed than in private enterprise economies, by virtue of governments' greater capacities to redistribute wealth in mixed economies.

Corporatism has a much less deleterious effect on market efficiency; greater collective gains can be realized in corporatist than in pluralist political economies. Wage earners can capture the greatest share of wealth in corporatist mixed systems, by virtue both of their greater organizational power *and* of governments' relatively greater capacities to redistribute wealth in such systems. Overall, the level and rate of societal consumption and wealth of future generations are greatest in corporatist-private enterprise systems and least in pluralist-mixed systems. The potential for maldistribution of wealth

97

Table 3. Welfare implications of four political-economic systems

Administrative Style	Private Enterprise Economy	Mixed Economy
PLURALIST		
Non-centralist	Social power concentrated in hands of private asset holders Capital market transactions and private investment decisions both a motor for the realization of Pareto gains in consumption and intergenerational equity, and a barrier to the realization of intragenerational equity between private asset holders and wage earners • Elections have some, usually minor, effects on government intervention and hence on the consumption rate and the character and stability of the intragenerational distribution of wealth • Greatest possibility of maldistribution of wealth between private asset holders and wage earners	Social power dispersed between private and public asset holders and, to some extent, political parties Productive efficiency and ameliorative effects of government market participation are major determinants of consumption rate and intergenerational equity; a greater share of output, earnings, and employment potentially available for intragenerational redistribution than in pluralist–private enterprise systems • Elections have major impact on effectiveness of government market participation and hence on productive efficiency, and on the character and stability of the intragenerational distribution of wealth • Some possibility of maldistribution of wealth between workers in private and public segments of economy
Centralist	Social power somewhat less concentrated; state administrators exert some influence over the allocation of some public resources Capital market transactions and private investment decisions play basically same role as above • State administrative elite often able to promote greater productive efficiency and greater consumption rate in comparison to pluralist–private enterprise systems with noncentralist administrative style • Elections have even less effect on the consumption rate and the intragenerational distribution of wealth	Social power dispersed between private and public asset holders, wage earners, and state administrators Determinants of welfare outcomes essentially same as above • State administrators are another participant in negotiations over the scope and operation of the government business sector • Elections still have major impact on welfare outcomes • Possibility of maldistribution of wealth between both managers and workers in the private enterprise and public enterprise segments of economy

between the private owners of firms and wage earners is greatest in pluralist–private enterprise systems and lowest in corporatist–mixed systems. Contrasts in the welfare outcomes of the four systems are

CORPORATIST

Non-centralist	Social power somewhat concentrated in hands of private asset holders and in producer group organizations	Social power somewhat dispersed between private and public asset holders, producer groups, and political parties

Capital market transactions and private investment decisions still major determinants of consumption rate and also a constraint on intragenerational redistribution of wealth; existence of official, organizationally strong producer group for workers enhances possibilities of greater equity in distribution of wealth between private asset holders and wage earners
• Producer group negotiations ameliorate labor-management conflict, stabilize investment, and help realize potentially superior consumption rate relative to pluralist–private enterprise systems; labor organization negotiates larger share of wealth for wage earners
• Elections have some impact on character and stability of distribution of wealth through political interconnections between parties and producer groups

Productive efficiency and ameliorative effects of government market participation are major determinants of the consumption rate and intergenerational equity; existence of producer groups, plus public production of large share of output, means potential for intragenerational equity between private asset holders and wage earners is greatest in these political economies
Role of producer groups same as for corporatist–private enterprise systems except that workers' organization potentially captures greater share of wealth for its constituents; and producer groups may be able to design and implement more effective market participation than parties and hence realize greater rates of consumption
• Elections have more impact on the level and distribution of wealth than in corporatist–private enterprise systems and less than in pluralist–mixed systems
• Greatest possibility of maldistribution of wealth between private enterprise and state enterprise workers

Centralist — Social power somewhat less concentrated than if administrative style is noncentralist; state administrators are potential ally of producer groups
Capital market transactions, private investment decisions, and producer groups negotiations play essentially same role as above
• State administrators assist or oppose producer group efforts to promote higher consumption and distributional equity
• Elections have less impact on the consumption rate and on the intragenerational distribution of wealth in comparison to corporatist-private enterprise systems with noncentralist administrative style

Social power somewhat dispersed between private and public asset holders, producer groups, parties, and state administrators
Determination of welfare outcomes essentially same as above
• State administrators participate in party and producer group negotiations over the scope and operation of state business sector
• Elections have somewhat less impact on welfare outcomes. The possibility of maldistribution between private enterprise and state enterprise workers is somewhat less than in corporatist–mixed systems with noncentralist administrative style

more pronounced under certain conditions pertaining to the character of state administration, nature of capital markets, degrees of societal consensus over the ends and means of government, and citizens' sense of "collective ownership efficacy" with regard to publicly owned assets. Finally, the interconnections between democracy and markets produce a skewed distribution of power—a "privileged position"—for private asset holders or owners and public enterprise workers in pluralist–private enterprise and corporatist–mixed systems, respectively; and elections have a major impact on intragenerational equity, if at all, only in pluralist–mixed systems.

PLURALIST–PRIVATE ENTERPRISE POLITICAL ECONOMIES

In this first system, welfare outcomes are outgrowths of market competition between privately owned firms for customers, competition between governments for the public revenues and employment opportunities generated by privately owned firms, and nonmarket competition between parties and interest groups for public services and income transfers. Competition between private firms is spurred by share trading among their private owners and by managers' desire to perform well in their segment of the labor market. This form of competition yields levels of production that represent Pareto improvements in earnings and in societal consumption, plus some market-determined blend of intergenerational and intragenerational equity.[1]

Citizens' demands for employment and for various public services spur governments to recruit privately owned firms to locate within their jurisdiction. Government success in this regard has direct effects on the welfare of its constituents—how many citizens are employed, how clean the air is, and so on—as well as indirect effects on how much revenue is available for financing public services and for redistribution through public agencies. Who benefits most from the provision of public services and from government redistribution of wealth over the short term depends, in some part, on the outcomes of pluralist political competition, for example, on the outcomes of electoral competition between political parties. The winners of electoral contests, to some extent, seek to enhance the welfare of their supporters

1. The notion of a market-determined distribution of income follows from the idea that when markets are in competitive equilibrium, the distribution of income depends on the distribution of asset holdings (including human capital) among consumers, the rental and wage rates for resources and labor, and consumer preferences about leisure and consumption.

at the expense of supporters of the losers. Stability in the welfare outcomes of pluralist–private enterprise systems thus implies that the market is essentially in competitive equilibrium. The net number of relocations of private firms into and out of government jurisdictions is effectively zero, and the distribution of political power among contending political parties and interest groups are essentially fixed.[2]

The structural and behavioral features of pluralist–private enterprise political economies determine the range of welfare outcomes that can be achieved. The severity of market failures and imperfections, in the absence of government intervention, constrains the possibilities of achieving particular levels and rates of societal consumption. Whether these structural defects can be overcome depends, in part, on whether pluralist politics enhances or undermines government's capacity to ameliorate market failures and imperfections. For instance, party leaders and their administrative appointees may simply lack the technical skill to reestablish marginal cost pricing in sectors characterized by natural monopoly or to promote the development of efficient asset markets. Hence the structural deficiencies of markets will not be overcome and, in turn, the welfare of current and future generations will be inferior to what it could have been in terms of short-term and long-term consumption.

The possibilities for redistribution of wealth in private enterprise economies hinge, to a substantial extent, on the mobility of private firms. Generally speaking, the greater the willingness and ability of private firms to relocate from one government jurisdiction to another, the more insecure wage earners are and the less the revenue available to finance public services and for redistribution. In addition, the more private investors respond to government taxation by disinvesting, the lower is the present value of wage earners' expected flow of wages and the less economic security they enjoy. In these ways welfare outcomes depend directly on the choices made by private firms rather than on the workings of electoral systems or on the results of interest group negotiations.

Because shareholder transactions encourage relocation and disinvestment, capital markets have a major impact on the distribution of wealth in this first kind of political economy. Financial markets make it easier for private asset holders to sell the equity they hold in private

2. The first condition here means that the level and rate of societal consumption are unchanging; no net change in firm relocation coupled with market equilibrium means that employment security is unchanging; and a balance of political power implies either that an incumbent party has achieved an intragenerational distribution of wealth that ensures its reelection or that the outcomes of elections result in the reshuffling of wealth between party constituents but not in an alternation of the overall intragenerational distribution of wealth.

firms and in that way to encourage managers to relocate the firms in jurisdictions that promise higher rates of return both because tax rates are lower and because the level of public services is higher. In the process, productive efficiency and hence Pareto gains in consumption may be realized. But at the same time, the potential for government-directed redistribution of wealth is diminished. A substantial amount of the social power in pluralist-private enterprise systems is therefore wielded through capital market transactions by asset holders and by the managers of private firms.[3] Indeed, the power that private asset holders exert over the distribution of wealth probably matches or exceeds the power wielded by political parties and political interest groups.[4]

Pluralist politics is important insofar as it affects the intertemporal choices governments make and the frequency with which governments attempt to alter the relative wealth of particular groups of citizens. The benefits from eliminating market imperfections usually do not accrue to society at the same time that market intervention occurs. Rather, government intervention usually produces Pareto gains in consumption at some future point in time. Such government decisions, therefore, are inherently intertemporal. The question is whether pluralist politics is conducive to making such choices or, more specifically, to what extent political parties and interest groups value future gains relative to current gains in consumption.

The answer depends on what discount rate party leaders, interest group representatives, and individual citizens apply to future societal gains in consumption, whether these people think they will be among those who will benefit from such gains, and how or if they take into account the gains of others—including future generations. If party leaders, interest group representatives, and individual citizens all apply a high discount rate to the likely outcomes of government intervention or show little concern for the well-being of the unborn, pluralist politics can be expected to produce a short-term orientation in government decision making. Structural defects in markets will be tolerated because for party leaders, interest group representatives, and individual citizens, the present value of future consumption gains

3. I assume a substantial amount of redistribution does not occur as a result of the philanthropy of private asset holders. Moreover, governments may choose redistribution through deficit spending (see note 8 below).

4. Of course, the argument that the power of asset holders matches that of political parties is not new. For instance, Boddy and Crotty (1975) argue that natural cycles in private enterprise economies are managed in a way that reinforces the power of capitalists through the repeated creation of a reserve army of workers; see also Lindblom (1977) and Cameron (1984). Another version of the argument is contained in Zysman (1983), who maintains that in pluralist–private enterprise systems with well-developed capital markets, responses to industrial change are "company-led."

is relatively low.[5] Under these conditions, electoral politics will focus more on intragenerational than on intergenerational equity issues, and shifts in the partisan composition of government will have little effect in themselves on the rate of societal consumption over time.

Of course, it is also possible that the leaders and supporters of one party will apply a lower discount rate than their opponents to potential gains in consumption, consider themselves and their offspring most likely to be the beneficiaries of societal gains in consumption, or be more concerned than the leaders and supporters of other parties about the welfare of future generations. In such circumstances, the election of this party might lead government to promote long-term consumption possibilities, whereas election of another party would lead government to tolerate market failure and to place a higher value on present consumption.[6] This shift in the temporal orientation of government is more likely if the electoral system is majoritarian in character; in such a case, parties will have more freedom to impose a different discount rate.

The possibility that parties may apply different discount rates to future gains in consumption raises the larger issue of how much consensus exists in a pluralist–private enterprise economy about what constitutes equitable market outcomes. Societal dissensus over the distribution of wealth means that parties, interest groups, and individual citizens will disagree about who should benefit from government intervention in the market. Consider disagreements about what constitutes an equitable intragenerational distribution of wealth. If the political resources of groups of partisans are roughly equal and the electoral system is of the majoritarian kind, party competition may result in frequent shifts in redistributive policies. One set of partisans might win an election and seek to bring about their conception of intragenerational equity, then another set of partisans could win an election and seek to bring about their different conception of intragenerational equity. However, note that by virtue of the capital mobility and ease of equity disinvestment private enterprise economies allow, the amount of revenue available for redistribution is relatively small. Hence even if parties have fundamentally different concep-

5. In this case "suboptimal" may be inappropriate since all members of society apply a very high discount rate to future consumption. Hence the present value of any government-induced gains in consumption is low relative to the market-determined level of consumption.

6. Arguments to the effect that, in private enterprise political economies, pluralist politics imparts a socially undesirable, short-term orientation to government intervention are advanced by Nordhaus (1975) and Chappell and Keech (1983). For a more circumspect analysis of this issue, see Alt and Chrystal (1983: chap. 10). The idea that some parties are oriented more to future gains in consumption and intergenerational equity concerns is implicit in Hibbs's classification of party goals (1977).

tions of intragenerational equity, elections will have little or no effect on the actual distribution of wealth among members of the current generation. Rather, elections will serve either to marginally enhance the wealth of supporters of the party that manages to remain in office for several terms or to reshuffle a small amount of public revenue back and forth between the same competing groups of partisans. In neither case will pluralist politics have a significant effect on the overall intragenerational distribution of wealth.

State administrative style can affect the welfare outcomes of pluralist–private enterprise systems. A centralist administrative tradition may improve the possibilities for and effectiveness of government promotion of productive efficiency. If administrators have the technical skill and are consistently deferred to by parties, interest groups, and voters, any socially deleterious myopia inherent in pluralist politics can be at least partially overcome. Centralist administrators will make intertemporal choices designed to ameliorate market defects and imperfections, and so improved rates of societal consumption will be realized over time. In fact, it is conceivable that, if administrative tradition is markedly centralist, government may apply a discount rate on future societal consumption that is lower than both the market and the nonmarket (politically induced) discount rates. Administrators might do so in the name of intergenerational equity, for example. In such a case a centralist administrative tradition would reduce the likelihood that elections might impart an intergenerationally inequitable, short-term orientation to government intervention in the market.

What are the implications of administrative tradition for the intragenerational distribution of wealth in pluralist–private enterprise political economies? Can centralist administrators circumvent the limits on redistribution that derive from the mobility of private capital and the ease of private disinvestment? The answers to these questions hinge on how mobile private firms are, on how well developed capital markets are, and on the willingness of administrative elites to promote a particular conception of intragenerational equity. To the extent that administratively directed market intervention enhances capital mobility by encouraging the frequent relocation of private firms or by promoting the development of capital markets that nurture and reinforce the power of private asset holders over managers, public policy may further undermine the security of workers and delimit government's ability to finance public services and to redistribute wealth. In sectors where administrators regulate the private production of particular goods and services, there are opportunities for publicly directed efforts to favor one group of citizens relative to another group, as through administratively mandated rate structures intended to favor certain consumers or through administrative promotion of private investment in particular regions of the government jurisdiction. In addition, because capital markets are not always perfectly developed, opportunities sometimes exist in the realm of financial intermediation for administrative rationing of investment capital to privately owned firms. In this case, the power of private owners is lessened somewhat by the substantial degree of control state administrators wield not only over the supply but also over the allocation of money and credit.[7]

Will the enhanced power of state administrators translate into attempts to benefit one group of citizens relative to another group? The answer depends on whether individual administrators believe that government has an obligation to promote a particular conception of intragenerational equity. There is no reason to believe they have such beliefs. In fact, state administrators may not make any effort to resolve competing equity claims within current generations; they may believe that markets are the best arbiter of intragenerational equity conflicts and therefore devote most of their efforts to helping society realize Pareto gains in consumption and achieve intergenerational equity. Only when prodded by party and interest group leaders will they intervene in ways that adjudicate competing intragenerational equity claims. Where administrative tradition is noncentralist, public authorities usually do not have the will to alter the intragenerational distribution of wealth.

In pluralist–private enterprise political economies, therefore, welfare outcomes are most likely to favor Pareto gains in consumption and intergenerational equity rather than intragenerational equity between the holders and nonholders of assets (that is, between private owners and wage earners). The possibility of severe market imperfections and failures means that lower levels of consumption may accrue to the corresponding societies than is technically feasible both in the short term and over time. Pluralism leads political parties, interest groups, and individuals to impose a high discount rate on future gains in consumption, or place comparatively little value on the welfare of future generations or both. Hence pluralism produces instability in public policies, which discourages long-term investment.

Generally speaking, pluralist politics does not have a significant effect on the intragenerational distribution of wealth in this first kind of system. This is true even if the constituents of some parties are committed to a major, short-term redistribution of income and even

7. See Zysman's discussion (1983) of the allocative power enjoyed by administrators in France and Japan by virtue of the credit-based financial systems of those countries.

if the election system is of the majoritarian type. The reason is that in pluralist–private enterprise political economies, firms' mobility and capital market transactions—the mechanisms that promote Pareto gains in societal consumption and intergenerational equity—delimit the possibilities for government redistribution of wealth. Wealth can only be "reshuffled" among wage earners, for instance. The power that private owners or asset holders have over managers amounts to power over society, in the sense they can implicitly bargain for a degree of redistribution that leaves intragenerational equity largely unaffected by pluralist politics.[8]

CORPORATIST–PRIVATE ENTERPRISE POLITICAL ECONOMIES

The welfare outcomes of corporatist–private enterprise systems are outgrowths of competition between privately owned firms for customers; of competition between governments for the public revenue and employment opportunities generated by privately owned firms; and of political competition between parties and interest groups for public services and income transfers combined with negotiations between official producer groups over wage rates and other facets of capital-labor relations. In corporatist–private enterprise systems, threats of disinvestment by private asset holders and managerial incentives spur market competition between private firms, in turn yielding Pareto gains in earnings and consumption. Also, governments recruit private firms to locate in their jurisdiction in an attempt to satisfy their constituents' demands for employment and for public revenue. But in the first type of political economy, who benefits from public services and public redistribution of wealth depends on the outcomes of elections and decentralized interest group lobbying alone; in the second type of political economy, negotiations between official producer group representatives have important effects

8. At first glance, the possibility of borrowing against the income of future generations—running up large government deficits—appears to offer incumbent political parties an opportunity to enhance the wealth of their constituents relative to the unborn and also relative to the wealth of both their political opponents and asset holders. However, if these deficits are financed through borrowing from private owners—the group that already holds the majority of the capital in the society—repayment of the public debt may impoverish future nonowners even more, since it conceivably will leave the original asset owners and their heirs comparatively better off than they were when they originally financed the consumption of the government's patrons. Thus there could be a shift in terms of the intragenerational distribution of wealth between asset holders and wage earners as a result of (public) deficit spending, but over the long term the superior share of wealth the former group enjoys will be preserved if not enlarged.

on the distribution of wealth. The welfare outcomes achieved in corporatist–private enterprise systems are partly a result of two, interconnected forms of political decision making which articulate and
aggregate the preferences of two, partially overlapping sets of
citizens.[9] Stability in the welfare outcomes of corporatist–private enterprise political economies thus implies that markets are essentially
in equilibrium, there is in effect no net relocation into and out of
government jurisdictions, the distribution of power between competing political parties is essentially fixed, and also the balance of power
within and between official producer groups is relatively stable.

The structural and behavioral features of corporatist-private enterprise systems determine the blends of collective gain and distributional equity that can be achieved in them. As regards the current
level of wealth and the distribution of wealth between generations,
the severity of market failures and imperfections is again important
insofar as such structural deficiencies define the feasible range of
earnings and consumption possibilities. Corporatism is socially beneficial because producer groups are better able than political parties
and interest groups to cope with these deficiencies. Normally the
technical expertise of producer groups and their staffs is superior to
that of political parties and interest groups, for example, because
producer groups have more experience with market failure and so
better understand how to cope with it. In two private enterprise
economies characterized by identical structural deficiencies, then, the
one with a corporatist form of political decision making offers its current and future generations higher levels and rates of consumption
because, from a technical standpoint, corporatism produces more effective market intervention than does pluralism.[10]

Corporatist–private enterprise systems produce a different range
of intragenerational welfare outcomes than do pluralist–private enterprise systems. Capital market transactions embody an important
kind of social power in them. By threatening to disinvest, asset holders again influence the location and investment decisions of private
managers, in turn affecting both wage earners' security and the
amount of revenue available for public services and for public redis-

9. See Panitch's explanation of the relation between parliamentary and corporatist
politics (1980:173); also Lehmbruch (1977), Jessop (1979), and Keeler (1981:181–82).
For a discussion of the linkages between social democratic party politics and labor organizations in Sweden see Korpi (1978: chaps. 3 and 10). A more aggregated, crossna-
tional study of the linkage between social democratic parties and corporatism and its
impact on the "governability" of industrial democracies can be found in Schmitter
(1981).
10. See, for instance, Farnleitner and Schmidt (1982:97); also Nowotny (1984:120–
21).

tribution. Private decisions to invest or disinvest therefore continue to affect the workings of markets and hence the pace and character of technological change, labor mobility, and other facets of market processes.[11] But, in pluralist–private enterprise systems, wage earners can challenge asset holders' power only through (decentralized) forms of collective action such as strikes and by voting for political parties that promise to promote wage earners' interests; in corporatist-private enterprise systems, by contrast, an organizationally autonomous and strong, official producer group also exists to promote their interests. As a consequence, the social power of wage earners relative to that of the owners and managers of private firms is greater than it is under pluralism. For example, labor militancy under corporatism is more threatening to private owners because labor leaders usually can organize a strike of much greater scope and severity than what the employees of a single firm or industry could organize on their own; the threat of a nationally coordinated strike is more imposing than the threat of any legislation workers and their representatives might be able to enact.[12] Under corporatism, then, it is possible to achieve a more equitable distribution of wealth between labor and capital than it is under pluralism.

How much greater is labor's share of wealth in corporatist–private enterprise as opposed to pluralist–private enterprise systems? The answer is a matter of debate. Some theorists contend that the differences in the shares of wealth captured by labor in the two economies are not great. Private enterprise economies preserve the (dis) investment privileges of private asset holders, wage earners rarely hold many capital assets or participate in capital markets, and capital markets allow those who own shares in firms to repeatedly exercise their power over managers; as a result, the relative bargaining power of producer groups remains heavily skewed toward employers (the private owners of firms). Hence labor's power to capture a significant share of societal wealth in private enterprise economies remains circumscribed regardless of the prevailing form of interest intermediation.[13] Other theorists maintain that corporatist–private

11. See Korpi (1978: chap. 6) and Pontusson (1984); also Hernes and Selvik (1981:117–18). Of course, in some cases workers hold equity assets through their pension funds, and through this kind of institution they engage in capital market transactions. Also, in some countries, such as Sweden, pension funds constitute a significant share of the assets of capital markets. (Since workers usually do not hold equity assets, and as the magnitude of pension fund transactions is not great, I discuss this factor with the Swedish case in Chapter 8.)

12. On the importance of organizational strength in general and the benefits Swedish labor gained from the creation of a national labor organization in particular, see Pizzorno (1981) and Korpi (1978), respectively.

13. For a discussion of the "positive-sum" nature of Swedish corporatism, see Korpi

enterprise systems produce intragenerational distributions of wealth substantially different from those in pluralist–private enterprise systems.[14]

The significance of corporatism lies in the way it shapes the blend of collective gain and distributional equity in private enterprise economies. Political parties and their appointees sometimes have the expertise to intervene in markets in ways that promote productive efficiency. But there is reason to doubt their ability to do so repeatedly in a way that amounts to genuine, welfare-enhancing intertemporal choice. Rather, political parties and interest groups normally enact policies that *retard* market processes and hence create inefficiencies, for instance, policies that preserve the jobs of workers in declining industries. In contrast, corporatism enhances the capacity of government to make effective intertemporal choices that promote productive efficiency and, in turn, help realize gains in earnings and consumption. Corporatism *reinforces* market processes by promoting labor mobility, for example. It also produces greater certainty than does pluralism about wage rates and about the likelihood of work stoppages. This, in turn, has a salutary effect on long-term business investment.

Corporatism transforms distributional conflict between employers and workers into a cooperative problem-solving venture that yields short-term and long-term gains to both groups. If both apply roughly the same discount rate on future gains in earnings and consumption and they agree about how much wealth should accrue to future relative to current generations, then producer groups can forge an agreement that imparts greater stability to labor-capital relations than may be possible under decentralized employee-employer bargaining, party politics, and interest group negotiation. In this way, corporatism appears to enhance the welfare of many citizens, including the unborn.[15]

This is not to say that corporatist politics yields just distributions of wealth or that it eliminates distributional conflict between or within producer groups. As I pointed out in Chapter 4, corporatism is not necessarily founded on complete consensus either within or between

---

(1978:199, 324–25). See also Przeworski (1980c:141). Radical evaluations of corporatism frequently stress the more regularized and potentially less risky disciplining of labor which the negotiations between producer groups allow. In its boldest form, this critique argues that corporatism is the "institutionalization of inequality" (Offe and Wiesenthal 1980; also Panitch 1980, 1981).

14. See Shonfield (1984: chap. 10), Katzenstein (1985), and Korpi (1980).

15. Thus, Offe (1981:143) argues, "it is not any specific characteristic of the policy area in question . . . that gives rise to corporatist structures but the failure of political parties to perform as agents of the 'formation of political will of the people' . . . and the 'functional gap in consensus building' that results." See also Korpi (1978: chap. 6).

producer groups. Members and leaders of producer groups frequently disagree about whether welfare outcomes are distributionally just. For example, disagreements arise from the fact that corporatist agreements frequently create and sustain substantial wage and profit differentials across certain sectors of the economy.[16] Also, political parties under corporatism continue to play an important role in deciding the ends and means of government intervention. And while parties and producer groups are often closely linked in terms of leadership and goals, there is no guarantee they will agree that the terms of corporatist bargains are distributionally just. Hence elections and parliamentary politics may produce public policies that undermine the terms of corporatist agreements or challenge the authority of producer group leaders. Such a challenge might be mounted if workers feel that labor leaders do not give them enough say in the operation of their organization; workers might support either certain factions of affiliated political parties or even opposition political parties in attempts to hold their producer group representatives accountable for certain of their decisions.

The important point is that in comparison to the first type of political economy, this second type more fully insulates labor-capital relations from the effects of electoral and parliamentary politics. In so doing, corporatist–private enterprise systems enhance the possibilities of achieving both Pareto improvements in earnings and consumption and a more equitable distribution of wealth between the owners of private firms and wage earners.

State administrative style affects the welfare consequences of corporatist–private enterprise systems in essentially the same ways as it affects those of pluralist–private enterprise systems. A centralist administrative style enhances a government's capacity to promote productive efficiency by providing additional expertise from which producer groups and political parties can draw (or to which they can defer) or by giving producer group representatives an ally with whom to oppose harmful adjustments in the long-term policies adopted by these officials. To the extent that producer groups and state administrators have more expertise than parties or unofficial interest groups, then, a centralist administrative style facilitates the realization of

16. The efforts of Austrian and Swedish labor organizations to improve the welfare of the lowest-paid workers and to avoid creating privileged groups of workers are discussed in Lacina (1983) and Korpi (1978: chap. 11). Conflict within the Austrian labor organization over which workers should bear the cost of industrial adjustment is studied by Andrlik (1983, 1984). On the general cohesiveness of European labor movements see Wallerstein (1984). Sabel mentions the splits within the business community which corporatism spawns (1981:215); see also Korpi (1978).

Pareto gains and intergenerational equity in corporatist–private enterprise political economies.

As regards intragenerational equity, a centralist administrative tradition can affect the durability of producer groups' agreements to create a particular distribution of wealth between private owners and wage earners. A centralist administrative style can help realize and enforce a corporatist bargain between producer groups. Or a centralist administrative elite conceivably can ally with a coalition of parliamentary groups to oppose an agreement worked out by producer groups. This attitude might take the form of administrative opposition to national wage and price setting and advocacy of a more decentralized approach to labor-management relations—that is, the creation of a more pluralist system. In this case the effect of an administrators' alliance with parliamentary groups is to reassert the limits on redistribution that are imposed by capital market transactions, firm mobility, and decentralized labor-management negotiations. However, state administrative support for a corporatist bargain may have a similar effect. Merely by regulating capital market transactions and the investment decisions of private firms, state administrators preserve barriers to intragenerational transfers of wealth.[17]

To reiterate, in corporatist–private enterprise systems it is possible to realize greater levels and rates of consumption, and hence intergenerational equity, than is possible in pluralist–private enterprise systems. This second type of political economy also allows for greater equity in the distribution of wealth between private asset holders and wage earners (non-asset holders). In so doing, corporatist–private enterprise systems diminish even further the effects of popular elections on the distribution of wealth. Popular elections continue to affect social welfare, in that they help resolve conflicts that are not (directly) subject to corporatist bargaining. Moreover, they may serve as an alternative, if less perfect, means through which producer group members can hold their representatives at least partly accountable for their actions. In this sense elections and parliamentary politics are both a source of legitimacy for corporatist political arrangements and an additional mechanism for deciding who benefits from government market intervention. But in comparison to pluralist–private enterprise systems, electoral and parliamentary politics here have less of an impact on the content and stability of welfare outcomes.[18]

17. See the structuralist interpretation of the consequences of state intervention in corporatist political systems in Panitch (1980).
18. For empirical evidence of the distributional gains labor makes through corporatist as opposed to pluralist political institutions see Korpi (1980).

Pluralist–Mixed Political Economies

The welfare outcomes of pluralist–mixed political systems are out-growths of market competition for customers between privately owned and publicly owned firms, government operation of certain publicly owned industries, competition between governments for the revenues and employment opportunities generated by private and public firms, and competition between parties and interest groups for public services and income transfers as well as for the locations and investments of public firms. Mixed economies are populated by both privately and publicly owned firms. Threats of disinvestment by private owners and labor market incentives for private managers spur competition between private firms. Threats of privatization and policy mandates from elected officials and state administrators encourage competition between public and private firms. Privatization threats and policy mandates also influence the way public firms attempt to solve the problems of external effects and increasing returns and, concomitantly, to resolve the distributional conflicts that emerge from those types of market failure. Competition between firms coupled with public firms' efforts to promote productive efficiency determine the overall level of market output, which, in turn, represents Pareto gains or losses in earnings and consumption.

Citizens' desires for certain welfare outcomes lead governments to recruit both private and public firms to locate within their jurisdictions. Their success in this regard once more has both direct and indirect effects on their constituents' welfare. The recruitment of public firms is bound up with the more general political process through which competing equity claims are negotiated. In particular, in mixed economies the distribution of wealth is a result not only of government transfers of wealth among citizens but also of the character of public production decisions, for example, the pattern of public investment. In pluralist–mixed political economies, then, the winners of electoral contests can seek to enhance the welfare of their supporters both by using tax revenue to provide them with services and income transfers *and* by directing public firms to employ and serve them at the expense of the supporters of the electoral losers.

Stability in the welfare outcomes of this third type of system thus implies, among other things, that there is a fixed partitioning of public and private firms; the mix of private and public production creates some equilibrium in the respective markets; the net number of relocations of public and private firms is essentially zero; and the distribution of power between contending political parties and interest groups is essentially fixed so that how citizens exercise their collective ownership rights does not appreciably affect the pattern of public or private production and consumption decisions.[19]

The range of welfare outcomes that can be achieved in pluralist–mixed political economies depends on the structural and behavioral features of these systems. Pareto gains in consumption and intergenerational equity hinge not only on how effectively governments intervene in markets but also on how effectively governments participate in markets. Productive efficiency is restored only if state businesses are operated in a manner that promotes marginal cost pricing, for example. To achieve Pareto improvements in consumption, parties and their appointees must have wider range of technical expertise than is required for intervention in private enterprise systems. They must be capable of creating and actually operating public businesses, rather than merely regulating private firms, in a way that restores efficiency. This is a challenging task because, by their very nature, mixed economies are often plagued by severe market imperfections. The absence or underdeveloped condition of capital markets, for instance, deprives political authorities of a natural benchmark for consumers' and private investors' rates of time preference. This and the related problems outlined in Chapter 3 mean that some party leaders have great difficulty formulating, let alone implementing, a program for the creation and operation of state businesses.[20]

In pluralist–mixed systems, the possibilities for redistributing wealth within current generations depend, in part, on the degree of mobility of private firms and also on the outcomes of party competition as that competition reflects citizen efforts to exercise public ownership rights toward certain private and public ends. The relative power of managers and workers in the state business sector is also an important factor affecting the intragenerational distribution of wealth in these systems.

In private enterprise economies, even those with corporatist political institutions, the ability of private asset holders to invest or disinvest, especially through capital markets, constrains government ability to redistribute wealth. This constraint is present in mixed economies as well, since a substantial number of firms are privately owned, and share trading, to some extent at least, encourages investment in jurisdictions with lower tax rates. But a substantial amount of the assets in mixed economies are owned collectively, and citizens, as collective

19. For some partitioning of the economy, that is to say, markets clear and political competition yields no substantial changes in this partitioning or, concomitantly, in the material or nonmaterial distribution of wealth.

20. Again, see Przeworski (1980a:49), Korpi (1978: chap. 4), and Tilton (1987).

holders of these assets, do not rely on capital markets to influence the behavior of public firms. Rather, they make their investment decisions through the same political process where distributional conflicts are negotiated; in the case at hand, through pluralist politics. Decisions about how much of firms' output can be taxed and exactly where firms will locate are made both by individual, private asset holders and by collective, public asset holders. How much of current earnings is reinvested (in the economy as a whole) for the sake of future consumption and wages is partly a matter for government to decide, not for private asset holders and managers to decide alone. Finally, in mixed economies, public managers and public enterprise workers often possess a relatively large amount of social power. Indeed, as I pointed out in Chapter 3, in some respects managers and workers in state-owned enterprises have more social power than their counterparts in private firms. For example, some workers in public enterprises possess a much more potent strike threat. In sum, social power is less concentrated in mixed economies; private asset holders—especially the owners of private firms—do not wield as much influence over the distribution of wealth in pluralist–mixed systems as they do in pluralist–private enterprise systems. As a consequence it is possible to achieve different distributions of wealth in the two political economies.

It follows that democratic politics has much more effect on social welfare in pluralist-mixed systems than in pluralist-private enterprise systems. Because elections and parliamentary politics serve as a means to exercise public ownership rights, citizens have more say over distributional issues in the former system. The realization of Pareto gains in consumption and earnings hinges much more directly on partisan consensus over the necessity for and future implications of public policies. Party consensus about the appropriate discount rate to apply to public investment decisions has more direct effects on productive efficiency and hence on consumption than the fiscal policies of governments in private enterprise economies. Partisan agreements in pluralist–mixed systems to apply a low social discount rate or to place little value on the gains that accrue to future generations translate directly into reduced public investment, reduced rates of consumption, and, conceivably, intergenerational transfers of wealth.[21]

21. This is not to say that fiscal policy in particular or political change in general has no impact on the behavior of private firms. Party competition certainly has effects, and they can differ from those which party competition has on the behavior of public enterprises; see the comparison in Mann (1974:441–42). But public firms are, to a somewhat greater extent, subject to democratic supervision; they are comparatively less able to relocate to jurisdictions where party competition has little or no effect on the financial performance and other aspects of state-owned enterprise.

Dissensus over the appropriate social discount rate to apply to public investment, or over the relative importance of intergenerational equity, produces the same outcome if elections repeatedly substitute one party for another and, in turn, public business policies are repeatedly revised. Dissensus over the distributional objectives of state-owned enterprise can also produce Pareto losses in consumption, if elections force public managers continually to revamp their business policies in ways that undermine efficiency, for example, to change their pricing policies or their investment location decisions so as to enhance the short-term consumption or employment security of the constituents of the victors of electoral contests. In such circumstances, pluralism in effect allocates the dividends and losses of nontradable collective assets between current and future generations and between different sets of public owners. Pluralism partially substitutes for capital markets in allocating the earnings and benefits from the public's shareholdings. In the process, pluralist politics serves as a counterweight to capital market transactions—and the power of private asset holders embodied in these transactions—in altering the possibilities for redistributing societal wealth.[22]

Exactly how pluralism allocates the dividends and losses of state-owned enterprise, and ultimately decides to retain or reprivatize the public's shareholdings, depends on party leaders' and citizen-voters' conceptions of the nature and value of collectively owned assets. Consensus over the objectives of state-owned enterprise requires some common understanding among party leaders and their followers about the broader meaning of voting in popular elections and, more specifically, about the relationship between electoral participation and the execution of public ownership rights. Voting in popular elections has to be conceived, in some part, as a collective stockholders' meeting that either decides the scope and operation of the state business sector or confers authority on elected officials and state administrators to monitor the performance of public managers.

When popular elections are conceived in this way, the outcomes of electoral competition can be roughly compared to the outcomes of meetings of the stockholders of private firms, with the distributional results revealing society's preference for government market participation in order to achieve particular welfare outcomes. Or, in the case of a mandate to restructure an economy toward a private enterprise form, elections can be seen as revealing a social preference to rely more on capital market transactions to shape welfare outcomes.

22. In other words, the range of distributional outcomes, in this third type of political economy, results more from both the workings of political (pluralist) and economic (capital market) institutions than from the latter alone.

Interpreted in this way, the continual reelection of Leftist political parties that support the creation and governmentally supervised operation of mixed economies in ways that expressly favor their constituents reveals a majority or plurality preference for an intra-generational distribution of wealth in which the relative material and nonmaterial wealth of certain (public enterprise) workers is enhanced at the expense of other citizens, especially the potential private owners of public firms. Similarly, election of a party advocating reprivatization of state businesses can be interpreted as a revealed majority or plurality preference for a shift in the blend of welfare outcomes toward one that places a greater emphasis on Pareto gains in consumption and intergenerational equity, a relatively greater share of wealth for the owners of private assets, and a smaller share of material and nonmaterial wealth for workers who support Leftist parties.[23]

But do citizens conceive of their votes in popular elections in this way? Do citizens make an explicit connection between electoral participation and the execution of public ownership rights? The answers to these questions are not clear.

It is true that the welfare consequences of state-owned enterprise are evident to some citizens. Where the issue concerns the location of state-owned enterprises and their investments, for example, citizen-owners often have a good sense of what they stand to gain in the way of employment security and higher wages.[24] There is also evidence that citizens see public ownership as a means of achieving increased and even more equitable consumption possibilities, for example, through their enhanced ability to convince public managers to adopt lower and more uniform user charges for various services and goods. Their ability to pursue and achieve these ends through electoral participation appears to vary, to some extent, with the level of government jurisdiction at which public ownership is promoted. In this sense, pluralism promotes political competition between the consumers or users and nonconsumers or nonusers of publicly produced goods and services.[25]

23. For example, some British Labour party activists see nationalization as a means of redressing the inequities suffered by coalminers under private ownership (interviews, London, October 1984). The broader connection between nationalization, altruism, and economic decline in Britain is explored by Alt (1979: chap. 14); see also Millward (1978).

24. Evidence of the citizens' realization of the potential benefits from public investment in the British nationalized industries is given in Dudley (1979); the explicit link between voting behavior and expected public investment in the (nationalized) British automobile industry is reported in Hart (1986).

25. Among studies that suggest citizens are able to discern enhanced consumption

In addition, party activists recognize the instrumental value of state-owned enterprise, and in some instances they are directly involved in supervising the operation of the state business sector. Hence there is reason to expect they will view elections and parliamentary politics as a sort of referendum on the operation of the state business sector. As we saw in Chapters 2 and 4, these individuals often have well-developed conceptions of the role state-owned enterprise plays in achieving partisan ends. They may consider themselves "brokers" for their constituents, overseeing the public business sector in a way that best serves their clients'—if not society's—interests. Seen in this way, elections allow citizen-owners to choose one set of party-public business managers over another and, in turn, to alter the resulting level and allocation of the dividends or losses from the collectively held asset.

There are other ways in which elections could hold party business managers accountable to public shareholders for the welfare consequences of state-owned enterprise. For example, a nonincumbent party might favor a dismantling of the state business sector. In an electoral system of the majoritarian type, this aim would pose a serious threat to the power and influence of state managers and the respective elected officials. Performance might improve accordingly. Also, there are cases in which the makeup of the supervisory boards for nationalized industries depends directly on electoral outcomes: the electoral fortunes of political parties translate into their controlling more or fewer seats on the bodies that supervise public enterprises. In such circumstances, the implications of voting are easier for citizens to discern, and there is more reason to believe that citizens view voting as, in part, an exercise in the execution of public ownership rights. In turn, state managers are held more accountable than they are in those systems where elections have less clear and indirect effects on the makeup of supervisory boards.[26]

Thus we have some reasons to believe that citizens view elections as a means of exercising their public ownership rights and that they place a high instrumental value on those rights. This phenomenon, which I call "collective ownership efficacy," is one facet of citizens' more general set of beliefs about the nature and value of political or nonmarket participation. It is not unique to the politics of mixed economies or to the problems of monitoring the performance of state

possibilities under public versus private ownership is Pashigian (1976); see also Mann (1974).

26. Austria's *Proporz* system has, until recently, provided for representation on the supervisory board of the state holding company for nationalized industries to be linked directly to the outcomes of popular elections. I examine this system more closely in Chapter 7.

enterprise. Private asset holders display a similar kind of ownership efficacy in their willingness to participate in stockholders' meetings; they also display market efficacy in their willingness to rely on capital market transactions to hold managers accountable for the performance of private firms. What is different about mixed economies is that this individual ownership or what we might call "market efficacy" is not a factor in holding state managers accountable for their actions. In this third political economy, state managerial accountability hinges, in part, on citizens' belief in the effectiveness of pluralist politics as a means of articulating and aggregating their preferences with regard to the scope and operation of public businesses.[27] Collective ownership efficacy therefore is a critical determinant of the welfare consequences of pluralist–mixed economies. To the extent that citizens actively participate in elections and engage in other kinds of political activities for the purpose of monitoring the scope and operation of the state business sector, we can refer to a "revealed social preference" for the achievement of a blend of collective gain and distributional equity distinct from that which can be achieved in private enterprise systems, especially pluralist–private enterprise political economies.

In practice, however, pluralist–mixed systems are unlikely to reveal such preferences. To begin with, popular elections involve a variety of issues, not simply those pertaining to the creation and operation of the state business sector. Unlike private stockholders, citizens, as collective owners of public assets, rarely have the opportunity to vote on issues pertaining to state-owned enterprise alone.[28] Even if they have well-defined views about the best scope and operation of state-owned

27. What distinguishes collective ownership efficacy from private ownership efficacy is that citizens link participation in nonmarket institutions with the dividends that accrue to them from holding a publicly owned asset, part of the value of which derives from the workings of market processes. Again, private asset holders also display collective efficacy in their willingness to participate in private stockholders' meetings. In this sense, both collective and private owners have the option of participating in a nonmarket political institution designed to hold managers accountable for the behavior of firms; and each kind of owner must weigh the benefits and costs of promoting personal interest in this way. But this is, ignoring the possibility of migration, the only means of ensuring accountability open to the owners of public firms; they do not have the option of participating in capital market transactions for this purpose. Private asset holders normally do have this second option, and it illuminates the phenomenon of market efficacy—private asset holders believe in the effectiveness of capital market transactions as a means of promoting their individual interests (as well as the interests of society).

28. There is, of course, the possibility of a regular referendum on the scope and performance of state-owned enterprise. We encounter this possibility in Chapter 7 in the discussion of the Austrian experience, and in Chapter 8, in a brief discussion of the Swedish proposal to create "citizenship funds."

enterprise, then, citizens may not be able to express those views effectively through the electoral process.

Second, the individual welfare implications of collective asset ownership are, in some ways, more difficult to discern than the individual welfare implications of private asset ownership. The owners of private assets can measure the value of their holdings in terms of the dividends those assets yield and the assets' present market value; the dividends that private asset holders earn are directly related to the number of shares they own. In contrast, the dividends that state-owned enterprises pay are allocated through a pluralist political process. And since ownership is collectivized, it is much more difficult for public owners to determine if they or others earn the share of dividends to which they are entitled. Moreover, citizens have different expectations about the allocation of public dividends: they do not necessarily expect all public asset holders to receive the same proportion of the dividends from public shareholdings, even though all citizens technically hold the same amount of public shares. Indeed, as I pointed out above, the motivation for creating state enterprises is, in part, an explicit concern for the welfare of other citizens.[29] For all these reasons, it may be difficult for party leaders and their followers to treat elections as a collective stockholders' meeting for state-owned enterprise.

These problems tend to produce a lack of collective ownership efficacy and, in turn, a distinctive set of welfare outcomes. Failure to make the connection between voting and accruing benefits from state-owned enterprise, a belief that the leaders of competing parties will not manage state-owned enterprise in substantially different ways, or the expectation that the dividends and losses from owning public assets will almost certainly be allocated to others—all could leave citizens with little efficacy insofar as execution of their public ownership rights is concerned. A substantial number of citizens therefore fail to articulate any preference regarding the operation of the state business sector.

But as we saw in Chapter 3, popular elections are essentially the only way public owners can influence state managers. So the lack of collective ownership efficacy exacerbates the behavioral problems associated with mixed economies. Productive efficiency suffers because citizen–collective owners fail to hold elected officials and public en-

29. Students of the politics of mixed economies who take as axiomatic the self-interested, somewhat myopic behavior of voter–public owners include Mann (1974) and Pashigian (1976). Peltzman's work (1971) and evidence discussed in note 23 above show that this axiom is unreasonable. Voters are explicitly concerned with the welfare of others; their views in this regard display an appreciation for the instrumental value of public ownership.

terprise managers and workers accountable for their performance. In turn, any one of those groups or a coalition of them can further their interests at the expense of other groups in society as well as at the expense of the population as a whole, for example, by eschewing those intertemporal choices which might augment societal consumption possibilities over the short or long terms. The lack of efficacy among citizen-owners under pluralism thus produces a blend of welfare outcomes in which the level and rate of societal consumption is lower than it might be either in a pluralist or in a corporatist private enterprise system, and one in which the intragenerational distribution of wealth favors public enterprise managers and workers and their partisan allies.

This conclusion follows only if one assumes that elected officials, public administrators, and public enterprise managers and workers act solely on the basis of their own short-term interests. There is no reason to assume, contrary to what some observers claim, that all these groups always behave in this way. One group that may be committed to the pursuit of Pareto gains in consumption and intergenerational equity is state administrators. As I stressed in Chapter 2, the managers of state-owned enterprises and the administrators who manage the state business sector often have well-conceived notions of the distributional outcomes government market participation should promote; these individuals seem to take a view of their role as operators of public firms different from that of their counterparts in private firms. Where state administrative style is of the centralist type, therefore, a pluralist–mixed economy might produce comparatively high levels and rates of consumption even though many citizens lack ownership efficacy. Alternatively, even though citizens lack a well-developed sense of the instrumental value of exercising their collective ownership rights through voting in popular elections, elections may produce such small electoral pluralities that party leaders are unable to force administrators to make any major changes in the scope and operation of the state business sector—or electoral systems are consensual in nature and hence limit the opportunities for major alterations in state-enterprise operations. The same is true with respect to any intragenerational equity objectives state managers might attempt to pursue. These objectives could differ from those to which elected officials are committed, and either low collective ownership efficacy or a consensual electoral system could enhance state managers' abilities to promote a particular intragenerational distribution of wealth.

Another possibility is that centralist administrative style amounts to a form of public owner deference: a substantial number of citizens genuinely trust state managers and workers to pursue welfare outcomes that are in some sense more just than what private managers and private asset holders might pursue if the same economy were of the private enterprise type. In this case, citizens might elect candidates who explicitly promise to preserve the autonomy of those who work in the state business sector, because they trust the judgment and approve of the history of performance of that sector. Of course, the difficulty citizens have in conceptualizing and articulating their public ownership rights could allow state administrators and managers to pursue objectives that are contrary to the preferences of a majority of public shareholders or to make it more difficult for certain parties to implement some citizens' preference for restructuring the economy toward a private enterprise form. This point again raises the prospect of public enterprise managers and workers able to capture a share of societal wealth exceeding what accrues to their counterparts in the private sector or what they could capture if the entire economy was of the private enterprise type.

In sum, the welfare consequences of pluralist–mixed political economies depend to a much greater degree on the workings of political institutions than do the welfare consequences of pluralist–private enterprise systems. Market processes still have an important impact on social welfare in this third type of political economy. The investment and disinvestment decisions of private asset holders have a direct impact on the level and rate of consumption, as well as on the overall amount of public revenue available to finance public services and income transfers and to finance some public investment.[30] However, a substantial number of firms are publicly owned, and hence investment and other public business decisions can be made through electoral and interest group politics. As a result, the potential exists for realizing a somewhat different set of welfare outcomes in pluralist–mixed as opposed to pluralist–private enterprise systems. In particular, because of the difficulties inherent in using popular elections to monitor public enterprise performance coupled with the general, short-term orientation of pluralist politics, pluralist–mixed systems will produce outcomes that are inferior on the first welfare criterion and somewhat superior on the second. Pluralist–mixed systems will produce relatively lower rates of collective gain and less intergenera-

30. How state-owned enterprises are created is important insofar as it raises, once again, the importance of financial markets in reinforcing the power of private asset holders over time. This issue is addressed in Chapter 9, where I briefly consider the role of international capital markets in financing state-owned enterprise. There is no reason why state-owned enterprise cannot be self-financing. Hence the implications of borrowing from and repaying private asset holders for the creation of a mixed economy need not necessarily arise.

tional equity than will pluralist–private enterprise systems. At the same time, pluralist–mixed political economies will produce somewhat more intragenerational equity. The beneficiaries in this case will be a certain segment of the workforce—state enterprise managers and workers—and their partisan allies.

CORPORATIST–MIXED POLITICAL ECONOMIES

The welfare outcomes of corporatist-mixed systems are outgrowths of market competition between privately owned and publicly owned firms for customers; government operation of certain publicly owned industries; competition between governments for the revenue and employment opportunities generated by private and public firms; and a combination of political competition between parties for public services, income transfers, and the location of and investments in public firms and of negotiations between producer groups over wage rates, prices, and other facets of capital-labor relations. Competition and cooperation between public and private firms once more affect the conditions under which markets in the mixed economy clear and hence the levels and rates of consumption that are achieved in this fourth system.

Citizens' demands for employment, public services, and other benefits spur governments to recruit firms, private and public, to locate in their jurisdictions. In turn, the distribution of wealth depends, as before, on the outcomes of this competition among governments. But in pluralist–mixed systems, who actually benefits from public services, government redistribution of wealth, and the public production of goods depends on the outcomes of this intergovernmental competition and on the outcomes of electoral competition. In corporatist–mixed political economies, by contrast, negotiations between producer groups also have important effects on the distribution of wealth. Welfare outcomes are outgrowths, in corporatist–mixed systems, of the interconnected workings of a broader set of political and economic institutions.

Stability in these outcomes implies, among other things, a fixed partitioning of public and private firms; the mix of private and public production creates some equilibrium in markets for the inputs and outputs of production and in consumer demand; the net number of relocations of public and private firms is essentially zero; the distribution of power between contending political parties is essentially fixed, so that electoral participation and citizen exercise of public ownership rights do not alter the pattern of private and public production; and a balance of power within and between official producer groups so that the terms of the corporatist bargain and its implications for the operation of the state business sector are continually adhered to by producer group members.

The structural and behavioral features of corporatist–mixed political economies produce a distinctive range of possible welfare outcomes. As in pluralist–mixed systems, state-owned enterprise affects the overall efficiency of the economy and, in turn, allows (or prevents) the achievement of Pareto gains in consumption. The challenge of managing the state business sector so as to realize such improvements in social welfare is present once again. Only now, the willingness and ability of producer group leaders to meet the challenge determines whether potential improvements in consumption will actually be realized.

Producer group representatives and their staffs can ally with or conceivably substitute for political parties in managing the state business sector in a fashion that promotes productive efficiency. There are good reasons to believe that producer groups are more willing and able to perform this task than political parties. The representatives of labor are often much more committed to public investment as a means of promoting the interests of their constituents than are parties, which must serve a multiplicity of interests. Also, the stability that corporatism imparts to economic policy making is more conducive to intertemporal choices like those embodied in public investment decisions, for example, to impose a low discount rate on the returns to future generations from public investments. Unlike political parties that must consider various short-term interests of their supporters, producer group representatives—especially labor representatives—often have a much clearer mandate to promote the long-term interests of their constituents. Producer group leaders have more faith in corporatism's capacity to formulate and implement medium- and long-term social policies; the success they have had in erecting and maintaining corporatist institutions makes them confident that they can design and enforce welfare-enhancing strategies for state-owned enterprise.[31] In mixed economies, corporatist politics thus may be more conducive to the realization of Pareto gains and the achievement of some form of intergenerational equity.

In corporatist–mixed systems the intragenerational distribution of wealth still depends, to some degree, on the mobility of private firms and hence on the social power of private asset holders. However, pol-

31. See, for example, Andrlik's summary (1983: chap. 3) of the rationale behind Otto Bauer's plan for achieving socialism, part of which provided for nationalizing Austrian industry.

itics has direct effects on intragenerational equity as well, since citizens now exercise their public ownership rights both through participation in elections *and* through participation in producer group organizations. The relative power of the workers in public enterprises can also be somewhat greater. Recall that in mixed economies, social power is somewhat more dispersed than it is in private enterprise economies; capital market transactions do not limit the possibilities for achieving intragenerational equity between the owners and nonowners of private assets in the former kind of economy to the same extent as they do in the latter. In addition, under corporatism the power of wage earners is comparatively greater than under pluralism, since there exists an organizationally autonomous, strong, official producer group that can promote wage earners' interests more fully than political parties can. The possibilities for achieving a more equitable distribution of wealth between private asset holders and wage earners are therefore greatest in corporatist—mixed political economies. The fact that a substantial number of firms are publicly owned, and therefore more the captives of government jurisdictions, together with the greater power corporatism affords wage earners gives that group the opportunity to capture a greater share of material and nonmaterial wealth than their counterparts in any of the other three political-economic systems. Through their corporatist wage and price agreements and their employment in publicly owned firms, wage earners have the potential to secure a comparatively greater share of current consumption and a greater employment security.

Whether this potential for greater intragenerational equity between wage earners and private owners (asset holders) is realized depends on how corporatist politics shapes the execution of public ownership rights in the mixed economy. The combination of electoral politics and producer group negotiations has direct effects on distributional equity in this case. Consensus among party and producer group leaders and their followers about the appropriate scope and ends of state-owned enterprise essentially produces a revealed social preference for a particular conception of distributional justice. The sorting out of welfare issues between parliaments and corporatist institutions and the implications of this sorting out for the erection and operation of the state business sector, under conditions of effective consensus, reflect some basic agreement among asset holders—private and public—about what distribution of wealth is socially most desirable.

On the other hand, disagreement over what constitutes distributional equity or over the appropriate scope and ends of public enterprise may produce instability in the goals and character of government market participation. But in this fourth kind of political economy, disagreement among parties and their leaders is potentially less destabilizing than in pluralist–mixed systems. The reason is that corporatist political institutions insulate state-owned enterprise from distributional conflict. The institutionalization of labor-capital relations means that distributional conflict, as expressed through elections and parliamentary politics, has less of an effect on public investment decisions as well as on economic policy in general. The existence of official, autonomous, and organizationally strong labor organizations means, for example, that the welfare of workers hinges less on the electoral success of those political parties which count wage earners among their constituents. In turn, the intragenerational benefits that accrue to wage earners—especially those employed in state-owned enterprises—are more immune to the operations of electoral and parliamentary institutions than they are in pluralist–mixed systems.[32]

The relative magnitude of the gains workers realize in corporatist–mixed economies ultimately depends on their and other citizens' conceptions of the nature and value of public ownership rights and on how that conception translates into certain forms of political behavior. In this system, citizens' preferences for certain welfare outcomes are expressed through a pair of elections rather than a single popular election. Corporatism provides citizens with an additional means through which to articulate their preferences regarding the scope and operation of government businesses.

For wage earners, in particular, corporatism provides another channel for voicing preferences regarding the scope and ends of state-owned enterprise and securing the differential benefits it provides to them in the way of employment security and consumption opportunities. For party leaders who are also producer group representatives, dual producer group-popular elections can provide a stronger mandate or a clearer statement of collective preference for altering or maintaining the operation of the state business sector.[33] Thus collective ownership efficacy may be more prevalent in corporatist than in pluralist–mixed systems. And as a consequence, state

32. For more general discussion of the relative insulation of economic policy making from parliamentary politics and elections in Austria, see Nowotny (1984) and Katzenstein (1984). This is not to say that parliamentary politics has no influence on economic policy, only that it has less influence there than in pluralist political systems. See Farnleitner and Schmidt's brief discussion of the tendency of Austria's social partners to anticipate parliamentary decisions or wishes (1982:96); see also Pelinka (1987).

33. The argument here is not just that two channels of interest articulation are better than one but also that producer group organizations genuinely complement elections in focusing public decision making on the important issue of the distribution of output, earnings, and employment in public firms within society.

managers may be held more accountable for their policies and for pursuing some set of socially preferred welfare objectives.

Do citizens consider the dual mode of political participation and other facets of corporatist politics as effective channels for exercising their public ownership rights? Do producer group and electoral politics work together in a harmonious fashion to help realize socially preferred distributions of wealth? The answers to these questions depend on the citizen–collective owners one focuses on. Wage earners employed in state-owned enterprises have a greater stake in overseeing the operation of the state business sector than do workers in the private enterprise part of the mixed economy. The former's wages and their long-term security are directly affected by public business decisions. Of course, the same is true of the employees of state-owned enterprise in pluralist–mixed economies. What is different about corporatist–mixed political economies is that for the respective public enterprise workers, political participation is more likely to have a direct impact on the way that dividends from state-owned enterprise are distributed. In corporatist–mixed political economies, public enterprise workers have both an incentive *and* a better chance to influence the investment and employment decisions of state business managers. Their relative wages and employment security do not hinge on the decisions of private asset holders, as they do for workers in private firms. Nor do they hinge solely on the vagaries of electoral and parliamentary politics, as in pluralist–mixed systems. Rather, in addition to being able to exercise their collective ownership rights through elections, in corporatist–mixed economies public enterprise workers have a powerful, official organization through which to press their particular demands on what are captive public businesses. In this fourth type of system, then, public enterprise workers can be expected to display a relatively greater amount of collective ownership efficacy than their counterparts in pluralist–mixed economies, especially at lower jurisdictional levels. Public enterprise workers and their producer group representatives will monitor public business decisions more closely than public enterprise workers and their representatives in pluralist–mixed economies; and, in turn, they will hold state managers more accountable for the welfare outcomes state-owned enterprises produce, at least with respect to their particular economic fortunes.[34]

34. That publicly owned firms are captives of national governments is important since it means that state enterprise workers do not have to cope directly with the private owners' power to disinvest. Evidence that state enterprise workers and their party and producer group leaders display much (collective ownership) political efficacy, especially at the regional level, is contained in Andrlik (1983).

Wage earners in the private enterprise segment of the corporatist–mixed economy cannot be expected to display the same degree of collective ownership efficacy. This other group of workers may not consider the combination of corporatism and electoral politics an effective means of executing public ownership rights. The complexity and uncertainty surrounding the effects of a dual mode of political participation on the scope and operation of the state business sector may leave this segment of the workforce no more efficacious than workers (the entire workforce) in pluralist–mixed political economies. Hence workers in private firms will not meaningfully execute their public ownership rights, and so state managers will not be held accountable by a substantial number of citizens. As a result, the relative influence public enterprise workers exert over the decisions of these managers and, in turn, over the distributional outcomes state-owned enterprises produce increases; this particular segment of the workforce has an opportunity to secure differential wage rates and a higher degree of economic security relative to their counterparts in the private enterprise sector of the economy.

Would workers in the private enterprise sector of the mixed economy be willing and able to oppose such a privileged position for public enterprise workers? The former group of workers has several options. First, employees of private firms can press labor and party leaders to increase their wages and to enhance the security of their jobs, for example, by providing public financial support for private firms. Unfortunately, some such demands will be inherently ineffective since, for the private segment of the economy, labor organizations and their partisan allies must contend with the social power of private asset holders and their representatives, who will oppose wage increases on the grounds that they jeopardize private profit rates and who will also guard private owners right to invest or disinvest. Public financial support for firms may also be difficult to secure because citizens have different expectations about what these entities are entitled to. Many citizens, including some workers in private enterprises themselves, will oppose this policy on the grounds that, in contrast to publicly owned firms, the benefits from private ownership accrue mainly to the private owners of firms.

Workers in private firms also have the option of pressing labor and party leaders to reduce the wages and economic security of public enterprise workers. The issue then is whether public enterprise workers, using their more potent strike threat, can deter labor and party leaders from attempting to redress the perceived maldistribution of wealth among wage earners. In a larger sense, private enterprise workers' ability to redress perceived inequities hinges on the balance of political power between them and public enterprise workers within the respective producer group and political parties.

Workers in private enterprise are in a different position from workers in state enterprise. The former usually exercise less social power through refusing to work and face more uncertainty about the effects of exercising their public ownership rights. Private enterprise workers, therefore, may be less willing to exercise their public ownership rights on behalf of any conception of distributional equity. In corporatist–mixed political economies, then, the performance of state managers will depend to a great degree on how workers in publicly-owned firms exercise their public ownership rights through both electoral and producer group institutions. The way these workers execute public ownership rights may also be a source of disagreements between members of labor organizations and, in turn, a factor that destabilizes corporatist politics.

State administrators can play an important role in negotiations among producer group and party leaders. Where state administrative style is centralist, political decision making about the scope and operation of the state business sector can be further insulated from parliamentary and electoral politics. Centralist administration can impart even greater stability to the terms of the corporatist bargain and to its application to state-owned enterprise. For example, state administrators can promote and then enforce a particular social discount rate for public investments and so help achieve welfare outcomes that producer group and party leaders have agreed to pursue.[35]

In this context, state administrators can actively oppose efforts by public enterprise workers to enhance their welfare at the expense of other citizens, especially at the expense of workers in the private enterprise sector. State administrators can promote norms of equity across different segments of the workforce, enlisting political allies for this purpose. In turn, the collective ownership efficacy of many citizens may be enhanced; more citizens might exercise their public ownership rights because they see state administrators as a potential ally for creating more just distributions of wealth, including more uniform wage rates and similar degrees of economic security across the private and public sectors of the economy.

The relative power of producer groups in corporatist mixed political economies makes it less likely that state administrators, including state managers, can exert the same amount of influence over public business decisions as they exert in pluralist–mixed political econo-

35. See, for instance, Grunwald (1977) and Lacina (1977, 1983).

mies. However much they may desire greater autonomy to pursue some self-conceived notion of distributional equity, state administrators in this fourth system must negotiate not only with political parties but also with labor and employer associations that have the capacity to promote the interests of their particular constituents. Also, the prospects for state elites' achieving autonomy purely through some popular deference to their administrative authority is dimmer in corporatist mixed political economies; deference of this kind can exist only if citizens withdraw their support for corporatist institutions, and this, by definition, is impossible.[36]

In sum, political institutions are important in mixed economies with corporatist political institutions, but for different reasons and with different welfare implications than in mixed economies with pluralist political institutions. Social power is somewhat less dispersed in corporatist mixed systems than it is in pluralist mixed systems, in that official producer groups exist to further the interests of particular segments of society. One consequence is the possibility of achieving distinctive welfare outcomes in corporatist mixed systems. To be specific, in the corporatist mixed political economy it is possible to achieve higher levels and rates of consumption than are usually possible in a pluralist mixed political economy, together with a more equitable distribution of wealth between the private owners of firms and wage earners than can be achieved in a pluralist private enterprise political economy.

The main reason for this state of affairs is that corporatism facilitates the long-term choices in public investment and other facets of state-owned enterprise activity which produce Pareto gains in consumption. And the existence of producer groups provides a more effective (additional) means through which citizens can exercise their public ownership rights over public firms and press for a greater degree of distributional equity between private owners and workers. Pluralist mixed political economies often exhibit a maldistribution of wealth between the managers of private and public firms, but this fourth type of political economy often exhibits a maldistribution of wealth between workers in state and in private firms. This is a cause and a consequence of the comparatively greater efficacy of public enterprise workers in exercising their public ownership rights.

---

36. If, as I assume in this subsection, the polity is corporatist, then there must be some substantial amount of deference to the authority of producer group leaders to negotiate economic policies, incuding state business policies. Otherwise the polity would be pluralist.

THE FOUR POLITICAL ECONOMIC SYSTEMS COMPARED

Different forms of democratic capitalism produce distinctive blends of collective gain and distributional equity. Figure 5 captures two main results of our analysis about these blends. First, all things being equal, the level and rate of societal consumption and hence the wealth of future generations are potentially greatest in corporatist–private enterprise political economies and least in pluralist–mixed political economies. Second, in reference to intragenerational equity between private owners and wage earners, the potential for maldistribution is highest in pluralist–private enterprise systems and lowest in corporatist–mixed economies. The first result follows mainly from the relative effectiveness of private share trading versus popular elections in relation to the problem of managerial control, on the one hand, and the long-term, market-reinforcing effect of corporatism versus the short-term, market-retarding effect of pluralism, on the other. The second result follows from the fact that the relative power of wage earners is greatest when they are represented by an official, organizationally strong producer group and there is a large amount of publicly owned assets. When most assets are owned privately and workers must exercise social power through decentralized forms of collective action and pluralist political institutions, as a group workers will capture a smaller share of societal wealth. In this context, the analysis suggests that as corporatism diminishes the power of private asset holders, so it enhances the power of wage earners. This effect is most clearly seen in corporatist mixed systems, where state enterprise workers enjoy a privileged position not unlike the position private asset holders enjoy in pluralist private enterprise systems.[37]

The analysis also shows that differences in the welfare outcomes of the four political economies depend on three related variables: administrative tradition, the degree of mobility of private firms, and the nature of mass attitudes and political behavior, more specifically, the degree of societal consensus over the ends and means of government intervention (market participation) and citizens' conception and valuation of collective ownership rights. Centralist administrative style can enhance the productive efficiency of markets in all four kinds of systems by improving the effectiveness of government market intervention or participation, or both. As a consequence, in the same kind

37. In this sense the gains workers make relative to private owners in private enterprise systems are offset, in some part, by the creation of a maldistribution of wealth between those employed in the public enterprise and those in private enterprise segments of the mixed economy. This argument implies that intragenerational equity is higher or "highest" only in corporatist–mixed political economies; these systems are *not* characterized by perfect intragenerational equity.

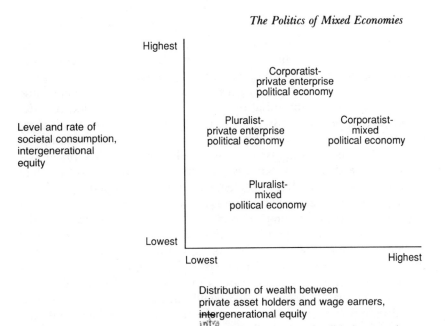

Figure 5. Contrasting welfare implications of the four types of political economies

of political economy levels and rates of consumption should be somewhat higher if administrative tradition is of the centralist type. The magnitude of the improvement in consumption is not necessarily the same in all four political economies, however. Gains from centralist administration may be greatest in private enterprise systems, since here the state elite does not have to operate businesses in the absence of clear benchmarks for discount rates for societal returns on public investments and so on; in pluralist mixed systems state administrators face just such a challenge, and they are also captives of governments. Hence, *ceteris paribus*, electoral and parliamentary politics are more likely to affect decisions in ways that effectively apply a higher rate of discount to the future societal returns from public investment and to the other social benefits state administrators might seek to produce.

As regards intragenerational equity, centralist administrative style is of less consequence in private enterprise than in mixed economies. Even state administrators who have well-defined conceptions of distributional equity are constrained by the power of private asset holders from promoting those welfare objectives in private enterprise economies, especially in pluralist private enterprise ones. In corporatist private enterprise systems an equity-conscious elite can ally with labor and other producer groups to promote what it sees as a more just distribution of wealth between private asset holders and wage earners. But again, state administrators remain constrained by private asset holders' ability to disinvest. In mixed economies, the power of centralist state administrators to promote a particular distribution of wealth is potentially greater than it is in private enterprise economies, since a substantial number of investment and location decisions are in public hands. The ability of centralist state administrators to influence the objectives and oversee the implementation of these public investments is greatest of all in corporatist–mixed systems because there they can ally with producer groups and insulate themselves from the effects of electoral and parliamentary politics to a much greater degree than in pluralist–mixed systems.

A second variable that affects the welfare outcomes actually achieved in the four political economies is the degree of capital mobility.[38] The greater the degree of capital mobility—because of the fuller development of capital markets or because of the greater willingness and ability of private owners to disinvest—the greater is the social power private asset holders wield, and the more inequitable is the distribution of wealth between them and wage earners. On the other hand, the more fully developed capital markets are, the more accountable private managers are to stockholders and, in the case of mixed economies, the better the information public administrators have about consumers' and investors' marginal rate of time preference. Hence, in principle, societal consumption and intergenerational equity are enhanced by greater mobility of private capital, in both private enterprise and mixed economies. Greater capital mobility retards the possibilities for achieving one kind of distributional equity while at the same time enhancing the possibilities for achieving another. This dual effect is more pronounced in private enterprise than in mixed systems, both because of the relative share of output and employment that is subject to private asset holders' control in the former and because efficient operation of state businesses is inherently more difficult to accomplish in the latter.

The third important variable affecting the welfare outcomes that actually occur in the four political economies is the nature of mass attitudes and political behavior. Two facets are especially important. First, the degree of societal consensus about the ends and means of government intervention (i.e., market participation) has an effect on the stability of public policy and, in turn, on the realization of Pareto gains in consumption. The tendency for dissensus to produce policies that diminish societal consumption rates is most marked where elec-

38. On differences in capital mobility in selected West European countries and the implications of these differences for the "privileged position of (private) business," see Bowler (1986).

tions have the greatest impact on the productive efficiency of the economy as a whole, that is, in pluralist–mixed systems. In such political economies, societal dissensus has more potential—through frequent, electorally induced changes in public policies—to retard the level and rate of societal consumption and to produce repeated, significant changes in the intragenerational distribution of wealth. Societal dissensus has the least effect on productive efficiency in corporatist–private enterprise systems, where government intervention and productive efficiency are most insulated from the effects of party and (unofficial) interest group competition. "Political business cycles," to the extent they are an outgrowth of societal dissensus over the ends and means of public policy, should be most evident in pluralist–mixed systems and least evident in corporatist–private enterprise systems.

Mass attitudes and political behavior affect welfare outcomes in a second way, by affecting the manner and extent to which public ownership rights are exercised in mixed economies. The productive efficiency of public firms and of mixed economies as a whole hinges, to some degree, on whether citizens hold public enterprise managers and workers accountable for their actions. Where collective ownership efficacy is high—citizens regularly exercise their collective ownership rights through electoral and other forms of political participation—accountability and productive efficiency are more likely to be achieved. But since citizens are inherently less likely to display collective ownership efficacy than to display private ownership efficacy, public enterprise managers and workers tend to be held less accountable for their actions than are their counterparts in private enterprises. Hence the level and rate of consumption in mixed economies are potentially somewhat less than what private enterprise economies can achieve.

Returning to the heuristic categorization of Figure 5, we find that contrasts in the collective-intergenerational welfare consequences of corporatist–private enterprise and pluralist–mixed systems are likely to be most pronounced when the following conditions apply: (1) administrative style is centralist in the former and noncentralist in the latter; (2) the corporatist–private enterprise system has a well-developed capital market and private investors in it are willing and able to disinvest in the face of government attempts to redistribute wealth, whereas the capital market of the pluralist mixed system is underdeveloped and its private investors are more captives of native governments; and (3) there is a high degree of societal consensus about the value of consumption now and in the future relative to income equality and employment security in the former system, and both a marked degree of societal dissensus about the objectives and operation of the state business sector and a low degree of collective ownership efficacy in the latter.

The contrasts in intragenerational equity between pluralist–private enterprise and corporatist–mixed political economies are likely to be most stark when (1) in the former system there is a centralist administrative elite committed to augmenting societal consumption and to promoting intergenerational equity but deferring to the market with respect to intragenerational welfare outcomes, and, in the latter system, there is a noncentralist administrative elite; (2) the pluralist–private enterprise system has a well-developed capital market and its private investors are willing and able to disinvest, whereas in the corporatist–mixed political economy capital markets are underdeveloped and private owners are less able and willing to disinvest; and (3) there is a high degree of societal consensus about the value of consumption now and in the future relative to income equality and employment security in the former political economy and both a high degree of societal consensus about the value of income equality and employment security relative to present and future consumption *and* a high degree of collective ownership efficacy in the latter political economy.

Differences in social welfare in *actual* pluralist–private enterprise, corporatist–private enterprise, pluralist–mixed, and corporatist–mixed systems can be traced, as the next chapters show, to the existence of various constellations of these three variables.

PART THREE

EVIDENCE

CHAPTER SIX

Welfare Outcomes:
Cross-national Evidence

The implication of the welfare taxonomy given in Chapter 5 is that, to the extent the four types of political economies exist in the Western world, there is *no* clear-cut relationship between our two welfare criteria. Relatively high and low levels of collective welfare are associated with relatively equal and unequal distributions of wealth (see Figure 5). If there is sufficient variation in administrative tradition, capital mobility, and citizens' attitudes and behavior toward state-owned enterprise, there will be marked contrasts in the welfare of different countries, especially in the welfare of countries with corporatist–private enterprise and pluralist–mixed systems and countries with pluralist–private enterprise and corporatist–mixed systems.

This chapter begins to establish the validity of the theory presented in Chapter 5. It examines societal welfare in Western industrialized countries and, in large part, confirms our theoretical expectations.

GAUGING SOCIAL WELFARE IN WESTERN DEMOCRACIES

Numerous, interrelated indicators show how wealthy countries are and how equitably wealth is distributed within countries. Levels of societal consumption, capital accumulation, and productivity all indicate how wealthy countries are; short-term rates of change in these and related variables indicate whether the material wealth of current generations is increasing or diminishing over time.[1] Levels and rates

1. Data on the Japanese case are included here, but only for purposes of exposition. I will make no effort to demonstrate the applicability of the theory in an Asian setting.

of change in such things as public debt, prices, crime, and air quality also tell us about the collective well-being of different societies.[2]

Long-term rates of change in consumption and other variables give us some idea of how equitably wealth is distributed across generations within countries. All things being equal, the greater the long-term rate of change in such variables as real per capita gross domestic product, the fairer is the relative share of wealth captured by successive generations.[3] Contrasts in such things as the scope of social insurance coverage also affect intergenerational distributions of wealth insofar as they produce differences in the nonmaterial gains that accrue to older age groups.[4] One summary indicator of this first dimension of societal wealth is the physical quality of life index; it treats such variables as life expectancy and infant mortality as surrogates for the overall level of societal well-being.[5]

Intragenerational equity consists of the ways various kinds of wealth are distributed within societies at certain stages in market and nonmarket allocation processes.[6] Pretax income shares indicate the primary or market-determined distribution of material wealth. Posttax shares of national income are indicators of secondary distribution; they give us some idea of how government transfers affect income inequality. The relative amount of posttax income accruing to the top 1 percent of the income scale and the ratio of shares of income of groups at the "semideciles" of the income scale can also be used to assess intragenerational equity within countries.[7] The level

2. Among the authors who evaluate societal welfare on the basis of trends in real per capita GDP are Heidenheimer, Heclo, and Adams (1983: Chap. 5), and Garret and Lange (1986). Cameron (1978) uses "Change in percentage of GDP, Private Sector Capital Accumulation, 1960–1975," in his cross-national assessment of the welfare consequences of government spending. Productivity measures are used to compare the performance of Western industrialized countries by Hollingsworth (1982) and by Magaziner and Reich (1982). The latter source also employs various measures of the quality of life, including crime statistics, for this purpose.

3. Liberal theory assumes that future generations have a right to a greater level of consumption than their predecessors. For instance, Arrow and Kurz's (1970) objective function was defined in terms of discounted per capita consumption rates. The practice of normalizing consumption and GDP with respect to population is quite common. See Magaziner and Reich (1982: Chap. 1), and Heidenheimer, Heclo, and Adams (1983: Chap. 5, Table 5.3).

4. For information on the scope and nature of social insurance coverage in Western industrialized countries, see Heidenheimer, Heclo, and Adams (1983: Chap. 7), and Esping-Andersen (1985).

5. See Morris (1979).

6. The following types of income equality are suggested by Kraus (1981).

7. A wide range of indicators is used to assess intragenerational equity. Heidenheimer, Heclo, and Adams (1983: Table 5.3) and Cameron (1978: Figure 4) both employ the ratio of posttax shares of the top and bottom quintiles of the income distribution. Hibbs and Dennis (1988) have used the ratio of the top 20 and bottom 40 percent of net income of families to chart trends in income inequality in the United States. Mag-

and rate of unemployment across groups and across sectors of economies is still another important indicator. Unemployment directly affects the economic security of individuals, groups, and communities; unemployment rates are thus indicators of the material and nonmaterial well-being of the corresponding segments of societies.[8] The effects of unemployment and other variables are mitigated, to some degree, by policies such as public employment insurance and public child support. These particular policies partially shelter such groups as unmarried, unemployed women—one of the most vulnerable segments of societies—from economic hardship. In so doing, they too shape secondary distributions of wealth.

Governments produce some public goods that are not characterized by jointness of supply or public goods that certain individuals may be prevented from consuming; hence the final distribution of wealth will also favor some groups of citizens relative to others. For example, the manner in which a public good is produced may make citizens who reside in a particular geographical location better or worse off, materially or nonmaterially, than those who reside in another location within the same government jurisdiction.[9] For this and

---

aziner and Reich (1982) present information about the share of income that accrues to the bottom 20 and 10 percent of the income scale. The same authors, Kraus (1981), and such government publications as the British Central Statistics Office's *Economic Trends* all report the shares of the group at the top 1 percent of the income scale. Other authors rely on the Gini index, percent difference of average taxes paid by high- and low-income households, variance in logs of income shares, or the semidecile ratio to compare the degree of income inequality in societies. See Korpi (1980), Hollingsworth (1982), Esping-Andersen (1985). Wiles (1974) makes a case for using the ratio of the income shares of the 5th and 95th percentile groups, rather than the Gini index, to assess income inequality. Brooks (1983) uses a combination of the Gini index and a posttax income shares ratio. My data emphasize those dimensions of social equality which Brooks calls "welfarist" and "egalitarian."

Radical theorists such as Bowles and Gintes (1982) show how conclusions about trends in income inequality rest, in part, on definitions of the income scale or income classes. In particular, these authors reach conclusions mildly different from those of their neoliberal counterparts (e.g., Fusfeld 1982: Chap. 28) about trends in income inequality in the United States, on the basis of a conceptualization that assesses the relative earnings of capital and labor rather than the relative earnings of groups with different income levels. Here I adopt the liberal approach to measuring income inequality.

8. The distributional consequences of unemployment are studied in Hibbs (1982a). See also Bluestone and Harrison (1982) and Nowotny (1982a).

9. The simplest way of classifying public goods is in terms of (a) whether they exhibit jointness of supply—whether, when units of the good are made available to one person, the same number of units can simultaneously be consumed by other people— and (b) excludability—whether individuals can be excluded from consuming a good by a price mechanism and by a legal system that legitimizes this price (Riker and Ordeshook 1973: Chap. 9). The idea that governments produce goods that have one or both properties and therefore produce differential gains or losses for particular groups of citizens, for instance, those located in close proximity to where the good is produced.

other reasons there always exist regional (intrajurisdictional) inequities in the way consumption, employment, air quality, and other facets of societal wealth are distributed.[10]

Some of the more commonly used measures of levels and distributions of societal wealth are displayed in Figures 6–11. These figures depict the blends of collective wealth and intergenerational and intragenerational equity which exist in democratic capitalist countries. They are neither definitive nor complete: important facets of both kinds of equity, such as income inequities across regions, are not incorporated in them. Because of the absence of cross-nationally meaningful measures of certain indicators for some cases—the absence of comparable income distribution estimates for Austria, for instance—certain countries are excluded from the displays.[11] Finally, the focus on nine- and twenty-three-year changes in per capita consumption and the limited availability of cross-national estimates of income equality obscure important temporal variations in social welfare. The British case is illustrative. There were major changes in societal welfare in Britain between 1968 and 1985 (Figure 12). For this reason, in some years this and other countries may rank differently on some or all of the measures on which Figures 6–11 are based; therefore the scatterplots in Figures 6–11 may be inaccurate to some degree.

Nonetheless, this welfare accounting is much more comprehensive than what other scholars have produced. It incorporates most of the single welfare criteria others use to evaluate national performance, and the patterns it produces are robust against alternative compositions of the two sets of indicators. It is therefore reassuring that the scatterplots confirm the predictions of Chapter 5: the figures show that there is indeed no clear-cut relationship between the two kinds of welfare. They also show that there are significant differences in the levels and distributions of wealth within Western industrialized countries. For instance, they indicate that, for all four definitions of intragenerational equity, there are major differences in the performance of Italy and Sweden. There is markedly less intragenerational equity in Italy than in Sweden, both in terms of selected measures of income inequality and in terms of ranked, composite measures of inequality.[12]

10. Thus government agencies such as the British Statistical Office in its *Economic Trends* and the Austrian Statistical Office in its *Statistische Übersichten* regularly report regional variations in employment and other variables.

11. The intragenerational equity indicators in the figures are those most often used in the political economy literature, and they do not cover the Austrian case. Chapter 7 reports several estimates of income equality for Austria, suggesting that Austria is relatively inegalitarian in this respect. See Brooks (1983:406) and Esping-Andersen (1985:242).

12. The relative position of countries such as Sweden was essentially the same under alternative schemes for combining indicators of intergenerational and intragenera-

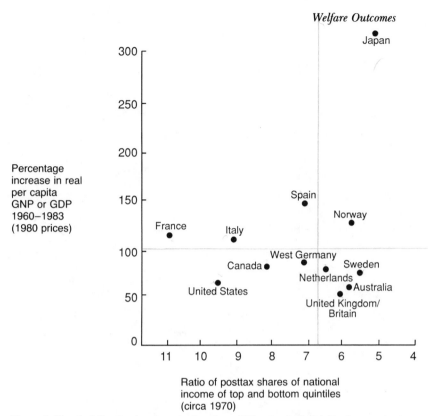

Welfare Outcomes

Figure 6. Blend of distributional equity in selected Western industrialized countries (two common indicators), 1960–1983
Sources: *International Financial Statistics,* 1983 Yearbook; OECD 1981.

There appears to be a somewhat greater degree of collective gain and intergenerational equity in Italy than in Sweden, but this difference is not as marked as that which exists between the respective scores and ranks for Italy and the United Kingdom. The United Kingdom performs worse than Italy in terms of *long-term* increases in real GDP per capita and in terms of overall rank on several indicators of intergenerational equity. The performance of the United Kingdom is inferior to that of Austria both in terms of increases in real per capita GDP and in terms of unemployment rates.[13] On the basis of these two in-

tional equity. For instance, Sweden's position is roughly the same for the six-country scheme in which the first welfare criterion is measured in terms of percentage increase in GDP (GNP) for 1960–1983 and 1974–1980; inflation, 1974–1980; and the physical quality of life index in 1975; and intragenerational equity is measured in terms of ratios and differences of posttax shares of the top and bottom quintiles, the Gini index of posttax shares, poverty levels, and unemployment rates for 1965–1982 and 1974–1980.

13. The percentage increases in real per capita GDP in the period 1960–1983 were about 56 for the United Kingdom and about 119 for Austria; for the period 1974–

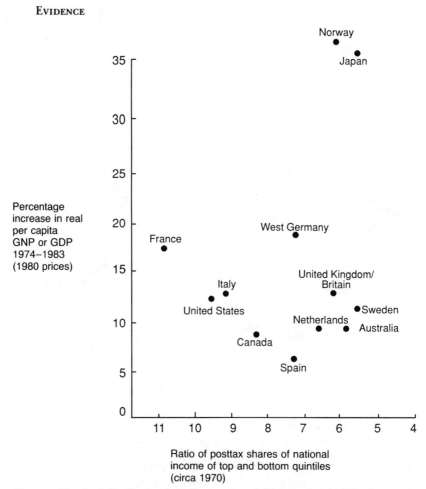

Figure 7. Blend of distributional equity in selected Western industrialized countries (two common indicators), 1970–1983
  Sources: International Financial Statistics, 1983 Yearbook; OECD 1981.

dicators, at least, Austria and the United Kingdom have different levels and distributions of wealth. Developments in Britain in the 1980s may have had the effect of reducing contrasts in intergenerational equity between the two countries while at the same time making contrasts in intragenerational equity more pronounced.[14]

1983, about 13 for the United Kingdom and 21 for Austria (1980 prices; *International Financial Statistics,* 1983, 1985). The average percentages of the total workforce unemployed for both the period 1965–1982 and the period 1974–1980 were about 5 for Britain and 2 for Austria (Cameron 1984; OECD 1982).

14. Of course, it could also be the case that, in recent years, the blends of social welfare in Austria, Italy, and Sweden evolved in such a way that despite some recent increases in real per capita GDP, redistribution of income, and so on, Britain's relative

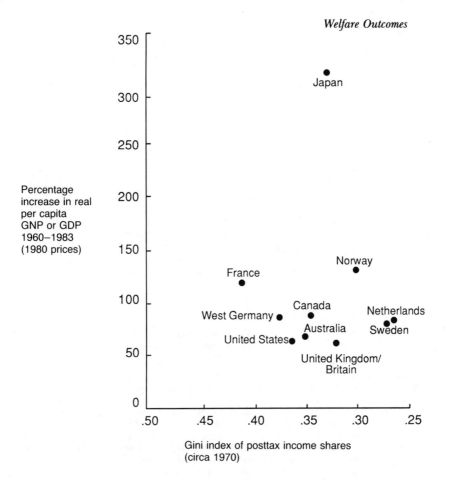

Figure 8. Blend of distributional equity in selected Western industrialized countries (two common indicators), 1960–1983
   Sources: International Financial Statistics, 1983 Yearbook; Korpi 1980.

Existing theories do not explain these patterns and changes in societal welfare. The main reason is that they rarely consider both welfare criteria at the same time. Rather, as suggested in Chapter 1, existing assessments of national performance usually focus exclusively on collective gains and losses in social welfare or on intragenerational equity.[15] The few investigations that consider both dimensions of so-

performance was essentially identical to what we observe for the periods 1960–1983 and 1974–1983.

15. Among authors who seriously consider both dimensions of social welfare are Cameron (1978), Heidenheimer, Heclo, and Adams (1983), Hollingsworth (1982), and Wilensky and Turner (1987). Among these, Hollingsworth (1982) provides the most balanced, in-depth evaluation of blends of distributional equity. His analysis is closest to that which appears in my Chapter 5 above. Also note that my ranking of countries conforms closely to those that appear in these works, for instance, Wilensky and

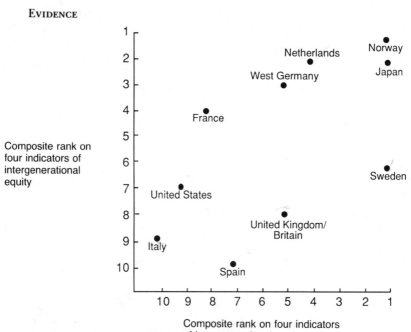

Figure 9. Blend of distributional equity in selected Western industrialized countries (composite ranking on several indicators), 1960–1983

Note: Indicators are ranked so that 1 represents the most equity. Composite rankings are formed by first ranking the countries for which data are available, averaging these ranks across indicators, and then reranking on the basis of these averages. Indicators of intergenerational equity are increases in real per capita GDP or GNP, inflation, and the physical quality of life; indicators of intragenerational equity include the ratio of posttax shares of national income received by top and bottom quintiles, the raw differences in these same shares, and average unemployment rates.

Sources: International Financial Statistics, 1983 Yearbook, 1985; OECD 1982; Morris 1979; OECD 1981; OECD 1976a; Cameron 1984.

cietal welfare usually take for granted the existence of a tradeoff between such things as per capita consumption and income equality. Yet such a tradeoff is not apparent in Figures 6–11. There is no obvious relation—visual or statistical—between collective gain and intergenerational and intragenerational equity; countries score high and low on both dimensions of societal welfare.[16]

Turner (1987: Table 1).

16. Perhaps the best-known case for the existence of such a tradeoff is Okun (1975). See also Brittan (1984). The quality of data and limited number of observations prohibit us from making any sound statistical inferences about the relationships depicted in Figures 6–11. Suffice it to say that for Figures 6 and 7, the correlations between indicators of collective gain and intergenerational equity and indicators of intragenerational equity are -.29 and -.31, respectively; neither of these correlations nor the corresponding regression estimates is statistically significant at the .05 level (either for the two-tailed test that follows from the previous chapter—the test that implies no relationship between the variables—or for the one-tailed test that follows from the conven-

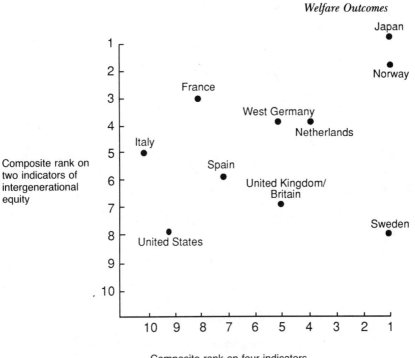

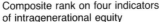

Figure 10. Blend of distributional equity in selected Western industrialized countries (composite ranking on several indicators), 1960–1983.

Note: Indicators are ranked so that 1 represents the most equity. Composite ranks are formed by first ranking the countries for which data are available, averaging these ranks across indicators and then reranking on the basis of these averages. Indicators of intergenerational equity are increases in real per capita GDP and GNP, whereas indicators of intragenerational equity are the ratio of posttax shares of national income received by top and bottom quintiles, the raw difference in these same shares, and average unemployment rates.

Sources: International Financial Statistics, 1983 Yearbook, 1985; OECD 1981; OECD 1976a; Cameron 1984; OECD 1982.

My welfare taxonomy (Figure 5) is consistent with this result. It predicts such distinctive blends of social welfare will be observed if the four different kinds of political economic structures exist and certain political-economic conditions hold in Western industrialized

---

tional wisdom and implies a negative relationship between them). The same result is obtained if Japan is deleted from the country sample in Figure 6, and if both Japan and Norway are deleted from the country sample in Figure 7. The Spearman Rank Order Correlation coefficients for Figures 9 and 10 are .63 and .26, respectively. Neither (rank order) correlation is statistically significant for a two-tailed test at the .05 level. The former is statistically significant for a one-tailed test (at the .05 level) of the hypothesis that there is a *positive* relationship between the two welfare criteria. For Figures 8 and 11, correlations of .038 and .040 (rank order) were obtained, respectively; neither correlation is statistically significant at the .05 level for a one-tailed or a two-tailed test. This result holds whether or not Japan is included in the country samples.

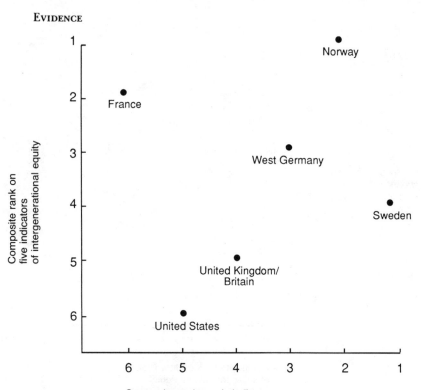

Figure 11. Blend of distributional equity in selected Western industrialized countries (composite rank on several indicators), 1960–1983

Note: Indicators are ranked so that 1 represents the most equity. Composite rankings are formed by first ranking the countries for which data are available, averaging these ranks across indicators, and reranking on the basis of these averages. Indicators of intergenerational equity are percentage increases in real per capita GNP or GDP, ratio of value of cash or tax allowance for children, index of social insurance coverage, and public debt per capita; indicators of intragenerational equity include ratios and raw differences in posttax shares of national income received by top and bottom quintiles, Gini index for posttax shares of national income, proportions of national populations in relative poverty, and average unemployment rates.

Sources: International Financial Statistics, 1983 Yearbook, 1985; OECD 1976b; Flora and Alber, 1981; von Beyne 1985; OECD 1981; OECD 1976a; Korpi 1980; Cameron 1984; OECD 1982.

countries. To be more specific, my welfare taxonomy predicts that, if the Western industrialized world includes the four systems and if certain political-economic conditions hold in regard to administrative tradition, capital mobility, and citizen attitudes and behavior toward state-owned enterprise, then there will be markedly different welfare outcomes in the four sets of countries, outcomes that do not present any grand tradeoff between collective welfare losses or gains and intergenerational and intragenerational equity.

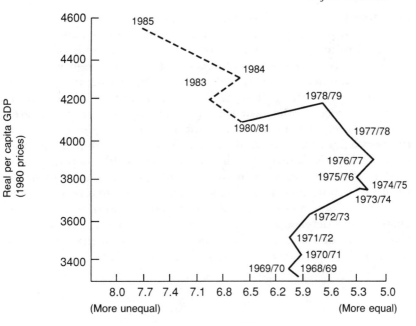

Figure 12. Evolution of social welfare in the United Kingdom (selected indicators), 1968–1985

Sources: For real per capita GDP figures, *International Financial Statistics*, 1983 Yearbook and March 1987. Income distribution figures for the years 1968–1981 are taken from articles entitled "The Distribution of Income in the UK," *Economic Trends*, May 1978, Table 5, p. 86; February 1981, Table A, p. 82; and July 1984, Table A, p. 97. For the years 1983–1985 these figures are taken from articles entitled "The Effects of Taxes and Benefits on Household Income," *Economic Trends*, December 1984, Table B, p. 95; July 1986, Table C, p. 103; December 1986, Table B, p. 97. The latter set of figures are based mainly on the imprecise Family Expenditure Survey; the former set of income distribution estimates incorporates several additional data sources, including the Inland Revenue's "Survey of Personal Incomes."

OUTCOME VERSUS PROCESS

The political-economic structures of and conditions in Western industrialized countries are those on which my taxonomy is based. There are systems of all four types, and there are variations in administrative style, capital mobility, and citizens' attitudes and behavior toward state-owned enterprise in North America and Western Europe. This much is clear. What is not clear is that the interconnections between ownership structures and modes of interest intermediation in Western countries actually *account* for the patterns in Figures 6–11. The welfare taxonomy and the analysis on which it is based are superior to its competitors only if I can demonstrate that expected differences in the workings of the four kinds of political economies are responsible for the contrasts we observe in Figures 6–11. For example, the theoretical investigation in Chapter 5 predicts that contrasts in the welfare of British and Austrian citizens result from differences in the structures of ownership and types of interest intermediation that exist in these two countries. It also alerts us to the possibility of certain kinds of maldistribution within these countries, among them inequities in the relative wealth of private asset holders and wage earners in the British case and inequities in the wealth of private enterprise and state enterprise workers in the Austrian case. The experiences of these and other countries must be examined to determine whether political-economic systems are responsible for the welfare outcomes we observe in the figures and whether these predicted inequities actually exist.

CHAPTER SEVEN

A Tale of Two Political Economies

This chapter demonstrates that British and Austrian performance on our welfare criteria derives from the fact that the two countries have pluralist–private enterprise and corporatist–mixed systems, respectively. It also shows that predicted inequities do exist in these two countries. The next chapter compares the British and Austrian experiences with those of Italy and Sweden, countries that have pluralist–mixed and corporatist–private enterprise systems. Together, the two chapters establish the validity of our analysis of the politics of mixed economies. More specifically, they show that blends of collective gain and distributional equity are outgrowths of the logical interconnections between countries' modes of interest intermediation and their ownership structures.

BRITAIN

Britain's political economy is of the pluralist–private enterprise variety. Producer groups are represented in the Trades Union Congress (TUC) and in the Confederation of British Industries (CBI). Membership in these organizations is fairly comprehensive; both have substantial financial resources and the ability to impose sanctions on nonmembers. But the TUC and the CBI are neither hierarchically structured nor well-disciplined. Rather, both are highly fragmented organizations. There are serious disagreements between the manufacturing and financial segments of the CBI, for instance, and wage negotiations are usually decentralized, with strikes often occurring spontaneously, without the approval of the leadership of the TUC. Efforts have been made to institute corporatist forms of interest intermediation in Britain. Even when the TUC and its Labour party allies agreed to do so, however, little real progress was made toward achieving corporatism. A few consultative bodies were created in the mid-1970s, but they were more experiments in concertation than in corporatism. The quasi-corporatist bodies created under the Labour government are now defunct, and most producer group and party leaders think it is unlikely these bodies will be recreated in the near future or outright oppose the idea. Thus Britain's polity remains basically pluralist.[1]

Britain has a highly developed private enterprise economy. This economy is composed of privately owned, mixed private and publicly owned, and nationalized firms. As I noted in Chapter 1, in the late 1960s and early 1970s the British nationalized industries employed a large number of workers, and they have, at times, accounted for as much as 20 percent of gross fixed capital formation. Also, in the late 1970s the government, through its National Enterprise Board and British Technology Group, became directly involved in risky business ventures, especially technology ventures. However, in comparative terms the British economy has never been highly mixed. In the late 1970s, for example, the relative importance of the British nationalized industries in terms of employment (8 percent), investment (20 percent), and output (11 percent) was only about half that of their counterparts in Austria and Italy, and since then the relative importance of the British nationalized industries has declined as private enterprise has become responsible for even greater shares of British investment and output. One reason is that since 1979 the British government has been actively denationalizing and privatizing the state's holdings. The architect of this privatization program is the Thatcher administration, which acknowledges that it will take time and a lot of money to return British public enterprise to the private sector but argues that this "is the price of the folly of public ownership."[2]

1. Major divisions within the CBI are analyzed by Leys (1985). Intraclass barriers to the development of corporatism—especially splits within the labor movement—are investigated by Cox and Hayward (1983). Cox and Hayward examine the Heath government's efforts to institute corporatist forms of bargaining and also the social contract struck between the TUC and the Labour party in the early 1970s. This contract was the basis for several experiments in "quasi-corporatism." Among party leaders who express doubts that relations between producer groups can be institutionalized in the near future is Roy Hattersley (1982). General treatments of British interest intermediation—treatments that stress the basically pluralist nature of British politics—include Schmitter (1981) and von Beyme (1983); see also Panitch (1980) and Lange (1984).

2. See Heald and Steel (1982:344). Summaries and evaluations of the Thatcher administration's privatization program include Redwood and Hatch (1982: chap. 7), Heald and Steel (1982), Brittan (1984), Abromeit (1986), and Hemming and Mansoor (1988). In 1970 the public corporations and general government accounted for about 44 percent of gross fixed capital formation (*Economic Trend Annual Supplement*

Because Britain has a pluralist–private enterprise political economy, we expect, *ceteris paribus*, that over time there will be greater collective gains in consumption and in intergenerational equity in Britain than in Italy (a pluralist–mixed political economy). We also expect that Britain's performance in terms of this first welfare criterion will be inferior to that of Sweden (corporatist–private enterprise), whereas it should roughly match that of Austria (corporatist–mixed).

In reference to intragenerational equity, our expectation is that wealth should be more maldistributed in Britain than in either Sweden or Italy (since labor is weaker and a greater share of investment decisions are in private hands in Britain). In addition, the Labour party's attempts to create corporatist political institutions and the Conservative party's rejection of this idea together with its active efforts to privatize public enterprises suggest that the British political economy is in some kind of disequilibrium. There appear to be fundamental disagreements about the best political-economic system for Britain and no lasting balance of power between the parties and interest groups that are promoting alternative systems. The changing blend of social welfare in Britain (see Figure 12) thus appears to be in some part both cause and consequence of changing electoral outcomes. Put another way, the trend in growth and income distribution in Britain appears to be the result not just of market forces but also of the outcomes of political competition between contending parties.

The patterns in Figures 6–11 are only partly consistent with our theoretical expectations. Britain matches Sweden and is slightly inferior to Austria in terms of consumption gains and intergenerational equity. Britain's performance on this welfare criterion is clearly not superior to that of Italy, however. In the period 1960–1983 the increase in real per capita GDP which occurred in Italy was almost twice that in Britain; for the years 1974–1983 the increases in real per capita GDP were roughly the same in these two countries. The degree of intragenerational equity in Britain in the 1960s and 1970s is greater than expected. Given the relative power of labor in Sweden and the relative size of the state business sector in Italy, we would expect income to have been more maldistributed in Britain (where labor is weaker and the economy is of the private enterprise type).

Developments in the last decade in Britain conform more closely to our theoretical expectations. As (quasi-)corporatist institutions have been dismantled and publicly owned firms have been denationalized

1985:51). But by 1980 this figure had fallen to 27 percent, a level maintained in 1983. For information on reductions in employment in nationalized industries, see the *Economist*, September 6, 1986, pp. 51–52, and November 22, 1986, pp. 60–61.

and reprivatized, British growth rates have increased—indeed, they have exceeded those of all other European countries—and, by several measures, wealth has become more maldistributed.[3] But in some respects these changes in social welfare are anomalous. There is evidence that the wealth of particular groups of wage earners, for instance, skilled manual workers, has increased both absolutely and in relation to the wealth of other wage earners under the Thatcher administration.[4] A pluralist–private enterprise political economy thus does not fully account for Britain's historical or cross-national performance.

To understand Britain's performance we need to examine more closely the structural and behavioral facets of its pluralist–private enterprise political economy. Britain has one of the most highly developed capital markets in the world. Hence we would expect the managers of British private firms to be held accountable for their decisions and, in turn, the economy to be highly efficient, producing more goods, higher consumption, and more jobs than the economies of most other Western countries (which have less well developed capital markets). But as the figures in the last chapter show—and the British themselves widely admit—until recently Britain's economy has been comparatively inefficient. In the late 1960s and 1970s Britain suffered from a "sickness" of low growth, high unemployment, and high inflation.

The causes of this sickness are not entirely clear. One group of writers attributes it to the very development of British capital markets. They argue that myopic investors—especially myopic institutional investors—are unwilling to finance private managers' efforts to

3. When different measures and aggregation schemes are used to define intragenerational and intergenerational equity, they render differences in the welfare of Swedish and British citizens more stark; cf. the positions of the two countries in Figures 11 and 12. The data on which these displays are based are not available for Italy and Austria; but see Wilensky and Turner (1987: chap. 2). Since 1981 British GDP has grown at a rate of almost 3 percent per year—almost twice the rate at which other European economies have grown (*Economist*, September 14, 1985, p. 61; April 4, 1987, p. 13). Note that in Figure 12 the ratio of posttax income shares of the top and bottom quintile increased from 5.8 to 6.6 between 1978/79 and 1981/82. The Gini index for posttax income shares by quintile groups increased from 33.5 to 36.0 in this period ("The Distribution of Income in the United Kingdom, 1981/82," *Economic Trends*, July 1984, p. 97). According to the *Economist* (September 7, 1985, p. 64), the wage share of domestic income fell from 69 percent to 64 percent in the first half of the 1980s: in 1985 the wage share was at a level comparable to what it was in the 1950s. The boom in the profits of British privately owned firms is traced to the increase in investment in the *Economist*, July 13, 1985, pp. 60–61; see also "Poor Man, Rich Man," ibid., June 29, 1985, p. 64.
    4. See, for example, Leys (1985).

restore the competitiveness of their firms. Hence these managers are unable to undertake the long-term investments required to restore productive efficiency and international competitiveness. Others reject the idea that British firms are "starved for capital." They place the blame for Britain's problems at the feet of its managers: managers are unwilling to invest, or managers are unable or unwilling to undertake effective investment, that is, investment that leads to lasting increases in net output. The proponents of this view maintain that a combination of the country's anti-industrial culture and managerial ineptitude explains British firms' poor performance in domestic and international markets in the late 1960s and 1970s and, by implication, explains the lower-than-expected gains in real per capita consumption and employment in that period.[5]

British governments have attempted to promote growth. Fiscal policies have aimed to create investment incentives and also to prevent public borrowing from crowding out private investment. These measures have generally had little lasting effect on the investment decisions of private managers. But the Thatcher government's changes in fiscal policy, particularly a reduction in the corporate income tax rate, do seem to have increased the level and rate of private investment and, in turn, fueled increases in per capita consumption.[6] The Thatcher administration hopes its privatization program will be a further stimulant to investment and growth insofar as it reduces the concentration of asset ownership in British capital markets and thus

5. An economic policy statement of the Labour party argues that British industry is starved for capital (*Economist*, September 28, 1985, pp. 16–17). In the 1970s the same argument was, in part, the basis for several Labour party proposals to nationalize British finance. See also the discussion of the low proportion of company financed R & D in Britain and the need to enhance capital market promotion of company R & D in the *Economist*, September 14, 1985, p. 20. The case against the capital starvation thesis is made by Coakley and Harris who argue there was a shortfall in the demand for investment funds (1983:11–12, 41ff.). These authors also contest the thesis that banks are deeply involved in the management of private firms. Samuel Brittan casts doubt on the idea that the level of investment has been too low in the United Kingdom. What is unique about the British experience, he argues, is the ineffectiveness of investment in terms of output generally (Brittan 1983:222–25). For a further exposition of the anti-industrial culture–managerial ineptitude argument see Sir Arthur Knight's Fairburn Lecture (1983).

6. The *Economist* attributes the upswing in investment of 1984 and early 1985 to the high profits British firms are making and also to the expectations of higher future earnings that resulted from the cut in the corporate tax rate. The *Economist* maintains that these new fiscal measures are much more efficient than previous measures (July 13, 1985, p. 61). The decline in private earnings preceded some of those changes in fiscal policy which, according to some observers, were intended to finance the increases in government spending in the 1960s and 1970s. See Hadjimatheou and Skouras (1979) and Brittan (1983). For the government's efforts to shape location decisions through fiscal policy see Grant (1984).

eliminates rigidities in those markets. Privatization is viewed, by the Thatcher administration, as promoting the ideal of a "shareholders' democracy" with an even greater degree of productive efficiency.[7]

British governments have also attempted to promote growth through public enterprise. In so doing they have gradually become directly involved in the operation of the nationalized industries. The nationalized industries originally were to be kept "at arm's length" from ministers and members of parliament; their boards relied on their own collective sense of the public interest in deciding how to manage the public enterprises. In the 1950s a Select Committee of Parliament was created to oversee the nationalized industries, and from time to time governments intervened in pricing and other managerial decisions. But for the most part, the managers of nation-alized industries were free to promote their own conception of the public interest.[8]

This situation changed in the 1960s and 1970s. Through a series of White Papers the nationalized industries became subject to various forms of government supervision and control. For instance, governments mandated required rates of return on public investments, the application of long-run marginal cost pricing and the use of test discount rates on new investment projects (the returns from which assumed this kind of pricing), and the use of cost-benefit analyses for a variety of managerial decisions. In the late 1970s a framework for operating the nationalized industries was announced which imposed strict external financing limits, required the use of ex-post required rates of return, and set both cost reduction objectives and objectives designed to increase the quality of services. In addition, the Monopoly and Mergers Commission and a variety of parliamentary committees became involved in the supervision of public enterprises. The Thatcher administration has called for more administrative and parliamentary supervision of the nationalized industries, including more regular and thorough reviews of the performance of board members.[9]

7. Britain's capital market is largely dominated by institutions rather than by individual stock holders. See the *Economist*, September 17, 1985, p. 65. On the Thatcher government's aim to create a shareholder's democracy see Abromeit (1986).

8. For the legal status of and intended operating guidelines for the nationalized industries in 1947–1961 see Garner (1985). The nationalized industries were not required even to reply to MPs' inquiries about their operations (Redwood and Hatch 1982: chap. 2). Public enterprises were to be operated in a manner that allowed them to break even after provision for depreciation at market cost.

9. Governments become more deeply involved in the operation of the nationalized industries both from the perceived need to coordinate different kinds of public borrowing and from a growing uneasiness about the wisdom of giving the boards so much autonomy. The first White Paper (1961) stipulated a minimum rate of return over

As the nationalized industries were held more accountable to public authorities for their decisions, so their financial performance began to deteriorate. For much of the 1960s the nationalized industries earned a positive rate of return, and in some respects they even outperformed private enterprise. Nationalized industries in manufacturing paid somewhat higher wages in this period, but they also had higher (labor) productivity growth than private industry. In the late 1960s the relative performance of the nationalized industries began to deteriorate, however. The industries' net earnings started to decline; despite a brief recovery in the early 1970s, they fell far below those of private industry. The principal reason for this deterioration in financial performance, many observers argue, was that after 1968 governments forced publicly owned firms to hold their prices at levels that did not cover the firms' costs; publicly owned firms were not allowed to charge prices that would earn a positive rate of return. This is not to say that all nationalized industries failed to earn a positive rate of return in this period; indeed, some publicly owned firms remained in the black after 1968. But the financial performance of the nationalized industries as a whole changed markedly in the 1970s as governments became more deeply involved in their daily operations and, in so doing, revealed a greater concern for price stability than for financial returns from the public's business ventures.[10]

---

five-year periods; the second White Paper (1967) required long-run marginal cost pricing, along with the use of a test discount rate on all new investment projects. In practice, however, boards had difficulty implementing these guidelines or simply ignored them. Provisions for conducting cost-benefit analyses for public investments were included in the second White Paper as well. Experience led in the late 1970s to an acknowledgment of the impossibility of separating commercial and noncommercial aspects of public enterprise performance and to the creation of a third framework for operating the nationalized industries. This framework, announced in the 1978 White Paper, made external financing limits one of the principal means by which governments could monitor and control investments by the nationalized industries. The White Paper reintroduced the notion of a required rate of return, but on the capital program of each industry as a whole and ex-post not ex-ante; it also established cost and quality of service objectives for public enterprise. See Garner (1985, 1979); Redwood (1980); and Redwood and Hatch (1982).

10. Redwood and Hatch (1982) summarize financial targets for and performance of British public enterprise in the 1960s and 1970s. Pryke (1981) reviews in detail the operation and performance of each nationalized industry. He shows that in several respects the performance of British Telecom, British Gas Corporation, and British Air has been superior to that of other public enterprises. He attributes some of the disparity to the ineptitude of managers in the remaining industries, especially to mistakes in planning of capital expenditure. Millward has produced some of the most systematic, macro-level evaluations of the performance of the public corporations. His work (1976, 1982) explicitly incorporates or at least acknowledges the different cost structures and unique political challenges faced by public as opposed to private firms. Reports on the recent performance of nationalized industries can be found in the *Economist;* for example, August 1, 1987, pp. 49–50, and December 19, 1987, pp. 49–50.

The Thatcher government has not reversed the trend toward greater involvement in the operation of the nationalized industries or showed any lesser willingness to use public enterprise to achieve its macroeconomic objectives. Indeed, under Margaret Thatcher the trend toward government involvement in the operation of public firms has accelerated, and nationalized industry financing has become the cornerstone of authorities' efforts to control public spending. In this context, Prime Minister Thatcher and her colleagues have made a concerted effort to improve the financial performance of the nationalized industries. But they have also sold off many financially profitable firms, and in the future there may be less room for improvement in the financial performance of the public enterprise sector as a whole.[11]

The key to understanding Britain's poor performance in terms of consumption gains and intergenerational equity in the 1960s and 1970s thus seems to lie in the peculiar behavior of its *private enterprises*—the unwillingness of private managers and owners to undertake new, productive investments—rather than any structural imperfections in Britain's economy. Capital markets might have spurred productive efficiency. But apparently there was little competition for investment funds in the 1960s and 1970s, and in fact there was a lack of demand for investment financing in this period.[12] On the surface the losses of British public firms translated into reduced consumption and future tax obligations for the unborn. Publicly owned firms produced lower financial returns in this period. But the performance of nationalized industries was, in some part, due to the government's decision to fight inflation, so we must balance any losses in public earnings against collective gains that accrued to British citizens from enhanced price stability.[13] Also governments, in the way they attempted to operate the nationalized industries, forced public firms to use social discount rates that bore a close relation to the market rate of social time preference, even though, as we learned in Chapter 3, one cannot always assume that the same rate should be

11. On the importance of nationalized industry financing in the macroeconomic strategy of the Thatcher administration, see Bruce-Gardyne (1984:62) and Brittan (1983:257).

12. Alt (1987) advances the thesis that financial interests' speculation in the value of the pound is responsible for the lack of competitiveness of British industry and, in turn, for the low growth rate and high rates of unemployment Britain has experienced since the early 1970s. I examine his argument in Chapter 10.

13. Cox and Hayward (1982:226–27) and Eltis (1979) argue that in the 1970s the performance of the nationalized industries had a deleterious effect on mass consumption and the British standard of living. Redwood (1980) stresses the burdens the nationalized industries place on consumers. These authors ignore the possibly salutary effects that the pricing policies of nationalized industries had on the inflation rate.

applied to both private and public investment. It could well be, then, that the government effectively forced the nationalized industries to use the wrong discount rate in this period.[14]

Either way, the investment and other policies of the nationalized industries must be evaluated in terms of their combination with private investment to produce Pareto gains and losses in consumption as well as other welfare outcomes. In this light, the most noteworthy fact about the British experience of the 1960s and 1970s is the steady decline in the rate of return from *private investment,* a decline that began in the late 1950s and reversed itself only in the 1980s. In view of the relative importance of private investment in the British economy, the stagnation of aggregate private investment and the erosion of private rates of return in this period seem to be the principal cause of Britain's relatively poor performance on the first welfare criterion.

According to some analysts, private managers failed to undertake viable new investments because of the way income was redistributed intragenerationally in Britain, or because government redistributed substantial amounts of wealth among various groups of citizens. Let us take a closer look at Britains' intragenerational distribution of wealth.

Government statistics indicate that between 1949 and 1981 there was a decline in the relative wealth of the richest British citizens. Similarly, the pay of British executives declined in comparison to the pay earned by their European and American counterparts. Transfers from the top income group have accrued more to upper or middle income groups than to lower income groups, and for this reason there were no major changes in the Gini index of post-tax income shares in Britain in the 1960s and 1970s. The top 1 percent income group earned over three times more income from investments than the top 25 percent income group; its investment income was more than four times greater than that of the next income group (second 25 percent). For the bottom income groups wages constitute the smallest share of income; national insurance retirement pensions and social security payments make up most of these individuals' income. Under the Thatcher administrations top income groups have recovered some of the losses they experienced since 1949 (see Figure 12). Also, there have been substantial increases in the profits share of national income.[15]

14. In practice the boards often found the mandated guidelines difficult to interpret and apply; in a great number of cases they apparently ignored the guidelines. See, for example, Garner (1985) and Redwood and Hatch (1982:74).

15. On the sources of pretax income in the United Kingdom see "The Distribution of Income in the UK, 1981/1982," *Economic Trends,* July 1984, Table D, p. 99. *Economic Trends* now publishes an annual survey of the effects of taxes and benefits on house-

In reference to nonmaterial wealth—for example, employment security—Britain has performed worse than most industrialized countries. The unemployment rate increased almost ninefold between 1965 and 1987, and there are marked contrasts in the regional distribution of unemployment. In the mid-1980s the unemployment rate in the North of England was almost two times what it was in East Anglia and the Southeast; the unemployment rate in Wales, the Northwest, and Scotland about one and one-half times higher. There is also a high incidence of youth unemployment in Britain. And since the investment boom of the mid 1980s has been labor-saving rather than labor-intensive, there is little prospect of reducing youth or adult manufacturing unemployment in the near future.[16]

The distinction between private asset holders and wage earners is made somewhat ambiguous by the fact that a substantial number of British workers benefit from membership in large pension funds. These pension funds own about 10 percent of the assets in Britain's capital market; about 50 percent of their holdings are in local company securities, but in recent years they have also been purchasing an increasingly large number of foreign securities. Workers do not directly control these funds. Rather, the pension funds' investment decisions are usually made by other institutions, such as banks. Hence it is difficult to interpret British pension funds as an instrument for counterbalancing the social welfare consequences of managerial decisions. Instead, the pension funds seem to be a means through which the relative wealth of a particular segment of the British workforce is enhanced relative to other segments that do not belong to these pension funds; if anything, they reinforce constraints on governmental redistribution of wealth.[17]

---

hold income. This survey indicates that cash transfers and "benefits in kind" raise the income share of the bottom quintile from less than 1 percent to about 7 percent and lower the Gini index for percentage of total household income from about .50 to about .33.

16. In 1965 Britain had an unemployment rate of 1.3 percent whereas in 1986 the rate was 11.4 percent (*Economic Trends*, May 1987, p. 38). For more information on employment, government efforts to create jobs, and the bleak prospects for increased employment in manufacturing, see the *Economist*, September 17, 1985, p. 40. The hardships faced by coal communities are described in ibid., November 22, 1986, pp. 60–61.

17. Coakley and Harris (1983) describe the relative importance of pension funds in British financial markets. They chart the increasing importance of the overseas investments of these funds (p. 39), the increase in investments in British companies (p. 101), and the willingness to turn over investment decisions to money managers (p. 111). This last phenomenon means that, in effect, British pension funds do not behave much differently than other financial institutions in promoting competition and productive efficiency and, by implication, constraining government efforts at redistribution. (That British pension funds act like other financial institutions was confirmed by several union officials in interviews in London, October 1984.)

Government fiscal policies have had some effects on the intragenerational distribution of wealth. Until recently, Britain had a comparatively progressive tax rate, and taxation does appear to substantially reduce the relative wealth of individuals in the upper percentiles of the income distribution. Taxation also appears to have eliminated, at least for a time, wage differentials between certain groups of workers. As regards regional inequities, the government has provided lucrative fiscal incentives for private firms willing to locate in areas with high levels of unemployment. It has also assisted private and public firms in these areas that face bankruptcy. On the other hand, the government's macroeconomic policies, especially its efforts to curb inflation, have yielded differential gains to those citizens who are more adverse to price changes than to unemployment.[18] This group includes individuals at the top of the income scale whose income derives in some substantial part from earnings on investments and also, to a lesser degree, that segment of the workforce which contributes to and earns substantial economic dividends from pension funds; it excludes manual workers and those who depend on government transfers.[19]

Through their policies the nationalized industries have also affected the intragenerational distribution of wealth. The price controls instituted through nationalized industries in the 1970s were one of the primary means by which British governments tried to control inflation. In recent years, the strict financial guidelines for nationalized industries have been an instrumental part of government efforts to cut public borrowing and thereby reduce inflationary expectations. Thus publicly owned firms have promoted the distributional outcomes associated with a low inflationary, high ("natural") unemployment environment. Beyond this, the nationalized industries have provided differential wage gains to particular sets of workers, enhanced the economic security of particular communities, and provided uniform consumption opportunities for the users of particular goods and services—especially those in rural areas.[20] The evolu-

18. See, for instance, Hibbs's discussion of the distributional consequences of inflation and unemployment in Britain (1982a).

19. The government's tax policy has restored earning differentials between certain segments of the workforce (Leys 1985). The government statistical service examined the sensitivity of income inequality indicators to superannuation contributions and other supplemental income in its article in the 1977 issue of *Economic Trends* (no. 290). In essence it found that this form of income does not appreciably affect the overall distribution.

20. One of the best-known differential wage increases for workers in British nationalized industry is the Wilberforce pay agreement in the coal industry in 1972 (see Pryke 1981). This and other large wage settlements lead Knight (1982), Silberston (1982), and others to take the validity of the Wellington-Winter effect for granted. For evidence that state-owned plant closures occurred more slowly and hence provided selected communities with comparatively more (short-term) security than industries that

tion of policies toward the nationalized industries—and the more enlightened scholarly evaluations of this evolution—show that from its inception, public enterprise has been intended to serve various equity objectives.[21]

The effects of the Thatcher government's privatization program on the intragenerational distribution of wealth are difficult to judge. Some workers in privatized firms have made income gains as a result of having moved to the private sector. Moreover, owners of the newly offered private shares in certain nationalized industries have seen the value of their private holdings multiply in a short period. But it remains to be seen whether privatization will have any lasting, *direct* effect on the overall distribution of wealth.[22]

The *indirect* effects of privatization are clearer. There are signs that the privatized firms are less subject to government control over investment and purchasing. In keeping with our theoretical expectations, privatized firms appear to be more willing and able to evade government directives than they were when nationalized. As more and more firms are returned, either partially or wholly, to the private sector, British governments will have to rely solely on fiscal instruments to influence the distribution of wealth; and the indications are that, thanks to privatization, they will be ever more constrained from doing so.[23]

---

were privately owned see Pryke (1981). This same outcome appears to occur as a result of the cross-subsidization of different segments of the same nationalized industries; for instance, communities with National Coal Board pits in South Wales appear to subsidize communities with pits in the Midlands (see Redwood 1980:63). The uniform pricing policies of various nationalized industries are stressed by Millward (1982:78). Pryke argues that these policies are responsible for the financial difficulties of several nationalized industries, especially insofar as they mean that public firms cannot fully recover the costs of serving rural customers.

21. More enlightened evaluations of the objectives of British public enterprise include Millward (1976, 1982), Roll (1982), Garner (1979, 1985), and also Lipton (1976). A less enlightened, narrow evaluation that does not consider, let alone adequately incorporate, the intragenerational equity objectives of public enterprise is Eltis (1979).

22. The financial gains that accrued to workers in the privatized National Freight Corporation are described in the *Economist*, August 24, 1985, p. 47. The same source reports that the new shareholders of British Telecom saw the value of their private holding more than double in the first nine months after privatization (ibid., September 7, 1985, pp. 91–92). The TUC charges that the private financial advisers to the Thatcher administration have been the prime beneficiaries of privatization (see Abromeit 1986:159–60). Brittan (1984; 1983: chap. 11) explores various methods of privatizing the nationalized industries and their potential effects on the overall distribution of income in Britain.

23. Evidence of British government difficulty in regulating the newly privatized British Telecom are described in the *Economist*, September 27, 1985, pp. 63–64, and July 18, 1987, pp. 48–49; see also the same source's brief report of the ease with which British banks avoid paying taxes (ibid., June 29, 1985, p. 64). Cox and Hayward (1982:228) make the more general argument that financial interests' autonomy prevents the British government from forcing labor and capital to implement a corporatist

The larger implication here is that British fiscal policy has been neither "neutral" nor fully redistributive. The active fiscal intervention of British political authorities coupled with the relatively progressive tax rates on personal income may have retarded productive efficiency and hence diminished collective consumption and intergenerational equity. The same fiscal measures and the policies of the nationalized industries appear to have produced a somewhat more egalitarian distribution of income than might be expected from the size of Britain's private enterprise sector and the well-developed nature of the country's capital market. But fiscal intervention and the management of the public enterprise sector have left intact major regional and demographic inequities. The privatization of the nationalized industries promises further to delimit British governments' abilities to promote particular blends of distributional equity, as we would expect; privatization makes the British system even more subject to capital mobility.

Are British governments aware of the effects their fiscal policies and policies toward the nationalized industries have had on social welfare? If privatization delimits their ability to shape distributions of wealth, why is privatization proceeding? The answers to these questions lie in the pluralist nature of British politics. The workings of Britain's pluralist political institutions and their interrelationships with the workings of certain economic institutions explain these policy outcomes.

In the postwar years and much of the 1950s, British citizens generally agreed about the ends and means of government intervention. To be sure, there were disagreements about the wisdom of certain government policies, and there was conflict between and within parties about the wisdom of nationalization. But for the most part, citizens and their representatives were committed to the same economic objectives through essentially the same kind of policies. Moreover, this consensus was rooted in a widespread trust in the managers of the nationalized industries and in a genuine concern for the welfare of the unemployed and of other less fortunate groups in British society. So despite periodic elections (and the absence of corporatist institutions) in Britain, there was a great deal of stability in the way governments intervened in the economy and in the welfare consequences of that intervention.[24]

---

economic strategy. Zysman (1983) makes essentially the same argument about the government's inability to implement an industrial policy.

24. In the late 1940s and 1950s there was little provision for supervising the activities of nationalized industries. Rather, there was a high degree of trust in the willingness and ability of state managers to pursue the public interest (Garner 1985). Alt (1979) analyzes the postwar history of British economic policy in terms of consensus

In the early 1960s this consensus began to erode, and political competition began to produce real changes in the nature and extent of government intervention and market participation. Labour governments began to promote industrial revitalization, first by promoting private business investment and then by engaging in indicative forms of planning. Labour party intervention reached its height in the mid-1970s when the second Wilson administration experimented with risky, high-technology state business ventures and also with quasi-corporatist forms of interest intermediation. Conservative governments attempted to control prices and wages, and they too sought to promote private business investment through various fiscal measures. But Conservatives were less willing to engage in industrial planning or to launch new state business ventures. Meanwhile, citizens displayed less concern for the plight of others as their own personal welfares began to deteriorate. The politics of economic decline became the politics of dissensus, and electoral competition produced increasingly significant changes in government policy.

Since the late 1970s there has been a further breakdown of the postwar consensus, and the balance of political power has become somewhat fluid. The party system itself has been transformed as the Social Democratic–Liberal Alliance and its private enterprise–social policy oriented constitutents have become a factor in British politics.[25] The last Labour government surrendered to a monetarist approach to macroeconomic policy, and a substantial portion of the Labour leadership has revised its commitment to nationalization. But many Labour party activists remain deeply committed both to full employment and to public ownership; some of them have promised to renationalize those publicly owned firms which have been sold off by the Thatcher administration.[26] Finally, and most important, the Conservatives under Margaret Thatcher have smashed the surviving vestiges of the postwar bipartisan consensus and embarked on a program of monetarist economic policy, supply side intervention, and privatization. In so doing, they have renounced both the economic

and dissensus on the means and ends of government intervention. He also charts the declining altruism of the British citizenry over the postwar period.

25. For the distinguishing political preferences of Alliance supporters relative to Labour and Conservative supporters—with regard to social policy and an enterprise-oriented economy—see the *Economist*, August 17, 1985, pp. 45–46.

26. The Labour leadership's renouncement of nationalization is described in the *Economist*, September 28, 1985, pp. 16–17; the same source, in its August 3 issue (pp. 51–52), describes a growing disenchantment inside the Labour party with economic technocracy. However, many Labour activists remain committed to renationalization (*Economist*, June 29, 1985, p. 61) and to the notion of "social ownership." See the *Economist*, February 13, 1988, p. 56. See also Abromeit (1986:168–70) and the *Economist*, July 18, 1987, pp. 47–48.

interventionism of their predecessors and the social spending plans of new challengers.[27] Thus over the last twenty-five years British politics has become marked by more and more dissensus and partisan conflict and, in turn, by greater instability in the motivation for an character of public policy.

It is this political instability and its effects on the workings of the economy that, according to many observers, explain the evolution of social welfare in Britain. The shifting balance of political power has either created too much uncertainty about the permanence of property rights and wage shares of workers or simply immobilized government, preventing authorities from intervening in ways that would produce lasting gains in societal consumption. The former problem made it impossible in the 1970s for private managers (and many investors) to plan ahead, for example, to predict accurately what new investments would yield in the way of earnings for their firms and for themselves. As a consequence, private enterprise managers invested in ways that sheltered their earnings from taxes and ensured a modicum of short-term gains to investors but that, over the long term, did little to enhance the competitiveness of their firms or of the British economy as a whole.[28]

Growing dissensus about who should benefit from growth (or lose least from economic decline) constrained public authorities from implementing any effective industrial policy. Governments were consistently prevented from undertaking those kinds of intervention which proved successful in other countries, where presumably questions of intragenerational equity were less important than the prospect of achieving collective gains in consumption. British democracy, in this sense, undermined the welfare of future generations; pluralist political competition kept governments "immobile" and hence prevented the kinds of intervention which would have yielded the future gains in welfare that the unborn deserve.[29]

27. A sympathetic review of Thatcher's policies is Bruce-Gardyne (1984); a more critical summary is Leys (1985). The "novelty" of the Thatcher administration's posture toward public ownership is stressed by the *Economist*, October 5, 1985, pp. 62–63, and Abromeit (1986).

28. For example, Brittan writes: "But a system of confused and unpredictable property rights under a nominally private enterprise system is highly discouraging to investment—and thereby also depressing to employment in the longer run" (1983:237). He argues that the SDP-Liberal Alliance promises to give Britain the stability of property rights required to realize consumption gains and employment opportunities. Various SDP party documents (Social Democratic Party 1984a,b; SDP/Liberal Alliance 1984) make the same promise. The SDP promises not to "ruin the nationalized industries by switching [their] ownership backwards and forwards," for example.

29. On the effects of dissensus and political immobilism on effective government promotion of growth and intergenerational equity in the 1970s, see Shonfield (1984) and Zysman (1983:229).

Governments' increased involvement in the operations of the nationalized industries was a cause and a consequence of this same sequence of events. Governments encouraged nationalized industries to adopt policies expressly designed to enhance the election prospects of incumbent politicians. In particular, both Conservative and Labour governments imposed a high discount rate on the potential losses of nationalized industries in order to slow closures and preserve jobs in their constituencies. In essence the Thatcher government applied a low discount rate to the long-term benefits from nationalization so that public enterprises could be sold off to middle- and upper-class constituents.[30]

Location and pricing decisions of the nationalized industries were also motivated by the electoral ambitions of governments. Investments in nationalized industries were targeted to particular constituencies in order to win votes. The Conservatives' greater aversion to inflation than unemployment and their tendency to reside in rural electoral districts may explain the respective governments' efforts to use the nationalized industries to achieve macroeconomic and regional objectives and, more specifically, to stabilize prices and to unify rate structures for the goods and services produced by public enterprises. Even the Thatcher government, with its willingness to tolerate somewhat higher prices for certain of the goods and services produced by nationalized industries, remains committed to uniform pricing and service for rural citizens. (It is generally agreed that uniform rate and service structures yield rural citizens real welfare gains relative to their urban counterparts insofar as they preserve marked disparities in the cost effectiveness of public enterprise production.) The Thatcher government's effort to increase the scope and complexity of government supervision of the nationalized industries could heighten the effects of electoral competition on these and other aspects of public enterprise in Britain.[31]

In its privatization program the Thatcher government reveals even more vividly its effort to reshape permanently the blend of collective gain and distributional equity in Britain. Thatcher's program for privatizing the nationalized industries is intended to eliminate

30. The case for politically imposed myopia in the investment decisions of nationalized industries is made by Rowley (1982) and Hindley (1982). See also Aharoni (1986:231, 237), Garner (1985), and Pryke (1981: chap. 10).

31. A thorough discussion of the aversion of British partisans to inflation and unemployment is provided by Hibbs (1982a). Evidence of the link between nationalized industry policies toward rural consumers and the electoral interests of the Conservative party can be found in Redwood and Hatch (1982:34), Heald and Steel (1982), Bruce-Gardyne (1984:85) and Pryke (1981:92–95). Thatcher government efforts to win votes and to discourage conflicts between regions in the United Kingdom are described by Hart (1986).

"forced ownership" of public shares in favor of dispersed, private ownership of assets; promote collective gains in consumption by reducing the role of public enterprise in the economy and by increasing the roles played by capital markets and private enterprise; eliminate private- and public-sector wage differentials through a reduction in union power in formerly nationalized industries; and, in general, reduce government's capacity to shape the intragenerational distribution of income through public enterprise. Privatization thus amounts to a renouncement of past government efforts to promote intragenerational equity in general and of the usefulness of public enterprise in particular. The privatization program affirms the belief of the Conservative party (and to some extent also the new Alliance) in the virtues of a private enterprise economy and of a market-determined distribution of income. In the scope of the current privatization program and the welfare outcomes it has produced we thus see illustrated the depth of the dissensus in Britain over the ends and means of government market intervention and market participation.[32]

Let us return to the questions raised about motivations for government intervention and market participation in Britain. It appears that authorities were all too aware of some of the consequences of their policies. There is no doubt that Labour and Conservative governments used fiscal policy and the nationalized industries to further the interests of their own supporters at the expense of the supporters of their opponents and, in this way, altered the distribution of wealth in Britain. The efforts of both parties to use fiscal policy for the purpose of reshaping the distribution of income in Britain speak for themselves. The use of the nationalized industries in the fight against inflation—especially by the Conservatives—also reveals an appreciation for the interconnected distributional and electoral consequences of economic policy.[33]

What neither the Labour nor the Conservative party seems to have fully realized is the effect electoral competition and the uncertainty it produced—about the flow of future earnings and about the very existence of private enterprise—had on the investment behavior and productive efficiency of private and public firms. Pluralist political

32. The Thatcher administrations' rationale for privatization and denationalization is summarized in Heald and Steel (1982), Brittan (1982), and Abromeit (1986). The first source stresses the desire to reduce government capacity to redistribute wealth. The third source notes that the rationale for privatization includes the need to reduce the power of trade unions in publicly owned monopolies.

33. This is not to say that Conservative governments believed they could ensure electoral victories in this way but rather that these kind of policies make a contribution to political success. On the *realistic* expectations of the Heath government with regard to its ability to control macroeconomic variables for political purposes see Alt (1979: chap. 7).

competition contributed to a persistent myopia in private investment behavior—a myopia that could be cured only by a second and then a third Thatcher administration committed to the continued use of monetarist economic policies, to particular fiscal policies, and to the implementation of an extensive, seemingly irreversible program of privatization. In addition, pluralist political competition undermined public enterprises' abilities to work in tandem with private enterprise by creating cycles in investment and pricing decisions which reshaped the intragenerational distribution of wealth in Britain but which also retarded productive efficiency.[34] In this way, the deepening disagreements between and within British political parties accelerated the decline of British industry and thus lowered collective consumption rates and employment rates.

The contrast between Britain's performance and that of other countries involves not only an outgrowth of the interconnected workings of its pluralist polity and private enterprise economy but also certain structural features of the British system, namely, British administrative tradition, the degree of capital mobility in the British economy, and the nature of citizens' attitudes toward collective ownership. These factors have much to do with, for instance, how stark the contrast in intragenerational equity is between countries with pluralist–private enterprise systems and countries with corporatist–mixed systems.

Britain's relatively poor performance in terms of aggregate consumption rates and intergenerational equity can be attributed, in some part, to its noncentralist administrative tradition. Britain has a well-developed administrative structure. Its administrators are as well-trained as any in the Western world. British public officials have actively promoted various forms of market intervention, and in this context they have occasionally advocated the pursuit of particular welfare outcomes. Since the late 1970s, for instance, the British Treasury has defended monetarist approaches to macroeconomic policy and imposed strict financial guidelines on the nationalized industries. The Treasury has allied itself with the Thatcher government in promoting reductions in public borrowing and spending, greater pro-

---

34. For example, Pryke (1981:87) reports that prior to the second Wilson government, several nationalized industries quickly hired new workers, only to lay off many of them several years later when the industries' deficits grew to intolerable levels. He also links recruitment drives in the nationalized industries to governmental financial rescues (p. 247; see also p. 233). King (1975) argues that voters consistently force governments to "meddle" in the operations of the nationalized industries. Knight (1982), Millward (1976), and Roll (1982) argue that government intervention in the operation of nationalized industries has occurred regardless of which party is in office but to different ends.

ductive efficiency in the nationalized industries, and privatization. In this way it has revealed a preference for a particular kind of political-economic system and, in turn, a particular blend of collective gain and distributional equity.[35]

Treasury officials have recently displayed the will and capacity to participate actively in the formulation of public policy and the restructuring of Britain's economy over the last decade, but most other public administrators have not. On the whole, British administrators have remained comparatively passive, failing to provide the policy direction their counterparts in other countries have provided. Public authorities have not attempted to formulate a national industrial plan, for example, let alone legislate for it.[36] Managers of nationalized industries have been supervised in an ad hoc and essentially incremental way; they have not been guided to any significant degree by an administratively conceived national strategy for employing nationalized industries on behalf of some socially preferred set of welfare outcomes. Indeed, the administrative structure of the nationalized industries was expressly designed to avoid central direction.[37] For their part, state managers have forged alliances with unions and communities with which they do business in an attempt to influence government decisions about how to operate the public enterprise. They have also altered their hiring and investment policies in anticipation of the success or defeat of particular parties and lobbied against privatization. But these political activities have been in keeping with the pluralist nature of British politics; they have not been guided by any larger, single strategy for promoting administrators' own interests or society's collective interests.[38]

35. See Goodin (1982) on the "mission" of British administrators. The rise of the Treasury Department in the making of economic policy is described in the *Economist*, June 1, 1985, pp. 60–61.

36. The structural weakness of British administrators, including Treasury, in the implementation of industrial policy is stressed by Zysman (1983), who argues that industrial change is company-led, not state-led, in Britain. See also the conclusion in Leys (1985).

37. Pryke (1981:249–50) argues that government attempts to exercise control over the investment decisions of public firms have been at best variable. Some apparently unwise investment projects have been killed by administrators, while other seemingly imprudent investment decisions have fallen through "large holes in the Whitehall sieve."

38. A general review of the interest group activities of the nationalized industries and their chairmen's group is Tivey (1982); see also Abromeit (1986). These and other authors (Pryke 1981: chap. 13; Rowley 1982; Bruce-Gardyne 1984:82) report that public management has often formed alliances with unions and consumer groups to oppose government policies toward their nationalized industry. The role of nationalized industries in the CBI is discussed in Tivey (1982). Community lobbying and negotiation with nationalized industries are analyzed in Dudley (1979).

Britain's administrative tradition thus has done little to offset the effects of dissensus and electoral competition on productive efficiency. The potential for public administrators to promote a particular conception of distributional equity has been realized only in recent years, in the form of a politically active British Treasury committed to furthering the Thatcher government's program for a more fully developed private enterprise economy. Beyond this increase in the power and influence of the British Treasury (the "rise of Great George Street"), Britain's noncentralist administrative style has had little effect on parties' efforts to reshape social welfare or on the way political disequilibrium has undermined the productive efficiency of the British economy.

The degree of capital mobility in the British economy has had two important effects on social welfare. First, although private firms' efforts to evade taxes and hedge against long-term uncertainties yielded them short-term gains, over time their behavior reduced their mobility and hence diminished their bargaining power vis-à-vis workers and governments. The repeated short-sightedness of private managers coupled with the growing obsolescence of their industrial plant gradually diminished their capacity to relocate to avoid paying higher taxes and wages. Their behavior forced many firms to remain in one location where their only choice was to eschew long-term investment for the sake of short-term earnings. In turn, private firms were prey to slightly higher wage rates than they might have been had they undertaken longer-term investments and become more competitive.[39] This is not to say that political disequilibrium led to investment behavior that eventually gave governments the freedom to create their preferred distributions of wealth. After all, the well-developed nature of British capital markets and relative viability of private enterprise presented formidable barriers to governmental redistribution. The point is merely that the barriers to redistribution were not as constraining as they might have been had a different pattern of private investment behavior occurred in the 1960s and 1970s.

Second, the Thatcher privatization program aims to enhance the capacity of capital markets in order to spur productive efficiency and improve the self-financing capacity of private firms. Achievement of the first objective will create more managerial incentives for relocation, whereas achievement of the second will enhance private firms' ability to relocate within and outside Britain. The consequence of privatization may be a higher rate of aggregate consumption, but privatization will also enhance capital mobility and therefore

39. That a decline in long-term profitability makes firms, for a period of time at least, prey to large wage settlements is argued by Lawrence and Lawrence (1985).

reduce government capacity to redistribute wealth intragenerationally. The Thatcher government and its allies, as pointed out above, are well aware of this fact. Indeed, it is one of the reasons for their advocating privatization.[40]

That societal dissensus about the means and ends of government intervention has had important effects on social welfare in Britain is already obvious. Insofar as citizens' conceptions of collective ownership rights are concerned, much evidence shows that a significant fraction of the British populace is committed to the principle of public ownership and also that these individuals believe that nationalized industries have improved their welfare and the welfare of other citizens.[41] What is unclear is the extent to which citizens are able to translate their commitment or opposition to nationalization into political actions that are designed to reward or to make state managers more accountable for their business decisions. It is also unclear whether this execution of collective ownership rights is to any extent responsible for the performance of nationalized industries. The links between electoral outcomes and the behavior of particular public firms, the popular support for privatization and the uses to which the government has put this support in dealing with nationalized industry representatives,[42] and the ways certain communities have lobbied nationalized industries for new investments[43] all suggest that some substantial number of citizens are willing to exercise collective ownership rights on behalf of particular welfare objectives. The debate over privatization seems to reveal widespread appreciation for the welfare implications of public ownership, as well. To the extent that nationalized industries have been involved in promoting collective welfare gains and in shaping distributional equity in Britain, then, there is some basis for interpreting their policies as revealing the preferences of different segments of the British citizenry. What remains to be shown is that collective ownership rights are executed regularly—as through popular opinion polls—with lasting effects on

40. Again, see Heald and Steel (1982) and Abromeit (1986). The Thatcher administrations' aversion to direct foreign investment, which is presumably highly mobile, should be acknowledged here. I return to this peculiarity of the British experience in Chapter 10.

41. See Figure 4. The salutary effects of nationalization on the welfare of miners and on mining communities was stressed in several interviews the author conducted in London in October 1984 with Labour party activists and union officials.

42. Tivey (1982:44) points out that the new threat of privatization has complicated nationalized industry–government relations insofar as it restrains state managers from demanding too much autonomy. See also Abromeit (1986).

43. Once more, see Dudley's (1979) description of the efforts of the community of Shelton to negotiate new and retain existing steel investments from the management of the corresponding publicly owned firm.

the operation and welfare consequences of public enterprise, or that citizens monitor relatively continuously the performance of nationalized industries. The results of relevant statistical analyses are consistent with those of Chapter 5: public opinion polls do not have lasting effects on the operation and performance of public investments. Rather, if citizens regularly execute their public investment rights, they are more likely to do so through interest group lobbying and related forms of political participation.[44]

In sum, until recently Britain has enjoyed somewhat less intergenerational equity and more intragenerational equity than expected, primarily because pluralist politics produced uncertainty about the long-term rate of return and the long-term existence of private enterprise. This uncertainty, in turn, retarded the rate of long-term investment, diminished productive efficiency, and reduced the growth in aggregate consumption while at the same time enhancing government capacity—but *not* empowering government—to redistribute income within current generations. The workings of Britain's pluralist political institutions are rooted in fundamental disagreements about the ends and means of government intervention and market participation and, concomitantly, about the best political-economic system for the country. Because of Britain's noncentralist administrative tradition, elements of the state have done little to ameliorate the effects of pluralist political competition (or enhance the effectiveness of capital markets as engines of productive efficiency locally). This is one reason why Britain's performance in terms of collective consumption gains was for much of the 1960s and 1970s inferior to that of other countries. Over time the reduced rate of long-term investment became to some degree self-perpetuating as it reduced private firms' capacity to relocate and thereby enhanced government capacity to redistribute wealth. Britain's somewhat better performance in terms of intragenerational equity is, in some part, attributable to this fact.

Finally, the collective ownership efficacy of part of the citizenry appears to have forced politicians and state managers to operate nationalized industries in ways that may have affected the distribution of wealth in Britain. So the existence of a substantial number of publicly owned firms also improved Britain's performance in terms of the intragenerational distribution of wealth, at least until the end of the 1970s. The recent turn toward a more *inequitable* intragenerational

44. For a statistical analysis of the effects of trends in popular approval and voting intentions on trends and welfare consequences of British investment, private and public, see Freeman and Alt (1987). Freeman (1988) analyzes the short-term effect of the 1979 election on the employment decisions of British native-private, foreign-private, and nationalized firms.

distribution can be traced in part to the current government program of privatization and financial management of the nationalized industries. This new stance toward public enterprise is best seen as only the most recent—if also the boldest—effort of one segment of the British citizenry to alter the distribution of wealth through the surrender of some collective ownership rights and more energetic execution of the ownership rights now in private hands.

AUSTRIA

Austria's political economy is of the corporatist–mixed variety. Producer groups are organized in a system of "chambers," representing business, labor, and agriculture. These chambers are publicly licensed; membership in them is compulsory. Business and labor are also organized in a small number of relatively centralized associations. In fact, the Austrian Trade Union Federation is one of the most authoritatively centralized labor associations in the world. Through the institution of joint commissions, producer group representatives set a large share of the prices and also many of the wage rates in the Austrian economy.

Negotiations between producer groups—or between the "social partners," as they are called—are not totally insulated from parliamentary and electoral politics. For one thing, some leaders of Austria's producer groups are also leaders of political parties. Hence they are concerned with the electoral consequences of producer group agreements. In addition, up until recently, Austria's *Proporz* system required that appointments to various government agencies and the supervisory boards of the nationalized industries be made in accordance with the relative strength of the parties within the Austrian Parliament. In this way electoral outcomes had direct effects on the operation and supervision of the state holding company.[45] Finally, through popular referenda citizens have challenged producer group and party leaders' decisions on several issues, among them development of nuclear power.

Producer group negotiations still have a great deal of influence on the making and content of public decisions in Austria, and so, in a

45. The Proporz system provided that most of the appointments to such entities as the Supervisory Board of the state holding company (OeIAG) were party representatives; the relative number depends on the strength of the parties within the Austrian Parliament. As a consequence of Proporz, elections had direct effects on the relative strength of the parties within state institutions. Whether these effects translated into major alterations in the decisions these bodies made, and hence into the welfare consequences of public policy in general and of state business operations in particular, is debatable. See Katzenstein (1984:73–78).

broad sense, politics is more corporatist than pluralist there. Indeed, the relative importance of the idea of a social partnership between labor and capital, the centralization of interest group representation, and the degree of coordination of conflicting interests make Austria's polity the prototype of social corporatism.[46]

Austria has a relatively well-developed, mixed economy with a large number of small and medium-size private enterprises. These firms are responsible for a major share of such services as mechanical engineering and metal fabrication. The Austrian economy also has several large domestic private and foreign private enterprises. For example, Siemens, the German multinational, is responsible for much of the electronics production and for the provision of electrical engineering services in Austria.[47] What is distinctive about the Austrian case is the scope of government market participation (see Table 4). State-owned enterprises produce not only most of the water, energy, transportation, and communication services in Austria but also a large amount of the manufactured goods. Moreover, they dominate the financial sector of the economy. Through its national holding company, the OeIAG, the state produces and markets steel, aluminum, copper, lead, coal, oil, chemicals, and other goods; it also markets various kinds of engineering services. Among the largest fifty firms in the economy, about two-thirds are owned and operated by the government. Overall, the social economy (*Gemeinwirtschaft*) is responsible for about a quarter of the jobs and net production value in Austria, and almost one-half of all investment decisions are in public hands. Over the past four decades a few publicly owned firms have been privatized; 40 percent of the shares in one of the nationalized banks have been sold off, as have 25 percent of the state airlines and a minority holding in the state oil company. But overall, the relative importance of state-owned enterprise has not changed appreciably. Austria has had a highly mixed economy.[48]

46. The social corporatist nature of Austria's polity is described by Pelinka (1987), Nowotny (1984), and Katzenstein (1984, 1985); see also Marin (1983) and Farnleitner and Schmidt (1982). In addition to Katzenstein's effort (1984) to place the Austrian polity in comparative perspective, see Schmitter's investigation (1981), in which he classifies Austria's polity as the most societal corporatist in the Western world. The links between the Austrian social partnership and the Austrian party system are described and analyzed in Katzenstein (1984: chap. 4).

47. For a brief discussion of the relative importance of small- and medium-scale private enterprise in Austria see Tomandl and Fuerboeck (1986: chap. 1) and Grunwald (1982b:130–31). The latter source contains information about the role foreign private enterprises such as Siemens play in the Austrian economy. See also the annual article "The Top 500" in the Austrian magazine *Trend*.

48. See Katzenstein (1984:49–53); Nowotny (1982b); Grunwald (1982a); and the annual reports of the OeIAG. The Centre for European Public Enterprise consistently identifies Austria as having, next to Italy, the most mixed economy in Europe (C.E.E.P.

Austria's corporatist–mixed political economy leads us to expect that it should outperform Italy (pluralist–mixed political economy) in terms of collective consumption gains and intergenerational equity. Austria should perform about the same as Britain and worse than Sweden on this first welfare criterion. The potential for achieving intragenerational equity between private asset holders and wage earners should be great in Austria. If this potential is realized, there should be a greater degree of intragenerational equity in Austria than in the other three countries. At the same time, Austria may suffer certain forms of maldistribution, as between the economic security and real income of workers in privately owned and publicly owned firms. Finally, the relative stability of the structure of the Austria economy over the last four decades suggests a similarly stable balance of political forces. Hence a relatively unchanging set of welfare outcomes has been achieved in Austria.

The data on Austria's economic performance are, to some extent, consistent with these theoretical expectations. In terms of gains in real per capita GDP, the United Kingdom's and Italy's performance, until very recently, has been inferior to that of Austria. Sweden has failed to outperform Austria in this regard as well. Austria has also outperformed all three countries in terms of public debt burden.[49] Data on the intragenerational distribution of wealth support our theoretical expectations in that Austria's unemployment level has been markedly lower than that of Italy, the United Kingdom, and most other industrialized countries; it has also been lower than in Sweden. On the other hand, Austria has one of the more *in*egalitarian income distributions of all Western democracies. My calculations for the year 1979, for example, suggest that the ratio of posttax

---

1973, 1976, 1978, 1981); see also the data in the *Economist,* December 21, 1985, p. 72. Data on the scope and activities of provincial and municipal public enterprise can be found in Kager (1983). The few episodes of privatization that have occurred in Austria are described in Platzer (1986) and Lacina (1977). Recent proposals to privatize part of the publicly owned oil company and several other state holdings are discussed briefly in *Austrian Information* 41(12), 1988, and Chapter 10 below. Nowotny (1982b:47) charts changes in relative importance of OeIAG industrial investment in the period 1973–1979. Grunwald (1982a:136) reports that between 1969 and 1977 the relative importance of state capital in terms of employment share increased from 26 percent to 28 percent while the importance of foreign capital increased in this respect from 18 percent to 28 percent and the importance of Austrian private capital decreased from 56 percent to 44 percent.

49. See, for instance, Pelinka (1987), Wilensky and Turner (1987), and Garret and Lange (1986). The very recent decline in Austria's relative growth rate is described in *Austrian Information* 41(4), 1988. The public debt has grown from 12.7 percent of GDP in 1970 to 42.0 percent in 1986 (*Economist,* November 11, 1986, pp. 36–40). However, even this level is only average by European standards. See also von Beyme (1985).

Table 4. The social economy (Gemeinwirtschaft) in Austria: Employment, salaries, investments, and production values (Late 1970s)

Economic sector		(1) Employees	(2) Wages and salaries	(3) investments	(4) Gross production value	(5) Net production value
Energy and water provision	absolute:	34.774	8,455.799	13,670.161	43,946.620	21,531.392
	% of economic sector:	96.5	97.8	97.0	95.6	97.5
Mining and extraction	absolute:	13,906	3,292.190	1,720.965	11,629.023	6,016.605
	% of economic sector:	64.6	69.5	65.7	69.2	66.7
Manufacturing and industry	absolute:	157.797	31,105.875	8,070.960	151,302.077	46,106.724
	% of economic sector:	18.3	24.2	27.0	27.8	24.4
Construction	absolute:	5,361	1,027.811	170.372	2,716.424	1,141.586
	% of economic sector:	2.3	3.1	3.4	3.1	2.5
Commerce and warehousing	absolute:	29,069	4,113.135	968.155	62,806.146	7,170.842
	% of economic sector:	8.7	9.3	8.0	11.7	8.6
Lodgings and restaurants	absolute:	2,321	275.950	30.351	627.786	311.301
	% of economic sector:	2.7	3.4	0.6	1.7	1.8
Transportation and communication	absolute:	154.359	27,799.808	13,123.355	39,218.989	28,213.222
	% of economic sector:	78.9	82.0	76.3	51.3	69.9
Finance, credit, and private insurance	absolute:	64,529	14,170.109	6,154.978	43,422.545	30,459.202
	% of economic sector:	64.8	70.7	70.6	68.1	71.8
Personel, social, and public services	absolute:	7,908	2,044.648	614.419	4,139.842	2,067.848
	% of economic sector:	14.4	32.5	38.2	28.6	23.7

Total social economy					
absolute:	470,024	92,285,525	44,523,716	359,809,452	143,018,722
% of trade and industry economy:	24.5	32.1	46.1	25.3	31.3

Note: The Austrian Social Economy is composed of state enterprises and state partnerships (from 50 percent); nationalized industries; the Austrian National Bank; nationalized banks (state portion: 60 percent) and partnerships (with at least 50 percent of nominal capital); enterprises and partnerships in the Bundesländer; municipal enterprises and partnerships; cooperatives and other enterprises.

Entries for columns 2–5 (wages, investment and gross and net production value) are in thousands of schillings.

The exact year for the data is 1976. However, the author indicates (1982b:21) that the scope of the social economy is essentially the same for the remainder of the decade.

Source: Nowotny (1982b), reprinted by permission of the author.

shares of income for top and bottom quintiles was about 9.[50] This finding suggests that Austria does not perform as expected on the second welfare criterion.

Finally, although some students of Austria's political economy argue there is an "equilibrium of power differences" within the country, it is not entirely clear from their accounts that this equilibrium explains the stable Austrian mix of public and private enterprise or, more important, how the corporatist–mixed character of Austria's political economy produces a relatively unchanging blend of welfare outcomes. Nor is it clear that the expected maldistributions of wealth exist in Austria. A deeper look into the structural and behavioral features and the welfare outcomes of Austria's corporatist–mixed political economy is therefore required to establish the validity of the theoretical account given in Chapter 5.[51]

By most standards, Austria has a highly efficient economy. In terms of growth in real per capita gross domestic product and productivity, for example, Austria consistently ranks near the top of the industrialized world.[52] Austria's capital market is quite small and underdeveloped, and so, though shareholder transactions encourage managerial efficiency to some degree, they are normally not credited for Austria's success on the first welfare criterion. Rather, Austria's superior growth and productivity are attributed to the "vitality" of its small- and medium-scale private businesses. In terms of the analysis in Chapters 3 and 5, what explains the economy's productive efficiency is the fact that many private managers own their enterprises

50. For performance on our second welfare criterion, see Pelinka (1987), Wilensky and Turner (1987), and Cameron (1984). For income distribution, in particular, see Esping-Andersen (1985:242) and Brooks (1983:405–6). My calculations are based on total income and tax data in *Lohn und Einkommensteuerstatistik*, 1979 (Vienna: Oesterreichisches Zentralamt, 1985), Table 2, p. xxv.

51. Peter Katzenstein, for example, writes that "the system of social and economic partnership reflects and shapes a policy process built around an equilibration of power differences not as an end in itself but as a means of assuring that the process of small-scale political conflict over carefully factored issues never ends" (1982:153). He argues that nationalization weakens the power of private business, but he does not attempt to show that public ownership is a necessary condition for the realization of Austria's distribution of wealth or to determine if those forms of maldistribution we uncovered in the section on corporatist–mixed political economies exist in Austria. Nor does Katzenstein explicitly show that the equilibrium of power differences is rooted in an appreciation for the welfare consequences of corporatist–mixed political economies. In what follows I show that Austrian elites do have an appreciation for the welfare implications of their political economy, including the need for some degree of public ownership if their welfare objectives are to be achieved; elites are also aware of the potential for the predicted forms of maldistribution between state enterprise and private enterprise workers.

52. On productivity, for instance, see *Austrian Information* 38(a), 1985, p. 5.

and that there are few layers of management within many Austrian private firms.[53]

The realization of collective and intergenerational welfare gains can also be attributed to the policies Austrian governments have adopted and to the management of the nationalized industries. Governments' schemes of indirect and direct financial intervention have produced one of the highest annual investment growth rates in the Western world. A wide range of fiscal incentives has made private reinvestment more attractive than savings or consumption, for instance. Because of its countercylical nature, fiscal policy has also stabilized business expectations and, in turn, smoothed investment and consumption patterns.[54]

Austrian governments have become directly involved in the allocation of credit as well. Public authorities have borrowed funds from international lenders and then channeled this "fresh capital" to particular firms and industries. In this way they have compensated for the weakness of Austria's local capital market and for the unwillingness or inability of private enterprises to borrow abroad. Government involvement in the acquisition and allocation of credit once again has been motivated by a desire to promote domestic investment and growth.[55] The international dimensions of "Austro-Keynesianism" involve commitment to a hard-currency policy—pegging the Austrian schilling to the deutschemark—and adoption of a monetary policy expressingly designed to shelter the local economy from the inflationary effects of foreign borrowing and deficit spending.[56]

53. The underdeveloped nature of Austria's capital market is stressed by Hankel (1981); the segmented, oligopolistic structure of its credit markets is stressed by Hodjera (1976:610–14). On the vitality of Austrian small- and medium-sized private enterprise see Grunwald (1982a, b), Tumlir (1982), and Vak (1982). Hankel (1981: chap. 1) points out that generally there is less managerial control in Austria than in Germany.

54. Hankel explains how fiscal policy has rendered reinvestment the most attractive option for Austrian entrepreneurs (1981:70–71). See the same source for a fuller exposition of the motivation behind Austrian fiscal policy; see also Katzenstein (1984:42–44) and Bowler (1986).

55. See Hankel (1981: chap. 3). See also Katzenstein (1984:76) and Grunwald (1982b). Although Austrian authorities are deeply involved in the acquisition and allocation of capital, they do not engage in any formal national investment planning. Rather, their industrial policy tends to be more incremental and restrained in the way industries are actually aided and promoted. See Katzenstein (1984: chap. 4).

56. Austro-Keynesianism is distinguished by its emphasis on price stability and its commitment to a hard-currency policy (Seidel 1982; see also Hankel 1981: chap. 5). The constraints that the hard-currency policy imposes on monetary policy are examined in Seidel (1982), Dreyer (1982), and Koren (1982). On the links between international capital movements and economic activity within Austria, see Hodjera (1976) and Penati and Dooley (1984). The results of the latter two studies are examined in greater detail in Chapter 10 below.

Austrian public enterprise has contributed to the realization of collective and intergenerational welfare gains. The Austrian legislation on nationalized industries stipulates that the state can influence the operation of the public business only through its role as a stockholder. For much of their history, therefore, the nationalized industries have been administered through various state ministries and trustee companies rather than through the Austrian Parliament. These ministries, like their counterparts in Britain, initially established an "arm's length relationship" with publicly owned firms. In contrast to what happened in Britain, however, this kind of relationship was maintained in Austria throughout much of the 1960s and early 1970s. In 1966 and again in 1970 the nationalized industries were organized into a state holding company, the Oesterreichische Industrieverwaltungs-Aktiengesellschaft (Austrian Nationalized Industries Holding Company, or OeIAG). At the same time, provision was made for annual reports to Parliament on the performance of the nationalized industries, for public audits of the nationalized industries, and for mandatory parliamentary approval of the sale of subsidiaries of nationalized industries. But beyond this, very few restrictions were placed on the operation of state-owned enterprise. Publicly owned firms were not required to pay dividends to the state; public managers were left relatively free to make the investment and purchasing decisions they judged to be in the best interest of their firms.[57] In the late 1970s, under the auspices of an amended OeIAG Bond Issue Law, the state holding company was given full auditing rights within the nationalized sector of the economy, and financing limits were established for the OeIAG group as a whole. But no effort was made to impose the financial constraints imposed on the British nationalized industries.[58]

Until the late 1970s the Austrian nationalized industries were considered among the most efficient publicly owned firms in the world. There has been relatively little controversy about whether or not they have promoted investment and growth. Throughout much of their history, Austrian publicly owned firms earned positive rates of return, and they managed to finance internally a large share of their investments and research and development. Thanks in part to the technological advantages they enjoyed, public firms also achieved a relatively high level of productivity. In addition, they employed

57. For an overview of the history of Austrian nationalized industry see Grunwald (1982a) and Katzenstein (1984: chap. 2). The differences in the British and Austrian experiences are recognized by Van der Bellen (1981:81).

58. For a brief summary of the provisions of the amended OeIAG Bond Issue Law see the *Annual Report of the OeIAG* (1983:9).

and trained a large number of youths through the apprentice system, thus providing real material and nonmaterial gains to younger generations.

The performance of the nationalized industries deteriorated in the aftermath of the oil price shocks of the 1970s. Declining demand for steel and other industrial products coupled with the nationalized industries' commitment to maintaining employment or even "hoarding" labor (see below) reduced the productivity of the OeIAG group (Table 5). Such enterprises as the Voest-Alpine steel combine suffered substantial financial losses and, despite extensive efforts to cut costs and to diversify into other forms of manufacturing, had to turn to the government for financial assistance. Public authorities granted subsidies to Voest-Alpine and to several other state-owned enterprises, while at the same time encouraging industrial adjustment and diversification. The decline in the financial performance of some Austrian nationalized industries should not overshadow the financial success of public firms such as OeMV and Chemie Linz—the state-owned oil and chemical combines—in this period or the fact that over the decade of the 1970s the OeIAG achieved real gains in productivity (Table 6). Also, the vigorous investment programs of Austria's nationalized industries have made their plants among the most modern in the industrialized world.[59]

Nationalized industries enhanced the productive efficiency of the Austrian economy in this period. By providing low-cost goods and services to other firms they contributed to higher earnings by the private sector and to private investors' propensity to reinvest. The anticyclical investments and stable pricing policies of the nationalized industries had important psychological effects on the private sector, offsetting the potentially harmful impact of the world economic crises of the 1970s on business expectations. At the same time the investments that nationalized industries made put them in a good position to exploit future upswings in the local and global economies as well as to produce goods and services at comparatively low cost over the short term. A mix of private and public enterprise thus appears to have allowed Austria to achieve a relatively high level of col-

59. The financial success of Voest-Alpine prior to the mid-1970s is evidenced by the fact that historically it had been able to fund 96 percent of its research and development internally (Katzenstein 1984: chap. 6). The more general success of the OeIAG group prior to the oil price shocks is stressed by Nowotny (1982a) and Kromer (1983). The latter gives a more detailed breakdown of the performance of Austrian nationalized industries in the 1970s, a breakdown that produces a more salutary evaluation of their relative performance than that given in Table 5. See Andŕlik (1983: chap. 7) for a detailed examination of productivity trends in Austria's steel industry during the 1970s.

Table 5. Development of employment, production, and productivity: OeIAG,[1] Austrian industry, and West German industry (1973 = 100)

	1973	1974	1975	1976	1977	1978	1979	1980
Employment								
OeIAG total (114,705)[2]	100	104	105	103	103	102	102	102
Total Austrian industry[3]	100	100	94	93	94	92	92	93
OeIAG portion	16.3	17.0	18.0	18.1	17.8	17.9	18.0	17.9
West German industry	100	97	91	89	87	87	87	88
Production								
OeIAG	100	103	93	97	98	103	109	114
Total Austrian industry	100	105	97	104	108	110	116	121
West German industry	100	98	91	99	102	103	108	108
Productivity[4]								
OeIAG	100	99	89	94	96	101	107	112
Total Austrian industry	100	105	103	112	115	120	126	130
West German industry	100	101	100	112	116	118	124	123

[1] excludes Boehler-Duesseldorf
[2] absolute number of employees
[3] excludes electric, gas, and water production, excludes construction industry
[4] Production per employee

Source: Nowotny (1982b), reprinted by permission of the author.

lective consumption and intergenerational equity in the 1960s and 1970s. According to some observers, this welfare outcome could not have been achieved if Austria had either a private enterprise or a socialist scheme of economic organization.[60]

This is not to say that government policies have been optimal in any sense or that the nationalized industries could not have promoted an even greater degree of productive efficiency, especially over the last fifteen years. Austrian authorities may have promoted excessive investment, and their failure to create a fully integrated capital market prevented Austria from realizing still greater gains in collective and intergenerational consumption.[61] There is also some debate both about the long-term welfare consequences of foreign indebtedness and about the wisdom of Austria's hard-currency policy, for example, whether pegging the schilling to the deutschemark has significantly retarded the competitiveness of Austrian industry.[62]

Whether nationalized industries have become inherently inefficient and hence prevented Austria from realizing higher levels of collective consumption is an issue of increasing controversy both within and outside Austria. In terms of productivity the performance of Austria's public enterprise has deteriorated since the mid-1970s. The question is whether the overall effects of the investment and other policies of the nationalized industries retarded the performance of the Austrian economy as a whole. It can be argued that the distinctive behavior of Austrian privately owned firms—their willingness and ability to reinvest in the face of economic crisis—is, in some substantial part, an outgrowth of the countercyclical behavior of Austrian publicly owned firms. It can also be argued that newly modernized, more fully diversified nationalized industries will help Austria preserve and secure a less volatile, comparatively high level of collective consumption in the future.[63]

60. The stabilizing and subsidizing effects of the nationalized industries' investment and pricing decision are stressed by Hankel (1981), Kromer (1983), Nowotny (1982a, b), Andrlik (1983:286–87), and Katzenstein (1984:76, chap. 6). The idea that Austria's mix of private and public enterprise yields welfare outcomes superior to those which could be achieved in either a private enterprise or a socialist economy is advanced by Nowotny (1982b:27).

61. See Hankel (1981: chap. 5).

62. Hankel (1981) argues that the decision to incur foreign debts was not irrational and that *inter alia* this decision actually improves the welfare of future generations. Katzenstein expresses some concern about the burden these external financial obligations pose for future generations. But he is quick to acknowledge that in relation to the debt burden of other countries, Austria's foreign obligations are not great (1984:235, 244). The wisdom of Austria's hard-currency policy is questioned by Artus (1982) and Willett (1982). Hankel defends the policy, arguing that it stabilizes business expectations (1981: chap. 1).

63. See Nowotny (1982b:27). The virtues of large size and of holding-company orga-

Table 6. Comparative productivity trends (turnover / employees) for Austrian state and local-private industry and West German industry, 1974–1981

Year	OeIAG Index	OeIAG without OeMV Index	Index for Business Groups of the Large Banks	Austrian Industry	West German Industry
1974	100.0	100.0	100.0	100.0	100.0
1975	102.7	100.9	108.7	104.2	104.8
1976	123.3	121.1	129.8	119.4	120.2
1977	128.7	124.4	131.0	125.9	127.3
1978	129.0	134.0	140.2	131.0	133.0
1979	157.8	151.4	156.8	146.8	146.6
1980	183.2	164.6	168.0	162.6	157.6
1981	217.7	185.0	192.8	176.7	169.1

Note: The large banks are The Creditanstalt–Bankverein and Länderbank. The Austrian state owns about half the shares in these banks (Platzner 1986:277–278).

Source: Kromer (1983), reprinted by permission of the director of the Ludwig Boltzman-Institute.

Austrians' concern for promoting intragenerational equity holds the key to explain the poorer financial performance of the nationalized industries in the late 1970s and 1980s and, in turn, to demonstrate the larger welfare implications for a country with a large state business sector. The few studies that include Austria conclude it has a relatively inegalitarian distribution of income. For instance, in 1979 the top 20.6 percent of the population had about 50 percent of the total income whereas the bottom 28.9 percent had about 6 percent. These and other facts lead several observers to conclude there is a stable, low degree of intragenerational equity in Austria and that governments' investment and growth-oriented policies have reinforced, not ameliorated, inequities in the material distribution of wealth.[64]

Insofar as employment security—one kind of nonmaterial wealth—is concerned, however, Austria clearly outperforms most other Western countries. Austria consistently has one of the lowest unemploy-

---

nization for public enterprise are mentioned by Short (1983:29) and by Mallon (1981:284), respectively. See also the more general discussion of the virtues of conglomeration in Millward and Parker (1983:211).

64. For income-distribution data see note 50 above. One example is Katzenstein's argument that "a decade of socialist rule has not altered the size of the wage share in national income, and Austria's growth policy has at best left unaltered the inegalitarian distribution of income and wealth. Indeed it is more likely that the policy has reinforced an inequality which the union movement is committed, at least in principle, to erase" (1984:39; see also Pelinka 1987:70 and Hankel 1981:56). Erich Andrlik draws essentially the same conclusion from an examination of wage and profit share data and a consideration of the degree of social mobility in Austria (1983:369).

ment rates in the West.[65] As in Britain, there are regional disparities in unemployment rates; for example, in the early 1980s the unemployment rate in Burgenland and Kärnten was more than twice as high as the rates in all but two other provinces. On the other hand, youth unemployment—a reflection also of intergenerational equity— is comparatively low in Austria; for the period 1975–1979, for instance, the unemployment rate for men and women under age twenty was less than 1 percent.[66] Because Austrian workers contribute to a number of large pension funds, the distinction between asset holders and wage earners is somewhat ambiguous. However, the Austrians themselves, and many students of Austria's political economy, measure intragenerational equity (in part) in terms of the relative shares of profits and wages in national income, suggesting that the distinction between private asset holders and wage earners is still meaningful.[67]

Government monetary and fiscal policies, if they have any major effects on the intragenerational distribution of wealth, probably reinforce income inequities. The extensive subsidies that authorities provide to private entrepreneurs appear to augment the share of material wealth that those private asset holders control. The government policy of going into debt on behalf of the private sector also reduces the economic uncertainty these asset holders face while simultaneously increasing the size of the economic burden on future generations of Austrian citizens. Government macroeconomic policies, to the extent they favor price stability at the expense of some jobs, may also have provided differential welfare gains to private asset holders.

Beyond these effects, government policies do not appear to have significantly altered the intragenerational distribution of wealth. The extensive support that the government provides to older age groups in the form of public pensions appears to amount more to an

65. Again, see Pelinka (1987), Wilensky and Turner (1987), and *Austrian Information* 41(4), 1988. Unemployment data are not always strictly comparable across countries; see Kosters (1982) and Payne (1979). There is little reason to suspect that Austria's superior performance is a statistical artifact, however. Also, Austria relies on a foreign workforce to adjust to economic downturns (see Butschek 1982), but the relative size and comparative treatment of the foreign workforce is different in Austria than in Switzerland, where noncitizens bear much of the brunt of economic adjustment. See ibid. and Katzenstein (1984, 1985).

66. The regional unemployment data are from *Statistiche Übersichten* 4/1983, Table 11.8. The rates are expressed as a percentage of the available (registered) workforce. Data on the rate of youth unemployment are taken from Butschek (1982:110). See the same source for a fuller discussion of Austria's exemplary performance on youth employment rates, part of which is attributable to an unusually low minimum wage rate.

67. See Hankel (1981:56).

intergenerational than to an intragenerational transfer of wealth. The same is true of other aspects of Austrian social spending, which are roughly commensurate with or inferior to those of other Western countries.[68]

Through their Labor Market Administration and Labor Market Promotion Scheme, public authorities have actively promoted the employment security of current generations. Financial support has been given to local and foreign firms that agree to locate and hire workers in particular regions, especially in rural areas. Public jobs have been created in all regions, but especially in those areas which have suffered most from industrial adjustment. By comparative standards, however, Austria's manpower programs are not particularly extensive. The relative importance of public employment is not that great, and unemployment insurance benefits are among the lowest in Europe.[69]

What accounts for Austria's exemplary performance in terms of employment security? For many years the nationalized industries made a concerted effort to create and preserve jobs and, by implication, to maintain the nonmaterial wealth (that is, economic security) of wage earners. The nationalized industries affect Austria's intragenerational distribution of wealth in various ways. The pricing behavior of public firms contributes to price stability and hence, to the extent it causes shortfalls in earnings and layoffs, to the provision of differential welfare gains to asset holders. At the same time the nationalized industries have paid their workers slightly higher wages and benefits than many private enterprises pay. For much of the 1960s and 1970s, for instance, the earnings of workers in state-owned enterprises were 10–15 percent higher than those of their counterparts in the private enterprise sector. State enterprise workers also had the opportunity to participate to a greater degree in the operation of their firms, allowing them to secure nonmaterial gains that did not accrue to private enterprise workers.[70]

68. See Katzenstein (1984:44–45), Tomandl and Fuerboeck (1986), and such general works as Heidenheimer, Heclo, and Adams (1983: chap. 7).

69. For a description of the rationale behind and workings of the Labor Market Administration and Labor Promotion Schemes, see Tomandl and Fuerboeck (1986: chap. 4). Butschek (1982) also reviews manpower policies in Austria. He stresses the relatively small size of such programs relative to those in other Western countries and the extent to which Austrian authorities monitor and promote the willingness to work. The difficulties of Austrian governments in the late 1970s and early 1980s in using fiscal incentives to ameliorate regional employment disparities are also described by Butschek (1982:119); see also Wilensky and Turner (1986:59).

70. Nowotny (1982a, b) emphasizes the demonstration effects of the pricing policies of nationalized industries and hence the role they have played in promoting price stability. However, he does not explore the distributional implications of inflation versus unemployment. The differential wage and benefit gains that workers in state-owned enterprises have made are described briefly in Andrlik (1983:282) and Lacina (1977).

It is the employment policy of the nationalized industries which has had the most significant impact on the wealth of wage earners. For much of their history, the Austrian nationalized industries have consistently protected jobs in the face of cyclical and, more recently, major structural changes in the economy. Nationalized firms have reduced their capacity far less and laid off far fewer workers than have private firms, local and foreign (see Table 5). In industries such as steel, publicly owned firms have accepted orders at prices below cost in an effort to maintain production levels and retain workers. They have also worked closely with public authorities to retrain and find alternative employment for workers whom they have laid off. As a result of these policies many communities within Austria appear to have been spared the economic and social upheavals experienced by communities such as those located in the Mahoning Valley in the United States. Some observers argue that since the employment policies of the nationalized industries have helped Austria avoid the problem of hysteresis—structural, long-term unemployment—they have served the interests of future generations as well.[71]

The slump in the financial performance of the nationalized industries can be traced, in part, to the commitment to create and preserve jobs. In the 1970s privately owned firms lowered production levels, disinvested from existing plants and left particular locations, diversified their private assets, laid off workers, and maintained financial returns. During the same period Austrian publicly owned firms maintained production levels, invested in existing plants and remained in particular locations, diversified the public's assets, maintained employment levels, and suffered a setback in financial

Note that the economic crises of the 1970s greatly diminished the ability of certain groups of state enterprise workers to preserve their wage and benefit advantage. In 1975, for example, workers in private firms, like the then quasi-nationalized tire manufacturer Semperit AG, were able to convince their management to make their annual bonuses a permanent part of their wages, whereas workers at VEW lost part of their bonuses (Andrlik 1983:292–93). The nationalized industries have been at the forefront of the movement to democratize Austrian firms to introduce social innovations. See the discussions in Katzenstein (1984:39), Grunwald (1982a, b), and Lacina (1977); see also Tomandl and Fuerboeck (1986: chap. 2).

71. Butschek (1982), Kosters (1982), and Arndt (1982:211) stress that the employment policies of the nationalized industries are important in explaining this aspect of Austria's performance. Public ministers and public managers explicitly acknowledge their intention to adopt employment policies that are expressly different from those which private firms adopt—especially small- and medium-sized private firms; see Lacina (1983) and Grunwald (1982b). The strategic guidelines of the OeIAG's policy explicitly acknowledge the holding company's responsibility to preserve employment in regions with a long industrial tradition (Austria's Nationalized Industries 1983:6). Details on how they have done so, especially within the steel industry, can be found in Andrlik (1983, 1984) and Nowotny (1982a, b). The point about hysteresis is made by Nowotny (1982b:32).

earnings. The nationalized industries thus provided nonmaterial wealth—employment and economic security—to particular groups of workers and particular communities. They did so at the expense of current and future consumption and public earnings. Meanwhile private enterprise maintained private earnings, and perhaps collective consumption now and in the future, at the expense of the employment security of its workforce and the communities where that workforce resided.

What is important for our purposes is that the blend of welfare outcomes realized in Austria in this period differed markedly from what was realized in Britain and other countries. Moreover, it was not fiscal policy or manpower programs but rather the behavior of the state business sector that was instrumental in bringing about this distinctive blend. All the evidence suggests that if Austria had had a private enterprise economy, the welfare consequences of the structural crises of the 1970s would have been quite different. In particular, industries that were privately owned would have emphasized preserving levels of collective consumption and private and public financial returns, and downplayed preserving employment and community security.[72]

The nature of Austrian politics has much to do with why fiscal and monetary authorities and the nationalized industries behaved as they did, and hence with why Austria has achieved its blend of social welfare. Until recently there has been much consensus in Austria about the ends and means of government market intervention and participation. Producer groups and political parties cooperated closely in the years following World War II. This cooperation spawned a social partnership between labor and capital and a grand coalition of political parties. Partnership was based on a compromise in which business supported the goal of full employment and tolerated nationalization while unions supported efforts to promote growth, tied their wage bargains to productivity gains, and largely abandoned efforts to eliminate inequities in the distribution of material wealth. This compromise was also based on a mutual perception of national vulnerability to world market and nonmarket forces and on a genuine concern for intergenerational equity. Nationalization, it was believed, would serve these ends as well as provide at least some workers with employment security.[73]

72. The nationalized industries laid off workers in relatively large numbers in the mid-1980s. I return to this and other recent developments in Chapter 10 below.

73. See, in particular, Katzenstein (1984:36, 72) and also Pelinka (1987), Arndt (1982:81), and Hankel (1981:185). Union leaders' commitment to full employment, and their perception that nationalization is instrumental in achieving this objective, is evident in statements such as the one Anton Benya, president of the Austrian Federa-

Political parties—whose structures and memberships are intimately connected to those of the major producer groups—have also displayed an unusual degree of consensus over economic and other issues.[74] The grand coalition of parties lasted for more than a decade, and it established important precedents for consultation and for accommodating conflicting interests within Austria. Even after the coalition disbanded in the mid-1960s, political leaders continued to actively seek the advice of their opponents on major issues. In addition, a large share of the legislation passed by Parliament was approved unanimously; for example, the financial support given to the nationalized industries in the late 1970s and early 1980s was endorsed by both of the major parties.[75]

The workings of Austria's political institutions reflect and enforce this consensus. Austria's democratic corporatist system is based on an ideology of social partnership, a mutual recognition of the authority of Austria's national producer groups, and a deep commitment to coordinate conflicting objectives through "continuous political bargaining between interest groups, state bureaucracies and political parties."[76] The partnership is based on the compromise described above, and unanimous agreement between the partners is usually required before the terms of the compromise are implemented. The chambers for business, labor, and agriculture and the trade union conferation enforce these national agreements in a way that reproduces the commitment to growth and full employment on the one hand and toleration of nationalization and indifference to income redistribution on the other. Labor organizations do so by sanctioning and regulating internal opposition to the terms of the national compromise.[77]

Unlike other countries, where popular elections can cause major alterations in public policies, Austria has elections that serve to stabilize or make only minor changes in public policies. A large number of

tion of Trade Unions, makes about the importance of the Austrian social economy (1982:10). The shared views of Austrian political parties are described in Chaloupek (1985).

74. The links between parties and producer groups are described in Chaloupek (1985) and Katzenstein (1984: chap. 2).

75. Andrlik (1983:144–45) reports that between 1966 and 1970 about 80 percent of legislation was passed with the votes of the two main parties; in 1971–1975 the proportion increased to 90 percent.

76. Katzenstein (1984:32).

77. See, for instance, Marin's discussion of the way in which the Austrian Trade Union Federation uses its central control over organizational resources to achieve "internal consensus formation" (1983:212–13). See also Tomandl and Fuerboeck (1986: chap. 1).

policy decisions are made outside the parliamentary arena in corporatist bodies, and Proporz translates electoral outcomes into only minor shifts in the balance of power on the supervisory boards of the nationalized industries and on other government bodies. In addition, there have been few deep divisions of opinion within the Austrian electorate concerning economic issues. The relative homogeneity of the Austrian public's conception of the ends and means of public policy and of nationalization appears to be a cause and a consequence of the real collective welfare gains Austrian citizens realized in the postwar era. Also important is a shared popular perception of national vulnerability to external economic and political forces. Popular consensus has made it difficult for radical parties that oppose the social partnership to achieve electoral success.[78]

The political consensus has broken down in the 1980s, and Austrian political institutions have displayed less capacity to manage social change. Disagreements have surfaced among producer groups and political parties over many issues, among them how best to manage the nationalized industries. These disagreements culminated in 1986 in a reorganization of the OeIAG and in a plan to privatize parts or all of several state holdings. Also, elections have produced popular challenges to the authority of the social partners and of elected officials. In 1983, for example, the Social Democratic party was forced, for the first time, to form a coalition with a minor party, the Freedom party (FPOe). Still, from a historical and comparative standpoint, Austrian politics has been marked by consensus and stability.[79] It is a politics rooted in a real balance of political power between producer groups and political parties.[80]

Austria's blend of social welfare in the forty years after the World

78. Thus while Lijphart classifies the electoral system as majoritarian, he is quick to point out the consensual nature of Austria's party politics (1984:64). For statistical evidence that the 1983 election had little effect on the behavior of Austrian firms, public and private, see Freeman (1988).

79. Recent changes in the fabric of Austrian politics and the potential welfare implications of those changes are examined in Chapter 10 below. Major disagreements over the nationalized industries have surfaced between political parties (Chaloupek 1985) and within and between producer groups (Andrlik 1983, 1984, 1985; Platzer 1986). These disagreements produced the 1986 OeIAG Law, which limits the use of Proporz and reorganizes publicly owned firms into six holding companies (see Itzlinger, Kerschbamer, and Van der Bellen 1988). In the fall of 1987, the OeIAG sold part of its interest in Austria's largest oil company, the Oesterreichische Mineraloeverwaltungs AG (*Austrian Information* 41(3), 1988:5). The government also plans to sell parts of the largest state banks, the state airline, and the state electrical works.

80. On the equilibrium of political forces within Austria in the postwar period in general see Katzenstein (1982:153). Marin (1983:200) stresses that the possibilities for achieving a balance or equilibrium of class forces is a defining feature of Austro-Marxism; see also Andrlik (1983).

War II, is an outgrowth of this politics of consensus and stability. The political compromise that the social partners forged not only provides private entrepreneurs with lucrative incentives to reinvest but also reduces their uncertainty about the rate of return from that reinvestment. Entrepreneurial risk is reduced because private owners can predict that certain monetary and fiscal policies will be maintained. Political leaders' long-term orientation in economic policy making—their willingness to impose a low social discount rate on future collective gains in consumption—assures private business that authorities will promote growth and investment and also that unions will contribute to this effort in their wage negotiations. In contrast to what happened in Britain and elsewhere, Austrian politics promotes private investment and the growth this investment engenders.[81]

The performance of the nationalized industries also reflects the character of Austrian politics. Political leaders consider the nationalized industries a means of pursuing collective, national interests as much as a means of pursuing the interests of a particular group of citizens. The investment and diversification policies of the nationalized industries, as explained above, show a real concern for promoting future gains in collective consumption and for diminishing the risks faced by the *public* owners of these industries. The autonomy leaders have given to public managers in these respects is further evidence of their commitment to promoting productive efficiency and to safeguarding the public's interest as a collective shareholder.[82]

The policies of the nationalized industries also reveal the partners' and the parties' commitment to employment security. Publicly owned firms delay closures and protect jobs, in keeping with the terms of the compromise forged between business and labor. Representation of political parties on the supervisory boards of the nationalized industries—especially representation of labor's allies within the two major parties, the SPOe and OeVP—ensure that the policies of publicly owned firms also serve this second welfare objective. As the corresponding enterprises are publicly owned, the managers themselves have fewer incentives to relocate rather than attempt to provide their workers with some degree of economic security. In this way, the nonmaterial well-being of at least one segment of the workforce has been preserved and defended in the face of economic change.

81. See the discussions in Hankel (1981: chap. 4), Frisch (1982:77), Chaloupek (1985:74), Tomandl and Fuerboeck (1986:25), and Braun (1986: chap. 10).
82. For instance, Katzenstein (1984:49) stresses that nationalization is a means of asserting national independence among nation-states more than it is a manifestation of the class struggle.

Producer group and party leaders are fully aware of the possibility of a maldistribution of wealth between state enterprise workers and private enterprise workers. They have denounced efforts to create a "labor aristocracy" in the nationalized industries. In addition, leaders have taken steps to lessen disparities in the earnings of workers in the two segments of the economy. For instance, agreements between national unions and employer associations have stipulated that both sets of workers should receive equal pay and benefits. The differences in the earnings of private enterprise and state enterprise workers appear to have arisen more because of the bargaining skill of local union organizations, and perhaps also the attitudes of managers of nationalized industries, than because political leaders have sought to create disparities. Nor have such differences arisen because state enterprise unions have used their more potent strike threat to gain a greater share of the material wealth that accrues to wage earners. In fact, there is little strike activity in Austria in any industry. Also, in the face of the financial problems nationalized industries encountered in the late 1970s, pension benefits for many state enterprise workers were substantially reduced. Generally speaking, the possibility of large disparities in the distribution of *material* wealth between the two groups of wage earners has not been realized.[83]

On the other hand, there clearly has been greater employment security in the nationalized industries, not only because of the smaller likelihood that publicly owned firms will relocate or close but also because of the seemingly more concerted effort of state managers to secure alternative employment for their workers. Therefore differences in the *nonmaterial* wealth accrue to the two groups of wage

83. Andrlik (1983: chap. 7) indicates that the negotiations between the national association of metal workers and their employers provided for equal rates of remuneration for private enterprise and state enterprise workers, but that the latter secured somewhat greater earnings than the former in local negotiations with employers. The aim of reducing wage differentials and other inequities between the two sets of workers has been voiced by Chancellor Kriesky and other leaders (see Nowotny 1982a:49). Lacina (1977) stresses the conscious efforts producer group leaders and other elites have made to avoid the creation of a "labor aristocracy" in the nationalized industries. Van der Bellen (1981:84) reports that wage differentials have been tolerated within state industries: "Employees in all the relatively monopolistic enterprises in State hands seem to enjoy similar wage advantages. Even the very centrally organized Trade Union Federation has tolerated these wage differences up to now." (He cites a 1980 study by Nowotny in this context. However, Nowotny, in an interview in Vienna, October 1984, said that the main differences in the earnings of workers in the state and private sectors of the economy lie in nonwage benefits and that these benefits have been substantially reduced in the face of economic crises of the late 1970s.) For Frisch (1982: 93) and Seidel (1982) the differentials between the earnings in the "exposed" and the "sheltered" sectors of the economy are an important potential source of political conflict.

earners. State enterprise workers enjoy greater employment security than private enterprise workers, apparently one reason why, wages being equal, a large majority of Austrian citizens express the desire to be employed in state-owned rather than private firms.[84]

Corporatist politics and the enduring consensus on which it is based have thus been partly responsible for Austria's performance on our two welfare criteria. The specific goals of the social partnership provide the motivation for the policies governments have pursued and for the way the nationalized industries have been managed. Producer and other groups have remained committed to these goals, and Austria's political institutions have enforced this commitment over time, explaining the role government intervention and market participation have played in promoting certain welfare outcomes. Corporatism facilitated the implementation of policies that ameliorated market failure and encouraged investment and productivity growth in the private sector. It also enhanced labor's power. Corporatism allowed producer groups to achieve not only a high aggregate level of employment but also a high degree of employment security for at least one substantial segment of the workforce, wage earners in nationalized industries. The latter welfare outcome is a significant improvement in the relative well-being of wage earners relative to private asset holders; it probably could not have been achieved had the respective industries not been nationalized.[85] Finally, despite the existence of a majoritarian political system, electoral politics did not substantially alter the motivation for government intervention or alter the way in which nationalized industries were managed. The reason is that for many years popular opinions about the government's policies and the behavior of the nationalized industries were relatively homogenous and unchanging. Also, Proporz translated electoral outcomes into only minor changes in the balance of political forces within the government and within the state business sector. The reorganization of the nationalized industries into a state holding company and the

84. A poll by the Sozialwissenschaftliche Studiengesellschaft found that in 1964, 49 percent expressed a clear preference for working in the nationalized industries whereas 22 percent said they would choose the job in private enterprise. By 1979 the percentage expressing a preference for employment in nationalized industries had risen to 54 whereas the percentage expressing a desire to work in the private enterprise sector had fallen to 18; in 1983, the figures were 53 percent and 20 percent respectively. The question the poll asked was: "Suppose that you were offered an equally well paying position in a private company and a state company. Which position would you take?"

85. Thus those accounts which stress unions' growth consciousness and indifference to material income redistribution overlook the substantial gains one large segment of the workforce has made in terms of nonmaterial wealth and how these gains are contingent on the existence of Austria's relatively large nationalized sector.

more general separation of issues between corporatist and parliamentary bodies appear to have contributed to this result as well.[86]

Austria's performance can also be attributed to the three structural factors discussed in Chapter 5. First, Austria's centralist administrators help formulate and enforce political compromise. Experts within the state and within producer groups helped design and implement policies that promote investment and growth. Political executives, including the chancellor, intervene in negotiations with managers, workers, and communities to enforce a few closures and mergers that promise to enhance productive efficiency. The managers of the nationalized industries have for a long time pursued policies that ensured their financial self-sufficiency and realized productivity gains. At the same time state bureaucrats adopted policies that created and preserved jobs. For instance, public managers worked closely with the Labor Market Promotion Board and other agencies in retraining and finding alternative employment for their workers.

The relative efficiency of Austria's economy is in part an outgrowth of the fact that a centralist tradition enhances the influence of the state bureaucracy in the continuous negotiations that occur in the country's corporatist political system.[87] The effectiveness of executive interventions and the financial success public managers have achieved historically are both cause and consequence of deference to state authority. If Austria had a noncentralist administrative tradition, the compromise forged by bureaucracy and social partners might have been much more difficult to enforce. For instance, managers in the nationalized industries would have had a more difficult task promoting growth in the 1960s and early 1970s: less deference to state authority would have made it more difficult for them to make decisions that promoted productive efficiency and financial self-sufficiency. Of course, this period saw general challenges to the authority of state managers and public authorities in general. But there have been comparatively fewer challenges to the decisions of public administrators in Austria; decisions have been easier to enforce there than in Britain, where administrative tradition is noncentralist.[88]

86. Farnleiter and Schmidt (1982) argue that the decisions of the joint commissions are largely insulated from the vagaries of parliamentary politics.

87. On the basically centralist nature of Austrian state administrative tradition see Katzenstein (1984:63). The executive plays a more important role than the legislature in Austrian politics (Nowotny 1984). The chancellor's role in promoting industrial adjustment in Austria is described briefly in Grunwald (1982b:144) and Katzenstein (1984:38). For the role of producer group, commission, and party experts—so-called political technocrats—in Austrian politics, see Nowotny (1984:123–24) and Katzenstein (1984); see also Andrlik (1983).

88. For discussion of the outlook of Austrian state business managers, including

The state bureaucracy is now becoming more influential—especially as regards the operation of the nationalized industries—and as a result the blend of social welfare may change somewhat. Illustrative of this development is the new practice of ostensibly suspending Proporz in appointing managers for the nationalized industries. This practice, if fully implemented, will increase the relative power of state managers and administrators over the operation of the state business sector. Elections will have even less effect on the operation of the nationalized industries; state managers will be more than ever accountable to ministers and to the central executive rather than to party officials. In turn, the state business sector may place somewhat greater emphasis on the realization of collective and intergenerational consumption gains and less on job creation and preservation.[89]

It remains to be seen whether the Proporz system will be ended and other institutional changes will occur. At this point, what is important is the fact that for much of the postwar era, the Austrian state bureaucracy has supported the terms of the political compromise. Administrators and public enterprise managers generally have not sought to forge any coalitions with groups that oppose the social partnership or that seek to change the partners' policies. Nor have administrators and state managers attempted to subvert these policies. Rather, they have promoted productive efficiency and job security in a way consistent with the content and the long-term orientation of public policy making. Hence Austria's centralist administrative tradition is a factor that, on balance, contributed to the realization of the welfare outcomes described above.

Austria's economic performance is also, in part, an outgrowth of the fact that its local private enterprises are comparatively immobile. Austrian private business is markedly national in its orientation. In comparison to its counterpart in countries such as Switzerland, Austrian private enterprise is inward-looking and illiberal. Austria's privately owned firms are simply less willing and able than other national business groups to relocate to foreign locations in search of

their "team spirit" and their willingness to promote a blend of intragenerational and intergenerational equity, see Grunwald (1977:21) and Lacina (1977, 1983). Nowotny reports that finance is the most influential of the Austrian ministries (1984:118). However, neither he nor other authors claim that Treasury officials are as influential as the social partners in determining the course of economic policy or the policies of nationalized industries. In this respect, the Austrian experience differs from the British.

89. Various other proposals would alter the structure of the institutions through which state managers are held accountable for their public business decisions. For instance, the FPOe has proposed that the director of the OeIAG be chosen every five years by popular election. See the statements of the political parties in *Gemeinwirtschaft und Politik* 1983.

more lucrative business conditions. In addition, Austrian private business is politically weaker than Austrian labor. The former's associations are not as centrally organized, and its political ally, the OeVP, is not as homogenous as its labor counterpart. The OeVP is even composed partly of labor groups that for years included a concern for job security in the party's programs.[90]

On the other hand, *foreign* private enterprises are willing and able to relocate in search of better business conditions, and they have come to control an increasingly large share of economic activity within Austria. In turn, public authorities have found themselves competing with other governments for direct foreign investments (that is, for the revenue and jobs those investments produce). And as predicted in Chapter 3, as this competition has become fiercer, authorities have found fiscal incentives increasingly ineffective in promoting employment and economic security. A comparatively low degree of *native private* capital mobility thus contributed to Austria's original success in achieving a relatively high degree of job security, because this condition gave public authorities greater power to influence the decisions of privately owned firms. But over time this power waned as the private enterprise part of the Austrian economy became more heavily populated by highly mobile foreign firms. Governments now have less ability to influence the location and other decisions of private enterprise, and they are much less able to achieve their welfare objectives in the foreign enterprise segment of the economy.[91]

Turning to the third structural factor—citizen support for and conception of public ownership rights—there clearly is popular support for nationalization in Austria. Opinion polls have shown that a majority of Austrians citizen support the concept of state enterprise (see Table 7). Until recently a majority also approved of the performance of nationalized industry managers. The economic crises of the 1970s heightened popular concern about unemployment and, as we

90. The distinctive character of Austrian private business is described in Katzenstein (1984, 1985). See also Bowler (1986) and the *Wall Street Journal,* May 20, 1987, p. 28. Katzenstein discusses the relative political weakness of local private business within Austria (1984:63); see also Chaloupek (1985).

91. Efforts to recruit foreign private enterprises to Austria are described in Katzenstein (1984: chap. 2); see also recent issues of *Austrian Information.* Andrlik (1985) reports the generous terms under which the quasi-nationalized enterprise Semperit AG was sold to the German (State) Continental Rubber Works in return for a promise to maintain employment levels in certain locations for at least ten years. Haschek (1982:194–95) describes the difficulties of Austrian authorities in using fiscal incentives to encourage foreign firms to locate in particular regions. He also reviews several studies that conclude that the net benefits from foreign private enterprise are less than the net costs.

Table 7. Support for the concept of state enterprise in Austria, 1964, 1979, and 1983 (percentages)

	1964				1979				1983			
	Advantageous	Disadvantageous	No Difference	Don't Know	Advantageous	Disadvantageous	No Difference	Don't Know	Advantageous	Disadvantageous	No Difference	Don't Know
Total sample	53	17	16	14	52	17	19	12	49	23	19	9
Men					54	22	17	7	51	24	18	7
Women					50	12	22	17	48	21	21	10
By party affiliation												
FPOe	37	32	21	10	34	24	32	11	41	29	27	2
KPOe	86	2	11	1	62	21	14	3	56	6	22	17
OeVP	20	43	19	18	20	33	32	14	21	41	28	11
SPOe	81	5	6	8	76	5	10	9	70	11	12	8
Nonaligned	33	15	29	23	41	20	22	17	41	25	24	10
By occupation												
Semiskilled					54	12	24	10	42	14	33	11
Skilled					64	14	16	7	61	19	13	8
Junior white-collar					58	21	19	3	52	31	11	6
White-collar (salaried)					58	15	18	8	49	25	18	8
Official									58	22	15	6
Retired					53	12	19	16	53	15	23	9
Housewife					54	11	18	18	54	14	22	9
Independently employed					30	42	21	7	27	51	17	6
Farmer					24	26	28	22	33	36	31	12
Other					43	14	22	21	43	28	16	11

Notes: Due to rounding, entries for given years do not sum to 100 percent. The specific question is: "Do you think that on economic grounds it is advantageous or disadvantageous that we have a state industry in Austria?" The sample sizes are 1,635, 1,993, and 2,245 for 1964, 1979, and 1983, respectively.

Source: Sozialwissenschaftliche Studiengesellschaft, used by permission of the director.

have seen, the nationalized industries played a major role in achieving comparatively high levels and more seemingly equitable distributions of employment. So there is some reason to believe that citizens see nationalization as a superior means of serving a social objective more important than fiscal policy alone. Indeed, a large share of citizens support financial aid to the nationalized industries on the grounds that it is a means to maintain jobs. This popular support for nationalization and the welfare outcomes it produces was also reflected, in the 1970s and early 1980s, in party consensus over the need to provide financial assistance to nationalized firms.[92]

While citizens do not express significantly less support for the concept of nationalization over the last decade, they have become less satisfied with the operation and performance of the nationalized industries during this period. By 1983, for instance, a majority of Austrian citizens gave state managers poor marks for the way they operate public firms. Also, large numbers of citizens support the plan to privatize parts or all of some state holdings. This growing dissensus about the operation and performance of the nationalized industries follows certain regional and occupational lines—lines that correspond to the constituency bases of the major political parties (see Tables 8 and 9).[93]

The dissensus about the operation and performance of the nationalized industries surfaced in disagreements within and between producer groups and parties about how best to restructure or reform the state business sector. The financial problems of some publicly owned firms caused disputes between worker councils and their constituen-

92. Other polls reveal that unemployment is considered by far the most important economic problem facing the country. In April 1984, for example, more than 60 percent of those polled named unemployment as the most serious problem and only 10 percent identified inflation as the second most serious problem (*Journal für Sozialforschung* 24, 1984, pp. 480–81). Also, a large number of citizens responded to the question of whether financial help should be given to nationalized industries by agreeing to the statement, "To guarantee jobs, help should be given in any case." These facts indicate that some substantial number of citizens appreciate the role of nationalized industries in promoting employment security.

93. A detailed description of how and why the financial problems of nationalized industries affect groups of workers and communities in different ways—and an analysis of the larger political implications of these effects—are in Andrlik (1983, 1984, 1985). More recent polls indicate that "ideologically speaking," 52 percent of the Austrian citizenry support privatization, 37 percent oppose it. Citizens are split with regard to the effects of privatization on such things as consumer service, but most agree that privatization will mean a loss of jobs (*Rundschau* 2, 1987, pp. 249–56). At the same time, 52 percent still say the nationalized industries should perform functions other than simply maximize profits, and of these respondents 83 percent and 65 percent say that other functions include promoting job security and small business, respectively (poll of 1,983 persons, January 1986, reported in Sozialwissenschaftliche Studiengesellschaft, internal report).

Table 8. Public evaluations of the management of Austrian state industries, 1979 and 1983 (percentages)

	1979				1983			
	Very Good, Good	Not Especially Good	Bad, Very Bad	No Opinion	Very Good, Good	Not Especially Good	Bad, Very Bad	No Opinion
Total sample	45	25	11	19	28	36	25	10
Men	45	28	14	12	28	36	29	6
Women	44	22	8	26	28	35	22	15
By party affiliation								
FPOe	22	27	28	22	24	34	36	5
KPOe	52	34	10	3	29	22	28	11
OeVP	21	35	21	23	12	39	40	10
SPOe	67	17	3	13	44	33	12	10
Nonaligned	30	29	14	28	16	38	33	12
By occupation								
Semiskilled	46	12	8	33	35	26	23	15
Skilled	57	22	10	12	34	38	23	5
Junior white-collar	47	34	11	7	23	37	37	4
White-collar	45	28	10	16	29	38	24	8
Official					31	38	26	5
Retired	52	19	6	24	34	34	19	13
Housewife	47	19	10	24	33	35	19	14
Independently employed	25	35	28	11	14	35	49	3
Farmer	27	32	17	23	15	31	37	16
Other	35	28	12	26	12	37	33	17
By region (state)								
Vienna	45	24	10	21	23	39	30	8
Burgenland	44	21	11	23	25	31	34	9
Upper Austria	44	28	12	16	34	35	17	14
Eastern Austria	44	26	14	15	31	41	21	8
Salzburg	42	25	12	21	32	29	31	9
Tirol	32	35	12	21	19	38	31	12
Vorarlberg	38	23	12	27	42	32	21	7
Steiermark	52	23	8	17	26	32	28	14
Kaernten	41	23	18	18	30	38	24	9

Notes: Rows may not add to 100 percent due to rounding. The specific question is: "What is your opinion about the management of the state industries in Austria?" The sample sizes are 1,993 and 2,245 for 1979 and 1983, respectively.

Source: Sozialwissenschaftliche Studiengesellschaft, reprinted by permission of the director.

Table 9. Public support for financial aid to Austrian state industries, Autumn 1983 (percentages)

	Unqualified Opposition	Qualified Support (Closure and financial self-sufficiency)	Qualified Support (Aid to private enterprise)	Unqualified Support (To guarantee jobs, help in any case)	Don't Know
Total Sample	12	33	27	37	6
Men	14	33	28	38	3
Women	11	33	26	36	9
By party affiliation					
FPOe	18	33	27	35	4
KPOe	12	23	15	42	19
OeVP	21	35	39	15	6
SPOe	5	31	18	55	5
Nonaligned	14	35	30	29	8
By occupation					
Semiskilled	12	17	31	51	6
Skilled	11	24	24	48	6
Junior white-collar	8	48	24	35	2
White-collar	9	37	29	36	4
Official	13	43	27	38	2
Retired	12	30	21	45	8
Housewife	8	34	23	38	11
Independently employed	23	32	43	18	3
Farmer	33	23	28	24	6
Other	12	37	30	30	9
By region (state)					
Vienna	12	41	28	34	5
Burgenland	16	36	27	38	4
Upper Austria	15	33	28	33	7
Eastern Austria	8	31	26	45	4
Salzburg	18	27	30	35	7
Tirol	13	33	21	35	11
Vorarlberg	16	32	33	33	6
Steiermark	10	27	27	42	6
Kaernten	13	31	22	39	6

Notes: Rows do not add to 100 percent because respondents were allowed to give two answers if they wished. The specific question was: "In order for the state industries to be 'stabilized' it is necessary for the national government to give them one billion schillings. What is your opinion about that?" Responses are classified as follows: "I completely reject that" (Unqualified Opposition); "Such help should be given only if the businesses which continually lose money are being closed and the remaining industries will be able to run without losses" (Qualified Support—closure and self-sufficiency); "The State Industries should be given money only if private enterprises are given the same amount of money" (Qualified Support—aid to private enterprise); and "To guarantee jobs, help should be given in any case" (Unqualified Support).

Source: Sozialwissenschaftliche Studiengesellschaft, reprinted by permission of the director.

cies as well as between unions and their Trade Union Federation officials over when and if certain plants should be closed and, if so, what assistance should be given to displaced workers. The parties have taken different stands about current and future policies toward the nationalized industries. In 1983, for example, the conservative People's party for the first time voted against financial aid to the Oe-IAG, and in the summer of 1985 it announced a privatization program. In December 1985 Social Democratic chancellor Sinowatz faced a vote of no confidence on the bill that provided additional financial support to the Voest-Alpine steel combine.[94]

This growing dissensus about the operation and performance of the nationalized industries reflects concerns about how best to hold state managers accountable for their business decisions or, more generally, about how citizens can best exercise their collective-ownership rights. According to the Austrian constitution these rights were to be exercised by government ministers, and in the 1950s both managers and labor leaders opposed efforts to create People's Shares in publicly owned firms. So for most of the postwar period citizens have had to rely on the political process—the combination of corporatist and electoral channels of interest articulation and aggregation—to evaluate state business managers. It is not clear how they have done so. Elections within labor organizations generally do not deal with larger issues but rather deal with firm- and community-specific issues. Workers show a willingness to participate in these elections. But their counterparts in the private enterprise sector tend to do the same, in part because Austrian law provides them with roughly the same amount of control over the operation of their firms. For these reasons, it is difficult to discern greater collective-ownership efficacy among state enterprise workers or to conclude that this efficacy is more fully developed than it is for workers in the private enterprise sector.[95]

There is some evidence of collective-ownership efficacy in Austria. The political negotiations over how the nationalized industries should respond to the crises of the 1970s reveal that citizens have some understanding of how to execute collective-ownership rights and that

94. The interest group politics surrounding closure and employment decisions of Austrian public, quasi-public, and some private firms are described and analyzed in Andrlik (1983, 1984, 1985). The OeVP's privatization proposal was by international standards quite modest. It provided for a slow process, one in which the government retains a majority holding in most firms. Also, as Platzer (1986:286) points out, even where the OeVP controls local government, it did not act quickly to implement its program.

95. On voting in union elections in Austria and how this voting creates islands of power within the country's neocorporatist political system, see Andrlik (1983: chap. 6).

they value these rights. In this period, interest groups mobilized in the communities where nationalized firms faced the prospect of closure or layoffs. These groups played an important role in collective decisions on the operation and hence the performance of public enterprises. Wage earners in the public enterprise sector and their labor and party representatives became deeply involved in deciding the fate of state-owned plants. These groups relied on *direct* negotiations and also on the threat of electoral retribution to persuade incumbent, national officials to delay layoffs and to increase investments in particular companies. In addition, Austrian political parties have developed plans for restructuring the nationalized industries in ways that expressly seek to improve the channels through which state managers are held accountable for their decisions, for example, to have the director of the state holding company stand for popular election every five years.[96]

Finally, throughout its history the institution of *Proporz*, to the extent it is widely understood and supported in Austria, translated citizen preferences directly into supervisory decisions that took into account concerns for achieving both growth and full employment. There is thus some reason to believe that wage earners in particular and citizens in general have some conception of collective-ownership rights and that they rely on a combination of corporatist and electoral institutions to exercise those rights in a way that reveals their preferred blend of collective gain and distributional equity. Seen in this light, the recent changes in the organization and performance of nationalized industries seem to indicate popular disagreement more about the ends to which nationalization should be put than about whether public authorities should exploit the power the nationalized industries give them to shape welfare outcomes.[97]

We need to determine about the Austrian experience whether state enterprise workers display a greater degree of collective-ownership

96. The 1983 issue of *Gemeinwirtschaft und Politik* contains statements by Austria's political parties concerning the scope and operation of state-owned industries. At the time all three major parties, the SPOe, OeVP, and FPOe, supported the principle of state-owned enterprise. They differed over imparting a longer-term orientation and, by implication, emphasizing Pareto gains in consumption and intergenerational equity in state business decision making (see especially the statement of the OeVP). Members of the Austrian Social Democratic party stressed that differences between parties and producer groups have to do more with the question of what blend of efficiency (Pareto gains) and (intragenerational) equity state enterprise should pursue than with whether the state should participate in markets. See Grunwald (1977) and Van der Bellen (1981).

97. Interestingly, a January 1986 poll of 1,983 Austrians revealed that 51 percent of respondents did not believe in doing away with partisan influence on the Board of the OeIAG. The more educated respondents were, the more likely they were to take this position. (Sozialwissenschaftliche Studiengesellschaft, internal report.)

efficacy than their counterparts in private firms. We also need to determine whether the difference in the way they value collective-ownership rights accounts for the greater employment security that state enterprise wage earners enjoy. In addition, we need to know whether elections regularly produce significant changes in the operations of nationalized industries and, if so, what the welfare implications of these changes are.[98] Only then will we be able to predict accurately the course and welfare consequences of current political developments involving the nationalized industries in Austria.

In sum, Austria's exemplary performance in terms of productive efficiency and employment security can be attributed to the way in which its corporatist politics combined with the workings of its mixed economy. Corporatism, and the consensus on which it was based, enhanced public authorities' ability to identify and implement policies that promoted growth and employment security. The large state business sector contributed to this welfare outcome insofar as the provision of autonomy to state managers coupled with a centralist administrative tradition allowed nationalized industries to promote growth in the private sector and to achieve productivity gains on their own. At the same time, because of a large state business sector, the state was less constrained in its efforts to promote full employment than if Austria had had a private enterprise economy. A relatively equitable distribution of *nonmaterial* wealth between private asset holders and wage earners—at least for the 1970s and early 1980s—

98. The problem of discerning differences in the collective-ownership efficacy of private enterprise and state enterprise workers is complicated further by the existence of splits between unions—splits that cut across the mixed structure of the economy. Because of the provision for codetermination in most firms and the relative immobility of local private enterprise, the size of firms and concentration of production may be more important determinants of workers' willingness to mobilize on behalf of their economic interests than whether the firm is publicly or privately owned. See Andrlik's (1985) account of political negotiations. There is much confusion about the impact of popular elections on the operation of nationalized industries. Taus (1983), the president of Austria's largest private company, and others suggest that the managers of public firms do not seem to be held accountable for their decisions, at least not in a manner comparable to private managers. Van der Bellen (1981) argues that Proporz minimizes the influence of politicians on the operation of nationalized industries. Interviews with SPOe officials and with the director of the OeIAG indicate that although elections may have had some effects on the pricing and investment decisions of public firms before the state holding company was formed, there are few such effects now. The major impact of elections is on employment policies, especially the timing of layoffs, reemployment assignment, and closure (see also Lacina 1983; Andrlik 1983:306–7, 360). The public statements of the FPOe—in particular, the rationale the party gives for adopting its proposals to reform the nationalized industries—and accounts of the *Economist* (November 30, 1985, p. 74) suggest that the effects of elections are much more regular and significant. Again, my statistical analysis (Freeman 1988) revealed little evidence that the 1983 election affected the employment policies of Austrian public and private enterprises.

has been achieved along with gains in collective and intergenerational consumption because a large number of investment decisions have been in public hands, and because labor has had the power to forge and enforce a compromise that produced this welfare outcome.[99] The fact that Austria does not have a particularly equitable distribution of *material* wealth therefore is a result more of the "growth consciousness" of its labor movement than of any structural constraint inherent in the nature of its economy or polity.

So much consensus about the concept of nationalization and labor's relative power suggest that in the near future politics—whether through producer group negotiation or through party competition— will revolve more around the relative emphasis on collective gains versus an equitable distribution of nonmaterial wealth than, as in Britain, about public authorities (and hence labor's) capacity to shape social welfare. In another important contrast, most Austrian nationalized industries are intact and still organized in the form of holding companies. Only a few Austrian publicly owned firms have been or will be privatized. Nor are publicly owned firms concentrated in declining sectors, like many of the remaining British nationalized industries. Austrian citizens, as public shareholders, are in a less risky, more diversified position than their counterparts in Britain. More broadly, they retain a greater capacity than British citizens to shape the intragenerational distribution of wealth.[100]

99. Foreign workers do not necessarily share in this security.

100. The increasingly undiversified nature of the British public's share holdings is evident in the *Economist*, December 21, 1985, p. 72.

Chapter Eight

The Italian and Swedish Experiences

ITALY

Italy's political economy is of the pluralist–mixed variety.[1] We expect Italy's performance on the first welfare criterion to be inferior to that of the other three countries. We expect greater intragenerational equity in Italy than in Britain, somewhat less in Italy than in Sweden, and markedly less in Italy than in Austria (see Figure 5). We also expect that, all things being equal, it is in Italy that political competition—especially elections—will have the greatest impact on welfare outcomes. That expectation grows stronger the more dissensus and political instability there is in Italy over the ends of government market participation. To the extent that Italian citizens lack a well-developed sense of collective-ownership efficacy and public enterprise managers are not encouraged to promote productive efficiency, the financial performance of state-owned enterprise should be comparatively poor. And state-owned enterprise should make a comparatively small contribution to collective consumption and to intergenerational equity.

The analysis in Chapter 6 only partly confirms these expectations. Austria outperforms Italy in increases in real per capita GDP both in 1960–1983 and in 1974–1983.[2] On this same indicator, however, Italy

1. That Italy's political system is pluralist is clear from comparative analyses such as Schmitter (1981); see also von Beyme (1983). Evidence of the highly mixed nature of Italy's economy is given in Chapter 1 above. Stefani (1986) stresses that in Italy privatization has meant an effort to improve the efficiency of public enterprise. It has also involved the sale of minority positions in the subsidiaries of state holding companies—sales designed to improve the financial condition of those companies.

2. More recent data on Italy's comparatively high rate of growth can be found in Italy Survey, *Economist*, February 27, 1988, p. 9.

outperforms both Sweden and Britain. Italy also ranks higher than Britain in its composite score on several indicators of collective welfare (see Figures 9, 10, and 11). Apparently there is less intragenerational equity in Italy than in Sweden; Italy has a higher unemployment rate than Sweden, for example.[3] But there also appears to be less intragenerational equity in Italy than in Britain, even though, according to the analysis in Chapter 5, there is greater potential for intragenerational redistribution of wealth in Italy than in Britain.

Italy's performance on the first welfare criterion can be traced in part to the relative vitality of its private enterprise sector, and also to the way its governments have intervened and participated in markets.[4] Italy's capital market is comparatively small and underdeveloped. Its private enterprise sector is composed of several large local business groups, a large number of small- and medium-sized firms, and a growing number of foreign firms. These privately owned enterprises are among the least regulated in the industrialized world. Like their counterparts in Austria, they have been efficient producers, especially over the 1980s, partly because the same individuals own and manage many of them—a close link between ownership and control in Italy compensates for the absence of a well-developed capital market. In addition, private entrepreneurs have in recent years cut capital and labor costs. For their part, governments have promoted private investment through a wide range of fiscal mechanisms. Public authorities' efforts to achieve price stability also appear to have encouraged private entrepreneurship.[5]

Italian public enterprises have received some of the credit for the country's economic development. In the 1950s state-owned enterprises undertook large, relatively productive investments in basic industries. They supplied low-cost inputs to private firms, and they helped stabilize the Italian economy. These investments and other policies of the public enterprises contributed to the overall efficiency of the economy and hence helped realize collective consumption

3. See ibid., p. 16.
4. There is some debate about the way the Italians adjust their GDP measures for black market activity. See the *Economist*, August 8, 1987, p. 14.
5. The relatively small, underdeveloped Italian capital market is described in the *Economist*, June 1, 1985, p. 66; September 14, 1985, p. S13; December 21, 1985, p. 77; and February 27, 1988, p. S15. Family ownership is stressed in the same source's articles on Italian businesses, for instance, on Montedison (October 18, 1986, pp. 69–70). Most students of Italian political economy recognize the important difference in the performance of small and medium versus large-scale private enterprise; see, for instance, Faini and Schiantarelli (1983). The *Economist's* Italy Survey describes the private sector productivity gains of the last decade (September 14, 1985, p. 54); see also ibid., August 8, 1987, pp. 14–15. Tumlir (1982:205–6) sees a parallel in the productive efficiency of small- and medium-scale private business in Italy and in Austria.

gains. As governments increasingly relied on the Italian state-owned enterprises for price control, countercyclical investment, and regional development, however, performance, as in Britain, began to decline. Little was done in the 1970s to arrest this decline. As a result, Italian state-owned enterprises were among the least financially self-sufficient in the industrialized world. They consistently made huge losses; they required large subsidies from an increasingly deficit-ridden federal budget to carry out their investment programs and to maintain their employment levels. In the 1980s, however, the financial performance of the state holdings has improved, in part because of the sale of minority positions in some of their subsidiaries.[6]

In spite of the financial condition of the public enterprise sector, the Italian economy as a whole performed relatively well in terms of growth and productivity in the 1960s and 1970s. Either the vitality of local private and foreign private investment compensated for the declining financial performance of public enterprise, or the relative efficiency of private enterprise was an outgrowth of the difficulties of Italian state business—that is, Italy's growth and productivity are, in some part, the result of private enterprise's having benefited from the factors that caused the financial problems of the public enterprises.

Italy's intragenerational distribution of wealth is comparatively inequitable. The shares of wealth that accrue to lower income groups in Italy are relatively small. The share of wages in national income is low as well. At the same time the Italian unemployment rate is by Western standards consistently high. There are stark disparities in the wealth of the citizens in the northern and southern halves of the country: since World War II, per capita income has been about 33 percent lower in the south than in the north. Unemployment rates have been three to four times higher in the south than in the north, and a high proportion of youth have been unemployed in the south.

6. The role of public enterprise in promoting growth and economic development in the 1950s and early 1960s is described in Posner and Woolf (1967); see also Holland (1972). Faini and Schiantarelli (1983:99) stress that in the 1950s and 1960s managers of public enterprises enjoyed a relatively high degree of autonomy and displayed genuine concerns for productive efficiency. They argue that public enterprise promoted the investment boom of the early 1970s and the growth that that boom produced. Fausto (1982) reviews the role public enterprise played in helping stabilize the Italian economy in 1968–1979; Italian public enterprise continues to play an active role in government efforts to control prices (*Economist*, September 14, 1985, p. 24). Fausto (1982) and Martinelli (1981) chart the effects of these and other policies on public enterprises' financial performance. The efforts made by Italian authorities to improve the financial performance of the state business sector are described by Stefani (1981). The enormous losses of Italian state industry in the 1970s are described in the *Economist* and in Monsen and Walters (1983). Recent improvements in financial performance are described in the *Economist*'s Italy Survey, February 27, 1988.

Government fiscal and employment policies have been aimed, to some extent, at redressing this and other forms of maldistribution. But the relative stability of income shares, unemployment levels, and regional disparities suggests that government efforts to promote intragenerational equity have been neither extensive nor effective.[7]

Public enterprises have played a role in efforts to redress regional inequities. State-owned firms have made large investments in the south, for instance, building new steel and chemical plants there. Much debate surrounds the motivation for and wisdom of government regional policies in general and about the welfare consequences of public investments in particular. Critics charge that the location decisions of Italian state-owned enterprises have undermined those firms' efficiency because, among other things, they have dispersed the production facilities of publicly owned firms and greatly complicated the organizational tasks that public managers face. Some critics even argue that the manner in which state-owned enterprises have promoted development in the south has actually reinforced regional inequities; for example, that publicly owned firms in the south, by providing low-cost industrial inputs to northern firms, have fueled growth and employment in the north while at the same time spawning few new business ventures and few new jobs in the south. Most observers agree that it has been much easier for governments to convince public enterprises as opposed to private enterprises to move their operations south. That is, the fact that many large industrial concerns are publicly owned in Italy is recognized as having greatly facilitated government efforts to locate new investments in the south. That public ownership facilitates government efforts to shape the location of investment is consistent with our theoretical expectations.[8]

7. Recent unemployment data are reported in the *Economist*'s Italy Survey, February 27, 1988, p. 16. For a brief summary of regional inequities see Wade (1979, 1982). Wade describes the fiscal and employment policies used to try to improve the distribution of wealth between the north and south. More general support for employment includes the Cassa Integrazione Guadagni (CIG), which has guaranteed as much as 93 percent of the salaries of industrial, construction, and agricultural workers who are made partially or wholly redundant. Regini and Esping-Andersen (1980:117–19) argue that the CIG has been a major impediment to labor mobility in Italy.

8. The role of public enterprise in promoting southern development is described by Faini and Schiantarelli (1983); see also Holland (1972). Wade (1982) argues that state-owned enterprises' investments in particular, and government regional policies in general, have served to perpetuate inequities in the welfare of citizens in north and south. Political authorities' efforts to channel investment to the south were greatly facilitated by Italy's mixed economy (see Wade 1982:121–22); also Faini and Schiantarelli (1983). Especially noteworthy is the fact that southern workers in Turin repeatedly struck Fiat to get that private firm to locate in the south, whereas politicians consistently thwarted public managers' efforts to place new steel and chemical plants in the north (see Wade 1979:207 and Wade 1982). More general efforts to use public enterprise to subsidize

What remains unclear is why, in spite of authorities' greater ability to influence a substantial share of investment decisions in the economy, overall wealth is so maldistributed.

The pluralist nature of its polity has much to do with why Italy performs as it does on both welfare criteria. The weak, fragmented character of Italy's labor movement rules out the kind of continuous political bargaining that occurs in Austria. Rather than participate in such bargaining, Italian workers tend to press their demands for higher wages and for job security through local collective bargaining and through strikes.[9] This orientation does not allow them to use the state business sector to promote the interests of wage earners as their counterparts in Austria do. Italian business and the state have no institutionalized form of cooperation. The major Italian employers' association, the Confindustria, helped enact a weak incomes policy in the mid-1970s, in the form of a wage indexation scheme. But beyond this measure, business has not actively cooperated with government as it does in corporatist systems. In this respect, business-government relations in Italy resemble those in Britain. Finally, few serious attempts at government planning have been launched by the Italian state. Public administrators have imparted no long-term orientation to government decision making in the same way or to the same extent as administrators in other countries.[10]

Partisan politics has important effects on the workings and welfare consequences of Italy's pluralist–mixed system. Since World War II, Italy has been governed by a series of coalition governments. Southern political factions have played a pivotal role in these coalitions; to stay in power, governments have had to maintain the support of these factions. Southern factions have delivered support in return for large public investments and other forms of government aid for their constituents. This is not to say that they or other factions dictate the course of economic policy and of market participation in Italy; an agreement to use public enterprise to fight inflation and to promote

various form of consumption (e.g., transportation) are described in Fausto (1982); see also the *Economist*, August 24, 1985, p. 59.

9. The relative political weakness of Italian labor and its comparatively high propensity to strike are clear from Korpi (1980), Schmitter (1981), and Hibbs (1978); see also Sabel (1981). Italian unions' attitudes toward social policy and their reactions to the economic crises of the 1970s are discussed in Martin and Ross (1980) and Regini and Esping-Andersen (1980). The former notes that Italian unions have been more interested in reform than in expansion of public enterprise (1980:59). The latter stresses that Italian unions have a greater distaste than their Swedish counterparts for welfarism (1980:114–15).

10. Italian unions have thwarted state holding companies' efforts to privatize subsidiaries. See Stefani's (1986) discussion of the political negotiations surrounding the SME and Maccarese farm cases.

aggregate investment was forged among several parties in the 1970s. Also, southern and other political factions have been unable to prevent state holding companies from reprivatizing and denationalizing several firms and banks in the mid 1980s. But in Italy's pluralist, multiparty polity, social power is dispersed in a way that consistently gives political factions the ability to veto substantial changes in the ownership structure in the Italian economy and to locate large public investments within their local jurisdictions. In this way, pluralist politics contributes to the increasing inefficiency of state-owned enterprise and hence to collective welfare losses, on the one hand, and to the protection of the material and nonmaterial interests of particular communities (especially in southern Italy), on the other.[11]

Structural conditions in Italy are also responsible for this welfare outcome. Italy's noncentralist administrative tradition makes state administrators unwilling or unable to challenge factional efforts to influence the investment decisions of public firms or the more general power that Italian parties wield over economic policy.[12] The underdeveloped nature of Italy's capital market, immobility of some privately owned firms, and comparatively oligopolistic character of the private enterprise sector all serve to reinforce the existing blend of social welfare. These factors heighten southerners' and others' concerns about the welfare implications of privatization. Political factions realize that privatization will limit their ability to influence investment decisions and hence shape welfare outcomes in Italy. But they also fear that privatization will enhance the power of particular business groups rather than that of a more dispersed group of asset holders. Differ-

11. For a detailed account of the way in which the pivotal position of certain southern political factions allows them to secure public investment within their political jurisdictions, see Wade (1982). More generally, see Mazzolini (1978:50–51). Grassini (1981) describes the political patronage system within the Italian state holding companies. Martinelli (1981:93–96) reports that Christian Democratic governments provided lucrative tax breaks and subsidies to private business in order to mollify their opposition to public enterprise. This report is consistent with the statements private entrepreneur Carlos de Benedetti made about the Italian political system: "The system has to give something to everybody involved to keep in power" (quoted in the *Economist,* September 14, 1985, p. S4).

12. Salvati (1981) shows how Italy's noncentralist administrative tradition produces different economic policies than France's centralist administrative tradition. Again, Wade (1982) reports episodes in which the Italian state and its allies were unable to prevent politicians from locating public investments in the south despite significantly higher financial costs. Salutary evaluations of the behavior of Italian state enterprise managers can be found in Holland (1972, 1974). Despicht (1972) goes so far as to argue that these managers operate publicly owned firms according to a Catholic social philosophy; see also Martinelli (1981:94). A more critical evaluation of Italian state managers—one that argues they have usurped their authority and harmed the public interest—is in Cavalieri (1977:447).

ences in the character of capital markets and in the structure of private enterprise sectors thus produce somewhat different evaluations of and propensities for supporting privatization in Italy than in Britain.[13]

Citizens' attitudes toward and conception of public ownership shape welfare outcomes in Italy. The widespread perception that public enterprise serves the collective, national interest by enhancing native control over investment decisions and over the economy in general provides additional barriers to privatization. Dissensus about the legitimacy of the equity claims of political factions prevents parties from using public enterprise to radically alter the intragenerational distribution of wealth. And the appreciation for the potential selective gains from public investment and the high degree of collective ownership efficacy of citizens of various political communities encourage repeated pressure on political representatives to exploit their pivotal position in Italian coalition governments in a way that undermines the efficiency of public enterprise and serves particularistic interests. The absence of any consensus-generating, corporatist institutions to oppose this kind of factional behavior—institutions like those in Austria, for example—means that party politics and public enterprise consistently produce the selective benefits that these political factions seek (apparently at the expense of collective welfare).[14]

The anomalies in Italy's performance thus can be attributed to the distinctive features of its pluralist–mixed political economy, especially to the character of its private enterprise sector and to the relative balance of political power within its pluralist political system. The vitality of the Italian private sector has produced unexpected collective gains in social welfare at the same time that, to some extent, it has offset the greater capacity for redistribution that the large state business sector affords public authorities. Those authorities—especially elected officials—have not made a collective effort to use the state

13. That is, the threat of oligopolistic control over investment decisions and of a further concentration of wealth among upper income groups is clearer in Italy because large family business groups exist within the private sector and Italy's capital market is quite small and underdeveloped. In Britain, in contrast, privatization of nationalized industry is ostensibly less of a threat to the welfare of middle and lower income groups because a more fully developed capital market can absorb the new shares and a somewhat less concentrated private enterprise sector poses less risk of oligopoly. See the *Economist*, Italy Survey, February 27, 1988, esp. p. 31.

14. The perception that Italian state-owned enterprise serves the national interest is discussed by Mazzolini (1978:20); see also Holland (1972:31–33) and Prodi (1974:52). The tendency of southern citizens to see voting and political influence as instruments for enhancing their personal wealth is stressed by Wade (1979:210). As links between parties and unions are more tenuous in Italy than in Austria and in Sweden (see Martin and Ross 1980), Italian wage earners may execute collective-ownership rights primarily through the electoral process.

business sector to provide wage earners as a whole with a greater share of material or nonmaterial wealth. Nor has labor used state-owned enterprise for this purpose. Rather, political factions have repeatedly struck bargains that use state-owned enterprise to enhance their particular interests. This outcome occurs, in part, because of the pivotal power these political factions consistently wield within coalition governments. In this sense, what distinguishes welfare implications from those of the state business sector in Austria is more the fact that the Italian state business sector has been politicized *in a pluralist fashion* than the fact that it has been politicized. In Austria, *Proporz* and other political institutions politicize the operation of public enterprise, but in a way that imparts a longer-term collective orientation to public investment decisions. The corporatist political framework in Austria, coupled with somewhat deeper consensus about the legitimacy of the demands of regional interests and a shared commitment to the pursuit of collective welfare gains and intergenerational equity, has discouraged the political factionalism that occurs in Italy and the welfare outcomes that factionalism produced.

Differences in the outcomes of political competition appear to explain the differences between welfare outcomes in Britain and in Italy. There is dissensus in both countries about the ends and means of government intervention and government market participation. Political competition has produced numerous coalition governments in Italy. But this competition has not altered the balance of power between the Italian political parties; the relative power of parties and party factions *within* coalitions has remained relatively stable. As a result, the structure of ownership rights and the course of economic policies have been more predictable in Italy than in Britain. In turn, the Italian polity has created greater confidence about expected future returns from private investment, and Italian private enterprise has undertaken more productive investment than British private enterprise. Admittedly, the closer link between private ownership and control in Italy has also contributed to its superior economic performance: the comparative dynamism of its structurally distinctive private enterprise sector undoubtedly helps Italy achieve greater gains in collective consumption at the same time that it makes it more difficult for public authorities to transfer wealth to wage earners. Only wage earners whose representatives are consistently pivotal in Italy's coalition government can use public enterprise to serve their particular interests.[15]

15. Italy and Britain both display a relatively high degree of societal unruliness and political instability (see Schmitter 1981:304–9). In Italy, however, this characteristic has not undermined the vitality of private entrepreneurship as it has in Britain. Private investors appear more certain than their counterparts in Britain about earning a pos-

SWEDEN

Throughout much of the postwar era Sweden has had a corporatist–private enterprise political economy.[16] We therefore expect Sweden in this period to outperform Austria, Britain, and Italy in collective welfare gains and intergenerational equity. We expect Sweden to achieve a degree of intragenerational equity superior to what exists in Britain and Italy. We expect somewhat less intragenerational equity in Sweden than in Austria (see Figure 5). We expect elections to have some impact on welfare outcomes in Sweden but not as much as in Italy or in Austria (because a greater share of investment decisions is in public hands in Italy and Austria). In Sweden, elections may produce minor alterations in the terms of the corporatist bargain, for example, in the distribution of wealth among wage earners. But elections should not undermine the otherwise long-term orientation of governments, affect the private sector's willingness to invest, or allow political factions to secure a disproportionate share of the power within or between parties and producer groups. In other words, we expect postwar elections to have had no major impact on the overall blend of social welfare in Sweden.

The data in Chapter 6 generally support these expectations. They indicate that in the 1960s and 1970s Sweden outperformed Britain on various measures of collective welfare gain and intergenerational equity. However, Sweden's performance was inferior to that of Italy and Austria on some of these same measures, among them per capita GDP growth. Intragenerational equity appears much higher in Sweden than in Italy, Britain, or even Austria: for instance, income is more equitably distributed in Sweden than in the other three countries (Figures 7 and 8).[17]

Sweden's performance on the first welfare criterion is attributable to the comparatively concentrated nature of its private sector and perhaps also to the way in which government has sought to promote

---

itive rate of return on long-term investments. This difference appears to be in some part a consequence of Italy's pluralist, multiparty polity.

16. The corporatist nature of postwar Swedish politics is described in Heclo and Madsen (1987), von Beyme (1983), and Schmitter (1981). Katzenstein (1985) argues that Sweden's polity occupies a middle ground between the liberal corporatism of Switzerland and the social corporatism of Austria. Monsen and Walters (1983:17) report that 30 percent of Swedish investment is public in nature. However, the *Economist* (August 1, 1987, p. 65) stresses that almost 90 percent of Swedish industry is privately owned. Descriptions of Swedish state enterprise can be found in Ohlin (1974), Törnblom (1977), and Höök (1980).

17. For a recent review of Swedish economic performance see Bosworth and Lawrence (1987). These authors chart a recent decline in investment and growth in Sweden. I examine this and related developments below and in Chapter 10.

and preserve distributional equity. Sweden's capital market is not particularly large, and its economy is dominated by a relatively small
number of family-owned business groups. Although in Sweden individuals may also own and operate their firms, these enterprises are
larger and somewhat less efficient than the small- and medium-sized
firms in Italy's and Austria's private sectors. On the other hand, the
British capital market is larger and much more fully developed than
the Swedish capital market, and Sweden has consistently outperformed Britain in terms of growth and productivity. So Sweden's performance on the first welfare criterion may be less an outgrowth of
the inefficiency of its private sector than the result of exceptional
performance by Austrian and Italian private enterprise.[18]

Swedish governments have done much to promote productive efficiency and its welfare consequences. Government policies have encouraged labor mobility, especially relocation of workers to more
successful firms in the private sector. Government solidaristic wage
policies have encouraged private investment insofar as they have en-
gendered, among private business, greater certainty about future
rates of return. Wage policy until the 1980s has had a salutary affect
on inflation. For many years national wage agreements have stabilized workers' and employers' demands for higher earnings and
prices, though there is evidence that the agreements had harmful effects on youth employment.[19]

Moreover, authorities have created special investment funds to offset shortfalls in private investment during recessions, and they have
provided a wide range of fiscal incentives to the private sector to encourage modernization and technological innovation. In addition,
public investment banks have been created to fund risky ventures that
promise to enhance the competitiveness of the Swedish economy.
These efforts to promote efficiency have not been guided by any coherent, national plan. Rather, these and other forms of government
intervention have tended to be more incremental and reactive in
character.[20]

18. Korpi (1978:103) stresses that the Swedish economy is dominated by fifteen to
twenty large family business groups. He contends that the private sector has become
more concentrated over the last few decades; see also the *Economist*, August 1, 1987,
pp. 63–65. Although governments originally encouraged mergers and other forms of
concentration (Katzenstein 1985:114–15), political authorities, including segments of
the center and conservative political parties, favor deconcentration (see Korpi 1978).
Apparently, Swedish businesses have merged in recent years in an effort to insulate
themselves from takeovers by wage earner funds. See Hansen (1985).
19. See Flanagan (1987) and Holmlund (1987).
20. For a review of Swedish economic policy in this period see Heclo and Madsen
(1987: chap. 2) and Rivlin (1987). The salutary effects of governments' labor market
policies on productive efficiency and on price stability are described in Rehn (1984),

Productive efficiency has also been promoted, albeit to a much lesser extent, through public enterprise. Since the late 1960s a number of publicly owned firms have been created to encourage industrial innovation. In an attempt to promote efficiency, Swedish state-owned enterprises have been organized into a holding company that resembles those which exist in Austria and in Italy. Efforts also have been made to recognize explicitly the financial repercussions of using Swedish state-owned enterprise to pursue employment and other "noneconomic objectives." In practice, financial losses have been suffered by Swedish publicly owned firms as a consequence of their efforts to combat unemployment and industrial decline (these losses have been smaller than those suffered by publicly owned firms in Italy and other countries). Also, in the mid-1980s the Swedish government allowed several firms to go bankrupt rather than subsidize the jobs concerned. Finally, as in other countries with state business sectors, the fact that Swedish public enterprises have not earned high rates of (financial) return does not mean they have necessarily retarded the growth and productivity of the economy as a whole. Indeed, some Swedish observers argue that, on balance, the historically small Swedish state business sector has contributed to the realization of collective welfare gains.[21]

Sweden has one of the most egalitarian intragenerational distributions of wealth in the Western world. The shares of material wealth that accrue to lower income groups are higher than in most other countries. The level of nonmaterial wealth—in terms of employment security, for example—is relatively high. Wage earners' welfare is enhanced by the fact that most of them belong to several large pension

---

Katzenstein (1985), and Martin and Ross (1980). A more critical evaluation of government wage and employment policies is Flanagan (1987). The rationale behind and activities of Sweden's Investment Reserve Fund and Sweden's public investment banks are described briefly in Katzenstein (1985: chap. 2); see also Eliasson (1965) and Bowler (1986). The general lack of coherency and direction in Swedish industrial policy is stressed by Pontusson (1984) and Katzenstein (1985).

21. Pontusson (1984) points out that state-owned enterprises were originally created to encourage industrial innovation and growth but quickly became involved in government efforts to provide job security to workers in declining industries. The government let Salens, the country's largest shipbuilder, go bankrupt in 1987 (*Economist*, August 1, 1987, p. 63). Törnblom (1977) reviews the financial principles that guide the operation of Swedish publicly owned firms. He argues that Swedish public enterprise has generally had a positive impact on both employment and growth. A generally positive evaluation of the larger effects of the nationalizations of the late 1970s is also given by Rehn (1984:150). More concrete evidence of the relative efficiency of Swedish public enterprise is manifest in the foreign competitiveness of its locomotives and other products (see the *Economist*, September 7, 1985, p. 34). For a brief description of the "tender system" by which Swedish public enterprise managers and government officials explicitly recognize the costs of pursuing different kinds of objectives, see Törnblom (1977); see also Mallon (1981).

funds that regularly earn dividends in local and foreign capital markets. Thanks to solidaristic wage policy, the same segment of the population receives a relatively uniform rate of renumeration for their
labor.

This is not to say there is intragenerational equity in Sweden.
About 1 percent of households own about 75 percent of Swedish industry. The gap between the share of material wealth that accrues to
this and other top income groups and to lower income groups has
remained unchanged for much of the last forty years. Also, there are
regional inequities in the distribution of wealth in Sweden, for example, in the employment security of citizens who reside in the northern and southern parts of the country. But again, in comparison to
the situation in Britain, Italy, and most other Western countries, the
intragenerational distribution of wealth in Sweden is relatively
equitable.[22]

Governments have done much to promote intragenerational equity
in Sweden. As mentioned, their labor market policies have both diminished disparities in the incomes of wage earners and reduced the
costs workers incur in attempting to find new jobs. An extensive system of transfer payments and public assistance has also been erected,
in part in an attempt to lessen the cost of seeking alternative employment as well as to make the distribution of material wealth more equitable, at least among wage earners. When wage earners have had
difficulty finding new jobs in the private sector, Swedish governments
have hired them. In fact, in the early 1980s about 40 percent of the
workforce was employed in the public sector. Since the Swedish state
business sector is smaller than in Italy and Austria, employment security has been provided more through fiscal means than through government market participation.[23]

State-owned enterprise has been deeply involved in the effort to
preserve and create new jobs, especially in depressed regions of the

22. The shape and relatively stable nature of Sweden's intragenerational distribution
of wealth is discussed briefly in Korpi (1978:103–4); see also Korpi (1980). Korpi and
others point out a highly inegalitarian structure of property ownership in Sweden
(1978:104); see also Ruth (1984:57) and Heclo and Madsen (1987:277). The size and
activities of Swedish pension funds are described briefly in Katzenstein (1985: chap. 3).
Korpi and others contend that the terms of the corporatist bargain served to exacerbate disparities in the wealth of urban and rural regions and also to diminish the quality of working conditions in Swedish industry (1978:322).

23. The role of government labor market policies in enhancing long-run employment security is discussed in Rehn (1984); see also Katzenstein (1985: chap. 2). The
idea that various social policies compensate workers for the costs associated with the
government's labor market policies is reviewed by Regini and Esping-Andersen (1980);
see also Rehn (1984) and Katzenstein (1985). The increasing importance of public employment in Sweden is charted by Bosworth and Lawrence (1987), Flanagan (1987),
Hansen (1985), and Pontusson (1984).

country. Publicly owned firms were created to lessen the effects of the crises in basic industries on the welfare of particular groups of workers and on particular communities. Publicly owned firms have been operated, to some extent, with conscious concern to ameliorate the more general inequities that exist in the regional distribution of wealth. In the process, their financial performance suffered—not to the same extent as their counterparts in Italy, perhaps, but at least to the same extent as in Austria. The losses of the Swedish state business sector might have been larger, of course, had public enterprises been one of the principal means through which Swedish governments sought to provide employment for those who could not find work in the private sector. But again, other forms of public employment were used for this purpose.[24]

The corporatist nature of Swedish politics explains why postwar governments adopted the policies they did and hence why this blend of social welfare occurred. Corporatist politics helped forge and reinforce a political compromise that emphasized collective welfare gains more than intragenerational equity and reliance on markets and market forces to realize producer groups' welfare objectives. For several decades Swedish unions and business agreed to tolerate income inequalities and seek mutually beneficial welfare outcomes such as growth and price stability. Government promotion of labor mobility, willingness to compensate workers for taking new jobs and for adjusting to industrial change, and efforts to rationalize the rate and pattern of private investment were accepted by business for the sake of higher profits and price stability. The financial success of some privately owned firms, increased concentration within the private sector, and actual relocation of workers to new jobs (within the private sector) were accepted by unions in the interests of growth and, for a time at least, long-term employment security.[25]

The terms of the corporatist political compromise reflect the social power of Swedish producer groups. The social power that Swedish unions wielded through their strong central organization and broad membership base allowed them to secure allegiance to the terms of

24. Törnblom (1977:4) describes the general employment objectives of Swedish public enterprises, especially their commitment to preserve and create jobs in particular regions. Höök (1980) details the employment and other policies of state-owned steel firms in the north of Sweden, and how these policies were bound up with the government's more general efforts to cope with the international steel crisis of the 1970s. The *Economist* (August 1, 1987, p. 63) reports that between 1977 and 1979 the government subsidy in shipbuilding and carbon steel amounted to about $64,000 per worker.

25. For an account of the "positive-sum" nature of corporatist politics in postwar Sweden, including labor unions' willingness to tolerate income inequality, see Korpi (1978:199, 231, 324–25); see also Katzenstein's account of cooperation between labor and capital in Sweden (1985: chap. 3).

national wage bargains and other facets of the compromise. Unions also had the power to bargain for some initial redistributions of wealth, for enhanced job security in the form of retraining schemes, and for the security provided by state pensions and various forms of public compensation. Because most investment decisions remained in private hands and few legal restrictions were placed on private firms, Swedish business also wielded a great deal of social power. In essence, Swedish business set the direction of industrial change, shaping the pattern of job relocation and other aspects of industrial change.

The relative stability of the intragenerational distribution of wealth in Sweden reflects the balance of power between producer groups. Union leaders' commitment to eliminating wage rate disparities may have produced greater equality among middle and lower income groups, but union policies did little to undermine the social power that private business wielded in the 1950s and 1960s. The relative mobility and concentration of private capital—both of which were actually encouraged by the unions and their party allies in this period—limited opportunities to redistribute wealth between wage earners and private asset holders. Because private business holders were unwilling to launch new or expand existing ventures, for example, many Swedes could not find jobs in the private sector. Governments were forced to pursue their employment objectives through the creation of an ever-larger number of public jobs.[26]

Growing awareness that the material distribution of wealth was not changing and that private ownership was the source of much social power led some unions, in the 1970s, to propose a radical alteration in the terms of corporatist compromise, namely, the creation of wage earner investment funds. These funds were to be formed out of the "excess profits" of private business and would eventually give unions a much greater say about the pattern and level of investment in the Swedish economy and, in turn, about the blend of social welfare in Sweden. This development has been both a cause and a consequence of the recent demise of the national wage bargain and other facets of the corporatist compromise. It is one reason why Swedish politics has become less corporatist and more pluralist in recent years, and why

26. Korpi (1980) stresses that the power labor wielded in Sweden's corporatist system has been instrumental in its achieving a comparatively egalitarian distribution of wealth. The same author elsewhere (1978: chap. 11) points out that Swedish unions have made concerted efforts to avoid creating privileged groups of workers in particular firms and industries. The limits of labor power in Sweden—the barriers to redistribution imposed by private capital mobility—are examined in Meidner (1978), Sabel (1981), and Pontusson (1987, 1984). The problems that an increased reliance on public employment posed for national wage negotiators are discussed in Hansen (1985); see also Flanagan (1987).

Swedish politics has become more like British and Italian politics and somewhat less like Austrian politics.

For much of the postwar era, however, party politics did not produce major changes in the blend of social welfare in Sweden. For several decades the Swedish party system, through the close links between unions and the Social Democratic party, helped formulate and enforce the terms of the corporatist bargain. The Social Democratic party held office for over forty years, and it made no serious effort to alter the structure of ownership rights or other essential features of the compromise between producer groups. In this period Swedish politics was more like Austrian politics—and less like British politics—in that elections tended to reinforce the corporatist agreement about which blend of social welfare should be pursued and about how governments could best pursue it. Nor did elections allow any Swedish political factions to secure disproportionately large, selective gains in welfare akin to those that southern factions in Italy secured through state-owned enterprise. Rather, Swedish elections reinforced, or left only slightly diminished, the long-term, efficiency-minded orientation of governments. In the quarter-century after World War II, parliamentary politics essentially finetuned the distributional consequences of the corporatist compromise.[27]

The structural features of Sweden's political economy have contributed to its performance. Sweden's administrative tradition, which is more centralist than noncentralist, has reinforced a concern with achieving collective welfare gains and intergenerational equity.[28] The mobility of capital, nationally and internationally, spurred efficiency at the same time that it limited the possibility of redistributing wealth beyond the terms of corporatist compromise. Only to the extent that Swedish firms suffered large losses in international markets or became dependent on government for assistance to compete effectively in those markets did authorities have opportunities to manage and

27. The role of the Swedish party system in reinforcing the terms of the corporatist compromise is examined in Korpi (1978). The same author charts the relatively unchanging character of Sweden's income distribution across postwar electoral history. Most studies of Scandinavian political economy either do not focus on patterns of intragenerational equity (Hibbs and Madsen 1981; Jonoug and Wadensjo 1979) or make questionable assumptions about the independence of electoral events across countries and over time within countries. Paldam (1979) is an example of the latter kind of study.
28. On Sweden's administrative tradition see Heclo and Madsen (1987: chap. 1) and Katzenstein (1985: chap. 4). The more general importance of the notion of guardianship in Sweden is discussed by Ruth (1984). Pontusson (1987, 1984) argues that Swedish unions lack a coherent vision and the technical expertise to use their pension funds so as seriously to challenge the privileged position of private business. He apparently does not see Swedish administrators as potential allies for unions; see also Heclo and Madsen (1987: chap. 6). Tilton (1987:144) argues that part of the opposition to state-owned enterprise derives from a fear of creating a powerful state bureaucracy.

transfer the wealth that private firms had accumulated. Lack of control over the allocation of capital undermined government capacity to shape the pattern of investment in the economy and hence to alter significantly the distribution of nonmaterial wealth. But again, for much of the postwar era unions and their Social Democratic allies tolerated capital mobility and intragenerational inequities for the sake of growth and price stability; they did not seek to create the capacity to shape intragenerational equity.[29]

Most observers agree that throughout the 1950s and 1960s there was much citizen support for the idea and terms of the corporatist compromise. In this period most Swedes apparently agreed it was best to pursue collective gains in consumption as well as other mutual interests while at the same time compensating wage earners who moved to new jobs within the private sector. They also supported policies designed to create more uniform wage rates and to enhance the economic security of lower income groups and, in some respects (for example, child allowances), the security of younger generations.

The late 1960s witnessed the birth of real dissensus within Sweden. Serious disagreements between unions and parties arose about the ends and means of government and about the structure of ownership rights within the Swedish economy. During this period governments began to experience difficulty placing workers in private firms, and unrest surfaced within and between unions over reduced wage differentials and other aspects of the corporatist compromise. This dissensus was eventually reflected in the outcomes of producer group negotiations and of electoral competition. The practice of forging national wage agreements and of striking bipartisan agreements over controversial political issues began to break down. In the mid-1970s the Social Democratic party lost office for the first time in forty-four years. When it returned to office in 1982 the party was forced to form a coalition government with a smaller party. In the interim Sweden was ruled by a coalition of center and conservative parties that, interestingly, nationalized several large private firms.

These events, coupled with the heated debate over wage earner funds, suggest that Swedish politics has had somewhat different effects on social welfare in recent years. For example, some commentators now see the political system as seriously undermining the long-term orientation of government decision making and, at the same

29. Clearly there are barriers to capital mobility in Sweden (Bowler 1986). From a comparative standpoint, however, Sweden has a well-developed private sector that is relatively international in character (Katzenstein 1985: chap. 3). Again, numerous authors argue that Swedish pension funds have had little impact on the overall pattern and rate of investment in Sweden; see Korpi (1978:319) and Pontusson (1987; 1984: fn. 6).

time, retarding investment, slowing growth, and threatening the survival of the welfare state. These Swedish political observers see the dual channels of representation—union and electoral—as providing citizens with opportunities to dismantle or prevent further expansion of the welfare state while simultaneously pursuing their personal self-interest. As they see it, there has been a breakdown of the consensus on which Sweden's corporatist–private enterprise political economy was based. This breakdown has produced an increasingly myopic pluralism that allows certain unions and interest groups to sacrifice collective short- and long-term interests for the sake of their immediate personal gain. In essence, Swedish politics has become more similar to British and Italian politics in its basic character and in its effects on social welfare outcomes.[30]

Disagreements about how best to structure ownership rights are at the heart of this dissensus. Swedish citizens, unions, and parties disagree about the wisdom of maintaining or expanding the state business sector and of creating wage earner funds. Conservative political parties have renounced the nationalizations of the late 1970s, and the Social Democrats have allowed some of these enterprises to go bankrupt. In addition, the Social Democrats are trying to increase the productive efficiency of the remaining public enterprises. It is unlikely, then, that party politics will produce expansion of the Swedish state business sector in the next few years. It is also unlikely that party politics will render the welfare consequences of the remaining Swedish public enterprises more like those we find in Italy. Rather, the welfare consequences of Swedish state-owned enterprise should resemble those unfolding in Austria, because Swedish unions and parties continue to display little affinity for nationalization and the influence of private enterprise–oriented administrators and experts is on the rise.[31]

Nevertheless, conservative parties did nationalize a large number of firms in the late 1970s, and the Social Democratic party has not

30. Katzenstein maintains that proportional representation systems stabilize their polities and promote a willingness to compromise (1985: chap. 4). He and others have noted that the conservative coalition of the mid-1970s did not behave in ways fundamentally different from those of their predecessors. However, these and other observers also recognize the possibility that recent developments in the party system indicate a genuine breakdown of consensus, especially a breakdown of the commitment to solidaristic wage bargaining and welfare state policies. See Heclo and Madsen (1987), Katzenstein (1985), Aimer (1985), Ruth (1984), and Rehn (1984). Hansen (1985) argues that dual forms of representation—corporatist and electoral—render Swedish politics increasingly myopic. See Bosworth and Lawrence (1987) on the recent fall off in investment and growth.

31. See Tilton (1987, 1979) and Heclo and Madsen (1987:330), respectively.

dismantled all of Sweden's state business sector. Nor has there been much support for privatization in Sweden.[32] It appears that there is some support for state-owned enterprise. If Sweden experiences more or deeper crises in the 1990s, its economy could therefore become more mixed. As the breakdown of corporatist politics seems to have proceeded further in Sweden than in Austria, and as the Swedish party system is somewhat more fragmented, factional behavior is more likely to occur in Sweden. Hence the particularistic welfare consequences associated with the operation of the Italian state business sector are more likely to occur in Sweden than in Austria. On the other hand, the Swedish labor movement is still more unified and actively involved in government decision making than its counterpart in Italy. For this reason, factional behavior and the welfare consequences it produces are less likely to occur in Sweden than in Italy.[33]

The idea of and debate over wage earner funds makes the Swedish experience unique. The analysis in Chapter 5 does not tell us exactly how union as opposed to popular control over investment decisions should affect distributional equity. Moreover, the deep dissensus within Sweden over the wisdom of creating such a mode of investment makes it difficult to predict the role that wage earner funds will play in the Swedish economy in the future. As noted earlier, the rationale behind wage earner funds is a recognition of the social power inherent in private investment decisions. The advocates of wage earner funds explicitly recognize the social power that private asset holders wield by virtue of their ability to directly influence investment decisions. In this respect the rationale for wage earner funds is consistent with the tenets of the analysis in Chapters 3 and 5.[34]

Our theory has more difficulty explaining other elements of wage earner funds. As the name implies, wage earner funds differ from state-owned enterprise in that they are designed to augment the social power of one segment of citizens rather than the power of the citizenry as a whole. Under the existing scheme, for example, five of the nine individuals on boards that manage the regional funds must be representatives of labor; the government can nominate only four

32. See Pontusson (1987:29).

33. This is not to imply that Austria is immune to particularistic or factional behavior. My discussion of the Austrian experience acknowledges the changes in Austrian corporatist politics and the possibility of just such an outcome with regard to the consequences of state-owned enterprise. Austria and Sweden are relatively immune to this kind of behavior and the outcomes that it produces because their political systems are still more corporatist than pluralist.

34. For example, Meidner writes: "We want to deprive the capitalists of the power they exercise by virtue of ownership. . . . We cannot fundamentally change society without changing its ownership structure" (quoted in Pontusson 1987:14).

members of each board. Popular elections therefore cannot change the makeup of the supervisory boards to the same degree they can change the makeup of the boards that supervise nationalized industries in Austria. The earnings or losses of the wage earner funds accrue to segments of labor or to labor as an organization rather than to the public treasury. It is therefore more the welfare of one or more segments of citizens than of the citizenry as a whole that wage earner funds enhance or diminish. At the same time Sweden has a small state business sector that is collectively owned and whose earnings and losses, in principle, do accrue to all citizens. Hence, through the dual channels of popular and producer group elections, Swedish citizens have opportunities to exercise collective control over a significant number of investment decisions and to accrue collective gains or losses from those public investments. Sweden thus differs in an important way from the other three countries we have examined because wage earners have these multiple opportunities to shape investment decisions.[35]

The calculus that Swedish citizens use in deciding how to execute their different ownership rights is not clear. Citizens, especially wage earners, face an even more complex task than their counterparts do in Italy and Austria, where there is more certainty about how political participation affects public investment decisions and other aspects of public enterprise operations. There, elections consistently give certain political factions an opportunity to use state-owned enterprise to serve their particular interests, or the composition of the bodies that supervise nationalized industries depends more directly on electoral outcomes. In Sweden, on the other hand, citizens must consider the way private, wage earner, and public investment decisions combine to produce different welfare outcomes. They must then decide how participation in producer groups and elections can alter the combination of investment decisions and bring about changes in the welfare outcomes those decisions create.[36]

35. For a discussion of wage earner funds and the political debate they have spawned within and among producer groups and parties in Sweden, see Heclo and Madsen (1987: chap. 6), Åsard (1986), and Aimer (1985); also, Pontusson (1987, 1984) and Hansen (1985). Aimer argues that "the future of [wage earner] funds therefore and, by implication, of socialist policies generally, depends much more on the distribution of political power in the parliamentary arena than on the functioning of the structure and norms of Swedish corporate pluralism" (1985:52).

36. Once more this conclusion is a matter of degree. Italy's electoral outcomes may be more predictable, but wage earner funds have not been created there; the role of Italian unions in shaping government intervention and market participation is clearer than it is in Sweden. In Austria, corporatist institutions have broken down to some degree, and there is some dissensus about the best way to structure ownership rights. But in comparison to Sweden, Austria offers more certainty about the reality and outcomes of corporatist negotiations and party competition, nor does it exhibit the same

Despite its complexity, the Swedish case conformed for several decades to our expectations about the workings and welfare consequences of corporatist–private enterprise systems. The power of Sweden's trade unions allowed them to achieve a higher degree of intragenerational equity than exists in Britain and in Italy, countries where labor is much weaker or less committed to distributional equity. It has also allowed Swedish unions to prevent the wholesale privatization that has occurred in Britain.[37] Throughout much of the postwar era, corporatist politics facilitated government promotion of labor mobility and other forms of market intervention that enhanced productive efficiency and allowed Sweden to achieve exemplary growth and employment. Finally, the debate over wage earner funds reveals an appreciation among Swedish citizens for the structural difference we expect between their political economy and that of Austria, namely, the greater social power wielded by private asset holders in Sweden. The case for wage earner funds recognizes that in mixed economies like Austria's, wage earners can play a greater role in shaping the intragenerational distribution of wealth. Those who wish to alter intragenerational welfare outcomes in Austria have a greater capacity to do so because a large state-owned sector already exists. There is also greater consensus in Austria than in Sweden and Britain about the need to retain this capacity. Swedes' appreciation for the welfare implications of different structures of ownership rights, and the nature of the disagreements among them about how to alter the existing system of ownership rights, amount to an endorsement of the results given in Chapters 3 and 5.

Should the Swedish state business sector remain at its current size, no further expansion of wage earner funds occurs, and Swedish corporatist political institutions remain at least partially intact, then the blend of social welfare should remain relatively stable. Sweden should continue to outperform Italy and Britain in terms of intragenerational equity because of the greater power wielded by labor and the modicum of public control over investment that exists in Sweden. It should continue to perform worse than Italy and perhaps begin to

---

degree of dissensus about how to structure ownership rights or the same degree of complexity in existing structures of ownership rights. Note the interesting parallel between the proposal for regular elections of the head of the Austrian OeIAG and Korpi's call for the creation of citizen funds (1978: chap. 11).

37. Evidence of the different orientations of Italian and Swedish labor unions toward "welfarism" is presented in Regini and Esping-Andersen (1980). Hansen (1985) explains why the balance of political power within Sweden rules out privatization and other policies that the Thatcher governments have adopted. Crouch (1980) explains why the more fragmented nature of the British TUC prevents it from implementing the wage bargains that its counterpart in Sweden has implemented.

fall behind Britain in terms of collective welfare gains and intergenerational equity, because of the deleterious effects of parliamentary and electoral politics on productive efficiency, including the productive efficiency of the Swedish state business sector.

PART FOUR

EXTENSIONS AND IMPLICATIONS

CHAPTER NINE

The Politics of Openness
and Foreign Public Enterprise

We have focused thus far on the inner workings of national political economies. But as I pointed out in Chapter 1, most economies are open to trade and investment. As a consequence, all governments must cope with the presence in their territories of firms that are owned and operated by the private citizens and *governments* of other countries. More generally, all governments must cope with the workings of international markets for goods and finance. Governments in mixed economies must decide how or whether to expand their public enterprises into foreign markets. When they decide to expand into other national economies, these governments must formulate an international business strategy that allows their public enterprises to compete with foreign private firms and multinational corporations as well as with other foreign public enterprises. How do these facts alter the results presented in Chapter 5? How do the politics of foreign public enterprise and of openness alter the range of welfare outcomes that can be achieved in each of the four types of political economy?

This chapter analyzes the politics of foreign enterprise from the perspective of a nation-state with an open economy.[1] In parts one and two, I examine the problems that foreign state enterprises create for governments in what are otherwise private enterprise economies

---

1. By "nation-state perspective" I mean the perspective of individuals who are citizens of and who generally define their welfare in terms of the performance of a sovereign state. An international perspective would entail (1) a more extensive study of the activities of state-owned enterprises in foreign (onshore) and in global (offshore) markets; (2), in conjunction with (1), a fuller incorporation of open macroeconomic theory (Dornbusch 1980); (3) an analysis of the welfare consequences of foreign state enterprise from the point of view of the global population; and (4) investigation of the ways that the policies of foreign state enterprise affect and are affected by defense and foreign policies. An international perspective would thus involve an examination of the

and for governments in mixed economies.[2] The workings and welfare consequences of the four basic political economies are briefly reexamined and the results of Chapter 5 amended.

The present chapter shows that (1) countries with pluralist–private enterprise political economies are more likely to achieve collective welfare gains through international trade than are countries with pluralist–mixed systems; (2) foreign state enterprise disinvestment is likely to spawn efforts to create privately owned and publicly owned national champions in private enterprise and mixed economies, respectively; (3) the rise of the two kinds of national champions constrains, in different ways, governments' abilities to bring about certain kinds of welfare outcomes; (4) distributional conflict is likely to be more intense and of a different character in open mixed than in closed mixed economies: the foreign public investments of native public enterprise are especially prone to produce conflicts of interest among wage earners; (5) results (3) and (4) are manifestations of a larger tension that arises over the desire to promote collective national interests through privately owned or state-owned national champions, on the one hand, and the desire to retain government capacity to maintain or create particular distributions of wealth intragenerationally, on the other; and (6) this tension destabilizes corporatist modes of interest intermediation.

Finally, the revised analysis again shows that fundamentally different blends of social welfare can be achieved in the four types of open political economy. However, it suggests that in some respects the contrasts between the four systems are more or less stark than we hypothesized earlier. Also, the politics of openness and foreign public enterprise enhances the privileged position of private asset holders in pluralist–private enterprise systems whereas it diminishes the privileged position of state enterprise workers in corporatist–mixed systems. Popular elections continue to have their greatest impact on distributional equity in pluralist–mixed political economies.

---

ways international institutions like the IMF and World Bank promote the expansion or dismantling of state-owned enterprises (Biersteker 1986) and the adoption of certain performance standards for them (Gray 1983), the legal status of state enterprise in international and regional treaty law (Holland 1974, Aharoni 1986, Hindley 1982), governments' attempts to create oligopolies or cartels made up of state-owned firms in particular sectors of the global economy (Lamont 1979, Shafer 1983), and the role of state-owned enterprise in foreign economic and defense policy. Such an analysis would indicate how state-owned enterprise creates opportunities for and imposes limits on global consumption gains, on the one hand, and facilitates or impedes global redistribution of wealth between transnational groups and countries, on the other.

2. In what follows the term "private enterprise economy" refers to a national economy composed of native-private, foreign-private, and foreign-public firms. The term "mixed economy" refers to a national economy composed of native-private, foreign-private, foreign-public, and native-public firms.

The Politics of Open Private Enterprise Economies

The case for private enterprise economies rests on the collective gains that current and future generations realize from market efficiency. Intragenerational equity is achieved in these systems through government taxation and transfer of wealth. Market failures are solved through various forms of government regulation of private enterprise. Asset markets ameliorate the problems posed by the separation of ownership and managerial control at the same time that they constrain government abilities to redistribute wealth through fiscal policy.

When this kind of economy is open, collective gains in consumption depend, in some part, on private firms' competitiveness and on the nation-state's comparative advantage in world markets. Collective gains in consumption also depend on the manner in which international financial markets channel funds for investment and payments financing to and from the national economy. In addition to other tasks, government must manage its external account so as to protect the competitiveness of its firms and, more generally, to "stabilize" its national economy (in the context of the prevailing exchange rate regime).[3]

As regards intragenerational equity, openness tends to produce high industrial concentrations, which in turn facilitate labor organizing and labor power. Openness makes workers more vulnerable to global trade and financial fluctuations. In turn, workers tend to recognize their mutual interests and demand more government assistance than they do in closed economies, for example, publicly funded retraining programs to help them relocate to more internationally competitive industries. As they are usually better organized than their counterparts in closed economies, wage earners in open economies are often able to secure this and other forms of government assistance. But because openness implies comparatively greater capital mobility, government is more constrained in open than closed economies in its ability to finance this assistance through taxation of private enterprise. Rather, governments often have to tax wage earners in the "sheltered sector" of the open economy. This practice makes it difficult to maintain unity within wage earner organizations.[4]

3. The distinction between firm competitiveness and comparative advantage is discussed by Zysman (1983). The same author makes the case for government promotion and creation of comparative advantage. "Stabilization" of an open economy entails (1) smoothing changes in prices and in the rate of growth, and (2) managing external payments in a way that prevents crises in the foreign (exposed) sector of the economy. See, for instance, Lindert and Kindelberger (1982: pt. 4).
4. For a discussion of the general political implications of openness see Cameron

The commercial orientation of many foreign state enterprises suggests they might be as efficient as private firms; for instance, foreign state enterprises raise funds in international capital markets, and some of their managers sell their services to local and multinational private firms, suggesting that these publicly owned firms adopt marginal cost-pricing policies. These facts also suggest that foreign state enterprises forge and maintain productive joint ventures with local private and foreign private firms. Ostensibly, then, their presence should not change the workings of a private enterprise economy to any substantial degree. Collective gains in consumption should still be realized when foreign state enterprises are present.

However, in practice foreign state enterprises may undermine the efficiency of private enterprise economies, because they often serve the noncommercial objectives of their home governments. Also, foreign state enterprises often depend on home governments for investment capital. And, as we learned in Chapter 3, governments have great difficulty determining what type of investment and how much of it to fund. For this and other reasons, managers of foreign state enterprise may be unwilling or unable to respond efficiently either to local market forces or to the fiscal incentives and regulatory directives of host governments. The result is a relatively less efficient national market and, from the perspective of the *host* nation-state, a collective loss in consumption.[5]

In private enterprise economies, capital mobility constrains governments' ability to tax and transfer wealth. Because they must compete for firms with governments in other political jurisdictions and because private firms can threaten not to invest in existing facilities, governments are able to redistribute only a limited amount of wealth among their citizens. Foreign state enterprises can often threaten to locate in other nation-states, and they too can refuse to reinvest in existing facilities. For various reasons they may be slower to make such threats than foreign private enterprise. Ultimately, however, the presence of foreign state enterprise leaves intact the constraints on government ability to tax and redistribute wealth.

The problem with foreign state enterprises runs deeper. Because such enterprises are owned collectively by the citizens of another nation-state, their policies are more blatantly redistributive than

---

(1978), Katzenstein (1985), and Wallerstein (1984).

5. Lamont (1979:12, 88–90, 114) presents evidence that foreign state enterprises behave as efficiently as local and foreign private firms. However, he and Mazzolini (1980) and Monsen and Walters (1983) provide more evidence that most foreign state enterprises are inefficient in comparison to foreign private enterprises. Reasons for this inefficiency are discussed below, in the section on mixed national economies.

those of foreign private enterprise. The threat of disinvestment by a foreign state enterprise pits the collective interests of the citizens of a foreign country against those of the host country more clearly than does the threat of disinvestment by a foreign private firm. The cross-nationally redistributive character of foreign enterprise is obvious when it is expressly a tool of economic nationalism. But it is also obvious when foreign public enterprises relocate or disinvest in order to serve the noncommercial objectives of their home government, for example, when a foreign public enterprise refuses to modernize plants in a host country in order to maintain jobs in its home country. The cross-nationally redistributive character of foreign state enterprise is also evident when these firms begin to acquire substantial shares of the natural resources of the host country. Foreign control over national resources is likely to be viewed as a clear threat to the welfare of current and future generations of citizens in the host nation-state.[6]

As I stressed in Chapter 3, the relocation and disinvestment decisions of foreign private enterprise are normally considered detrimental to the interests of the citizens of the host country and to the interests of the affected employees and communities. But this perception is counterbalanced, to some degree, by the belief that the foreign private enterprise responds to (politically neutral) international market forces rather than to any particular cross-national redistributive objectives of its owners. Moreover, international market forces are believed to produce some collective welfare gains for the host nation-state. Since foreign public enterprises often do not respond to these forces, their contribution to the realization of these collective gains is more difficult for citizens to discern. For these reasons, all things being equal, the citizens of host countries will be more aware of and opposed to the constraints imposed by foreign state enterprise on government capacity to redistribute wealth than they are to the constraints imposed by foreign private enterprise.[7] The manner in which

6. As regards economic nationalism, consider a statement by French president François Mitterrand: "I am opposed to an international division of labor and production, a division that is decided far from our shores and obeying interests that are not our own. We are not a pawn in the hands of those who are more powerful than we. This must be made clear, *and for us nationalization is a weapon to protect France's production apparatus*" (quoted in Monsen and Walters 1983:29–30, my emphasis). Less provocative but still important are such episodes as the Norwegian government's directing Norsk Hydro to disinvest from its Colorado mines and to concentrate on the development of Norway's North Sea oil (Lamont 1979:125).

7. "All things being equal" here refers to the number of workers and communities affected by the disinvestment, geographical dispersion of those workers and communities, and so on. These factors are stressed in the section on open mixed economies and in the case studies in Chapter 10.

governments actually cope with foreign public enterprise depends on the type of interest intermediation that exists within the open private enterprise economy.

The Open, Pluralist, Private Enterprise Political Economy

In open, pluralist, private enterprise political economies, welfare outcomes are an outgrowth of market competition between firms, competition between governments for firms, and electoral and interest group competition between political parties. Because elections may produce major shifts in public policies, government may be incapable of making the intertemporal choices required to ameliorate structural imperfections in the private enterprise economy. This inability will occur if there is marked dissensus about the ends and means of public policy among citizens and their parties and if the electoral system is majoritarian in character. In such circumstances pluralist politics will diminish the effectiveness of policies designed to enhance the international competitiveness of particular private firms and produce collectively harmful, speculative flows of capital into and out of the national economy.

Through the power they wield within pluralist institutions, some groups will be able to secure protection from the effects of international trade. In this way, electoral and interest group politics will affect the intragenerational distribution of wealth and prevent the realization of some gains from trade. The effects of dissensus and the scope of protectionism will be less where a powerful centralist state administration is committed to the promotion of collective, national welfare or intergenerational equity. Either way, pluralist politics will have a minor impact on the current distribution of wealth, because in this first type of political economy investment decisions remain in native private and in foreign private and public hands. Moreover, private enterprise and foreign public enterprise can relocate to other countries to avoid government taxation.

To the extent that pluralist politics does produce genuine uncertainty about the course of government policies, it can be expected further to undermine the efficiency of foreign public enterprise. Pluralist politics in the host country will discourage long-term investment by foreign public enterprises and make it more difficult for them to forge productive joint ventures with local private firms. As regards intragenerational equity, foreign public enterprise managers must answer to some degree to officials in their home governments; as a result they may be slower to react to host government taxation and regulation. Hence, over the short term, opportunities are per-

232

haps somewhat greater for particular governments to tax and redistribute the earnings of foreign public enterprise. In these ways, foreign public enterprise can render pluralist politics even more unstable than it would otherwise be and, in turn, produce collectively harmful welfare outcomes.

Over the medium and long term, however, foreign state enterprise tends to stabilize pluralist politics. The cross-nationally redistributive character of foreign state enterprise encourages political consensus within the home country. Foreign state enterprises, to the extent they disinvest or threaten to do so, increase awareness of the common or national interests of host citizens vis-à-vis interests of the citizens of other nation-states. The efforts of foreign state enterprises to evade taxation encourage party agreements on behalf of collective-national rather than particular-constitutency interests. In this first kind of political economy these agreements may take the form of a commitment to promote the growth and expansion of privately owned national champions that can compete with foreign state enterprises as well as with foreign private enterprises. Short of this, foreign state enterprises' efforts to evade taxation mute, to some extent, the opposition to disinvestment threats and to the relocation decisions of local private firms. Once more, the policies of local private firms are ostensibly less detrimental to collective national interests or less blatantly redistributive (cross-nationally).

Over the long term this promotion of private national champions or a greater tolerance for private disinvestment and relocation further limits government abilities to redistribute wealth. The growth of private national champions yields some benefits to the citizens of the home nation-state as well as to the employees of the respective firms. But the economy as a whole becomes more open and hence more vulnerable to external trade and financial fluctuations. At the same time the large, privately owned national firms themselves become even less subject to taxation and transfer. Hence government capacity to redistribute wealth is further reduced; elections reassign smaller amounts of wealth among an increasingly insecure national populace.

The Open, Corporatist, Private Enterprise Political Economy

The primary difference between the open, corporatist political economy and the one we have just examined is the fact that welfare outcomes now derive, in part, from producer group negotiations. As a result, government usually has greater capacity to make the kind of intertemporal choices that enhance market efficiency and realize gains from trade. Wage earners are also able to capture a somewhat greater share of national wealth, materially and nonmaterially, than are their counterparts in pluralist private enterprise economies.

Openness poses new problems for governments in this second kind of political economy. Although it makes it somewhat easier for labor to organize itself, over time openness creates tensions within labor organizations. More specifically, over time it becomes increasingly difficult for labor leaders to maintain good relations with business leaders and to maintain the support of the rank and file in the exposed and sheltered sectors of the open private enterprise economy.[8]

Corporatist politics is more conducive to foreign state enterprise efficiency than is pluralist politics. The greater stability of this second form of interest intermediation facilitates foreign public enterprise planning. For instance, joint ventures with local private firms are relatively easier to consummate, because greater certainty about wage costs exists under corporatism. On the other hand, labor's greater social power in these political economies means that foreign public enterprise must pay a slightly higher price to locate in these countries. All things being equal, government has somewhat more power to tax and transfer the earnings of foreign public enterprises as well as to demand certain concessions from them.

Although foreign public enterprise imparts stability to pluralist policy making, it generally destabilizes corporatist politics. For a time, foreign public enterprises may be willing to cooperate with the corporatist partners in a particular country. Over the long term, however, pursuit of the interests of its home citizens (foreign public owners) will spawn efforts to defend national interests by promoting the development and expansion of private national champions. These efforts exacerbate conflicts of interest between workers in exposed and sheltered segments of the national economy and intensify the behavioral problems associated with corporatism. The promotion of private national champions again increases the relative wealth but also the vulnerability of the employees of those firms. This strategy undermines labor representatives' commitment to protect the particular interests of native wage earners; it makes it increasingly difficult for labor leaders to maintain their authority over those segments of the rank and file directly harmed by the expansion of the private national champion as well as those segments that question the utility of corporatism as a means of promoting class interests.

8. On the divisions that protectionism creates among producer groups, and also the incentives that openness spawns for the creation of corporatist institutions, see Wallerstein (1984). Katzenstein (1985) analyzes how corporatist institutions cope with this problem and, in turn, avoid the collective welfare losses produced by protectionism.

A strong centralist administration committed to promoting collective national interests and intergenerational equity will render ever more severe the problems faced by labor leaders. In these circumstances the private national champion may display even less concern for the interests of native wage earners, rendering labor leaders' efforts to promote the interests of native wage earners even more suspect. Over the long term the promotion of privately owned national champions may produce some collective gains for the host nation-state. But, once more, these gains come at the expense of economic security of workers in the respective industries and bring with them a reduction in government capacity to redistribute wealth. In this way foreign public enterprise spawns a series of events that diminishes labor power in corporatist–private enterprise political economies.

THE POLITICS OF OPEN MIXED NATIONAL ECONOMIES

Mixed economies differ from private enterprise economies in that, in the former, welfare outcomes depend to a much greater degree on government production of goods and services. Governments promote market efficiency by creating and operating publicly owned firms, public enterprises designed to ameliorate the problems of increasing returns and external effects. Intragenerational equity is promoted directly through the employment, pricing, and purchasing decisions of public enterprises, as well as through the taxation and transfer of the earnings of privately owned and publicly owned firms.

Openness complicates governments' tasks, as it does in private enterprise economies. Governments must again take the balance of payments into account when formulating fiscal policies, for instance, and they must still decide whether to promote the international competitiveness of privately owned firms. Distinctive about mixed economies are the challenges openness poses for the operation and possible transnational expansion of public enterprises. In open mixed economies governments must consider the effects of native public enterprise operations (local and foreign) on the balance of payments. They must also cope with the effects that external market forces have on the performance of their public businesses.[9] In addition, openness raises the possibility of direct public investment in other countries. Foreign public investment affects the welfare of native citizens somewhat differently than foreign private investment. The former type of

---

9. "Local operation" means operation within the boundaries of a particular nation-state. Operations within the boundaries of a nation-state other than that which owns the state enterprise are referred to as "foreign operations."

investment spawns different sorts of distributional conflicts within the nation-state.

Open mixed economies are generally less efficient than open private enterprise economies. In principle native state enterprise can both ameliorate the structural defects in the national market and compete successfully in international markets. The result is a more efficient national mixed economy and the realization of collective gains from trade. Native state enterprise succeeds in world markets, for example, when governments are sensitive to their natural resource endowments and to the structure of international trade in those resources. When they possess the technological know-how, there are few substitutes for their natural resources, and the processing of those resources is not vertically integrated, governments can create public enterprises that succeed commercially in international markets—a proposition to which the commercial success of certain state-owned mining ventures at home and abroad attests. Where governments lack the technical skill or international marketing networks to go it alone in foreign markets, joint ventures between native and foreign private firms can help realize gains from international trade. The durability and commercial success of some ventures in mining and mineral processing demonstrate the viability of this alternative method of promoting collective national welfare through native state enterprise.[10]

Normally, however, native public enterprises realize fewer gains from international trade than do private enterprises. Governments create native public enterprises that usually do not compete effectively with multinational private enterprises. Native public enterprises usually do not have the technical know-how to produce goods and services efficiently or possess the networks through which to sell those products abroad. Also, the structural and behavioral problems associated with public enterprise are more severe at the international level. For instance, governments can rely to a lesser extent on international capital markets to determine an appropriate discount rate for foreign public investment.[11]

10. On conditions under which state-owned mining ventures are most likely to be commercially viable see Shafer (1983). An interesting comparison of the commercial fortunes of state-owned potash and asbestos business ventures can be found in Laux and Molot (1987: pt. 2). See Chapter 8 of the same source for a discussion of the virtues and pitfalls of state-private joint ventures; see also Evans (1979) and Lamont (1979: chap. 8).

11. Shafer (1983) analyzes the commercial mistakes that various African and Latin American governments made in launching state-owned international business ventures and the collective welfare losses that resulted. Recent attempts to erect vertically integrated, export-oriented state-owned steel industries are evaluated in Vernon and Levy

Even if native state-owned enterprises possess the requisite technology and marketing networks, they still have to cope, to a greater extent than their private competitors, with their governments' efforts to use them to serve such noncommercial aims as preserving jobs in local communities. As a result, native public enterprises generally have more difficulty in exploiting foreign investment opportunities, diversifying, and taking other actions that might enhance their international competitiveness.[12]

In the national mixed economy, native public enterprises often limit citizens' consumption possibilities, because their output is usually more costly than that of firms in other countries. The output of foreign producers could be substituted (imported) for the output of native public enterprise, giving citizens additional consumption possibilities and, conceivably, enhancing the long-run efficiency of the national economy. In this sense the inefficiency of some native public enterprise produces additional welfare losses for the citizenry as a whole. Citizens are deprived not just of the consumption possibilities that could be achieved from more efficient operation of publicly owned firms in international markets but also of the consumption possibilities that imports of some native public enterprise goods and services might provide.[13]

For reasons given above, the foreign state enterprises that do business in the mixed national economy are usually inefficient. Therefore foreign state enterprises also reduce the consumption possibilities available to host citizens. Moreover, these firms are less subject to host government control, and so host governments are often unable to promote their efficiency even if they want to do so.

In sum, all things being equal, open mixed economies are likely to be more inefficient than open private enterprise economies. In open mixed economies, collective welfare outcomes are likely to be inferior in the sense that the foreign and local operations of their native public enterprises provide citizens with fewer collective consumption pos-

---

(1982). The general problem of determining an appropriate discount rate for public investment was discussed in Chapter 3. Problems here include the fact that international capital markets are also imperfect and participants are usually not constituents of the government owning the public enterprise that seeks to borrow in them. Hence interest rates in international credit markets may bear little relation to the current and future preferences of the involved government and its constituents.

12. Mazzolini (1979a, 1980) argues that state-owned enterprises are slow to react to international investment opportunities and, for this and other reasons, generally more inefficient than multinational private corporations. Vernon and Levy argue that one of the reasons for this inefficiency is the tendency of state-owned enterprises to treat labor costs as fixed in the face of declining international demand (1982:184). See also Aharoni (1986:373).

13. The argument that native public enterprise distorts free trade and produces collective welfare losses is advanced by Breton (1964) and Hindley (1982).

sibilities than would be possible under native-private and foreign-private production of the respective goods and services.

On the second dimension of societal welfare, governments retain a greater capacity to redistribute wealth intragenerationally in open mixed economies than in open private enterprise economies. As native public enterprises expand into international markets, their managers may be able to insulate themselves to some degree from government interference. For example, managers may be able to obtain financing for their foreign investments in international capital markets and thus undermine the authority of the officials who manage public financial resources at home. In this and other ways state managers may be able to capture a share of wealth that is markedly greater than their counterparts in native private enterprises.[14]

However, top state managers are usually appointed by the home government, and that same government must often guarantee loans from international creditors. As a result, home authorities can influence the foreign operations of native public enterprise. Through these and other mechanisms home officials force native state enterprise managers to serve distributional aims within the home country to a much greater degree than they force native and foreign private enterprise managers to do so. For instance, home governments may refuse to guarantee international bank loans or to help their state managers negotiate trade agreements with foreign governments unless some local operations are adjusted to better serve the interests of certain native communities. Foreign private firms tend to enjoy more autonomy from home governments in their dealings with international creditors and with foreign governments. They are not as constrained by the distributional consequences of their international business activities within their home country. Consequently, governments in open private enterprise economies have less capacity to shape the national distribution of wealth than their counterparts in open mixed economies.[15]

14. Breton (1964) and Shafer (1983) maintain that the foreign operations of state-owned enterprises afford certain groups within society—especially middle-income groups—and state managers opportunities to capture a greater share of societal wealth than might be possible in an open private enterprise economy. Hindley (1982) argues that in an open mixed economy, state enterprise workers enjoy a privileged position relative to other workers. He maintains that these privileged workers benefit at the expense of all other consumer-citizens.

15. Mazzolini's (1979a, 1980) work describes the numerous ways in which governments are able to influence the foreign operations of native public enterprises. He attributes the comparatively inefficient nature of public enterprise operations in large part to this intervention. Vernon argues that public enterprise behavior is an outgrowth of unceasing bargaining between state managers, government bureaus, ministers, and politicians. He writes: "The evidence seems to point to the general conclusion that the special relationships between state-owned enterprises and governments based

The intragenerational welfare outcomes of open mixed economies differ in important respects from those of closed mixed economies. First, the foreign investment decisions of native public enterprises spawn different, potentially more intense distributional conflicts in open than in closed mixed economies. The international marketing activities of native public enterprise generally serve both collective and particular interests; for instance, they earn all citizens foreign exchange at the same time that they enhance the welfare of the employees of the state-owned firm concerned. As we have seen, these collective gains may be viewed as a form of international income redistribution. In these circumstances the native public enterprise may be viewed as a champion of the collective welfare of *all* the citizens of the nation-state.[16]

The foreign investments of native public enterprises potentially enhance citizens' collective welfare as well. These investments promise to solidify the enterprises' market niches and eventually to yield a stream of earnings to current and to future generations of native citizen-owners. However, these foreign public investments also yield benefits to the citizens of other countries, seemingly at the expense of some citizen-owners in the home country, namely, the inhabitants of communities where the native public enterprise produces goods at home. Or the foreign investments of the native public enterprise may make it difficult to redress distributional inequities in the home country in that they deplete the supply of financial resources or international credit available for local public investment or public spending. Here again, the perception may be that native public enterprise is enhancing the welfare of foreign individuals at the expense of certain citizen-owners in its home country.

The situation is different in closed mixed economies and in open private economies. In closed mixed economies, public enterprise investment decisions have distributional consequences that are expressly national in character. Public investment decisions have no direct, immediate effect on the economic welfare of any foreign citizens. Rather, in closed mixed economies the investment and location

---

upon such bargains are *more extensive and more intensive* than those made with private enterprise" (1979a:10, my emphases). See also Aharoni (1986).

16. One basis for creating public enterprise national champions is the belief that the long-term benefits from foreign private control over certain kinds of production—in terms of gains from taxation and redistribution and "free trade"—are less valuable than the short-term collective benefits from native state control, in spite of inefficiencies associated with native public enterprise. See, for instance, the discussion of the rationale for state takeover of the Saskatchewan potash industry in Laux and Molot (1987). The idea that public enterprise national champions can serve the collective interest by capturing the natural resources of other countries is discussed by Mazzolini (1979a:19–20).

decisions of native public enterprises enhance the welfare of some citizens of the home nation-state; and through their political institutions, citizens have a say in these location decisions. In open private enterprise economies, the foreign investments of some native private firms may enhance the welfare of the citizens of some other country at the expense of the citizens of the home country. But those who suffer because of this foreign investment do not collectively own the respective firm, and as a consequence, they normally do not expect to have much say in location decisions.

In open mixed economies, on the other hand, a group of citizens, by virtue of their status as collective owners of the enterprise, has a say in the operation of the native public enterprise. These individuals' welfare is directly harmed by the foreign investments of native public enterprises at the same time that the welfare of some foreign, nonowning individuals is enhanced.

Second, the possibility of foreign public investment diminishes the power of some state enterprise workers in mixed national economies. Employees of the state firms that operate infrastructural facilities within the national economy retain a disproportionate share of social power. These workers still wield a potent strike threat. The strike threat of state enterprise workers in the exposed sector of the mixed economy is markedly less potent. These workers now must cope with the fact that militancy encourages foreign public direct investment by native public enterprises.

To be sure, state enterprise workers in the exposed sector are more powerful than employees of most local and all foreign private enterprises. State enterprise workers in the exposed sector of the mixed economy, because they are collective owners of their firm, have a greater say in the investment decisions of their firms than do workers in private firms. But the possibility of direct foreign public investment nevertheless exists in open mixed economies. And because it does, state enterprise workers in the exposed sector of the economy are less powerful than their counterparts in the sheltered sector of the open economy. The possibility of foreign public investment also makes managers of native state enterprises in the exposed sector more powerful than their counterparts in the sheltered sector. The lines of distributional conflict and distribution of social power are thus different in open and closed mixed economies.

The presence of foreign, state-owned enterprise within mixed economies complicates matters even further. The investments of foreign public enterprise heighten concerns about transfers of wealth to the inhabitants of other countries at the same time that they enhance the welfare of particular communities within the open mixed econ-

omy. Disinvestment threats by foreign public enterprises limit government capacity to redistribute these firms' earnings over the short
term. Whether these threats spawn efforts to create native-private or
native-state enterprise champions depends on the prevailing constellation of political and economic forces.[17] What is important here is
that open mixed economies offer a clear alternative to creating privately owned national champions, more specifically, to creating the
kind of national champion that over time diminishes government capacity to redistribute wealth. Open mixed economies offer the option
of creating *state-owned* national champions. And for reasons given
above, a state-owned firm can be used more easily than a private national champion to promote intragenerational equity within the home
nation-state. Hence, all things being equal, governments threatened
with foreign public enterprise disinvestment retain a greater capacity
to redistribute wealth intragenerationally in open mixed than in open
private enterprise economies.

The problem with state-owned national champions is that they reinforce the tension between the pursuit of collective intergenerational
and particular intragenerational welfare concerns. To promote a
state-owned national champion, governments must formulate and implement an international business strategy, necessarily undermining
government's willingness and ability to pursue distributional aims
within the home country. And because the strategy almost always entails foreign public investment, it expressly harms some of the collective owners of the native public champion. In this way, foreign public
(and private) enterprise threats to disinvest spawn a series of events
with the potential to exacerbate distributional conflict within open
mixed economies.

The workings and welfare consequences of open mixed economies
ultimately depend on what type of interest intermediation exists
within a particular nation-state. Pluralism and corporatism have different implications for the foreign operations of native public enterprise and for the way in which the associated tension over the pursuit
of collective and particular interests is resolved.

The Open, Pluralist, Mixed Political Economy

In open, pluralist kinds of mixed economy, welfare outcomes are
outgrowths of market competition between firms, government regulation of firms and operation of public enterprises, competition
among governments for firms, and electoral and interest-group com-

17. See Freeman (1987).

petition. Elections have their greatest impact on the intragenerational distribution of wealth in this case, especially if there is societal dissensus over the ends and means of government market participation. Openness provides opportunities to enhance collective welfare through international trade. Openness and pluralism together encourage distributional conflicts between groups in the exposed and sheltered sectors of the mixed economy, including conflicts between state enterprise and private enterprise workers.

Pluralism generally contributes to the inefficiency of public enterprise in open mixed economies. Pluralism forces public officials to respond regularly to the wishes of their constituents. As voters, these constituents decide whether or not to reelect incumbents. Such decisions are based, in part, on the performance of native public enterprise. Many observers contend that voters define good performance in terms of short-term personal benefit; voters supposedly display little appreciation for the collective or intergenerational welfare consequences of public enterprises' local and foreign operations. Thus government officials who want to be reelected supposedly must see that native public enterprises provide short-term benefits to their particular constituents. Hence they must discourage efforts to make native public enterprise internationally competitive; for instance, officials must anticipate the employment effects of native public enterprise operations within local constituencies. They must intervene in operations such as purchasing and investment decisions if those decisions threaten job losses and hence vote losses in the next election. Again, public officials presumably interfere even if these decisions promise to yield real benefits to the citizenry as a whole or to future generations of citizens. In this way, pluralism renders native public enterprise operations inefficient both at home and abroad. It follows that any foreign public enterprise operating in a national mixed economy will operate inefficiently as well if its home polity is pluralist.[18]

At the heart of this argument are two alternative sets of assumptions. The first includes the premise that as voters, citizens place little value on future returns from public enterprise, especially returns to future generations. Voters value the short-term benefits that derive from native public enterprise, especially the benefits that accrue to

18. Mazzolini (1979a) discusses the effects that the supposedly short-term orientation of pluralist politics has on public enterprise efficiency, particularly on the international competitiveness of state-owned firms. He stresses the short-term orientation of politicians, their desire for visible results, and their partisan orientation. Mazzolini argues that politicians and voters generally restrain public enterprise and its managers from taking what are otherwise sound, foreign business investments. See also Laux and Molot (1987: chap. 8).

them at the expense of other citizens, born and unborn. Voters regularly execute their collective ownership rights through elections, and the exigencies and nature of electoral politics are such that officials must intervene in the operations of native public enterprise in order to serve their constituents' short-term, selfish interests. A related set of assumptions includes the ideas that citizens do not understand how native state enterprise operations affect their welfare, and that only a few citizens execute their ownership rights through elections. Rather, party activists are the ones who interfere in native public enterprise's local and foreign operations in order to secure crucial, swing votes that ensure their reelection.

Both sets of assumptions were evaluated in Chapters 4 and 5. That evaluation stressed the importance of the degree of dissensus about the rationale for and objectives of public enterprise. It also stressed the difficulty of executing collective ownership rights through elections and other forms of pluralist politics. Among our conclusions were: (1) as owners of public enterprises, citizens are not necessarily purely self-interested and myopic—there is the possibility of genuine consensus over the ends of public enterprise; (2) if citizens genuinely disagree about the ends of public enterprise, there is no reason to expect different parties to manage the public enterprise sector in the same way; and (3) elections are highly imperfect means through which to exercise collective ownership rights—so imperfect, in fact, that citizens are liable to display little efficacy in this regard; hence politicians have an opportunity to pursue their own personal interests through public enterprise.

These conclusions have several implications for our analysis of open, pluralist mixed political economies. First, pluralism affects some kinds of public enterprise operations more than others. In particular, pluralist politics is liable to have fewer effects on the operations of state-owned firms that mine and trade natural resources. The reason is that the location of production is not subject to public choice: nature determines the location of mineral deposits. Also, natural resource ventures are more likely to be viewed as collective assets than are other kinds of public enterprise. Living and future citizens have a clearer claim on the benefits that derive from the development of natural resources than on the benefits from other forms of public enterprise. The collective sense of vulnerability often associated with openness therefore makes it likely that multiparty agreements can be forged to create and to foster the international competitiveness of public enterprise. Pluralist politics may affect the way in which the earnings of these firms are allocated within the home nation-state, but local and foreign operations will probably be only marginally affected by partisan competition. In turn, collective gains and intergenerational equity can potentially be achieved through these state-owned enterprises.[19]

In most other cases, pluralism undermines the efficiency and international competitiveness of state enterprise. Location decisions are more arbitrary: for example, in contrast to mining, mineral processing can be carried out in more than one locality or region of a country. The collective and intergenerational benefits from these kinds of production may also be more difficult to assess. At the same time the location of public enterprises within particular communities promises to greatly enhance the welfare of some citizens at the expense of others. Conversely, the decision to undertake foreign public investment clearly harms the short-term interests of particular citizens. Groups and communities therefore have clearer incentives to form political coalitions to promote or oppose these kinds of public enterprise operations as compared to the development and export of natural resources.

The power of the coalitions that form on behalf of certain public enterprise decisions depends on the number of constituents involved. The larger the coalition, the more political power it may exert. However, because of the way pluralist institutions work, a small but *pivotal* coalition may be able to exercise tremendous influence over the operations of native public enterprises. A small political faction may demand curtailment or even abandonment of public enterprises' foreign activities in return for their support for an incumbent coalition government.

Foreign public investment, as pointed out above, is likely to be especially controversial. Because of the nature of foreign public investment it is probable that workers and communities will execute their collective ownership rights against such investment, arguing that their local interests should be served rather than those of foreign communities. After all, the affected citizens own the enterprise, and their particular interests are directly threatened by the foreign public investment. If these coalitions block such investments, they may succeed in maintaining their share of the national intragenerational distribution of wealth, at least over the short term. In the process, however,

19. For the consensual basis for the creation of state-owned mining ventures in Canada see Laux and Molot (1987). See also Breton (1964) and Chandler (1982). Mazzolini (1979a) acknowledges the bipartisan support for these kinds of "primary" public enterprise ventures. He argues that this support derives in part from the fact that location decisions are determined by nature rather than by more ambiguous microeconomic criteria.

their action may render the native public enterprise less competitive internationally, imposing a collective welfare loss on the citizenry of the nation-state as well as on future generations of citizens. The indications are that under pluralism most ruling political coalitions curtail foreign public investment. Hence, it appears pluralism tends to impose collective welfare losses and, in effect, create intergenerational inequity in open mixed political economies.

It follows from the analysis in Chapter 5 that in open pluralist mixed economies, the intragenerational distribution of wealth is in some part an outgrowth of the prevailing balance of electoral forces or of the outcomes of coalition politics. Different political coalitions will form to encourage or to block changes in the local and foreign operations of native public enterprises. These coalitions may contain groups from the largest, most exposed sectors of the open economy, including segments of the state enterprise workforce. These groups are directly affected by changes in native public enterprise operations, as well as by international business developments, and they have greater collective ownership efficacy than other citizens do.

The pivotal nature of some political factions allows them to exercise a degree of influence disproportionate to their size. If the populace disagrees about the most equitable blend of distributional equity, elections may change the makeup of the ruling coalition; elections may alter the identity or relative power of these pivotal factions. In turn, the operational decisions of native public enterprises will change to reflect the new constellation of interests in the ruling coalition. The intragenerational distribution of wealth will shift as public enterprises alter their purchasing and investment decisions to enhance the welfare of different individuals, communities, and regions. State enterprise workers may have somewhat greater collective ownership efficacy than private enterprise workers, that is, they may be more willing to join coalitions that promote changes in their firms' operations; and in some cases they may wield a potent strike threat. But beyond this, state enterprise workers will not play a role markedly different from that of other interest groups. Ultimately, they must build and participate in political coalitions like other workers.[20]

20. For example, Lamont argues with respect to state enterprise joint ventures that "an election can throw the best-laid plans awry. It is a tribute to public enterprise management that such a destructive shift in the home government–state enterprise nexus has been held to a minimum"(1979:114). (In various passages Lamont contradicts himself, implying that in fact home government interference occurs regularly with deleterious effects on state enterprise performance.) Hindley (1982:120) also links electoral outcomes and the performance of public enterprise. The effects of the federalist character of many pluralist political systems on provincial public enterprise operations are studied in Laux and Molot (1987). The more general idea that native enterprise oper-

The welfare consequences of foreign public enterprise operations are difficult to predict in this case. Foreign disinvestment threats may be less potent because the affected individuals and communities now have the option of demanding expansion of native public enterprises in their jurisdiction. When such demands are met, they enlarge the native public enterprise sector and enhance the economic security of groups of citizens. Intragenerational equity is in this sense preserved by the possibility of answering foreign public enterprise's threats to disinvest with native public investment.

The long-term effects of foreign disinvestment threats may be less salutary, however. Unless natural resource development is involved, any newly created or expanded native public enterprise is liable to be the object of distributional conflict. Hence it will be very difficult to turn the enterprise into a champion of national interests. Over the long term, then, threats by foreign public enterprises to disinvest are likely to enlarge the size and diminish further the competitiveness of native public enterprise. Competing equity claims among living citizens may be more fully adjudicated in these circumstances, but in the process, collective welfare losses and intergenerational inequity are likely to occur.

In sum, open pluralist mixed systems are likely to be more inefficient than open private enterprise systems in that they fail to realize gains from trade or to pursue foreign public investment opportunities. The principal reason is that pluralist politics undermines the international competitiveness and long-term efficiency of native public enterprise. This effect is likely to be most pronounced in nation-states where citizens genuinely disagree about what constitutes a just blend of social welfare. The foreign operations of native public enterprise can be expected to be severly curtailed and most inefficient in these cases.

The intragenerational distribution of wealth in this third type of political economy is potentially more equitable than it is in open pluralist private enterprise political economies. In open pluralist mixed systems, native citizens have the ability to influence a large share of investment decisions. But this ability does not guarantee citizen efficacy with respect to the execution of collective ownership rights. Hence there remain, as in the case of closed pluralist mixed political economies, opportunities for state managers and public officials to capture a large share of societal wealth.

---

ations are an outgrowth of political coalition building within the home country is advanced by Evans (1979) and Vernon (1979:10).

The Open, Corporatist Mixed Political Economy

In political economies that are open, corporatist, and mixed, welfare outcomes are an outgrowth of the same factors that apply to pluralist mixed systems, together with those which stem from producer group negotiations and elections. Public enterprise operations are partly the result of the ways citizens execute their collective ownership rights, but these rights are executed through dual channels of representation. Openness helps labor organize workers at the same time that it eventually creates conflicts of interest between workers in the sheltered and the exposed sectors of the economy. In this fourth kind of political economy, labor leaders must cope with these conflicts of interest.

Corporatism facilitates intertemporal choices that enhance the international competitiveness of public enterprise. As a consequence, open corporatist mixed political economies are potentially more efficient than open pluralist mixed economies. Collective ends are easier to pursue under corporatism because the authority of producer group leaders is more secure than that of popularly elected officials. Producer group leaders face less risky electoral contests than do public officials, and they are therefore freer to promote the international competitiveness of native public enterprise. Support for the requisite purchasing and investment decisions of native public enterprises can be more easily generated through producer group organizations, if need be by compensating affected workers and communities. In addition, joint ventures with privately owned firms are more easily arranged and medium-range public investment planning is more feasible than in pluralist mixed systems. Operations of native public enterprise are liable to be more efficient than those of public enterprises from pluralist mixed political economies. Operations of foreign public enterprises from countries with corporatist political systems are likely to be comparatively more efficient as well.[21]

In terms of the distribution of wealth between wage earners and private asset holders, the prospects for intragenerational equity remain greatest in corporatist mixed economies. Wage earners have a greater capacity to achieve distributional equity in open corporatist mixed systems than in the other three open political economies. However, openness creates serious problems for wage earners and their representatives.

---

21. Most of the authors cited above fail to distinguish the operations of state-owned enterprises from corporatist countries from those of state-owned enterprises from pluralist countries. As we shall see, there are good reasons to believe the two kinds of public enterprises perform differently in international markets.

Openness creates new, potentially destabilizing conflicts of interest among wage earners. These conflicts exacerbate the behavioral problems associated with corporatism. Openness produces an additional cleavage within labor organizations, namely, conflicts of interest between workers in sheltered and exposed sectors of the economy. The interests of state enterprise workers in the sheltered sector differ substantially from those of workers in the exposed sector, as well as from workers in private enterprise. State enterprise workers in the sheltered sector retain a potent strike weapon, but those in the exposed sector have a less effective strike weapon. The latter workers are still liable to exercise their collective ownership rights more effectively than are workers in private enterprise. Hence they are likely to be "privileged" to some degree relative to their private enterprise counterparts. However, the possibility of foreign public investment makes them generally less powerful than in closed corporatist mixed systems. In principle, then, state enterprise workers in the exposed sector are able to capture a smaller share of societal wealth.

This situation greatly complicates the tasks facing labor leaders. It makes it more difficult for them to legitimize their positions of authority, since policy decisions inevitably serve the interests of one segment of the workforce rather than the other. In particular, decisions regarding the operations of native public enterprise are bound to spawn serious controversies between segments of the rank and file. Consider, for example, the decision to endorse foreign public investment by a native public enterprise. For reasons given above, affected state enterprise workers are likely to oppose such an action and press labor leaders to protect their short-term interests rather than serve the interests of foreign individuals. Workers in private enterprise and in sheltered public enterprises may endorse such investment, however, on the grounds that it promotes collective welfare or intergenerational equity. Other social groups may endorse foreign public investment for the same reasons. Labor leaders then face an impossible situation: no matter what they decide, they will serve the interests of some major segment of the workforce at the expense of another.

Centralist state administrators may help labor leaders cope with such dissension. State administrators may support the pursuit of collective gains and intergenerational equity through public relations campaigns, and administrators can help labor leaders find financial resources with which to compensate the workers harmed by the foreign operations of native public enterprises. But over the long term, state administrators are unlikely to reduce the tensions that inevitably arise within the labor producer group. Eventually some substantial segment of the workforce must suffer while another segment bene-fits, thereby undermining the authority of labor leaders.

Threats by foreign public enterprises to disinvest also destabilize corporatist politics over the long term. In the short term these threats may facilitate producer groups' efforts to promote collective national interests. To the extent these threats tend to enlarge the na-tive public enterprise sector, however, they increase the share of the workforce in the exposed sector of the economy. More workers be-come directly affected by foreign public investment decisions and other efforts to enhance the international competitiveness of native public enterprise. Increased tension within labor organizations and the delegitimation of labor leadership inevitably result.

In sum, open corporatist mixed political economies tend to be more efficient than their open pluralist counterparts, and the intra-generational distribution of wealth is likely to favor wage earners in open, corporatist mixed systems more than in the other three open systems. The intragenerational distribution again will favor state en-terprise workers to some degree, especially state enterprise workers in sheltered segments of the economy. In other respects the intragen-erational distribution will depend on the balance of electoral forces within producer groups and within the nation-state as a whole. Over time, in fact, electoral politics is likely to have a greater impact on the operations of native public enterprise, and hence on the prevailing blend of social welfare, because over time corporatism is liable to break down as conflicts of interest between workers become more se-vere. In the process, it is likely that native public enterprise will be-come less internationally competitive. Hence over the long term the gains from trade in corporatist–mixed political economies may be only slightly greater than those made in pluralist–mixed political economies.

IMPLICATIONS

The analysis in this chapter leaves the results in Chapter 5 basically intact. Our study of the politics of foreign public enterprise and openness again indicates that pluralist–mixed political economies produce the smallest collective consumption gains and intergenera-tional equity of the four systems. Whether collective welfare is most enhanced in corporatist–private enterprise systems depends on the capacity of this mode of interest intermediation to cope with the new and more intense distributional conflicts that openness creates. Our analysis suggests that openness produces tensions within producer groups, especially within national labor organizations. To the extent these tensions undermine the effectiveness of corporatist institutions and increase the influence that electoral and party politics have on public enterprise operations, the performance of corporatist–private enterprise political economies on the first welfare criterion will be similar to that of pluralist–private enterprise systems.[22]

Intragenerational inequity between wage earners and private asset holders is again most pronounced in pluralist–private enterprise political economies, because openness further restricts governments' capacity to tax and transfer wealth in these systems, either by default or by design (the deliberate creation of privately owned national champions that are less easy to tax and to regulate). The superiority of corporatist–mixed political economies in this respect again hinges on how well producer group leaders cope with the distributional conflict that openness produces. The potential for maldistributions of wealth between state enterprise and private enterprise workers is still present, but openness creates new conflicts of interest between workers in the exposed and sheltered sectors of the economy. These two lines of conflict destabilize corporatism, render political decision making more pluralist, and hence diminish the contrasts between intragenerational welfare outcomes in pluralist–mixed and corporatist–mixed political economies.

Figure 13 summarizes the effects of the politics of foreign public enterprise and openness on the potential in the four systems for achieving different blends of social welfare. Contrasts between these political economies are more or less stark under the conditions outlined above. For example, centralist state administrators committed to the promotion of collective consumption gains and intergenerational equity through international trade increase the likelihood that a pluralist–private enterprise system will perform better on the first (vertical) welfare criterion and worse on the second (horizontal) welfare criterion. A high degree of linkage between national and international capital markets further limits governments' capacities to achieve intragenerational equity in these political economies. Such linkage makes it even easier for private investors to disinvest in order to avoid taxation and regulation. Finally, popular dissensus over the objectives of native public enterprise is likely to exacerbate the effects of pluralism on the efficiency of mixed economies. In turn, the inferiority of pluralist–mixed systems with respect to the first

22. Or differences in performance will depend on what kind of electoral system exists in both systems. See Rogowski (1987).

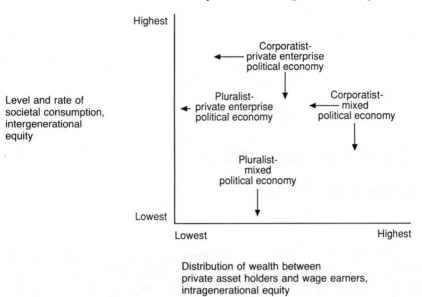

Figure 13. Long-term effects of openness on the welfare consequences of four basic types of political economies

welfare criterion is more marked than it would be if there were societal consensus about the objectives of public enterprise, at home and abroad.

One of the main implications of this revised analysis is that openness—particularly those features pertaining to the foreign operation of public enterprises—creates dissensus within political economies, especially among wage earners. Foreign public enterprise operations eventually make it more difficult for labor leaders to maintain their authority over the rank and file in open corporatist–mixed systems. Hence it becomes more and more difficult for them to promote market efficiency and collective welfare gains through corporatist institutions. Ultimately, then, the contrasts between the workings of pluralist–private enterprise and pluralist–mixed political economies may be most germane for our evaluation of democratic capitalism.

CHAPTER TEN

The Tale of Two Political
Economies Revisited

Our revised welfare taxonomy better accounts for the performance of Britain and Austria. Anomalies in Britain's and Austria's performance can be partly explained in terms of the politics of openness and foreign public enterprise. These political factors are also important in the Italian and Swedish cases.

BRITAIN

Britain's political economy is pluralist–private enterprise, and Britain performs as expected on both welfare criteria in comparison to Sweden and Austria. However, its performance is inferior to that of Italy with respect to collective gains and intergenerational equity, and until recently it achieved a somewhat higher degree of intragenerational equity than expected. These anomalies are partly attributable to the relative inefficiency of British private enterprise. Pluralism is, in some part, responsible for this inefficiency. It undermines the efficiency of private investment because it creates uncertainty about the long-term structure of property rights. As a result of the comparatively poor performance of private enterprise, the British economy is less productive than expected. British firms are somewhat immobile, and hence governments have somewhat greater capacity to redistribute income than expected.

Britain has a moderately open economy. The volume of its trade is roughly half of its gross domestic product; its nontariff barriers are relatively low.[1] No foreign public enterprises appear among the top

1. See the World Bank's *World Tables*, 1984 (Washington, D.C.) and *World Development Report*, 1984 (Washington, D.C.: World Bank), Table 2.5.

hundred firms in Britain, and only a handful among the top five hundred.[2] Some nationalized firms and parastatals are active in world markets. In the mid-1980s, for example, British Leyland and Rolls Royce were among the top ten British exporters; British Petroleum consistently ranked as one of the largest firms in Europe as well as in the world.[3] Because of the absence of a well-developed foreign public enterprise sector, we focus here on the political implications of the openness of Britain's economy and of the international activities of its native privately owned and publicly owned firms.[4]

Britain's relatively poor performance on the first welfare criterion derives in part from the fact that since World War II its firms have not competed effectively in world markets. Its multinationals have concentrated their activities in declining or stagnant industries. They have also displayed a lack of entrepreneurial spirit insofar as the development of new markets and technologies is concerned. The nationalized industries have tried to formulate international business strategies but, at the same time, they have lobbied for protection against foreign imports. And, as I pointed out in Chapter 7, nationalized industries have been forced to maintain economic security of workers and communities at home and also to keep their domestic prices low. Their foreign business ventures and attempts to forge joint ventures with local and foreign private firms have been largely unsuccessful as a result. By all indications, they and their private counterparts have realized comparatively fewer gains from international trade than firms in other countries.[5]

2. Included in the top five hundred British companies for 1984–1985 are several French foreign (para)state enterprises (Elf Aquitaine, no. 114; Total, no. 143; Renault, no. 232, and Total Marine, no. 357) and one Norwegian state firm (Norsk-Hydro, no. 333). Two Italian firms, Montedison and Alfa Romeo, rank 767th and 933d, respectively, in the top thousand firms in Britain in these years. See *The Times 1000* (London, 1985).

3. The relative importance of these and other Company Act or parastatal firms is evident from the figures given in the introduction to *The Times 1000*. Rolls Royce and British Petroleum are both being privatized by the Thatcher administration: see the *Economist*, April 9, 1987, pp. 65–66; August 31, 1987, p. 14; September 5, 1987, pp. 72, 76.

4. I have found no reference to political conflicts over the activities of foreign public enterprise in Britain. Nor were these activities brought up by interviewees in London in autumn 1984.

5. For a discussion of noncompetitiveness of British multinationals see the *Economist*, December 12, 1985, p. 77. International activities of nationalized industries are reviewed by Ezra (1982); he describes the foreign activities of the National Coal Board in detail. Pryke (1981) mentions the harmful effects of employment and other policies on the international competitiveness of British nationalized industries. He stresses the need for joint ventures with Japanese firms in the auto industry, for instance. Hindley (1982) provides a more general review of the ways in which government intervention in the operations of nationalized industries undermines their international competitiveness and produces collective welfare losses.

International financiers are often blamed for the poor performance of British firms. International banking is a major source of exchange earnings for Britain. Also, in recent years British firms, including nationalized industries, have been able to secure investment capital in offshore markets. These ventures into offshore capital markets, according to some observers, have enhanced the efficiency of the firms involved. But other observers suggest that the same markets have also driven up the value of the pound and in turn inflated the price of British goods and services. A lack of international competitiveness of British exports has been the result. The effects of speculation in the pound after the discovery of North Sea oil are illustrative. By all indications, speculation inflated prices of British goods and services to such a degree it nullified any advantages firms enjoyed as a consequence of government subsidies. In this way, international financial transactions have prevented British private and public enterprise from realizing the short- and medium-term gains from trade realized in other countries.[6]

To the extent that international financial transactions render British private firms uncompetitive and immobile, they tend to enhance government ability to shape the intragenerational distribution of wealth. The noncompetitiveness of British private firms makes their disinvestment threats less potent than if they could easily relocate in other countries. Also, nationalized industries provide opportunities for protecting the welfare of particular workers and communities. As a result, pluralist politics has had a greater impact on the distribution of wealth in Britain than we would expect on the basis of the analysis in Chapter 5. In this way our incorporation of the politics of openness helps explain Britain's unexpected performance on the second welfare criterion in the 1970s.

In other respects openness restricts British government capacities to alter the intragenerational distribution of wealth. British financiers for many years have enjoyed the freedom to invest overseas, allowing them to escape government efforts to tax and redistribute their wealth. Indeed, in this respect the barriers to intragenerational redistribution are greater in Britain than in almost any other industrialized country. Banking capital, for example, is the least integrated with any national industrial capital, and it displays comparatively little

6. Nationalized industry and parastatal borrowing in international capital markets is briefly described by the *Economist*, August 30, 1986, p. 68. Alt (1987) argues that currency speculation after the North Sea oil discoveries is largely responsible for the decline in the competitiveness of British industry and the consequent high unemployment. See also the *Economist*, October 5, 1985, p. 63. On the general importance of financial services in the British economy and for British trade, see the *Economist*, December 7, 1985, pp. 70–71; August 15, 1987, p. 44.

long-term commitment to develop any particular national economy. In addition, British money managers have invested an increasingly large share of wage earners' pension funds in foreign markets, so that workers, through their own foreign transactions, further restrict government capacity to redistribute wealth. These developments combine with the privatization of many nationalized industries— privatization accomplished, in part, through "international offers" to foreign investors—to give current and future British governments less ability to shape the intragenerational distribution of wealth than their predecessors. The politics of openness implies that recent, theoretically consistent trends in social welfare are likely to persist in Britain (cf. Figures 12 and 13).[7]

Britain's pluralist political system is partly responsible for these events. Political parties have endorsed or tolerated the international activities of British financiers. The consensus of the 1950s and 1960s included a commitment to maintaining the value of British currency, which aided British financial interests at the same time that it reduced the international competitiveness of British goods and services and produced some collective welfare losses. As popular consensus eroded in Britain, some elements of the Labour party charged that financiers were "starving" local private entrepreneurs—financiers were refusing to finance local private investment. But a government commission and Labour "radicals" were unable to show that financiers had refused to provide capital to domestic investors, or that financiers were deeply involved in the operations of many domestic producers. Rather, as I pointed out in Chapter 7, the problem was lack of demand for investment capital and lackluster managerial performance.[8] In addition, in the 1970s and 1980s the speculative behavior of financiers was tolerated by both parties. The Thatcher government has actually encouraged such behavior by opening international financial markets further, for example, by eliminating regulatory restrictions on overseas transactions and by inviting in more foreign financial interests. These policies are rooted, in part, in the desire to serve the interests of Thatcher's constituency and also to promote the long-term efficiency of the British economy.

As regards the nationalized industries, the consensus of the 1950s and 1960s promoted the international expansion of parastatal national champions such as British Petroleum. The perception of mu-

7. For a more general review of the activities of international financiers and the constraints these activities impose on British governments, see Marsh and Locksley (1983) and Coakley and Harris (1983). The latter source discusses the increasingly international nature of pension fund investment in Britain; see also the *Economist*, April 4, 1987, p. 76.
8. The capital starvation thesis is reviewed in Coakley and Harris (1983).

tual strategic interests in energy production led parties to help British Petroleum capture a substantial share of the world market in certain commodities. It also led parties to tolerate a comparatively high degree of autonomy for BP managers. The same bipartisan consensus appears to underlie recent efforts to restrict foreign private ownership of certain industries and to incorporate international considerations into regulatory decision making.[9]

With regard to other nationalized industries and other parastatals, parties agreed to support some managers' efforts to develop an international business strategy, and in the face of declining world demand for some goods, parties tolerated substantial reductions in the numbers of workers employed in such nationalized industries as steel. At the same time, however, parties forced nationalized industries to sacrifice some of their international marketing efforts and foreign investments on behalf of short-term, local interests. Some nationalized industries were forced to buy the output of others rather than import the same goods more cheaply from overseas. Inefficiency and a collective welfare loss no doubt resulted from these practices. In this way pluralist politics sanctioned and reinforced the effects of international financial activity on the competitiveness of British industry.[10]

The blend of welfare outcomes in Britain is partly the result of the power that certain political factions exercise within the polity. Policies toward the nationalized industries reflect the power that such factions wield. The coal industry is illustrative. It was protected from foreign competition and many of its inefficiencies were tolerated because of the power of coal unions and mining communities. This power was exercised through the Labour party and through the use of a potent strike threat. In effect, state enterprise workers in this industry were able to capture some of the wealth of the workers in other state industries as well as impose some collective welfare losses on British society as a whole.[11]

International financiers and their allies also wield power within British politics. The commitment to maintain the value of the pound and the toleration of international currency speculation reflect the influence of financial groups within both political parties, especially

9. The consensual basis for the creation of and support for British Petroleum's international business strategy is described in Lamont (1979:27) and Aharoni (1986:355). See also the discussion of the common perception of a threat of foreign control over certain kinds of mineral development in Chapter 9 above.

10. Again, see Hindley (1982).

11. For many years, of course, there was widespread popular support for differential gains to coalminers; cf. Chapter 7 above. Also, chairmen of the National Coal Board were particularly adept at negotiating beneficial treatment from elected officials and state administrators. See, for instance, Monsen and Walters (1983:60–63).

the Conservative party. Financial interests benefit directly from speculation and fees for handling privatizations, indirectly from the price stability that often accompanies an overvalued exchange rate. The constituency of the Conservative party also includes a segment of the workforce, more specifically, skilled workers who have benefited from the party's fiscal policies and from lower inflation rates. As noted in Chapter 7, these workers are part of the coalition the Thatcher administration represents. They appear willing to support Thatcher in return for absolute gains in real income—or gains relative to other workers—and the preservation of the value of their material assets. Admittedly, skilled workers in some industries are less secure today as a consequence of their firms' being privatized or forced to compete with foreign firms. But they are not as insecure or as poor as many unskilled workers in private and privatized firms. The welfare of the latter group of workers has not been enhanced by the Thatcher administration; they are not implicitly members of that government's coalition. Thus the intragenerational distribution of wealth again mirrors the makeup of the political coalition that holds positions of authority in Britain's pluralist polity.[12]

Our three structural factors are all relevant here. To the extent that the British Treasury supplies technocratic justification for opening the British economy or helps "mystify" the workings of international capital markets, it reinforces the influence of financial interests. In turn, international transactions limit the blends of social welfare that can be achieved in Britain.[13] The greater mobility of capital and the international expansion of newly privatized firms like British Petroleum make the barriers to redistribution of wealth in Britain even more severe now than earlier. Whether further opening of the economy and privatization will make British firms more competitive and hence realize comparatively greater gains from trade remains to be seen. Some observers suggest the financial sector itself may be the engine of growth insofar as it ushers in and enhances the efficiency of a new service economy. Either way, wealth has been redistributed to financial interests and skilled workers at the expense of industrial interests and unskilled workers. Electoral competition is unlikely to reverse this outcome in the future.[14]

12. On the direct and indirect influence of financial interests in British politics see Moran (1981) and Marsh and Locksley (1983).

13. Moran (1981) and Coakley and Harris (1983:220–21) describe the role of the Bank of England in articulating and defending financial interests within British governments. The implication is that the Treasury is an implicit ally of skilled workers.

14. There is some question whether electoral competition ever had major impacts on international financial transactions. See Freeman and Alt (1987), where the effects of political uncertainty are studied in the context of a seven-variable vector autoregres-

Dissensus among British citizens will no doubt have welfare consequences. It will undermine the competitiveness of the remaining nationalized industries and prevent them from developing an effective international business strategy. In the process some small number of state enterprise workers and their communities will no doubt maintain a higher degree of economic security than their counterparts in private industries. But since this sector has shrunk in size and parties are unwilling or unable to renationalize many firms, there is good reason to believe that the effects of pluralism on the overall efficiency of the British economy will diminish. The economic well-being of unskilled workers and their communities will be increasingly undermined in coming years.

In sum, the British experience demonstrates the validity of our revised account of pluralist–private enterprise economies. It confirms the importance of openness—especially of international financial transactions. Openness affects the efficiency of the British economy and limits the possibilities for redistributing wealth intragenerationally. The British case also confirms our revised expectations about the possibility for consensus on state development of natural resources (the case of British Petroleum); and it confirms our expectations about the effects of pluralism on the international competitiveness of state-owned firms. In this context, the relationship between the power of particular factions and coalitions and the intragenerational distribution of wealth has been established. Last, in what it suggests about trends in and the effects of openness, our discussion implies that the British case should conform more closely to our theoretical expectations in the future. As an increasingly open, pluralist–private enterprise system, Britain should perform somewhat better on the first welfare criterion and somewhat worse on the second in coming decades.

AUSTRIA

Austria has a corporatist–mixed political economy and performs as expected on the first welfare criterion. Austria has achieved collective welfare gains and a degree of intergenerational equity that match or exceed those of Britain, Sweden, and Italy. The degree of employment security is higher in Austria than in most Western industrialized countries; however, indications are that income is more maldistrib-

sive model that includes exchange rates.

utcd intragenerationally than expected. The revised analysis in Chapter 9 suggests that Austria's performance in these respects is not only an outgrowth of the workings of its corporatist polity and mixed economy but also, in some part, an outgrowth of the international activities of its state-owned enterprises and the general openness of its mixed economy.

Austria's economy is relatively open. The sum of its imports and exports is roughly equal to three-quarters of its GDP.[15] Austria's nontariff barriers are moderately high for imports from developed countries though somewhat lower for imports from developing countries. Among small West European countries, Austria has one of the highest tariff walls.[16]

Native public enterprises are active in international markets. In the 1980s the state holding company, OeIAG, has accounted for about one-fifth of Austria's exports, and some of its main subsidiaries have sold more than half their output overseas. These and other publicly owned firms have made direct foreign investments in North America, Africa, and Asia. The OeIAG is participating in venture capital enterprises in the United States and Germany, and it has also floated several large international bonds to help finance its restructuring efforts. Few foreign public enterprises appear among the top hundred firms in Austria, and only several more among the top five hundred. There is no well-developed foreign public enterprise sector in Austria.[17]

Austria's exemplary performance on the first welfare criterion derives in part from its firms' international competitiveness. Austrian private and public enterprises have captured niches in a number of international markets and opened new markets in Eastern Europe, the Soviet Union, and East Asia, resulting in a steady flow of export earnings. With the help of the government, Austrian firms have also been able to secure loans in international capital markets. These

15. See the World Bank's *World Tables, 1984* (Washington, D.C.).
16. *World Development Report, 1984* (Washington, D.C.: World Bank), Table 2.5. On high tariff walls in Austria see Katzenstein (1984:53).
17. See *OeIAG Annual Reports* for data on the relative importance of nationalized industry exports and the activities of Austrian public firms in international goods and money markets. The top hundred firms in Austria in 1985 (*Trend*, December 1985) included British Petroleum (43), the BMW Group (52), and AGIP (70). Among the next four hundred were Donau Chemie (Rhone Poulenc/Frankreich, 156), Renault (191), and CII–Honeywell Bull (444). I have found no studies of the foreign public enterprise sector in Austria. Interviews with Austrian state managers, administrators, and party and union officials revealed few concerns about foreign state enterprise. The one exception was the state steel combine's slight preference for joint ventures with foreign private rather than foreign public firms. The former are believed to have a stronger market position and a greater technological advantage in the world economy (Interview, Linz, November 1986). This perception is consistent with our evaluation of the relative efficiency of foreign public enterprises; see Chapter 9 above.

loans have been used to modernize existing plants and thus to increase the long-term competitiveness of Austrian enterprises. As we noted in Chapter 7, neither accomplishment has come at the expense of price stability. Rather, a relative low rate of inflation has been achieved in Austria as a result of the way governments have coordinated their hard-currency and Keynesian fiscal policies and secured "fresh capital" in international credit markets. Once more, the motivation for government policies is, in part, the perceived need to compensate for the underdeveloped character of Austrian financial markets and the inward-looking nature of domestic financial institutions.[18]

Although nationalized industries have contributed to Austria's export earnings and to the modernization of Austria's capital stock, in the 1980s they have suffered large financial losses. Some foreign investments have failed; two publicly owned firms lost several hundred million schillings speculating in international oil markets. OeIAG subsidiaries have also suffered losses because of shortfalls in world demand for their products. These shortfalls have been caused by developing countries' debt-based inability to import and by fluctuations in the value of Western currencies, especially in the relative value of the dollar. But the largest losses have been incurred as a consequence of the way the nationalized industries responded to the collapse of international iron and steel markets. Decisions to delay adjustment to world market developments have produced unprecedented losses. These deficits have been financed through a series of large "shareholder contributions" by the Austrian state.

The nationalized industries have attempted to improve their international competitiveness. They have developed new international marketing strategies; for instance, they have introduced project "packages"—a bundle of construction and engineering services for sale to developing countries. The OeIAG has also developed long-term restructuring plans designed to enhance the productivity of metal processing and other industries; diversified into industries in which international market trends counterbalance those in iron, steel, and related industries; and adopted more systematic and stricter internal accounting procedures. It remains to be seen whether these policies will restore the financial self-sufficiency and improve the international competitiveness of nationalized industry. Either way, Austria's performance on the first welfare criterion will continue to

18. There is some evidence that Austria's exports became slightly less competitive as a result of appreciation of the schilling, but this development was counterbalanced by a relative decline in unit labor costs. See Braun (1986: chap. 19).

depend, to a substantial extent, on how well its public and also private enterprises perform in world markets.[19]

On the second welfare criterion, Austria's performance in terms of employment is, in part, an outgrowth of native firms' propensity to produce goods and services at home rather than in foreign countries. Among small countries Austria is unusual in the degree to which its businesses produce and invest *within* national boundaries rather than abroad. The controversies that foreign direct investment spawns about whether it serves the interests of foreign citizens at expense of particular native citizens arise infrequently in Austria.[20]

The nationalized industries are no exception in this regard. OeIAG subsidiaries have made foreign investments in several countries, justifying these investments in terms of such standard microeconomic considerations as the cost of transporting finished products and access to raw materials. Some labor leaders have supported these foreign public investments, but direct foreign public investment constitutes a small share of total public investment. The OeIAG makes most of its investments within Austria's boundaries. Moreover, the plan for restructuring steel and other industries provides for additional *national* investment of considerable magnitude.[21] And proposals for joint ventures with foreign firms, mostly foreign private firms, often provide for majority control by OeIAG subsidiaries with provisos for local investment and job guarantees. Despite an expressed commitment to "internationalize" nationalized industry, most public investments will be undertaken within national boundaries. This fact, coupled with the parties' continued opposition to foreign

19. The importance of international market trends for the commercial fortunes of OeIAG subsidiaries is continually stressed in the holding company's annual reports (for example, the 1985 report, pp. 42, 91). See the same sources for descriptions of nationalized industry planning, diversification—especially out of steel production—and internal accounting efforts. One of the principal restructuring schemes is the "Corporate Plan, Measures and Self-Financing Needs for Restructing the Nationalized Industries," which was passed in 1983. The state authorized the OeIAG to borrow up to 16.6 billion schillings to implement this plan. In so doing the government urged "efforts . . . to *internationalize [nationalized] industry* so that Austria can reap benefits that are also achieved by other small states through the international activities of domestic enterprises" (*OeIAG Annual Report, 1984*, p. 97, my emphasis). For an evaluation of this part of restructuring see Itzlinger, Kerschbamer, and Van der Bellen (1988: sect. 3.5).

20. On the comparatively low level of foreign production and direct foreign investment by Austrian business—especially in relation to Swiss business—see Katzenstein (1985:51–52). See also Hankel (1981:69), Bowler (1986), and *Wall Street Journal*, May 29, 1987, p. 28.

21. For example, the government's contribution to restructuring the state steel combine, Voest-Alpine, is almost ten times greater than to any other subsidiary of the OeIAG (*OeIAG Annual Report, 1984*, p. 86). Most of this investment is targeted for areas hardest hit by the collapse of world iron and steel markets.

control of major industries, means that governments will retain their ability to create and maintain jobs and, in this way, to shape the intragenerational distribution of wealth within Austria.

Austria's corporatist polity has helped realize gains from trade and maintain the capacity to shape the intragenerational distribution of wealth. The social partners and political parties have been mutually committed, for some time, not just to exploit Austria's natural resources—as through the State Mining Fund, for instance—but also to keep Austrian industry internationally competitive. This commitment is evident in the manner in which real wages have been adjusted to reflect trends in Austria's relative production costs, as well as in the substantial export assistance governments have given to private and public firms. It is also evident in the way governments have consistently promoted modernizing local investments and encouraged joint ventures between native and foreign firms. Moreover, the plan to restructure the nationalized industries is ostensibly an attempt to enhance the international competitiveness of Austria's public enterprises. All these developments indicate that Austria's corporatist political system is conducive to the realization of collective gains from international trade.[22]

Whether state enterprise workers in iron, steel, and other industries should be sheltered from the effects of international market developments has caused increasing controversy within and among producer groups and political parties. Throughout much of the 1970s and 1980s there was widespread support for the idea of providing these workers and their communities with economic security. The social partners and the political parties agreed to give affected public enterprises large subsidies to offset the effects of the collapse of the world steel market. Only in the mid-1980s have serious conflicts arisen within labor and the Socialist party over whether the corresponding groups of workers and communities have a right to economic security or to the same share of societal wealth they enjoyed in the 1960s and 1970s.

The fact that the welfare of these workers and communities has been promoted for so many years, in the face of the collapse of international iron and steel markets, reflects the power that segments of the workforce and their local political allies wield within the Austrian polity. In contrast to such industries as textiles, where production is

22. See Katzenstein (1984, 1985) and Grunwald (1980), who argue that the social partners share a deep, mutual sense of economic vulnerability. This sense of vulnerability is also evident in public statements by political parties about the international competitiveness of the nationalized industries. See, for example, the rationale each provides for its restructuring proposals in the symposium in *Gemeinwirtschaft und Politik* (January 1983).

dispersed and workers are unorganized, iron and steel production is concentrated in politically pivotal regions of the country, and iron and steel workers are highly organized and politically influential with labor organizations. Believing they have a right to economic security regardless of trends in world markets, political factions—local alliances of workers and local party officials—have exploited their dual channels of representation so as to block layoffs and benefit cuts in publicly owned firms. National union and political officials explicitly recognize the collective intergenerational welfare implications of failing to respond to world market developments. But many agree that workers have a right to job security. Either way, they face electoral defeat unless they meet these factions' demands.

Finally, because these firms are publicly owned and most investment is located within Austria, state managers have difficulty relocating to other countries where unions and their allies do not wield so much social power. In Austria's mixed economy, these firms are captives of the polity; they cannot move to other national jurisdictions without the approval of producer groups and political parties. Labor leaders have a much greater say in the operations of these publicly owned firms than their counterparts in the same sector of private enterprise economies. But as the analysis in Chapter 9 predicts, this "say" forces labor leaders to choose between the interests of some segments of the workforce and national collective interests.[23]

New *public* investments have been launched in those regions most affected by the collapse of world iron and steel trade, showing that the same political factions continue to be powerful in Austria. Although this restructuring program provides for the elimination of some jobs and thus diminishes the relative security of the respective unions and communities, it nevertheless represents a long-term commitment to the economic well-being of those regions at the expense of other regions and of future generations (for example, from foregone foreign public investments). In the way it is being financed the investment program also represents a transfer of, or at least a claim on, the wealth from future generations.[24] The new plan for the

---

23. Contrasts in the power of different unions to extract policy concessions from labor and party officials in the face of world market trends are analyzed by Andrlik (1985). He stresses the size and concentration of union membership within particular regions of Austria as well as unions' ability to build political alliances within those regions.

24. To the extent the wealth of future generations is diminished by the failure to undertake more commercially viable foreign public investments, these political factions diminish the wealth of future Austrian citizens still further. Senior labor leaders stress the return to future generations from the political deradicalization of young workers in these depressed areas (interview, Vienna, November 1986).

nationalized industries thus reflects the relative power of state enterprise workers and their local allies in showing that, in the face of world market developments that have clear collective and generational welfare implications, state enterprise workers and their local allies can secure a greater degree of economic security in open corporatist–mixed systems than their counterparts in the same sectors of open pluralist–private enterprise systems. In pluralist–private enterprise systems such as the United States and Britain there is no comparable public investment program.

Structural factors are relevant in the Austrian case. The greater emphasis on technocratic, centralist administration of the nationalized industries is rooted in a commitment to realize greater collective gains from international trade over the medium and long term. The new managers and administrators of the nationalized industries are confident they can make their firms more competitive in international markets and in that way augment Austria's wealth. In this vein, they promise to undertake commercially viable, direct foreign public investments and to participate in lucrative joint ventures with foreign enterprises, public and private. These new managers and administrators are allies of those national officials who are committed to insulating the nationalized industries from the vagaries of producer group and party politics.[25]

Whether the operations of nationalized industries actually will be reoriented in this way, and whether collective national objectives will be promoted at the expense of particular regional interests, depends on the character and distribution of popular opinion in Austria. As noted in Chapter 7, there are signs that large numbers of citizens no longer support nationalized industries' efforts to protect the economic well-being of state enterprise workers. Real conflicts of interest have surfaced between state enterprise workers in the exposed sector of the economy and other workers in Austria. Many citizens now support the pursuit of collective, national interests through more commercially viable, internationally competitive nationalized industries. They may elect union and parliamentary officials who will encourage nationalized industries to pursue these ends at the expense of state enterprise employment.

On the other hand, powerful unions and local political parties remain committed to protecting the welfare of particular segments of

25. Interviews (Vienna, November 1986) with national labor leaders and federal ministers reveal that Austrian officials are confident the new operating procedures for the OeIAG will insulate state managers from the vagaries of union and popular elections and eventually enhance the international competitiveness of the nationalized industries.

the workforce and certain regions of Austria. National union leaders and political officials must maintain the support of these factions if they are to maintain their authority within their producer groups and political parties. It is unlikely they can do so *and* commit nationalized industries to pursue collective national objectives. For example, existing and other, latent, political factions will probably frustrate state managers' plans to undertake new foreign public investments or to negotiate commercially attractive joint venture agreements. Political factions will demand local public investments and also Austrian control—majority ownership—in larger joint ventures with foreign firms. To meet these demands, national union leaders and party officials will intervene in the nationalized industries on behalf of particular interests. The consensual basis for corporatist politics will thus be further undermined, and Austrian governments' capacity to make collectively beneficial intertemporal policy choices will suffer. In such circumstances, electoral outcomes could have a more substantial impact on the operations of nationalized industries and hence on the distribution of wealth in Austria.

International market trends will also have a major impact on the fortunes of nationalized industry. To the extent these trends further erode the financial viability of Austrian publicly owned firms, they may solidify the collective sense of urgency that motivates current efforts to restructure nationalized industry. The demands of state enterprise workers in iron, steel, and other depressed industries and their local allies might be further delegitimized in these circumstances. Corporatist institutions would be stabilized, and the new managers of nationalized industries would have an easier time pursuing commercial objectives, perhaps even in launching more small foreign public investments. These might be the effects of, for example, a prolongation of the international debt crisis and continued erosion of the value of the dollar and other major trading currencies.

A more commercially fortuitous set of international market developments (an amelioration of the debt crisis and sustained rise in the value of the dollar) will have the opposite effect: an upswing in demand for the products of the nationalized industries will encourage political factions to press their demands for economic security and in that way exacerbate conflicts within and between producer groups. But the same effect could occur even in the absence of such world market developments if the new managers and administrators are successful in improving the competitiveness of publicly owned firms. To be more specific, attempts to insulate the nationalized industries from party and producer group politics which produce commercial success invite "politicization" on the grounds that Austria can again afford to provide certain workers and their communities with economic security. And because of the nature of public ownership and power that corporatism—even in a diluted form—affords workers, state managers can do little to escape this influence.

In sum, the Austrian experience confirms the possibility of using state-owned enterprise to realize gains from trade and to shape the intragenerational distribution of wealth. In relation to the British experience, the Austrian case shows that public enterprise can be internationally competitive, at least in certain industries. It also shows that the effects of international financial transactions on the competitiveness of national industry may be lessened through a combination of hard-currency and Keynesian economic policies and public ownership. As noted above, the OeIAG's commercial fortunes are affected by currency fluctuations, but these fluctuations are the result of forces beyond the control of Austrian governments and their publicly owned financial institutions. Austria's few native private financial institutions do not influence the international competitiveness of Austrian business enterprises to the extent that their counterparts influence the competitiveness of British enterprises. Nor do Austrian financial institutions constrain their government's ability to promote the welfare of certain workers and their communities.

The Austrian case confirms that, in mixed economies, openness destabilizes corporatism, creating conflicts of interests between state enterprise and private enterprise workers. As the analysis in Chapter 9 predicts, openness forces labor leaders to choose between collective interests and intergenerational equity, on the one hand, and particular regional interests, on the other. Austria's new, public investment plan and its delay in responding to the collapse of international iron and steel markets illuminate the substantial power that a segment of the workforce can wield in an open, corporatist–mixed system. No segment of the British workforce has or is likely to have this much power. Indeed, in Britain privatization aims to prevent workers from obtaining the kind of power that Austrian workers have.

The larger implication is that not all workers are powerless in the face of international market developments. Some workers in some political economies can capture or retain a significantly greater degree of economic security than others. In so doing, however, these more powerful state enterprise workers may retard their country's performance on the first welfare criterion and simultaneously weaken corporatist institutions. In turn, over the long term, workers as a whole are less powerful. Hence the country concerned may eventually perform worse on the second welfare criterion as well. This is what the future may hold for Austria.

266

BRITAIN AND AUSTRIA IN COMPARATIVE PERSPECTIVE

Italy

Pluralist politics has more direct effects on the international performance of the Italian than the British economy, because of the differences in openness and structure of the two economies. Both countries have financial markets and large, private multinationals that compete in world markets. But Italian financial markets are less developed and less international in character than the British. Moreover, in Italy several large, publicly owned holding companies also compete in world markets.[26] Distinctive about Italy is the degree to which pluralist politics affects the competitiveness of these holding companies and, in turn, the international performance of the Italian economy as a whole.

Foreign investment is illustrative. As noted above, capital flows into and out of the British economy as a result of the decisions of private financiers and private industrialists. The Thatcher administrations' privatization program has given the British government less and less say about the *allocation* of investments within and outside Britain; most of these decisions are in private hands. In Italy, by contrast, public authorities have much more say about how capital is allocated internally and externally because many financial institutions and large business enterprises are owned by the state. In practice, Italian governments have often prevented publicly owned firms from making foreign investments and forced state holding companies to make new investments at home. The result is a set of native firms less competitive than the private firms in many pluralist–private enterprise economies. For example, Italian publicly owned firms' productive facilities are often more inefficient than those of their private competitors, who are freer to build efficient facilities abroad.

Restraints on the foreign investments of Italian publicly owned firms are outgrowths of the workings of Italy's polity and, by implication, of the welfare concerns outlined in Chapter 9. Coalitional politics allows pivotal factions to secure local public investments that enhance the welfare of their constituents at the expense of the constituents of other political factions and of Italian society as a whole. As I noted in Chapter 8 this local public investment often occurs in

26. The enduring difference between the ownership structures of the British and Italian economies is stressed by Stefani (1986:244). The Italian state oil company ENI is compared to the once state-owned British Petroleum by Noreng (1981). As regards the international activities of the Italian state holding companies, the Instituto per la Recostruzione Industriale, IRI, operates almost four hundred subsidiaries worldwide; 30–40 percent of its revenue is generated from foreign customers. IRI alone accounts for about 8 percent of Italy's exports (*Economist*, February 28, 1987).

the south of Italy, in the constituencies of Socialist party deputies who demand and receive the "direct returns" that only local or native investment can produce.[27] These same factions and their allies—some of which are unions—have succeeded in creating new publicly owned firms in response to takeovers and new investments by foreign private firms. The same political coalitions have thwarted efforts to forge joint ventures between publicly owned firms and foreign private enterprises.[28]

In Britain, however, it is now much more difficult for similar factions to secure public investment. Although their country too has a pluralist political system, British political factions have much more difficulty preventing foreign investment by British firms and financiers—because the British political system is more majoritarian and hence less conducive to vetos by small factions and, more important here, because most British firms now are privately owned and hence less subject to direct government influence. Thus Italians may suffer collectively from the greater capacity of political factions to influence the investment decisions and international competitiveness of a large number of publicly owned firms; nevertheless, the same factions are able to secure a greater degree of economic security than their counterparts in parallel industries and regions of Britain.

Overall, Italian wage earners are not likely to secure economic security to match that of Austrian wage earners, because modes of interest intermediation in Austria and Italy are quite different. In particular, the existence of corporatist institutions in Austria makes its wage earners, as a group, likely to secure more benefits from state-owned enterprise than those in Italy. Austrian citizens as a whole are likely to obtain more collective benefits from state-owned enterprise than Italian citizens, as well.

Austria's polity has also imposed restraints on foreign public investment, as we have just seen, and Austrian political factions have fought for and secured large public investments in their communities. Certain regions of Austria have therefore maintained their share of economic wealth in the same way as certain regions of Italy. Generally speaking, however, Austria's corporatist political institutions ap-

27. Prodi (1974:55) writes: "To retain legitimacy, the [Italian] public enterprise must concentrate on increasing domestic employment and developing depressed areas at home. In the foreign field, success has depended on capabilities of a different sort. Moreover, success has not brought direct return to the political apparatus. *Accordingly, the public enterprise has had little incentive to invest significant financial resources in achieving success abroad*" (my emphasis). A more recent discussion of the political restraints on foreign public investment in Italy can be found in Mazzolini (1979a, 1980).

28. See Chapter 2 and Freeman (1987). As regards political opposition to joint ventures between Italian public enterprises and foreign private enterprises, see Italy Survey, *Economist*, February 27, 1988, p. 32.

pear better suited to promote the international competitiveness of its publicly owned firms than are Italy's pluralist political institutions. For example, the decentralized, uncoordinated behavior of Italian unions toward state-owned enterprise produces more myopic, inefficient types of public business behavior than the more centralized policy making of Austrian unions. In addition, Austrian corporatism insulates state managerial decision making from interest-group politics better than the Italian system does, producing more efficient foreign public investments and public trading activity.

The financial difficulties of the Austrian OeIAG in the 1980s suggest that corporatism is not entirely conducive to international competitiveness. Corporatism may well substitute one source of inefficiency—a lack of public accountability—for another—the influence of political factions. Both corporatist and pluralist institutions may produce publicly owned firms unable to compete with multinational, privately owned firms. As a matter of degree, at least, the international competitiveness of publicly owned firms appears to vary depending on whether the home polity is pluralist or corporatist.[29]

In brief, some of the anomalies in Italy's performance can be expected to disappear in coming years. The Italian growth rate and its level of public indebtedness should become inferior to those of Britain, where the economy is becoming much more open and private enterprise–oriented than the Italian. Continued disunity among wage earners gives us no reason to expect relative improvements in the degree of intragenerational equity in Italy, even though its economy is likely to remain highly mixed. Rather, only those communities that represent pivotal political factions in Italy's pluralist political system will benefit from the greater capacity of the Italian government to shape this dimension of social welfare. In a broad sense, then, there may be a more equitable distribution of wealth in Italy than in Britain. But Italy's performance on this second welfare criterion is likely to be inferior to that of Austria and Sweden because wage earners as a group wield greater power in these two countries.

Sweden

Changes in the structure of ownership in its economy in the 1980s make Sweden particularly difficult to interpret. In the 1970s and early 1980s Sweden had some large state-owned firms active in shipping and other international businesses. The Swedish government

29. Compare, for example, Mazzolini's (1980) and Stefani's (1986) accounts of union behavior toward state-owned enterprise in Italy with Katzenstein's (1984) discussion of union behavior toward Austrian nationalized industries.

also contemplated large public investment programs akin to those launched in Austria. But as I noted in Chapter 8, Swedish governments have reduced the scope and curtailed the international activities of state-owned enterprise since then. They have not created the large, internationally active state holding companies that exist in Italy and Austria.[30]

Rather, as predicted in Chapter 9, Swedish governments have responded to competition from foreign multinationals by promoting privately owned national champions. This policy has led to increased foreign private investment overseas and, by implication, to a reduction in government's ability to influence the behavior of native firms. In this respect, the Swedish case tends to resemble the British: citizens stand to realize collective gains through the activities of its large private national champions, but they are also less able to promote intragenerational equity through government taxation of native firms.[31]

Several mitigating factors exist in the Swedish case, however, and they make the Swedish experience resemble more the Austrian than the British experience. First, despite a breakdown in the national wage bargain and conflicts that have surfaced within the labor movement, Swedish wage earners remain more powerful than their counterparts in pluralist private enterprise systems. Swedish labor organizations and their allies still wield a potent strike threat, and so wage earners in Sweden can extract more concessions than wage earners in Britain from their private national champions. In addition, Swedish wage earners remain committed to a comparatively high degree of intragenerational equity, and their new investment funds and large pension funds give them some ability to promote their vision of distributional justice by allocating capital to those regions and communities hardest hit by international market trends. Finally, despite some attempts to encourage foreign investment in the Swedish economy, capital remains largely in native hands. As a consequence, Swedish wage earners do not have to cope with the financial speculation that produced high levels of British unemployment.[32] For all these

30. See the *Economist*, August 1, 1987, pp. 63–65, and Höök's (1980) discussion of the aborted Steel Plant 80. See also Törnblom (1977).

31. See Katzenstein (1985:113–15) and such works as Bowler (1986:167) and Pontusson (1987:16).

32. Efforts to open Swedish financial markets are discussed in the *Economist*, June 21, 1986, p. 82. As regards restrictions on foreign ownership of Swedish private firms, see ibid., August 1, 1987, pp. 63–65, and Nordic Survey, November 11, 1987, p. 10. The importance of the government's exchange rate policy in this context is stressed by Flanagan (1987:161).

reasons Sweden is likely to continue to outperform other countries on the second welfare criterion.

As I predicted in Chapter 9, Sweden may perform relatively worse on the first welfare criterion in coming years. The country has performed worse in terms of investment and growth in recent years, and Sweden has also accumulated a moderately large public debt.[33] In addition, the promotion of private national champions will make it increasingly difficult for governments to reduce this debt through the taxation of large native firms. Growing conflicts between unions and regions in Sweden make it unlikely that corporatist institutions or political parties will be able to cut government spending to any great degree. Hence the financial burdens on future generations of citizens are likely to persist.[34] Moreover, the absence of a vital, small private enterprise sector means that the national economy may not produce the internal growth rates that Italians and Austrians enjoy.[35] It is not clear that wage earner funds can fill this void in the Swedish economy, let alone promote internationally competitive business ventures like those the Austrian state has launched in its iron and steel industry. In fact, implementation of the original wage earner fund proposal could produce a highly segmented economy with two sets of firms holding different orientations and objectives. A loss of gains from trade might result in such circumstances.

On the other hand, the decision not to undertake massive public investments in ailing industries could pay off for the Swedes. The public investment of the Austrian government could fail, leaving Austrians with financial obligations akin to those of Swedes and also substantially reduced gains from trade. In other words, the Swedes might benefit more in collective terms than the Austrians because they have taken a decentralized approach to collective investment. The Swedes have many more internationally viable multinational firms, so as a collectivity they may face fewer risks than the Austrians. The Austrians must rely on their state-owned industries to realize gains from trade to a much greater degree than the Swedes, who rely on private national champions for this purpose.

In sum, by virtue of the power its labor movement retains, Sweden can be expected to continue to outperform many other countries on the second welfare criterion. Its performance on the first welfare cri-

33. See Rivlin (1987) and Bosworth and Lawrence (1987).

34. On the increasing prevalence of union rivalry in Sweden see "Nordic Survey," *Economist*, November 11, 1987, p. 8. For analyses of the causes and effects of union rivalry see Calmfors (1987) and Holmlund (1987).

35. The relative weakness of Swedish small business is stressed by the *Economist*, August 1, 1987, pp. 63–65.

terion is contingent on the fortunes and generosity of its privately owned national champions and on the development of its local small business sector.

The politics of foreign public enterprise and openness refines our understanding of the workings and welfare consequences of our four political-economic systems. However, it leaves the principal result of Chapter 5 intact: there are fundamental differences in the blends of social welfare that the four political economies can achieve. These differences are illuminated by what we have learned about governments' diminished abilities to shape intragenerational distributions of wealth in Britain and Sweden, on the one hand, and the power of political factions or segments of the workforce to promote their own economic security in Italy and Austria, on the other. Armed with this knowledge about differences in the four systems, we now return to the questions posed in Chapter 1 about the compatibility of democracy and capitalism and about the virtues of democratic socialist alternatives.

CHAPTER ELEVEN

Democracy and Capitalism

This book casts new light on the debates between liberal and radical political economists. By identifying both collective and distributional welfare consequences of different systems, the analysis clarifies the controversy between the two schools of political economy. We now better understand the relative virtues of private enterprise and mixed economies in relation to pluralist and corporatist politics. The importance of certain structural conditions, both economic and political, is also clear, as are the intervening effects of openness and foreign public enterprise on the welfare consequences of different systems.

Our taxonomy shows that liberals fail to appreciate the welfare implications of alternative ownership structures and the different ways alternative political systems cope with societal dissensus. The case for democratic corporatism is sound insofar as it recognizes that pluralism undermines efficiency or corporatism's greater orientation toward collective gain and long-term rates of societal return. The case for democratic corporatism also recognizes the greater potential power of wage earners in corporatist systems relative to their counterparts in pluralist systems.

What advocates of corporatism fail to appreciate are the welfare implications of mixedness and the destabilizing effects of foreign public enterprise. Because a substantial number of firms are essentially immobile in a mixed economy, the power of wage earners is greater in corporatist–mixed systems than in corporatist–private enterprise systems. In other words, there are important differences between democratic corporatist systems in the potential for maintaining or promoting the wealth—for example, employment security—of some segments of the workforce. There is also the potential for markedly different, politically important distributional conflicts among workers in corporatist–mixed and corporatist–private enterprise political economies. These conflicts are distinctive, in part, because the politics of openness and foreign public enterprise differ in the two systems. Theoretical reasons for these differences were laid out in Chapters 5 and 9, and evidence that these differences are real was presented in Chapters 7, 8, and 10.

We now see that the other main strain of liberal thought—the case for enlightened consensus and private enterprise—rests on very weak analytic and empirical footings. Advocates of this second form of democratic capitalism appreciate only the virtues, not the drawbacks, of private enterprise. They display little appreciation for the problem of promoting intragenerational equity in the face of capital mobility, for example. These liberal thinkers essentially ignore the distributional implications of financial market transactions in particular and of international business transactions in general. The analyses in Chapters 3, 5, and 9 make it clear that capital mobility constrains governments' capacity to redistribute wealth. The evidence in Chapters 7, 8, and 10 show not only that these constraints are real but also that they are explicitly recognized by governments in democratic capitalist countries.

The existence of genuine societal dissensus over the ends and means of government is also ignored by these liberals. Our studies of the British and Austrian experience leave little doubt that substantial segments of the citizenry—especially in Britain—disagree about what constitutes a fair distribution of wealth. Also, substantial numbers of citizens in both countries do not believe that market distribution is "natural" or "just." Chapters 7 and 10 raise serious questions about these and other societies' abilities to articulate any collective will through electoral or other political processes. Rather, these chapters suggest that dissensus spawns different coalitions of interest groups and producer groups, depending on whether the political system is pluralist or corporatist in nature. These coalitions, in turn, promote changes in or the preservation of prevailing distributions of wealth. Coalitions' abilities to achieve their goals depend, in some part, on whether their economies are mixed. If their economies are of the private enterprise type, coalitions are constrained by the higher degree of private capital mobility: that is, coalitions cannot, through government action, achieve their preferred distribution of wealth. Contrary to what these liberals argue, then, private enterprise is not necessarily the most preferable type of economic structure, and decision making by enlightened consensus is sometimes impossible.

The welfare taxonomy in Chapter 5 illuminates strengths and weaknesses in radical thought. The taxonomy implies that the idea that democratic corporatism is the least undesirable form of demo-cratic capitalism is only partly correct. In comparison to pluralist–private enterprise systems, both types of corporatist systems have the potential to provide workers with a larger share of societal wealth. Corporatist–private enterprise systems—at least closed systems of this kind—also promote greater collective gains and intergenera-tional equity than the other three kinds of political economies. But again, the analysis shows important differences *between* democratic corporatist political economies. The blends of collective gain and dis-tributional equity that can be achieved in corporatist–private enter-prise systems are potentially quite different from those which can be achieved in corporatist–mixed systems. The latter kind of system al-lows for a privileged segment of the workforce, state enterprise work-ers. In turn, the lines of distributional conflict *among* workers and within society at large differ in corporatist–private enterprise and corporatist–mixed political economies. Openness and foreign public enterprise affect distributional conflicts among workers and between workers and private owners differently in the two systems.

Regarding the case for democratic socialism, the investigation re-veals some of the virtues and also some new problems with proposals to create a democratically planned, mixed, market-oriented economy (for example, Nove 1983). This vision of democratic socialism pro-vides for a pluralist kind of politics to guide public investment plan-ning and macroeconomic policy making, and a mix of private and public enterprise where the scope of private enterprise is limited.

Our welfare taxonomy supports the argument that government in such a system will have a greater capacity to shape social welfare than government in a private enterprise economy, even if both economies are open. The analysis indicates that coalitions of interest groups will have much greater capacity to promote their particular interests in pluralist–mixed than in pluralist–private enterprise systems. In these ways, the case for democratic socialism is supported.

What is not supported are radicals' claims about the efficiency of pluralist–mixed systems. The analysis in Chapters 5 and 9 raise seri-ous questions about the collective and intergenerational welfare con-sequences of creating a pluralist–mixed system. The problems of holding the managers of large-scale public enterprises accountable for their decisions, through elections and other political institutions, and of the power that pivotal interest groups wield in pluralist polit-ical systems suggest that pluralist–mixed systems will produce collec-tive and intergenerational welfare outcomes inferior to those of the other three systems. Our investigation of the politics of openness and foreign public enterprise produces essentially the same result. For instance, the analysis in Chapter 9 suggests that foreign investment decisions of publicly owned firms are very likely to yield smaller gains from trade and lower rates of return than are the decisions of private enterprises.[1]

Corporatist–mixed systems are potentially a preferable democratic socialist alternative insofar as this first welfare criteria is concerned. But as I pointed out in Chapter 1, radical writers never seriously consider combining a corporatist form of politics with a mixed economy. Rather, they base their case for democratic socialism on the virtues of pluralist politics alone, making little or no reference to the problems associated with pluralist–mixed political economies.

The welfare taxonomy in Chapter 5 is based on an improved analysis of the interconnections between market processes and democratic political processes. Out of this analysis emerges a better understanding of the senses in which state-owned enterprise and privately owned enterprise are incompatible with democracy.[2]

State-owned enterprise is incompatible with democracy to the extent that state managers and state workers regularly violate the preferences of a substantial number of citizens. We have seen that these two groups have the incentive, and for various reasons the capability, to resist citizens' efforts to alter public enterprise behavior. That is, both state managers and state workers enjoy a "privileged position" in terms of the social power they wield in mixed economies. However, we have also seen that in at least one country, Austria, substantial numbers of citizens tolerate if not support the privileged position of these groups, especially the position of state enterprise workers. These citizens believe that public enterprise is the best means of promoting the wealth of the respective segments of the workforce. They express these beliefs through their support for political parties or leaders of producer organizations. Public enterprise activity in this case is essentially the revealed preference of a *part* of the citizenry for using public ownership rights to promote the welfare of some workers. As such, public enterprise activity is compatible with democracy.

1. In contrast to Bergson (1978) and Kornai (1980), who stress the welfare consequences of managerial behavior in socialist systems, I stress the welfare consequences of the behavior of political factions, especially in relation to the workings of political institutions. Needless to say, both factors are important.

2. For example, Dahl (1985: chap. 2) defines a democratic association as one in which there is a need to make binding collective decisions and in which principles of equality, liberty, and fairness apply. For him, the criteria for a democratic process include equal votes, effective participation, enlightened understanding, final control of the agenda by the demos, and inclusiveness of representation. State-owned enterprise and privately owned enterprise are incompatible with democracy to the extent they violate conditions and criteria of this kind.

The incompatibility of state-owned enterprise and democracy is clearer with respect to the privileged position of state managers. We have uncovered very little evidence that citizens believe state managers are entitled to a large share of societal wealth. Rather, most of the evidence suggests that citizens believe state managers do not perform their jobs adequately and, by implication, capture an unfair share of societal wealth. We have also uncovered evidence that citizens are not able to hold state managers accountable for their behavior through electoral and other democratic political institutions.[3] For example, it appears state managers regularly thwart citizen efforts to monitor the rate of return on public investment or to improve the quality of public services. This evidence implies that public enterprise activity reveals the preferences of state managers rather than the preferences of any large segment of the citizenry. Doctrines such as Morrisonianism expressly deny democratic control; the presumption that state-owned enterprise and democracy are incompatible is evident in the design of the institutions that manage public firms.

State managerial control is not the only source of incompatibility. The status of state enterprise workers is problematic: because of the position they occupy in the mixed economy (see Chapters 3 and 5), state enterprise workers are more able to resist efforts to redistribute or diminish their wealth than are private enterprise workers. That is, they can more easily ignore changes in popular opinion or resist policy changes enacted by those segments of the citizenry which harbor less altruistic attitudes toward them. This is especially true if state enterprise workers occupy pivotal positions within producer group organizations in corportist systems. In such a case, state enterprise workers can preserve their wealth more easily than their counterparts in pluralist systems.

In principle, the power of state enterprise workers is diminished by openness, for openness spawns demands for the pursuit of collective gain through international trade and state enterprise investment in other countries. In effect, openness delegitimizes the privileged position of at least some state enterprise workers (see Chapter 9). At the same time public enterprise investment in foreign countries and the international activity of public enterprise in general increase the power of some state managers. Hence, overall, state enterprise decision making remains or becomes even more immune to democratic supervision, preserving the power of state enterprise workers in the closed part of mixed economies. In this sense some segment of

3. The results of statistical analyses of the British and Austrian experiences are consistent with the idea that state managers can essentially insulate themselves from electoral politics. See Freeman and Alt (1987) and Freeman (1988).

the workforce remains able to thwart government attempts to diminish its share of societal wealth, for example, through strikes in public monopolies.

Finally, there is evidence that elections and other forms of democratic politics are highly imperfect means of executing public ownership rights. The problems of holding state enterprise managers and workers accountable for their actions are, as we have seen, both a cause and a consequence of a low degree of collective ownership efficacy on the part of citizens. The deeper problem lies in the nature of elections and interest-group politics, the infrequency of their occurrence and uncertainty about the consequences of collective action. State-owned enterprise is incompatible with democracy in this case because electoral institutions are not well suited to supervising it.[4]

In these ways we have found support for liberals' claim that state-owned enterprise is incompatible with democracy. This support raises serious questions about the possibility of creating democratically planned mixed economies. We have also found some support for radicals' charge that private enterprise is incompatible with democracy. The issue is whether the owners of private firms and private managers regularly violate the preferences of large numbers of citizens, especially citizens who prefer to collectively own the respective firms. In particular, if private owners and private managers consistently prevent some large segment of the citizenry from creating a preferred distribution of wealth or from owning some set of firms collectively, they violate conditions for democratic control. State-owned enterprise is, in this case, more compatible with democracy because it gives government the capacity to serve the ends of citizens, and by its nature public enterprise better represents these citizens' preferences with respect to ownership rights than private enterprise can hope to do. State-owned enterprise is more compatible with democratic planning than private enterprise in these circumstances.

The problems with the radical argument lie in its focus on ownership rights alone and its failure to consider seriously citizens' preferences with respect to private property. Incompatibility does not necessarily derive from the power of private asset holders; it may derive from the power of private managers. If firms are very large and

4. There is a need to incorporate in the analysis institutional innovations that have been proposed for managing collectively owned assets in Austria and Sweden, for instance, the proposal for direct election of the director of the OeIAG and of the directors of pension funds. These innovations could conceivably produce changes in the blend of welfare outcomes in these two countries over both the short and the long term. They might also promote a greater sense of collective-ownership efficacy among citizens and therefore a greater degree of accountability among state managers and state enterprise workers.

financial markets underdeveloped, the source of incompatibility is again managerial control: the power of managers to set agendas, falsify financial performance, and so on frustrates *both* private *and* public control. Because international trade promotes increases in scale, it reinforces managerial power and further undermines private and public control of private enterprise (see Chapter 9). Many radicals do not appreciate the problem that managerial control poses for democracy, especially in an open economy. Democratic planning is frustrated by managerial control as well as by private ownership.[5]

Also important is the issue of how citizens view property rights, private and public. To argue that privately owned enterprise is incompatible with democracy implies that most, if not all, citizens want to own collectively a large number of firms and that these citizens do not support a fully market-determined distribution of wealth. Yet as we saw in Chapter 7, in Britain many workers support a party that is creating a private enterprise economy. The same workforce holds private assets in the form of pension funds that invest in private capital markets in Britain and other countries. Finally, much survey evidence suggests that citizens in some countries expressly support market-determined distributions of wealth, that is, individuals flatly reject the idea that government should intervene in markets, let alone participate in markets, in order to alter the distribution of wealth.[6] If citizens, including wage earners, hold these views and their political system is democratic, the economic structure must be for some period of time oriented toward private enterprise. Otherwise, citizens' preferences will not have been represented. Of course, citizens who want a mix of private and public ownership are entitled to have their preferences represented as well. So, if the former group privatizes firms in such a way as to prevent renationalization (Chapter 7), they expressly violate democratic norms. Both sets of popular preferences must be represented over time if democracy truly exists. Radicals have not come to grips with the real possibility that a substantial number of citizens have a genuine preference for private ownership and a market-determined distribution of income. This possibility makes it clear that private enterprise is not necessarily incompatible with democracy.

5. The work of Lindblom (1977) is illustrative. He advocates protections against private business privilege (in terms of private investment rights). But he does not provide for protections against managerial control, private or public. A more enlightened approach is taken by Langer (1964), Dahl (1982, 1985), and Wright (1984).

6. The implications of Chong et al.'s (1983) study of Americans' attitudes toward private property are important, as is Lane (1986) on Americans' support for market-determined distributions of wealth.

In sum, the compatibility issue is more complex than both schools assume. In some ways, privately owned enterprise and state-owned enterprise are both compatible with democracy, in other ways both are incompatible with democracy. Compatibility hinges on a set of factors involving the prevalence of managerial control (in general), the relative privilege of private owners on the one hand and state enterprise workers on the other, citizens' preferences regarding the structure of ownership rights, and citizens' willingness and ability to execute those rights through political and economic institutions.

Under certain conditions any of the four systems could be more compatible with democracy than the others. Consider, for instance, the liberal and radical ideals of a pluralist–private enterprise system and a pluralist–mixed system. It follows from our analysis that the former system would be more compatible with democracy than the latter system if the following conditions applied: for the pluralist–private enterprise system, (1) the economy is composed of small-scale, privately owned firms that are relative immobile; (2) most citizens own some part of these privately owned firms and ascribe to a market-determined form of distributional equity; and (3) citizens regularly express their preferences through an election system that has desirable qualities (clarity of responsibility, opportunity for choice, decisiveness, and effectiveness of representation);[7] whereas for the pluralist–mixed system (1) state-owned enterprises are very large, and they are monopolies within the national economy; (2) state enterprise workers are highly organized whereas private enterprise is small-scale and private enterprise workers are disorganized; (3) citizens are deeply divided in their preferences with regard to ownership rights and the means and ends of government; and (4) citizens display little collective ownership efficacy, and elections lack some or all of the desirable properties listed above. Then the pluralist–private enterprise political economy is likely to be more compatible with democracy in the sense that collective decisions are more binding and representative in it than in the pluralist–mixed political economy; in the latter, state enterprise workers and state managers are likely to *continually* thwart democratic control more than private owners and private managers are likely to do in the former.

A pluralist–mixed political economy might be more compatible with democracy than a pluralist–private enterprise economy if an alternative set of conditions holds: for the pluralist–mixed economy, (1) state-owned enterprises are small-scale and capable of making a few foreign investments; (2) state enterprise workers are not organized

7. See Powell (1986).

into any unified, single organization; (3) privately owned enterprise is also small-scale and incapable of undertaking many foreign investments; (4) most citizens prefer to hold a combination of private and public ownership rights, and most own some part of the private enterprises in addition to the public enterprises; and (5) citizens display a high degree of collective ownership efficacy and elections have desirable properties; whereas for the pluralist–private enterprise system, (1) private enterprises are large-scale and make many foreign investments; (2) private ownership is concentrated in a few hands, or capital markets are underdeveloped; (3) workers are highly disorganized; (4) there is dissensus about how ownership rights ought to be structured; and (5) citizens display little efficacy, and elections lack desirable properties. Now the pluralist–mixed political economy is more likely to be compatible with democracy than the private enterprise–political economy; private owners and managers are likely to continually thwart democratic control in the latter system whereas neither private owners, managers, nor state enterprise workers are liable to do so (continually) in the former.

Even in ideal comparisons of this kind, compatibility will always be a matter of degree. To some extent all four kinds of political economies will be incompatible with democracy. The issue is which political economy is least incompatible under prevailing economic and political conditions.

But is this all we can say? Does one of our political economies promote *more* just welfare outcomes than the others? Is one of our political economies *more* compatible with democracy under *most* prevailing conditions? We should eventually be able to answer both questions in the affirmative.

The Relative Virtues of Corporatist–Mixed Political Economies

Desiderata: Social Welfare and Democracy

The most desirable political economy has three properties. First, it promotes the most intergenerational equity or, more generally, the system that is intergenerationally most just. As noted in Chapters 3 and 4, there is no cross-culturally and atemporally meaningful concept of intergenerational equity. But it is clear that the actions of current generations affect the welfare of future generations. Hence living generations are obliged to behave justly toward future generations, especially those generations which are adjacent to or overlap with living generations and so share a common moral language and sense of justice with them.[8]

What we know about Western citizens' conceptions of the ends and means of government tells us that the most desirable political economy produces the greatest increase in level of material wealth over the next twenty-five years or so and also promotes the postmaterialist values of younger generations, for instance, their desire for a clean environment. This political economy promotes the highest possible degree of intergenerational justice.

Second, the most desirable political-economic system achieves the highest possible degree of intragenerational equity. Intragenerational equity is another multifaceted and mutable concept. It has meritocratic, egalitarian, welfarist, and emancipatory dimensions. The focus in this book is on the second and third of these dimensions. My analysis emphasizes the potential for redistributing wealth between private asset holders and wage earners (egalitarianism) and for making citizens secure economically, especially making their jobs secure (welfarism).

Although the attitude of Western publics toward income equality is ambiguous, many citizens clearly believe that people are entitled to certain basic goods and services. Also, in many cases citizens believe they are entitled to economic security, including a job that is guaranteed for some period of time. These social rights are defining elements of the democratic citizenship, elements that embody the prevailing conception of civic morality in Western countries. The best political economy is therefore one that creates the greatest degree of intragenerational equity in this sense, or the system that gives government the greatest capacity to satisfy citizens' basic needs, provide employment security, and (perhaps) create a fair distribution of wealth.[9]

Third, the most preferable political-economic system is most democratic in the sense that, over time, it represents the preferences of most groups in society and preserves citizenship rights. Fair representation means that all groups' preferences are articulated and eventually—within their lifetimes—acted upon. The preservation of citizenship rights means that regardless of which group comes to power, all citizens retain their civil, political, and social rights.

8. See Ball (1985:334). Nove (1983) also focuses on the possibility of creating feasible socialism within a *single* generation. I take the improvement of the material and nonmaterial welfare of one's children and grandchildren as the closest thing we have to a universally desirable welfare outcome.

9. See Marshall (1950), Flora and Alber (1981), and Esping-Andersen (1985). Nove's plan for feasible socialism also acknowledges the importance of employment security, in item (h) in his plan (1983:227–28).

The results of this part of our investigation were discussed above under the notion of "compatibility." In brief, we focused on the willingness and ability of some groups—managers, asset holders, and state enterprise workers—to undermine the workings of the democratic process. We found that under certain conditions, all three groups may prevent the preferences of other groups from being represented; all three groups, in effect, may make collective decisions nonbinding and unrepresentative. The same three groups may also deprive citizens of their social rights, for example, private asset holders may refuse to provide some citizens with job security either directly by suddenly firing workers or indirectly by refusing to finance public programs designed to enhance employment security. To the extent that managers, asset holders, and state enterprise workers do such things over a substantial part of a generation's lifetime, they in effect tyrannize other citizens. The best political economy minimizes prospects for this tyranny. That is, the best system minimizes the social power of managers, private asset holders, and state enterprise workers so as to diminish the likelihood of these kinds of tyranny.[10]

As well as minimizing prospects for tyranny, the best system promotes civic consciousness. The idea of a moral community among living and adjacent generations rests on the existence of common attitudes and beliefs among most citizens, a common sense of harmonious interest and moral obligation toward other citizens, living and unborn. It is this civic orientation which makes democratic politics possible, in the sense that opposing groups tolerate the actions of incumbent groups and incumbent groups do not tyrannize other groups. The most preferable political system most fully manifests and promotes this crucial, attitudinal underpinning of democracy.[11]

The Virtues of Corporatist–Mixed Political Economies

As regards our welfare criteria, we found no tradeoff between the two kinds of equity (see Chapter 6). Rather, two political economies achieve *both* intergenerational and intragenerational equity at the same time. Corporatist–private enterprise and corporatist–mixed systems both appear to be as desirable as or more desirable than pluralist–mixed and pluralist–private enterprise systems. Our analysis of the politics of openness and foreign public enterprise suggests that over the long term corporatist political economies may perform

10. Dahl (1982, 1985) stresses that group tyranny is possible in all social systems, including democratic socialist systems.
11. On the importance of civic orientation in democracy see Dahl (1982: chaps. 6 and 7).

about as well as pluralist–private enterprise systems on the first welfare criterion. It also suggests that the superior performance of corporatist–mixed systems on the second welfare criterion should remain intact; the politics of openness and foreign public enterprise does not undermine the respective governments' capacity to achieve a *comparatively* higher degree of intergenerational equity. In terms of welfare outcomes, then, corporatist–mixed political economies appear to be the most desirable form of democratic capitalism.

The superior performance of corporatist–mixed political economies derives from the fact that these systems are as democratic as, if not more democratic than, the other political economies. To reiterate, the primary sources of political tyranny in the four political economies are: for the corporatist–mixed case, the power and privilege of state enterprise workers and their labor and state managerial allies; for the pluralist–mixed case, the power of pivotal groups but especially the power of state managers; for pluralist–private enterprise systems, the power of private asset holders and private managers; and for corporatist–private enterprise systems, the power of organized labor as a whole and the power of private asset holders and private managers.

Some of the economic conditions that affect these tyrannies are relatively uniform across countries. For instance, the large size of many private and public enterprises makes the power of state enterprise workers, public and private managers, and private asset holders likely to be great in all political economies. The effects of scale are, in effect, uniform for all four cases. Accordingly, this economic factor does not help us determine which system is likely to be more democratic.[12]

Financial market development, on the other hand, does have important effects on the nature and severity of political tyranny. The more developed a system's financial markets are, the more the threat to democracy derives from the social power of private asset holders rather than the power of private managers. In other words, the source of political tyranny, especially in private enterprise systems, differs depending on the character of the financial market. But the potential for political tyranny exists regardless of the condition of financial markets. Private asset holders or the managers of large privately owned firms are always able to resist collective decisions to redistribute wealth or to provide employment security.

12. The challenge to democracy comes from the universally large scale of business enterprises, public or private. See Langer (1964); see also Dahl (1985: Intro.). That government can channel international funds to small-scale private enterprises rather than large-scale public enterprises must eventually be considered, however.

Most mixed economies do not have well-developed financial markets. However, private asset holders in mixed economies, even though they have no market in which to trade shares in their (normally small-scale) private enterprises, can still wield social power by threatening to disinvest in response to the tyranny of state enterprise workers and managers. These threats may spur private enterprise workers to oppose the actions of their state enterprise counterparts. In this sense, financial market underdevelopment permits some diffusion of social power in mixed economies. However, a well-developed financial market could conceivably provide counterweight to the power and influence of state enterprise workers and state managers, especially in corporatist–mixed political economies.[13]

The notion of collective ownership efficacy and its relation to civic orientation is an even more important determinant of how democratic mixed systems are relative to private enterprise systems. As we have seen, citizens have a greater capacity to *collectively* shape the welfare of living and future generations in mixed economies than they have in private enterprise economies. Democratic institutions can facilitate citizens' efforts to do so by holding state enterprise workers, state managers, and producer group leaders accountable for their actions. Institutional innovations such as those mentioned in Chapters 7 and 8 may help bring about an even greater degree of popular control over the state enterprise. Finally, mixed ownership structures by their very nature give people a direct stake in collective decision making insofar as state enterprise offers citizens the prospect of earning collective returns on public investments as well as an ability to affect directly the economic security of their other citizens. In principle, then, citizens have real material and nonmaterial—especially moral—incentives to hold these groups accountable for their actions.

In the end, however, it is up to citizens to exercise their public ownership rights. Citizens must come to understand how their votes in popular and producer group elections affect public business activity and, in turn, the welfare of living and future generations. If citizens fail to view the execution of public ownership rights as a civic responsibility, there is no reason to assume that mixed economies, pluralist or corporatist, will necessarily be more democratic than private enterprise economies.[14] Rather, mixed political economies will merely be associated with a different kind of tyranny. And the relative per-

13. In this sense, the development of a larger local or regional financial market in Austria (Hankel 1981) could both promote collective gains in welfare and provide safeguards against political tyranny by state enterprise workers and their allies.

14. Lange (1984) demonstrates that, in some important respects, labor organizations in corporatist countries are more democratic than those in pluralist countries.

formance of the four systems will be an outgrowth of the civic orientations of technocrats or private owners rather than of the preferences of their citizens. Our choice among these systems then will amount to a choice among different forms of technocratic, not democratic, capitalism: systems that yield different blends of collective gain and intergenerational and intragenerational equity, depending on whether the technocrats who manage them are producer group leaders, state managers, or private managers and owners and on the particular skills and civic orientations of these managers rather than on the civic orientations of the citizenries.

Despite our discouraging findings about citizens' willingness and abilities to manage public enterprise through electoral and other political institutions, and about the effects international factors have on corporatism, there are reasons to believe that mixed economies could be democratically controlled. The Austrian and, to a lesser extent, Swedish and British experiences suggest that citizens value and exercise their public ownership rights in ways that display genuine civic orientations. For example, the Austrian case suggests that in corporatist systems, citizens rely on dual channels of representation to hold state enterprise workers and managers accountable for their actions. In addition, groups within these systems appear to be working on institutional innovations that may produce a greater degree of collective ownership efficacy and democratic control in mixed economies. With such innovations, Austria's corporatist–mixed system could conceivably come closer to the democratic ideal.

In sum, corporatist–mixed political economies can and will function more democratically than other political economies, especially private enterprise economies. They yield superior welfare outcomes because they better represent and nurture citizens' civic morality. The tentative conclusion of this book, therefore, is that the most desirable form of democratic capitalism is a corporatist–mixed system. This kind of political economy is not perfect. Its superior performance derives primarily from its ability to provide employment security for a substantial number of citizens; by no means does it ensure genuine democratic planning of economic or any other activity, and its virtues relative to the democratic socialist ideal remain to be firmly established. But on balance, and in comparison to the other three political economies, the corporatist–mixed system yields superior welfare outcomes because it best approximates the democratic ideal.

References

Aberbach, J., R. Putnam, and B. Rockman. 1981. *Bureaucrats and Politicians in Western Democracies.* Cambridge: Harvard University Press.

Abromeit, H. 1986. "Privatization in Great Britain." *Annals of Public and Co-operative Economy* 57 (2): 153–179.

Adar, Z., and Y. Aharoni. 1980. "Risk Sharing by Managers of State Owned Enterprises." Mimeo. Tel Aviv, June.

Aharoni, Y. 1986. *The Evolution and Management of State-Owned Enterprises.* Cambridge, Mass.: Ballinger.

———. 1983. "Comprehensive Audit of Management Performance in U.S. State Owned Enterprises." *Annals of Public and Cooperative Economy* 54 (1): 73–92.

Aimer, P. 1985. "The Strategy of Gradualism and the Swedish Wage Earner Funds." *West European Politics* 8 (3): 43–55.

Alt, J. E. 1987. "Crude Politics: Oil and the Political Economy of Unemployment in Britain and Norway." *British Journal of Political Science* 17 (2): 149–200.

———. 1979. *The Politics of Economic Decline: Economic Management and Political Behavior in Britain since 1964.* New York: Cambridge University Press.

Alt, J., and A. Chrystal. 1983. *Political Economics.* Berkeley: University of California Press.

Andrlik, E. 1985. "Centrifugal Tendencies of the Austrian Economic and Social Partnership." Mimeo. Vienna, November.

———. 1984. "Die Sozialpartnerschaft in der Wirtschaftskrise: Der Fall VEW (1975–1984)." *Journal für Sozialforschung* 24:395–422.

———. 1983. "The Organized Society: A Study of 'Neo-Corporatist' Relations in Austria's Steel and Metal Processing Industry." Dissertation, M.I.T.

Arndt, S., ed. 1982. *The Political Economy of Austria.* Washington, D.C.: American Enterprise Institute.

Arrow, K. J. 1981. "On Finance and Decision Making." In *State-Owned Enterprise in the Western Economies,* ed. R. Vernon and Y. Aharoni, pp. 63–69. New York: St. Martin's.

Arrow, K. J., and M. Kurz. 1970. *Public Investment, the Rate of Return and Optimal Fiscal Policy.* Baltimore: Johns Hopkins University Press.

287

REFERENCES

Arrow, K. J., and R. C. Lind. 1970. "Uncertainty and the Evaluation of Public Investment Decisions." *American Economic Review* 60 (3):364–378.
Artus, J. R. 1982. "Commentary." In *The Political Economy of Austria*, ed. S. Arndt, pp. 35–41. Washington, D.C.: American Enterprise Institute.
Åsard, E. 1986. "Industrial and Economic Democracy in Sweden: From Consensus to Confrontation." *European Journal of Political Research* 14:207–219.
Austrian Documentation. 1984. *The Rational Approach to Labour and Industry: Economic and Social Partnership in Austria.* Vienna: Federal Press Service.
Bacon, R., and W. A. Eltis. 1976. *Britain's Economic Problem: Too Few Producers.* London: Macmillan.
Baer, W., and A. Figueroa. 1981. "State Enterprise and the Distribution of Income: Brazil and Peru." In *Authoritarian Brazil*, ed. T. C. Bruneau and P. Faucher, pp. 59–84. Boulder, Colo.: Westview.
Ball, T. 1985. "The Incoherence of Intergenerational Justice." *Inquiry* 28:321–337.
Barry, N. 1983. "Review Article: The New Liberalism." *British Journal of Political Science* 13(1):93–123.
Bean, C. R. 1981a. "A New Approach to the Empirical Investigation of Investment Expenditures: A Comment." *Economic Journal* 91(361):104–105.
———. 1981b. "An Econometric Model of Manufacturing Investment in the U.K." *Economic Journal* 91(361):106–121.
Beesley, M., and S. Littlechild. 1983. "Privatization: Principles, Problems and Priorities." *Lloyd's Bank Review*, July, pp. 1–20.
Beesley, M., and T. Evans. 1981. "The British Experience: The Case of British Rail." In *State-Owned Enterprise in the Western Economies*, ed. R. Vernon and Y. Aharoni, pp. 117–132. New York: St. Martin's.
Behn, R. 1981. "Policy Analysis and Policy Politics." *Policy Analysis* 7(2):199–226.
Benya, A. 1982. "ÖGB und Gemeinwirtschaft." In *Die Österreichische Gemeinwirtschaft*, p. 10. Vienna: Jugend & Volk.
———. 1975. *Gewerkschaften in der Gessellschaft von heute.* Vienna: Europa.
Berger, S. 1981. "Regime and Interest Representation: The French Traditional Middle Classes." In *Organizing Interests in Western Europe*, ed., S. Berger, pp. 83–102. New York: Cambridge University Press.
Bergson, A. 1978. "Managerial Rewards in Public Enterprises." *Journal of Comparative Economics* 2:211–225.
Bierstecker, T. 1986. "The Politics of Stabilization." Paper delivered at the Annual Meeting of the American Political Science Association, Washington, D.C.
Birch, A. 1984. "Overload, Ungovernability and Delegitimation: The Theories and the British Case." *British Journal of Political Science* 14(2):135–160.
Block, F. L. 1977. *The Origins of International Economic Disorder: A Study of United States International Monetary Policy from World War II to the Present.* Berkeley: University of California Press.
Bluestone, B., and B. Harrison. 1982. *The Deindustrialization of America: Plant Closings, Community Abandonment and the Dismantling of Basic Industry.* New York: Basic Books.
Boddy, R., and J. Crotty. 1975. "Class Conflict and Macro-Policy: The Political Business Cycle." *Review of Radical Political Economics* 7(1):1–19.
Bosworth, B., and R. Lawrence. 1987. "Adjusting to Slower Economic Growth: The Domestic Economy." In *The Swedish Economy*, ed. B. Bosworth

and A. Rivlin, pp. 22–54. Washington, D.C.: Brookings.

Bowler, S. 1986. "Corporatism and the 'Privileged Position' of Business." *West European Politics* 9(2):157–175.

Bowles, S., and H. Gintes. 1982. "The Crisis of Liberal Democratic Capitalism: The Case of the United States." *Politics and Society* 11(1):51–93.

Braun, A. Romanis. 1986. *Wage Determination and Incomes Policy in Open Economies.* Washington, D.C.: IMF.

Breton, A. 1964. "The Economics of Nationalism." *Journal of Political Economy* 72(4):376–386.

Bristow, J. A. 1966. "State Enterprise in the Republic of Ireland." *Annals of Public and Cooperative Economy* 37(1):25–41.

Brittan, S. 1984. "The Politics and Economics of Privatization." *Political Quarterly* 55(2):109–129.

———. 1983. *The Role and Limits of Government: Essays in Political Economy.* Minneapolis: University of Minnesota Press.

Brooks, J. 1983. "Left Wing Mobilization and Socioeconomic Equality: A Cross National Analysis of the Developed Democracies." *Comparative Political Studies* 16(3):393–416.

Bruce-Gardyne, J. 1984. *Mrs. Thatcher's First Administration: The Prophets Confounded.* London: Macmillan.

Brus, W. 1985. "Socialism—Feasible and Viable?" *New Left Review* 153 (September-October):43–62.

Burawoy, M. 1985. *The Politics of Production: Factory Regimes under Capitalism and Socialism.* London: Verso.

Burawoy, M., and J. Lukacs. 1985. "Mythologies of Work: A Comparison of Firms in State Socialism and Advanced Capitalism." *American Sociological Review* 50:723–737.

Butschek, F. 1982. "Full Employment during Recession." In *The Political Economy of Austria*, ed. S. Arndt, pp. 101–129. Washington, D.C.: American Enterprise Institute.

Calendar, G. S. 1902. "The Early Transportation and Banking Enterprises of the States in Relation to the Growth of Corporations." *Quarterly Journal of Economics* 17 (November):111–162.

Calmfors, L. 1987. "Comments." In *The Swedish Economy*, ed. B. Bosworth and A. Rivlin, pp. 174–181. Washington, D.C.: Brookings.

Cameron, D. 1984. "The Politics and Economics of the Business Cycle." In *The Political Economy*, ed. T. Ferguson and J. Rogers, pp. 237–262. Armonk, N.Y.: M. E. Sharpe.

———. 1978. "The Expansion of the Public Economy: A Comparative Analysis." *American Political Science Review* 72(4):1243–1261.

Cassesse, S. 1981. "Public Control and Corporate Efficiency." In *State-Owned Enterprise in the Western Economies*, ed. R. Vernon and Y. Aharoni, pp. 145–156. New York: St. Martin's.

Cavalieri, D. 1977. "The Crisis in the System of State Share Holdings in Italy." *Annals of Public and Cooperative Economy* 48(4):436–449.

C.E.E.P. (Centre for European Public Enterprise). 1973, 1976, 1978, 1981. "Public Enterprise in the European Community." London: British Section of C.E.E.P.

Chaloupek, G. 1985. "The Austrian Parties and the Economic Crisis." *West European Politics* 8(1):71–81.

Chandler, M. 1982. "State Enterprise and Partisanship in Provincial Politics."

REFERENCES

Canadian Journal of Political Science 15(4):711–740.

Chappell, H., and W. Keech. 1983. "Welfare Consequence of the Six-Year Presidential Term Evaluated in the Context of a Model of the U.S. Economy." *American Political Science Review* 77(1):75–91.

Chirot, D. 1987. "Ideology and Legitimacy in Eastern Europe." *States and Social Structures Newsletter* 4 (Spring):1–4.

Choksi, A. M. 1979. "State Intervention in the Industrialization of Developing Countries: Selected Issues." *Staff Working Paper* no. 341. Washington, D.C.: World Bank.

Chong, D., H. McCloskey, and J. Zaller. 1983. "Patterns of Support for Democratic and Capitalist Values in the United States." *British Journal of Political Science* 13(4):401–440.

Chubb, B. 1970. *The Government and Politics of Ireland*. Stanford: Stanford University Press.

Coakley, J., and L. Harris. 1983. *The City of Capital*. London: Basil Blackwell.

Cochran, N. 1980. "Society as Emergent and More than Rational: An Essay on the Inappropriateness of Program Evaluation." *Policy Sciences* 12(2):113–129.

Copeman, H. 1981. *The National Accounts: A Short Guide*. London: Central Statistical Office.

Corti, G. 1976. "Perspectives on Public Corporations and Public Enterprise in Five Nations." *Annals of Public and Cooperative Economy* 47(1):47–86.

Cox, A., and J. Hayward. 1983. "The Inapplicability of the Corporatist Model in Britain and France: The Case of Labor." *International Political Science Review* 4(2):217–240.

Cox, R. 1984. "Notes on the Emerging Global Class Structure." Paper presented at the Annual Meeting of the American Political Science Association, Washington, D.C.

Coyle, P. 1973. "Ireland." In *The Evolution of Public Enterprise in the Community of Nine*, pp. 169–177. Brussels: European Center for Public Enterprise.

Crouch, C. 1980. "Varieties of Trade Union Weakness: Organized Labour and Capital Formation in Britain, Federal Germany and Sweden." In *Trade Unions and Politics in Western Europe*, ed. J. Hayward, pp. 87–106. London: Frank Cass.

Cubbin, J., and D. Leach. 1983. "The Effect of Shareholding Dispersion on the Degree of Control in British Companies." *Economic Journal* 93:351–369.

Dahl, R. 1985. *A Preface to Economic Democracy*. Berkeley: University of California Press.

——. 1983. "Communication (Reply to Manley)." *American Political Science Review* 77(2):386–389.

——. 1982. *Dilemmas of Pluralist Democracy: Autonomy vs. Control*. New Haven: Yale University Press.

Dahl, R., and C. Lindblom. 1976. *Politics, Economics and Welfare*. Chicago: University of Chicago Press.

Dahrendorf, R. 1959. *Class and Class Conflict in Industrial Society*. Stanford: Stanford University Press.

Despicht, N. 1972. "Diversification and Expansion: The Creation of Modern Services." In *The State as Enterpreneur*, ed. S. Holland, pps. 127–164. London: Weidenfeld & Nicolson.

Dornbusch, R. 1980. *Open Economy Macroeconomics*. New York: Basic Books.

Dreyer, J. 1982. "Commentary." In *The Political Economy of Austria*, ed. S.

Arndt, pp. 22–25. Washington, D.C.: American Enterprise Institute.

Dudley, G. 1979. "Pluralism, Policymaking and Implementation: The Evolution of the British Steel Corporation Development Strategy with Reference to the Activity of the Shelton Action Committee." *Public Administration* 57 (Autumn):253–270.

Dupuy, A., and B. Truchil. 1979. "Problems in the Theory of State Capitalism." *Theory and Society* 8(1):1–38.

Dye, T., and H. Zeigler. 1988. "Socialism and Equality in Cross-National Perspective." *PS: Political Science and Politics*, Winter, pp. 45–56.

Eliasson, G. 1965. *Investment Funds in Operation*. Stockholm: National Institute for Economic Research.

Ellman, M. 1980. "Against Convergence." *Cambridge Journal of Economics* 4(3):199–210.

Eltis, W. 1979. "The True Deficits of Public Corporations." *Lloyds Bank Review* 1:1–20.

Esping-Andersen, G. 1985. "Power and Distributional Regimes." *Politics and Society* 14(2):223–256.

Evans, P. 1979. *Dependent Development: The Alliance of Multinational, State and Local Capital in Brazil*. Princeton: Princeton University Press.

Ezra, D. 1982. "The Mixed Economy and British Trade." In *The Mixed Economy*, ed. Lord Roll, pp. 206–223. London: Macmillan.

Faini, R., and F. Schiantarelli. 1983. "Regional Implications of Industrial Policy." *Journal of Public Policy* 3(1):97–118.

Farnleitner, J., and E. Schmidt. 1982. "The Social Partnership." In *The Political Economy of Austria*, ed. S. Arndt, pp. 87–100. Washington, D.C.: American Enterprise Institute.

Fausto, D. 1982. "The Finance of Italian Public Enterprises." *Annals of Public and Cooperative Economy* 53(1):3–24.

Flanagan, R. 1987. "Efficiency and Equality in Swedish Labor Markets." In *The Swedish Economy*, ed., B. Bosworth and A. Rivlin, pp. 125–173. Washington, D.C.: Brookings.

Flanagan, R., D. Soskice, and L. Ulman. 1983. *Unionism, Economic Stabilization and Incomes Policies: European Experience*. Washington, D.C.: Brookings.

Flora, P., and J. Alber. 1981. "Modernization, Democratization and the Development of Welfare States in Western Europe." In *The Development of Welfare States in Europe and America*, ed. P. Flora and A. Heidenheimer, pp. 37–80. New Brunswick, N.J.: Transaction.

François-Marsal, F. 1973. *Le dépérissement des entreprises publiques*. Paris: Calmann-Lévy.

Freeman, J. 1988. "Elections, Interest Intermediation and the Employment Decisions of British and Austrian Firms." Manuscript. Minneapolis: University of Minnesota.

———. 1987. "The Origins of Mixed Economies." Revised version of a paper originally presented at the 12th Annual Meeting of the International Political Science Association, Rio de Janeiro.

Freeman, J., and J. Alt. 1987. "The Politics of Public and Private Investment in Britain." Revised version of a paper originally presented at the Annual Meeting of the Western Political Science Association, Eugene, Oregon.

Freeman, J., and B. Job. 1979. "Scientific Forecasts in International Relations: Problems of Definition and Epistemology." *International Studies Quarterly* 23:113–144.

REFERENCES

Freeman, J., and E. Wilson. 1986. "It Isn't Enough to Bring the State Back In." Paper presented at the Annual Meeting of the American Political Science Association, Washington, D.C.

Frey, B., and F. Schneider. 1978. "A Politico-Economic Model of the United Kingdom." *Economic Journal* 88(350):243–253.

Frisch, H. 1982. "Macroeconomic Adjustment in Small Open Economies." In *The Political Economy of Austria*, ed., S. Arndt, pp. 42–55. Washington, D.C.: American Enterprise Institute.

Frohlich, N., and J. Oppenheimer. 1978. *Modern Political Economy*. Englewood Cliffs, N.J.: Prentice-Hall.

Furubotn, E. 1985. "Long Swings in Economic Development, Social Time Preference and Institutional Change: Comment." *Journal of Institutional and Theoretical Economics* 141:36–40.

Fusfeld, D. 1982. *Economics: Principles of Political Economy*. Glenview, Ill.: Scott, Foresman.

Garner, M. 1985. "The Government Control of Public Corporations in Britain: A History and an Evaluation." Paper presented at the 13th World Congress of the International Political Science Association, Paris.

———. 1979. "The White Paper on the Nationalized Industries: Some Criticisms." *Public Administration* 57 (Spring):7–20.

Garret, G., and P. Lange. 1986. "Performance in a Hostile World: Economic Growth in Capitalist Democracies, 1974–1982." *Journal of Politics* 47:517–543.

Goodin, R. 1982. "Rational Politicians and Rational Bureaucrats in Washington and Whitehall." *Public Administration* 60 (Spring):23–41.

Grant, W. 1984. "Large Firms and Public Policy in Britain." *Journal of Public Policy* 4(1):1–17.

Grassini, F. 1981. "The Italian Enterprises: The Political Constraints." In *State-Owned Enterprise in the Western Economies*, ed. R. Vernon and Y. Aharoni, pp. 70–84. New York: St. Martin's.

Gray, C. 1983. "Toward a Conceptual Framework for Macroeconomic Evaluations of Public Enterprise Performance in Mixed Economies." Departmental Memorandum. Washington, D.C.: International Monetary Fund.

Grunwald, O. 1982a. "Die Verstaatliche Industrie." In *Die österreichische Gemeinwirtschaft*, pp. 223–240. Vienna: Jugend & Volk.

———. 1982b. "Austrian Industrial Structure and Industrial Policy." In *The Political Economy of Austria*, ed. S. Arndt, pp. 130–149. Washington, D.C.: American Enterprise Institute.

———. 1980. "Steel and the State in Austria." *Annals of Public and Cooperative Economy* 51(4):478–491.

———. 1977. "The Austrian Nationalized Industries." Manuscript. Lisbon: Instituto das Participações do Estado.

Hadjimatheou, G., and A. Skouras. 1979. "Britain's Economic Problem: The Growth of the Non-Market Sector?" *Economic Journal* 89 (June):392–401.

Hall, P. 1986. *Governing the Economy: The Politics of State Intervention in Britain and France*. New York: Oxford University Press.

Hamermesh, D. S. 1975. "The Effect of Government Ownership on Union Wages." In *Labor in the Public and Nonprofit Sectors*, pp. 227–255. Princeton: Princeton University Press.

Hankel, W. 1981. *Prosperity amidst Crisis: Austria's Economic Policy and the Energy Crunch*, trans. J. Steinberg. Boulder, Colo.: Westview.

Hansen, B. 1985. "Consonance between Election Campaign Issues and Actual Policy Choices in Sweden's Welfare State." Paper presented at the Annual Meeting of the American Political Science Association, New Orleans.

Hart, J. 1986. "British Industrial Policy." In *The Politics of Industrial Policy*, ed. C. Barfield and W. Schambra, pps. 128–160. Washington, D.C.: American Enterprise Instutute.

Hartz, L. 1968. *Economic Policy and Democratic Thought*. Chicago: Quadrangle.

——. 1948. *Economic Policy and Democratic Thought: Pennsylvania, 1776–1860*. Cambridge: Harvard University Press.

Haschek, H. 1982. "Trade, Trade Finance, and Capital Movement." In *The Political Economy of Austria*, ed. S. Arndt, pp. 176–198. Washington, D.C.: American Enterprise Institute.

Hattersley, R. 1982. "Politics and the Mixed Economy." In *The Mixed Economy*, ed. Lord Roll, pp. 113–127. London: Macmillan.

Hawley, E. 1975. "The New Deal and Business." In *The New Deal: The National Level*, ed. J. Braemen, R. Bremmer, and J. Brody, pp. 50–82. Columbus: Ohio State University Press.

Heald, D., and D. Steel. 1982. "Privatising Public Enterprise: An Analysis of the Governments' Case." *Political Quarterly* 53(3):333–349.

——. 1981. "The Privatization of U.K. Public Enterprises." *Annals of Public and Cooperative Economy* 53(2):351–368.

Heclo, H., and H. Madsen. 1987. *Policy and Politics in Sweden: Principled Pragmatism*. Philadelphia: Temple University Press.

Heidenheimer, A., H. Heclo, and C. Teich Adams. 1983. *Comparative Public Policy: The Politics of Social Choice in Europe and America*. 2d ed. New York: St. Martin's.

Hemming, R., and A. Mansoor. 1988. *Privatization and Public Enterprise*. IMF Occasional Paper no. 56. Washington, D.C.

Hernes, G., and A. Selvik. 1981. "Local Corporatism." In *Organizing Interests in Western Europe*, ed. S. Berger, pp. 103–119. New York: Cambridge University Press.

Heurtibise, A. 1978. "The Place of Public Enterprises in the Economy." *Annals of Public and Cooperative Economy* 49(3–4):309–343.

Hibbs, D. A. 1982a. "Economic Outcomes and Political Support for British Governments among Occupational Classes: A Dynamic Analysis." *American Political Science Review* 76(2):259–276.

——. 1982b. "On Demand for Economic Outcomes: Macroeconomic Outcomes and Mass Political Support in the United States, Great Britain and West Germany." *Journal of Politics* 44(2):426–461.

——. 1982c. "The Dynamics of Political Support for American Presidents among Occupational and Partisan Groups." *American Journal of Political Science* 26(2):312–332.

——. 1981. "Economics and Politics in France: Economic Performance and Mass Political Support for Presidents Pompidou and Giscard d'Estaing." *European Journal of Political Research* 9:133–145.

——. 1979. "The Mass Public and Macroeconomic Performance: The Dynamics of Public Opinion toward Unemployment and Inflation." *American Journal of Political Science* 23(4):705–731.

——. 1978. "On the Political Economy of Long-Run Trends in Strike Activity." *British Journal of Political Science* 9(2):153–175.

——. 1977. "Political Parties and Macreconomic Policy." *American Political Sci-*

ence Review 71(4):1467–1487.

Hibbs, D. A., and C. Dennis. 1988. "Income Distribution in the United States." *American Political Science Review* 82(2):467–490.

Hibbs, D. A., and H. J. Madsen. 1981. "Public Reactions to the Growth of Taxation and Government Expenditure." *World Politics* 33(3):413–435.

Hindley, B. 1982. "The Mixed Economy in the International Context." In *The Mixed Economy*, ed. Lord Roll, pp. 187–205. London: Macmillan.

Hodjera, Z. 1976. "Alternative Approaches in the Analysis of International Capital Movements: A Case Study of Austria and France." *IMF Staff Papers* 23:598–623.

Holland, S. 1974. "Europe's New Public Enterprises." In *Big Business and the State*, ed. R. Vernon, pp. 25–44. Cambridge: Harvard University Press.

Holland, S., ed. 1972. *The State as Entrepreneur: New Dimensions for Public Enterprise: The IRI State Shareholding Formula* London: Weidenfield & Nicolson.

Hollingsworth, J. R. 1982. "The Political Structural Basis for Economic Performance." *Annals of the American Academy of Political and Social Science* 459 (January):28–45.

Holmlund, B. 1987. "Comments." In *The Swedish Economy*, ed. B. Bosworth and A. Rivlin, pp. 181–184. Washington, D.C.: Brookings.

Holton, R. 1986. "Industrial Politics in France: Nationalization under Mitterrand." *West European Politics* 9(1):67–80.

Höök, E. 1980. "Steel and the State in Sweden." *Annals of Public and Cooperative Economy* 51(4):493–506.

Inglehart, R. 1985. "Aggregate Stability and Individual-Level Flux in Mass Belief Systems: The Level of Analysis Paradox." *American Political Science Review* 79(1):97–116.

———. 1981. "Post-Materialism in an Environment of Insecurity." *American Political Science Review* 75(4):880–900.

———. 1977. "Value Priorities, Objective Need Satisfaction and Subjective Satisfaction among Western Publics." *Comparative Political Studies* 9(4):429–458.

International Monetary Fund. 1983, 1985. *International Financial Statistics.* Washington, D.C.

Itzlinger, A., R. Kerschbamer, and A. Van der Bellen. 1988. "Verstaatliche Industrie." Manuscript. Vienna.

Jackman, R. 1986. "Elections and the Democratic Class Struggle." *World Politics* 39:123–146.

———. 1980. "Socialist Parties and Income Inequality in Western Industrial Societies." *Journal of Politics* 42:134–149.

Jacobsen, J. K. 1980. "Chasing Progress: The Politics of Industrialization in Ireland, 1958–1978." Dissertation, University of Chicago.

Jessop, R. 1979. "Corporatism, Parliamentarism, and Social Democracy." In *Trends toward Corporatist Intermediation*, ed. P. Schmitter and G. Lehmbruch, pp. 185–212. London: Sage.

Jones, L. P. 1981a. "Toward a Performance Evaluation Methodology for Public Enterprises: With Special Reference to Pakistan." Paper delivered at the International Symposium on the Economic Performance of Public Enterprise. Islamabad, Pakistan, November 24–28.

———. 1981b. "Public Enterprise for Whom? Perverse Distributional Consequences of Public Operational Decisions." Paper delivered at the Conference on Problems and Policies of Industrialization in an Open Economy.

Istanbul, Turkey, August 29–24.

Jones, L. P., ed. 1982. *Public Enterprise in Less-Developed Countries.* New York: Cambridge University Press.

Jonoug, L., and E. Wadensjo. 1979. "The Effect of Unemployment, Inflation and Real Income Growth on Government Popularity in Sweden." *Scandinavian Journal of Economics* 81(2):343–353.

Judge, G., et al. 1985. *The Theory and Practice of Econometrics.* 2d ed. New York: Wiley.

Kager, M. 1983. "Ausgabengebarung und Investitionsverhalten von Ländern und Gemeinden im Konjunkturverlauf." In *Gemeinwirtschaft und Konjunkturverlauf*, pp. 1–66. Vienna: Ludwig Boltzmann, Institue für Wachstumsforschung.

Karl, B. 1976. "Philanthropy, Policy Planning and the Bureaucratization of the Democratic Ideal." *Daedulus* 105(4):129–149.

Katzenstein, P. 1985. *Small States in World Markets: Industrial Policy in Europe.* Ithaca: Cornell University Press.

——. 1984. *Corporatism and Change: Austria, Switzerland, and the Politics of Industry.* Ithaca: Cornell University Press.

——. 1982. "Commentary." In *The Political Economy of Austria*, ed. S. Arndt, pp. 150–155. Washington, D.C.: American Enterprise Institute.

Keeler, J. 1981. "Corporatism and Official Union Hegemony: The Case of French Agricultural Syndicalism." In *Organizing Interests in Western Europe*, ed. S. Berger, pp. 185–208. New York: Cambridge University Press.

King, A. 1975. "Overload: Problems of Governing in the 1970's." *Political Studies* 23(2–3):284–296.

——. 1973. "Ideas, Institutions, and the Policies of Government: A Comparative Analysis." *British Journal of Political Science* 3:291–313, 409–423.

Knight, A. 1983. "Ideas and Actions: How to Improve Industrial Performance." The Fairburn Lecture. Lancaster University, January 28.

——. 1982. "The Control of the Nationalized Industries." *Politics Quarterly* 53(1):24–34.

Koren, S. 1982. "Austrian Monetary and Exchange Rate Policies." In *The Political Economy of Austria*, ed. S. Arndt, pp. 26–41. Washington, D.C.: American Enterprise Institute.

Kornai, J. 1980. *The Economics of Shortage.* Amsterdam: North-Holland.

Korpi, W. 1983. *The Democratic Class Struggle.* London: Routledge & Kegan Paul.

——. 1980. "Social Policy Strategies and Distributional Conflict in the Capitalist Democracies: A Preliminary Comparative Framework." *West European Politics* 3(3):296–316.

——. 1978. *The Working Class in Welfare Capitalism: Work, Unions, and Politics in Sweden.* London: Routledge & Kegan Paul.

Kosters, M. 1982. "Commentary." In *The Political Economy of Austria*, ed. S. Arndt, pp. 124–129. Washington, D.C.: American Enterprise Institute.

Kraus, F. 1981. "The Historical Development of Income Inequality in Western Europe and the United States." In *The Development of Welfare States in Europe and America*, ed. P. Flora and A. Heidenheimer, pp. 187–238. New Brunswick, N.J.: Transaction.

Kristensen, O. 1982. "Voter Attitudes and Public Spending: Is There a Relationship?" *European Journal of Political Research* 10:35–52.

Kromer, R. 1983. "Ansatz einer vergleichenden Strukturanalyse der offentlichen Wirtschaft und der Gesamtwirtschaft für den Zeitraum von 1974–1981." In *Gemeinwirtschaft und Konjunkturlauf*, pp. 67–99. Vienna: Ludwig Boltzmann, Institut für Wachstumsforschung.

Kuisel, R. 1981. *Capitalism and the State in Modern France: Renovation and Economic Management in the Twentieth Century.* New York: Cambridge University Press.

Lacina, F. 1983. "Interview." *Gemeinwirtschaft und Politik* 1:9–14.

——. 1977. *The Development of the Austrian Public Sector since World War II.* Technical Papers Series no. 7. Office of Public Sector Studies, Institute of Latin American Studies, University of Texas, Austin.

Lafferty, W., and O. Knutsen. 1985. "Postmaterialism in a Social Democratic State." *Comparative Political Studies* 17(4):411–430.

Lamont, D. F. 1979. *Foreign State Enterprises: A Threat to American Business.* New York: Basic Books.

Lancaster, K. 1973. "The Dynamic Inefficiency of Capitalism." *Journal of Political Economy* 81(5):1092–1109.

Lane, R. 1986. "Market Justice, Political Justice." *American Political Science Review* 80(2):383–402.

Lange, P. 1984. *Union Democracy and Liberal Corporatism: Exit, Voice and Wage Regulation in Postwar Europe.* Western Societies Program Occasional Paper no. 16. Center for International Studies, Cornell University, Ithaca, N.Y.

Lange, P., and G. Garrett. 1987. "The Politics of Growth Reconsidered." *Journal of Politics* 48:257–274.

Langer, E. 1964. "Nationalization in Austria." *Annals of Public and Cooperative Economy* 35:115–163.

Laux, J., and M. Molot. 1987. *State Capitalism: Public Enterprise in Canada.* Ithaca: Cornell University Press.

Lawrence, C., and R. Lawrence. 1985. "Manufacturing Wage Dispersion: An End Game Interpretation." In *Brookings Papers on Economic Activity*, ed. W. Brainard and G. Perry, pp. 47–116. Washington, D.C.: Brookings Institution.

Layard, R. 1986. *How to Beat Unemployment.* Oxford: Oxford University Press.

Lehmbruch, G. 1977. "Liberal Corporatism and Party Government." *Comparative Political Studies* 10(1):91–126.

Lemass, S. F. 1969. "The Role of the State-Sponsored Bodies in the Economy." In *Economic Planning and Development*, ed. B. Chubb and P. Lynch, pp. 277–295. Dublin: Institute of Public Administration.

Leys, C. 1985. "Thatcherism and British Manufacturing." *New Left Review* 15 (May-June):5–25.

Lijphart, A. 1984. *Democracies: Patterns of Majoritarian and Consensus Government in 21 Countries.* New Haven: Yale University Press.

Lindbeck, A. 1974. *Swedish Economic Policy.* Berkeley: University of California Press.

Lindberg, L., et al. 1975. *Stress and Contradiction in Modern Capitalism: Public Policy and the Theory of the State.* Lexington, Mass.: Lexington Books.

Lindblom, C. 1982. "The Market as a Prison." *Journal of Politics* 44(2):324–336.

——. 1980. *The Policy Making Process.* 2d ed. Englewood Cliffs, N.J.: Prentice-Hall.

——. 1977. *Politics and Markets: The World's Political-Economic Systems.* New York: Basic Books.

———. 1965. *The Intelligence of Democracy: Decision-Making through Mutual Adjustment*. New York: Free Press.

Lindert, P., and C. Kindelberger. 1982. *International Economics*. 7th ed. Homewood, Ill.: Irwin.

Lintner, J. 1981. "Economic Theory and Financial Management." In *State-Owned Enterprise in the Western Economies*, ed. R. Vernon and Y. Aharoni, pp. 23–53.

Lipton, M. 1976. "What Is Nationalization For?" *Lloyds Bank Review*, July, pp. 33–38.

Litterman, R. B. 1984. "Forecasting and Policy Analysis with Bayesian Vector Autoregressive Models." *Federal Reserve Bank of Minneapolis Quarterly Review* 8(4):30–41.

Magaziner, I., and R. Reich. 1982. *Minding America's Business: The Decline and Rise of the American Economy*. New York: Harcourt Brace Jovanovich.

Mallon, R. 1981. "Performance Evaluation and Compensation of the Social Burdens of Public Enterprises in Less Developed Countries." *Annals of Public and Cooperative Economy* 52(3):281–300.

Mandel, E. 1986. "In Defense of Socialist Planning." *New Left Review* 159 (September-October):5–37.

Manley, J. 1983. "Neopluralism: A Class Analysis of Pluralism I and II." *American Political Science Review* 77(2):368–383.

Mann, P. C. 1974. "User Power and Electrical Rates." *Journal of Law and Economics* 17(2):433–443.

Marglin, S. 1963. "The Social Discount Rate and the Optimal Rate of Investment." *Quarterly Journal of Economics* 77(1):95–111.

Marin, B. 1983. "Organizing Interests by Interest Organizations: Associational Prerequisites of Cooperation in Austria." *International Political Science Review* 4(2):197–216.

Marsh, D., and G. Locksley. 1983. "Capital in Britain: Its Structural Power and Influence over Policy." *West European Politics* 6(2):36–60.

Marshall, T. H. 1950. *Citizenship and Social Class*. Cambridge: Cambridge University Press.

Martin, A., and G. Ross. 1980. "European Unions in Economic Crisis: Perceptions and Crisis." In *Trade Unions and Politics in Western Europe*, ed. J. Hayward, pp. 33–67. London: Frank Cass.

Martinelli, A. 1981. "The Italian Experience: An Historical Perspective." In *State-Owned Enterprise in the Western Economies*, ed. R. Vernon and Y. Aharoni, pp. 85–98. New York: St. Martin's.

Mazzolini, R. 1980. "European Government-Controlled Enterprises: An Organizational Politics View." *Journal of International Business*, Winter, pp. 48–58.

———. 1979a. "European Government-Controlled Enterprises: Explaining International Strategic and Policy Decisions." *Journal of International Business*, Winter, pp. 16–27.

———. 1979b. Review of Lamont's *Foreign State Enterprise*. *Political Science Quarterly* 94:712–713.

Meidner, R. 1978. *Employee Investment Funds: An Approach to Collective Capital Formation*. London: Allen & Unwin.

Miliband, R. 1969. *The State in Capitalist Society*. London: Weidenfeld & Nicolson

Miller, N. 1983. "Pluralism and Social Choice." *American Political Science Review* 77(3):734–747.

Million, J. W. 1896. *State Aid to Railways in Missouri*. Chicago: University of Chicago Press.

Millward, R. 1982. "The Comparative Performance of Public and Private Ownership." In *The Mixed Economy*, ed. Lord Roll, pp. 58–93. London: Macmillan.

——. 1978. "Public Ownership, the Theory of Property Rights and Public Corporations in the U.K." *Salford Papers in Economics* 78–1. Salford University.

——. 1976. "Price Restraint, Anti-Inflation Policy and Public and Private Industry in the United Kingdom, 1949–1973." *Economic Journal* 86 (June):226–242.

Millward, R., and D. Parker. 1983. "Public and Private Enterprise: Comparative Behavior and Relative Efficiency." In *Public Sector Economics*, ed. R. Millward et al., pp. 199–274. London: Longman.

Moe, R. 1982. "Federal Government Corporations: The Quest for Theory." Paper presented at the Annual Meeting of the American Political Science Association, September 2–5, Washington, D.C.

Monsen, R. J., and K. D. Walters. 1983. *Nationalized Companies: A Threat to American Business*. New York: McGraw-Hill.

——. 1979. "State-Owned Firms: A Review of Data and Issues." *Research in Corporate Social Performance and Policy* vol. 2:125–156. Greenwich, Conn.: JAI Press.

Moran, M. 1981. "Finance Capital and Pressure-Group Politics in Britain." *British Journal of Political Science* 11(3):381–404.

Morris, M. D. 1979. *Measuring the Condition of the World's Poor: The Physical Quality of Life Index*. New York: Pergamon.

National Academy of Public Administration. 1981. *Report on Government Corporations*, vol. 1. Report prepared for Office of Management and Budget. Washington, D.C.: National Academy of Public Administration.

Neuman, M. 1985. "Long Swings in Economic Development, Social Time Preference and Institutional Change." *Journal of Institutional and Theoretical Economics* 141(1):21–35.

Nordhaus, W. 1975. "The Political Business Cycle." *Review of Economic Studies* 42:169–190.

Noreng, Ø. 1981. "State-Owned Oil Companies: Western Europe." In *State-Owned Enterprises in the Western Economies*, ed. R. Vernon and Y. Aharoni, pp. 133–144. New York: St. Martin's.

Nove, A. 1983. *The Economics of Feasible Socialism*. London: Allen & Unwin.

Nowotny, E. 1984. "Institutionen und Entscheidungsstrukturen in der österreichischen Wirtschaftspolitik." In *Handbuch der österreichischen Wirtschaftspolitik*, pp. 118–132. Vienna: Manz.

——. 1982a. "Nationalized Industries as an Instrument of Stabilization Policy: The Case of Austria." *Annals of Public and Cooperative Economy* 53(1):41–58.

——. 1982b. "Gemeinwirtschaft in Österreich-Umfang und Bedeutung für die Volkswirtschaft." In *Die österreichishe Gemeinwirtschaft*, pp. 19–38. Vienna: Jugend & Volk.

——. 1978. "Verstaatlichte und private Industrie in der Rezession—Gemeinsamkeiten und Unterschiede." *W.I.S.O.* 3(2):71–95.

O'Connor, J. 1973. *The Fiscal Crisis of the State*. New York: St. Martin's.

Offe, C. 1983. "Competitive Party Democracy and the Keynesian Welfare

State: Factors of Stability and Disorganization." *Policy Sciences* 15(3):225–246.

——. 1981. "The Attribution of Public Status to Interest Groups: Observations on the West German Case." In *Organizing Interest in Western Europe*, ed. S. Berger, pp. 123–158. New York: Cambridge University Press.

——. 1975. "Theory of the Capitalist State and the Problem of Policy Formation." In *Stress and Contradiction in Modern Capitalism*, ed. L. Lindberg et al., pp. 125–144. Lexington, Mass.: Lexington Books.

Offe, C., and H. Wiesenthal. 1980. "Two Logics of Collective Action: Theoretical Notes on Social Class and Organizational Form." In *Political Power and Social Theory*, ed. M. Zeitlin, 1:67–115. Greenwich, Conn.: JAI Press.

Ohlin, G. 1974. "Sweden." In *Big Business and the State*, ed. R. Vernon, pp. 126–141. Cambridge: Harvard University Press.

Okun, A. M. 1975. *Equality and Efficiency: The Big Trade-Off.* Washington, D.C.: Brookings.

Olson, M. 1982. *The Rise and Decline of Nations.* New Haven: Yale University Press.

Organization for Economic Co-Operation and Development. 1982. *Historical Statistics, 1960–1980.* Paris.

——. 1981. *The Welfare State in Crisis.* Paris.

——. 1976a. *Occasional Studies: Income Distribution in OECD Countries.* Paris.

——. 1976b. *Public Expenditures for Income Maintenance Policies.* Paris.

Österreichische Industrieverwaltungs-AG. 1983. "Austria's Nationalized Industries." Vienna.

Paldam, M. 1979. "Is There an Electoral Cycle? A Comparative Study of National Accounts." *Scandinavian Journal of Economics* 81(2):323–341.

Panitch, L. 1981. "Trade Unions and the Capitalist State." *New Left Review* 125 (January-February):21–43.

——. 1980. "Recent Theoretizations of Corporatism: Reflections on a Growth Industry." *British Journal of Sociology* 31(2):159–187.

Pashigian, B. P. 1976. "Consequences and Causes of Public Ownership of Urban Transit Facilities." *Journal of Political Economy* 84(6):1239–1259.

Payne, J. 1979. "Inflation, Unemployment, and Left-Wing Political Parties: A Reanalysis." *American Political Science Review* 73(1):181–185.

Pelinka, A. 1987. "The Austrian Social Partnership: Stability versus Innovation." *West European Politics* 19(1):63–75.

Peltzman, S. 1971. "Pricing in Public and Private Enterprises: Electric Utilities in the U.S." *Journal of Law and Economics* 14(1):109–147.

Penati, A., and M. Dooley. 1984. "Current Account Imbalances and Capital Formation in Industrial Countries, 1949–1981." *I.M.F. Staff Papers* 31(1):1–24.

Pissardes, C. 1980. "British Government Popularity and Economic Performance." *Economic Journal* September, pp. 569–581.

——. 1972. "A Model of British Macroeconomic Policy, 1955–1969." *Manchester School* 40:245–259.

Pizzorno, A. 1981. "Interests and Parties in Pluralism." In *Organizing Interests in Western Europe*, ed. S. Berger, pp. 249–286. New York: Cambridge University Press.

Platzer, R. 1986. "The Privatization Debate in Austria." *Annals of Public and Cooperative Economy* 57(2):275–291.

Pontusson, J. 1987. "Radicalization and Retreat in Swedish Social Democracy." *New Left Review* 165 (September-October):5–33.

——. 1984. "Labor and Industrial Policy in Sweden." Paper presented at the Annual Meeting of the American Political Science Association, Washington, D.C.

Posner, M. 1981. "Running Public Enterprises: Theory and Practice." *Annals of Public and Cooperative Economy* 52(1–2):17–25.

Posner, M., and S. J. Woolf. 1967. *Italian Public Enterprises.* London: Duckworth.

Poulantzas, N. 1973. *Political Power and Social Classes*, trans. T. O'Hagen. London: New Left Books.

Powell, G. B. 1986. "Models of Citizen Control through Elections." Paper presented at the Annual Meeting of the American Political Science Association, Washington, D.C.

Price, V. 1981. *Industrial Policies in the European Community.* New York: St. Martin's.

Prodi, R. 1974. "Italy." In *Big Business and the State*, ed. R. Vernon, pp. 45–63. Cambridge: Harvard University Press.

Pryke, R. 1981. *The Nationalized Industries: Policies and Performance since 1968.* Oxford: Martin Robertson.

Przeworski, A. 1986. "Some Problems in the Study of the Transition to Democracy." In *Transitions from Authoritarian Rule: Comparative Perspectives*, ed. G. O'Donnell, P. Schmitter, and L. Whitehead, pp. 47–63. Baltimore: Johns Hopkins University Press.

——. 1982. "Investment Policies and Their Political Determinants." A proposal submitted to the National Science Foundation, February.

——. 1980a. "The Material Basis of Consent: Economics and Politics in a Hegemonic System." *Political Power and Social Theory* 1:21–67.

——. 1980b. "Social Democracy as a Historical Phenomenon." *New Left Review* 122 (July-August):27–58.

——. 1980c. "Material Interests, Class Compromise, and the Transition to Socialism." *Politics and Society* 10(2):125–154.

Przeworski, A., and M. Wallerstein. 1987. "Why Is There No Alternative?" Mimeo. University of Chicago.

——. 1986. "Revolutionary Demands." Paper presented at the Annual Meeting of the Midwest Political Science Association. Chicago.

——. 1985. "Popular Sovereignty, State Autonomy and Private Property." Revised version of a paper presented at the workshop Political Practice and the Reconstruction of Democratic Theory. Instituto Universitario Europeo, Florence.

——. 1982a. "The Structure of Class Conflict in Democratic Societies." *American Political Science Review* 76(2):215–238.

——. 1982b. "Democratic Capitalism at the Crossroads." *Democracy*, July, pp. 52–68.

Quirk, J. P. 1982. *Intermediate Economics.* 2d ed. Chicago: SRA Associates.

Rae, D. 1979. "The Egalitarian State: Notes on a System of Contradictory Ideas." *Daedulus* 108 (Fall):37–54.

Raiffa, H. 1981. "Decision Making in State-Owned Enterprise." In *State-Owned Enterprise in the Western Economies*, ed. R. Vernon and Y. Aharoni, pp. 54–62. New York: St. Martin's.

Redwood, J. 1980. *Public Enterprise in Crisis: The Future of the Nationalized Industries.* Oxford: Blackwell.

Redwood, J., and J. Hatch. 1982. *Controlling Public Industries.* Oxford: Blackwell.

Regini, M., and G. Esping-Andersen. 1980. "Trade Union Strategies and Social Policy in Italy and Sweden." In *Trade Unions and Politics in Western Europe*, ed. J. Hayward, pp. 107–123. London: Frank Cass.

Rehn, G. 1984. "The Wages of Success." *Daedalus* 113(2):137–168.

Riker, W., and P. Ordeshook. 1973. *An Introduction to Positive Political Theory.* Englewood Cliffs, N.J.: Prentice-Hall.

Rivlin, A. 1987. "Overview." In *The Swedish Economy*, ed. B. Bosworth and A. Rivlin, pp. 1–21. Washington, D.C.: Brookings.

Rogowski, R. 1987. "Trade and Democratic Institutions." *International Organization* 41(2):203–224.

Rohatyn, F. 1983. *The Twenty-Year Century: Essays on Economics and Public Finance.* New York: Random House.

Roll, E. 1982. *The Mixed Economy.* London: Macmillan.

Rowley, C. 1982. "Industrial Policy in the Mixed Economy." In *The Mixed Economy*, ed. E. Roll, pp. 35–57. London: Macmillan.

Ruth, A. 1984. "The Second New Nation: The Mythology of Modern Sweden." *Daedalus* 113(2):53–96.

Sabel, C. 1981. "The Internal Politics of Trade Unions." In *Organizing Interests in Western Europe*, ed. S. Berger, pp. 209–244. New York: Cambridge University Press.

Sachs, I. 1964. *Patterns of Public Sector in Underdeveloped Economies.* New York: Asia Publishing House.

Salvati, M. 1981. "May 1968 and the Hot Autumn of 1969: The Responses of Two Working Classes." In *Organizing Interests in Western Europe*, ed. S. Berger, pp. 331–366. New York: Cambridge University Press.

Sandmo, A., and J. H. Dreze. 1971. "Discount Rates for Public Investment in Closed and Open Economies." *Economica* 38(152):395–412.

Schloss, H. H. 1977. "Public Enterprise as a Form of Business Enterprise: Role, Purpose and Performance." *Annals of Public and Cooperative Economy* 48(3):299–305.

Schmitter, P. 1981. "Interest Intermediation and Regime Governability in Contemporary Western Europe and North America." In *Organizing Interests in Western Europe*, ed. S. Berger, pp. 287–330. New York: Cambridge University Press.

——. 1979. "Still the Century of Corporatism?" In *Trends toward Corporatist Intermediation*, ed. P. Schmitter and G. Lehmbruch, pp. 7–52. London: Sage.

Seidel, H. 1982. "The Austrian Economy: An Overview." In *The Political Economy of Austria*, ed. S. Arndt, pp. 7–21. Washington, D.C.: American Enterprise Institute.

Sen, A. K. 1967. "Isolation, Assurance and the Social Rate of Discount." *Quarterly Journal of Economics* 81(1):112–124.

——. 1961. "On Optimizing the Rate of Saving." *Economic Journal* 71:479–496.

Shafer, M. 1983. "Nationalizing the Multinationals." *International Organization* 37(1):93–120.

Shonfield, A. 1984. *In Defense of the Mixed Economy*, ed. Zuzanna Shonfield. New York: Oxford University Press.

——. 1965. *Modern Capitalism: The Changing Balance of Public and Private*

Power. New York: Oxford University Press.

Short, R. P. 1983. "The Role of Public Enterprise: An International Statistical Comparison." Departmental Memorandum. Washington, D.C.: International Monetary Fund.

Silberston, A. 1982. "Steel in a Mixed Economy." In *The Mixed Economy*, ed. E. Roll, pp. 94–112. London: Macmillan.

Sinn Fein Workers Party. 1975. "The Public Sector and the Profit Makers." *Studies in Political Economy* no. 2. Dublin: Repsol.

Skocpol, T. 1980. "Political Response to Capitalist Crisis: Neo-Marxist Theories of the State and the Case of the New Deal." *Politics and Society* 10(2):155–201.

Smith, Adam. 1920. *The Wealth of Nations*, vol. 2. 2d ed. London: Methuen.

Social Democratic Party. 1984a. *Policies for Competitiveness.* Green Paper no. 17. London: S.D.P.

——. 1984b. *Industrial Strategy.* Policy Document no. 2. London: Jaguar.

Social Democratic Party/Liberal Alliance. 1984. *Working Together for Britain.* London: Jaguar.

Spitäller, E. 1982. "Commentary." In *The Political Economy of Austria*, ed. S. Arndt, pp. 98–100. Washington, D.C.: American Enterprise Institute.

Statistik årbok för Sverige. 1971, 1974, 1975. Årgång 58, 61, 62. Stockholm: Statistiska centralbryån.

Stefani, G. 1986. "Privatizing Public Enterprises in Italy: the case of state holdings." *Annals of Public and Cooperative Economy* 57(2):231–251.

——. 1981. "Control Mechanisms of Public Enterprises." *Annals of Public and Cooperative Economy* 52(1):49–71.

Stern, G. 1987. "The Federal Budget's Effects on Intergenerational Equity: Undone or Not Undone?" *Federal Reserve Bank of Minneapolis Quarterly Review* 11(1):2–6.

Stoffaes, C., and P. Gadonneix. 1980. "Steel and the State in France." *Annals of Public and Cooperative Economy* 51(4):405–422.

Strom, K. 1986. "Party Competition in Open Economies." Paper presented at the Annual Meeting of the Midwest Political Science Association, Chicago.

Suleiman, E. 1974. *Politics, Power and Bureaucracy in France: The Administrative Elite.* Princeton: Princeton University Press.

Taus, J. 1983. "The Influence of Politics on the Private Economy and the Public Economy: A Comparison." *Gemeinwirtshaft und Politik*, January, pp. 15–18.

Thonet, P. J., and O. H. Poensgen. 1979. "Managerial Control and Economic Performance in Western Germany." *Journal of Industrial Economics* 29(1):23–27.

Thurow, L. 1980. *The Zero-Sum Society: Distribution and the Possibilities for Economic Change* New York: Basic Books.

Tilton, T. 1987. "Why Don't the Swedish Social Democrats Nationalize Industry?" *Scandinavian Political Studies* 59:142–166.

——. 1979. "A Swedish Road to Socialism: Ernst Wigforss and the Ideological Foundations of Swedish Social Democracy." *American Political Science Review* 73(2):505–520.

Tinbergen, J. 1972. "The Optimal Organization of the Economy." In *Public Expenditure Analysis*, ed. B. S. Sahni, pp. 21–35. Rotterdam: Rotterdam University Press.

——. 1963. "The Organization of the Economy in the Service of Man—A

General Review." *Annals of Public and Cooperative Economy* 34 (January-March):96–109.
——. 1959. *Selected Papers*, ed. L. H. Klassen, L. M. Koyck, and H. J. Wittereen. Amsterdam: North-Holland.
Tivey, L. 1982. "Nationalized Industries as Organized Interests." *Public Administration* 60 (Spring):42–55.
Tomandl, T., and K. Fuerboeck. 1986. *Social Partnership: The Austrian System of Industrial Relations and Social Insurance*. Ithaca, N.Y.: ILR Press.
Törnblom, L. 1977. "The Swedish State Company Limited Statsforetag AB, Its Role in the Swedish Economy." *Annals of Public and Cooperative Economy* 48(4):451–461.
Tulkens, H. 1976. "The Publicness of Public Enterprise." In *Public Enterprise: Economic Analysis of Theory and Practice*, ed. W. Shepherd, pp. 23–32. Lexington, Mass.: D. C. Heath.
Tumlir, J. 1982. "Commentary." In *The Political Economy of Austria*, ed. S. Arndt, pp. 204–206. Washington, D.C.: American Enterprise Institute.
Turner, J. 1978. *Labour's Doorstep Politics in London*. Minneapolis: University of Minnesota Press.
Vak, K. 1982. "The Competitiveness of the Austrian Economy." In *The Political Economy of Austria*, ed. S. Arndt, pp. 150–175. Washington, D.C.: American Enterprise Institute.
Vallet, C. 1983. "Resolution of Conflicts of Interest in the Ownership of a Firm: The Case of Mixed Firms." *Annals of Public and Cooperative Economy* 54(3):255–269.
Van der Bellen, A. 1981. "The Control of Public Enterprises: The Case of Austria." *Annals of Public and Cooperative Economy* 52(1–2):73–100.
Véliz, C. 1980. *The Centralist Tradition of Latin America*. Princeton: Princeton University Press.
Vernon, R. 1981. "Introduction." In *State-Owned Enterprise in the Western Economies*, ed. R. Vernon and Y. Aharoni, pp. 7–22. New York: St. Martin's.
——. 1979. "The International Aspects of State-Owned Enterprises." *Journal of International Business Studies* 10(3):7–15.
Vernon, R., and B. Levy. 1982. "State-Owned Enterprises in the World Economy: The Case of Iron Ore." In *Public Enterprise in Less Developed Countries*, ed., L. Jones and Associates, pp. 171–190. New York: Cambridge University Press.
Vernon, R., ed. 1974. *Big Business and the State*. Cambridge: Harvard University Press.
Vernon, R., and Y. Aharoni, eds. 1981. *State-Owned Enterprise in the Western Economies*. New York: St. Martin's.
Violette, E. M. 1918. *A History of Missouri*. Boston: D. C. Heath.
von Beyme, K. 1985. "The Role of the State and the Growth of Government." *International Political Science Review* 6(1):11–34.
——. 1983. "Neo Corporatism: A New Nut in an Old Shell?" *International Political Science Review* 4(2):153–172.
Von Furstenberg, G. M., and B. G. Malkiel. 1977. "The Government and Capital Formation: A Survey of Recent Issues." *Journal of Economic Literature* 15:835–878.
Wade, R. 1982. "Regional Policy in a Severe International Environment: Politics and Markets in South Italy." *Pacific Viewpoint* 23(2):99–126.
——. 1979. "Fast Growth and Slow Development in South Italy." In *Underde-*

veloped Europe: Studies in Core-Periphery Relations, ed. D. Seers, B. Schaffer, and M. Kiljunen, pp. 197–221. London: Harvester.

Wallerstein, M. 1987. "Unemployment, Collective Bargaining and the Demand for Protection." *American Journal of Political Science* 31(4): 729–752.

——. 1984. "Micro-Foundations of Corporatism: Formal Theory and Comparative Analysis." Paper delivered at the Annual Meeting of the American Political Science Association, Washington, D.C.

——. 1982. "The Welfare Economics of Capital Accumulation: A Literature Review." Paper presented at the Annual Meeting of the American Political Science Association, Denver, Colo.

Walters, K. D., and R. J. Monsen. 1979. "State-Owned Business Abroad: New Competitive Threat." *Harvard Business Review*, March/April, pp. 160–170.

Weaver, R. 1987. "Political Foundations of Swedish Economic Policy." In *The Swedish Economy*, ed. B. Bosworth and A. Rivlin, pp. 289–324. Washington, D.C.: Brookings.

Wilensky, H., and L. Turner. 1987. *Democratic Corporatism and Policy Linkages*. Berkeley, Calif: Institute for International Studies, University of California.

Wiles, P. 1974. *Distribution of Income, East and West*. New York: American Elsevier.

Willett, T. 1982. "Commentary." In *The Political Economy of Austria*, ed. S. Arndt, pp. 56–60. Washington, D.C.: American Enterprise Institute.

Wright, E. 1984. "A General Framework for the Analysis of Class Structure." *Politics and Society* 13(4):383–423.

Zysman, J. 1983. *Governments, Markets and Growth: Financial Systems and the Politics of Industrial Change*. Ithaca: Cornell University Press.

——. 1977. *Political Strategies for Industrial Order: State, Market and Industry in France*. Berkeley: University of California Press.

Zysman, J., and S. Cohen. 1983. "Double or Nothing: Open Trade and Competitive Industry." *Foreign Affairs* 61(5):1113–1139.

Index

Aberbach, J., 93n
Abromeit, H., 150n, 154n, 160n, 162n, 163n, 165n, 167n, 169n
Adams, C. Teich, 68n, 138n, 143n, 184n
Adar, Z., 75n, 76–77n
Aharoni, Y., 11n, 74n, 75n, 76–77n, 86n, 164n, 228n, 237n, 239n, 256n
Aimer, P., 219n, 221n
Alber, J., 282n
Alberta Heritage Fund, 85n
Alt, J. E., xi, 50n, 86n, 88n, 103n, 116n, 156n, 161–62n, 165n, 170n, 254n, 257–58n, 277n
Andrlik, E., 29n, 110n, 123n, 126n, 179n, 181n, 182n, 184–85n, 187n, 188n, 192n, 194n, 196n, 199n, 201n, 263n
Arndt, S., 185n, 186n
Arrow, K. J., 24–27, 30n, 31–32, 71n, 72n, 76n, 138n
Artus, J. R., 181n
Åsard, E., 221n
Austria: capital market and mobility, 176–77, 193–94, 260, 285n; corporatism, 170–71, 186–92, 200–201, 265–66; electoral system, 9, 187–92; as laboratory for study of democratic socialism, 13–14; mixed economy 171, 263–64; nationalized industries (state-owned enterprises) 178–81, 184–86, 189, 259–66; openness of economy, 259–66; party politics, 188–89, 193n, 194, 199, 200–201, 262; Proporz, 117n, 171, 188, 191, 193, 200–201, 210; public opinion about nationalized industries

(state-owned enterprise), 188, 194–201, 264–65; state administrators, 48–49, 192–93, 264; state enterprise workers, 190–91, 199–201, 264–66; workings of political economy and social welfare, 8n, 173–77, 285, relative to Britain, 141, 151, 266, 272, relative to Italy, 173–74, 268–69, 272, relative to Sweden, 173–74, 272, relative to United States, 264
Austrian Trade Union Federation, 171, 187n
Austro-Keynesianism, 177

Baer, W., 34n
Ball, T., 8on, 84–85n, 282n
Barry, N., 22n
Beesley, M., 29n
Behn, R., 93n
Benya, A., 89n, 186–87n
Berger, S., 90n
Bergson, A., 276n
Biersteker, T., 228n
Birch, A., 6n
Block, F. L., 47n
Bluestone, B., 3n, 139n
Boddy, R., 102n
Bosworth, B., 211n, 214n, 219n, 271n
Bowler, S., 132n, 177n, 194n, 213n, 218n, 261n, 270n
Bowles, S., 43n, 139n
Braun, A. Romanis, 189n, 260n
Breton, A., 78n, 237n, 238n, 244n
Bristow, J. A., 28n
Britain: capital market and mobility, 168–69, 254; as laboratory for study

305

Britain (*cont.*)
of democratic socialism, 14;
nationalized industries, 154–56,
160–66, 253; neoliberal account of
mixed economy, 28; openness of
economy, 252–58; party politics,
150–66, 171, 255–57; pluralism,
149–50, 161–63, 255–58; privatization, 11, 150–54, 160, 255, 266;
public opinion about nationalized
industry (state-owned enterprise),
16–17, 116n, 163n, 169–70; state
administrators, 166–68, 257;
Thatcher administrations, 48,
150–66, 171, 255–57; workings of
political economy and social welfare,
140–42, 147, 157–58; relative to
Austria, 141, 151, 266, 272, relative
to Italy, 141, 151, 267, 272; relative
to Sweden, 151, 272
British Petroleum, 253, 256, 258
British sickness, 6, 152
Brittan, S., 6n, 88n, 144n, 150n, 153n,
156n, 160n, 163n, 165n
Brooks, J., 8n, 13n, 67n, 94n, 139n,
140n, 176n
Bruce-Gardyne, J., 156n, 162n, 164n,
167n
Brus, W., 8n, 18n
Butschek, F., 183n, 184n, 185n

Calender, G. S., 14n, 40n
Calmfors, L., 271n
Cameron, D., 102n, 138n, 142n, 143n,
144–46n, 176n, 228–29n
Canadian Crown Corporations, 28n
capital markets: in mixed economies,
61–62; in private enterprise
economies, 61–62
capital mobility: barrier to redistribu-
tion, 15, 68–69, 77–78, 105–6, 132;
and democracy, 274, 284
capital starvation thesis, 255
Cassesse, S., 31n
Cavalieri, D., 208n
Chaloupek, G., 187n, 188n, 189n, 194n
Chandler, M., 244n
Chappell, H., 103n
Chong, D., 85n, 279n
Chrystal, A., 88n, 103n
Chubb, B., 31n
citizenship rights, 282–86
civic consciousness, 283, 286
Coakley, J., 153n, 158n, 255n, 257n
Cochran, N., 93n
collective ownership efficacy: 117–20,
133, 243–45, 278, 285–86; in

Austria 199–200; in Britain,
169–71; in corporatist–mixed vs.
pluralist–mixed systems, 125–28
Confederation of British Industries,
149–50, 167n
Confindustria, 207
consensual political systems, 5, 18, 82, 87
corporatism: destabilization, 248; in
liberal theory, 4–5; and
management of state business
sector, 123–29, 247, 269; in open
mixed systems, 247–49; in radical
theory, 7, 275; and wage earners'
share of societal wealth, 108. *See
also* corporatist–mixed political
economy; corporatist–private
enterprise political economy
corporatist–mixed political economy:
compatibility with democracy and
desirability, 281–86; openness of,
247–49; state administration in,
128–29, 248–49; workings and
welfare consequences of, 122–30,
133–34, 247–49
corporatist–private enterprise political
economy: compatibility with
democracy and desirability, 283–86;
openness of, 233–35; state administration in, 110–11, 235; workings
and welfare consequences of,
106–11, 130, 133–34, 233–35, 275
Corti, G., 6n, 31
Cox, A., 150n, 156n, 160–61n
Cox, R., 89n
Coyle, P., 28n
Crotty, J., 102n
Crouch, C., 222n
Cubbin, J., 66n

Dahl, R., 3n, 6n, 7n, 8n, 11n, 14n, 32n,
35n, 276n, 279n, 283n, 284n
Dahrendorf, R., 49n
democracy, 276n
democratic corporatism. *See* corporatism; corporatist–mixed political
economy; corporatist–private
enterprise political economy
democratic pluralism. *See* pluralism;
pluralist–mixed political economy;
pluralist–private enterprise political
economy
Dennis, C., 138n
Despicht, N., 41n, 78n, 208n
direct foreign investment: motivation for
state-owned enterprise, 27–28, 32,
48; problem for class compromise
theory, 47–48

Dooley, M., 177n
Dornbusch, R., 227n
Dreyer, J., 177n
Dreze, J., 69n, 71n, 72n, 77n
Dudley, G., 116n, 167n, 169n
Dupuy, A., 38

electoral systems, 82; and behavior of
    state managers, 29, 50; and
    workings and welfare consequences,
    of corporatist–mixed systems,
    124–28, of corporatist–private
    enterprise systems, 111, of
    pluralist–mixed systems, 115–22,
    133, 242–44, of pluralist–private
    enterprise systems, 102–4, 232. *See
    also* consensual political systems;
    majoritarian political systems
Eliasson, G., 213n
Ellman, M., 24n
Eltis, W., 78n, 156n, 160n
Esping-Anderson, G., 86n, 89n, 138n,
    139n, 140n, 176n, 206n, 207n,
    214n, 222n, 282n
Evans, P., 236n, 246n
Evans, T., 29n
Ezra, D., 253n

Faini, R., 204n, 205n, 206n
Farnleitner, J., 107n, 125n, 172n, 192n
Fausto, D., 13n, 31n, 72n, 78n, 205n,
    206–7n
Figueroa, A., 34n
Flanagan, R., 92n, 212n, 213n, 214n,
    216n, 270n
Flora, P., 282n
France: electoral system, 9; financial
    system, 105n; origins of mixed
    economy, 28, 48; state admin-
    istrators, 93n, 94n
Freeman, J., xi, 53n, 94n, 170n, 188n,
    201n, 241n, 257–58n, 268n, 277n
Frey, B., 88n
Frisch, H., 189n, 190n
Frohlich, N., 26n
Fuerboeck, K., 172n, 184n, 185n, 187n,
    189n
Fusfeld, D., 139n

Gadonneix, P., 13n
Garner, M., 154n, 155n, 157n, 160n,
    161n, 164n
Garrett, G., 138n, 173n
Gintes, H., 43n, 139n
Goodin, R., 167n
Grant, W., 153n
Grassini, F., 28n, 31n, 208n

Gray, C., 72n, 76n, 228n
Grunwald, O., 128n, 172n, 173n, 177n,
    178n, 185n, 192–93n, 200n, 262n

Hadjimatheou, G., 153n
Hamermesh, D. S., 50n, 79n
Hankel, W., 14n, 49n, 63–64n, 177n,
    181n, 182n, 183n, 186n, 189n,
    261n, 285n
Hansen, B., 212n, 214n, 216n, 221n,
    222n
Harris, J., 153n, 158n, 255n, 257n
Harrison, B., 3n, 139n
Hart, J., 79n, 116n, 164n
Hartz, L., 14n, 40n
Haschek, H., 194n
Hatch, J., 6n, 73n, 76n, 150n, 154–55n,
    157n, 164n
Hattersley, R., 150n
Hayward, J., 150n, 156n, 160–61n
Heald, D., 29n, 48n, 150n, 164n, 165n,
    169n
Heclo, H., 68n, 138n, 143n, 184n, 211n,
    212n, 214n, 217n, 219n, 221n
Heidenheimer, H., 68n, 138n, 143n,
    184n
Hemming, R., 11n, 71n, 150n
Hernes, G., 108n
Heurtibise, A., 35n
Hibbs, D. A., 85n, 86n, 91n, 103n, 138n,
    139n, 159n, 164n, 207n, 217n
Hindley, B., 164n, 228n, 237n, 238n,
    245n, 253n, 256n
Hodjera, Z., 177n
Holland, S., 28, 31n, 49n, 77n, 78n,
    205n, 206n, 208n, 209n, 228n
Hollingsworth, J. R., 138n, 139n, 143n
Holmlund, B., 212n, 271n
Holton, R., 29n, 41n, 86n
Höök, E., 211n, 215n, 270n
hysteresis, 185

Inglehart, R., 85n
Instituto per la Reconstruzione
    Industriale (IRI), 267n
Ireland, Republic of: origin and support
    for mixed economy, 28n, 89n;
    worker involvement in state
    enterprise management, 41n
Italy: capital markets and mobility, 72n,
    204; as laboratory for study of
    democratic socialism, 13n, 14n,
    nationalized industries (state-owned
    enterprises), 204–6, 207–10,
    267–69; openness of economy,
    267–69; party politics, 13n, 39, 88,
    207; pluralism, 203n, 207;

Italy (*cont.*)
  privatization, 11, 203n, 208–9;
    radical account of mixed economy,
    39, 48–49; workings of political
    economy and social welfare, 204–6,
    relative to Austria, 200, 203,
    268–69, 272, relative to Britain,
    141, 151, 203–4, 209n, 210, 267,
    272, relative to Sweden, 140,
    203–4, 269, 272
Itzlinger, A., 188n, 261n

Jackman, R., 7n, 87n, 94n
Jacobsen, J. K., 28n, 89n
Jessop, R., 107n
Job, B., xi
Jones, L. P., 34n, 76n, 78n
Jonoug, L., 217n

Kager, M., 173n
Karl, B., 93n
Katzenstein, P., 5n, 13–14n, 16n, 29n,
    89n, 94n, 109n, 125n, 171n, 172n,
    176n, 177n, 178n, 179n, 181n,
    182n, 183n, 184n, 185n, 186n,
    187n, 188n, 192n, 194n, 211n,
    212–13n, 214n, 215n, 216n, 217n,
    218n, 219n, 228–29n, 234n, 259n,
    261n, 262n, 269n, 270n
Keech, W., 103n
Keeler, J., 107n
Kerschbamer, R., 188n, 261n
Keynesiansim, in radical theory, 36,
    43–49
Kindelberger, C., 228n
King, A., 166n
Knight, A., 153n, 159n, 166n
Knutsen, O., 85n, 86n
Koren, S., 177n
Kornai, J., 276n
Korpi, W., 69n, 86n, 91n, 107n, 108–9n,
    110n, 111n, 113n, 139n, 143, 146,
    212n, 214n, 215n, 216n, 217n
Kosters, M., 183n, 185n
Kraus, F., 138n, 139n
Kristensen, O., 86n
Kromer, R., 179n, 181n, 182
Kuisel, R., 29n, 49n, 79–80n, 89n, 90n,
    93n, 94n
Kurz, M., 24–27, 32, 71n, 72n, 138n

Lacina, F., 28n, 29n, 79n, 110n, 128n,
    173n, 184n, 185n, 190n, 193n, 201n
Lafferty, W., 85n, 86n
Lamont, D., 228n, 230n, 236n, 245n,
    256n
Lancaster, K., 67n

Lane, R., 85n, 279n
Lange, P., 92n, 138n, 150n, 173n, 285n
Langer, E., 15n, 28n, 41n, 49n, 72–73n,
    77n, 279n, 284n
Laux, J., 11n, 28n, 85n, 236n, 239n,
    242n, 244n, 245n
Lawrence, C., 168n
Lawrence, R., 168n, 211n, 214n, 219n,
    271n
Leach, D., 66n
Lehmbruch, G., 107n
Lemass, S., 28n, 47n
Levy, B., 236–37n
Leys, C., 150n, 152n, 159n, 162, 167n
Lijphart, A., 5n, 87n, 90n, 188n
Lind, R. C., 76n
Lindblom, C., 3n, 7n, 11n, 57n, 93n,
    102n, 279n
Lindert, P., 228n
Lintner, J., 25n, 30n, 71n
Lipton, M., 160n
Locksley, G., 255n, 257n

Madsen, H. J., 211n, 212n, 214n, 219n,
    221n
Magaziner, I., 138–39n
majoritarian political systems, 5, 18, 82,
    87, 232
Malkiel, B. G., 25n, 27n, 68n, 71n
Mallon, R., 76n, 182n, 213n
managerial control: in corporatist–
    mixed vs. pluralist–mixed systems,
    124–27; and democracy, 277–81; in
    mixed economies, 72–78, 238; in
    pluralist–mixed vs. pluralist–private
    enterprise systems, 121–22; in
    private enterprise economies,
    64–66; problem in the study of
    political economy, 15. *See also*
    ownership rights
Mandel, E., 7n, 15n, 18n
Manley, J., 18n
Mann, P. C., 114n, 116–17n, 119n
Mansoor, A., 11n, 71n, 150n
Marglin, S., 67n, 77n
Marin, B., 172n, 187n, 188n
Marsh, D., 255n, 257n
Marshall, T. H., 282n
Martin, A., 207n, 209n, 212–13n
Martinelli, A., 28n, 39n, 41n, 205n,
    208n, 209n
Mazzolini, R., 31n, 88n, 89n, 208n,
    209n, 230n, 237n, 238n, 239n,
    242n, 244n, 268n, 269n
McCloskey, H., 85n
Meidner, R., 216n, 220n
Miliband, R., 39n

Miller, N., 18n
Million, J. W., 14n, 40n
Millward, R., 61n, 63n, 65n, 66n, 67n,
    68n, 70n, 71n, 74n, 76n, 116n,
    155n, 160n, 166n, 182n
Mitterrand, F., 231n
mixed economy: definition, xi, 228n;
    explanation for, class compromise
    theory, 42–44, classical liberal
    theory, 25, functional theory, 36,
    neoliberal theory, 27–28; structural
    and behavioral barriers to
    efficiency, 71–76; workings and
    welfare consequences of, 69–80,
    235–41. *See also,* corporatist–mixed
    political economy; pluralist–mixed
    political economy
mode of interest intermediation, 82, 90–
    92. *See also* corporatism; pluralism
Moe, R., 40n
Molot, M., 11n, 28n, 85n, 236n, 239n,
    242n, 244n, 245n
Monsen, R. J., 6n, 8n, 11n, 29n, 205n,
    211n, 230n, 231n, 256n
Moran, M., 257n
Morris, M. D., 138n, 144
Morrisonianism, 277

Neuman, M., 68n
Nordhaus, W., 103n
Noreng, Ø., 267n
Nove, A., 7n, 11n, 18n, 275, 282n
Nowotny, E., 12, 47n, 107n, 125n, 139n,
    172n, 173n, 179n, 181n, 184n,
    185n, 190n, 192n, 193n

O'Connor, J., 37n
Oesterreichische Industrieverwaltungs-
    Aktiengesellschaft (OeIAG), 10–12,
    172, 178–82, 188, 200, 222n,
    259–61, 269
Offe, C., 7n, 36n, 37–39, 42, 44n,
    91–92n, 109n
Ohlin, G., 211n
Okun, A., 22n, 144n
Olson, M., 91n
openness: and politics of mixed
    economies, 229–49
Oppenheimer, J., 26n
Ordeshook, P., 139n
ownership rights: and democracy, 279;
    foreign public, 240–41; public,
    117–20, 124–29, 133, 243–44;
    separation from managerial
    control, in private enterprise
    systems, 57, 64–66, in mixed
    systems, 64–66

Paldam, M., 217n
Panitch, L., 89n, 107n, 109n, 111n, 150n
Parker, D., 61n, 63n, 65n, 66n, 67n,
    68n, 70n, 71n, 74n, 76n, 182n
Pashigian, B. P., 116–17n, 119n
Payne, J., 183n
Pelinka, A., 91n, 125n, 172n, 173n,
    176n, 182n, 183n, 186n
Peltzman, S., 30–31, 50, 74n, 119n
Penati, M., 177n
People's shares, 41n, 199
Pizzorno, A., 93n, 108n
Platzer, R., 173n, 188n, 199n
pluralism: in liberal theory, 4–5, 273;
    and management of state business
    sector, 100–103, 105–6, 243; in
    open mixed systems, 242–46; in
    radical theory, 7
pluralist–mixed political economy:
    compatibility with democracy and
    desirability, 283–86; openness of
    241–46; state administration in,
    120–21; workings and welfare
    consequences of, 112–22, 133–34,
    241–46
pluralist–private enterprise political
    economy: compatibility with
    democracy and desirability, 281–86;
    openness of, 232–33; state
    administration in, 104–6, 232;
    workings and welfare consequences
    of, 100–106, 130, 133–34, 232–33
Poensgen, O. H., 65n, 66n
political business cycles, 133
political parties, 86; technical expertise
    vs. that of producer groups, 109
Pontusson, J., 108n, 213n, 214n, 216n,
    217n, 218n, 220n, 221n, 270n
Posner, M., 32n, 77n, 86n, 205n
Poulantzas, N., 37n
Powell, G. B., 9n, 280n
Price, V., 31n, 32n, 79n
private enterprise. *See* privately owned
    enterprise
private enterprise economy: definition,
    xi, 228n; structural and behavioral
    barriers to efficiency, 62–66;
    workings and welfare consequences
    of, 60–69, 229–32, 237–38. *See also*
    corporatist–private enterprise
    political economy; pluralist–private
    enterprise political economy
privately owned enterprise: behavior in
    comparison to state-owned enter-
    prise, 11–13; compatibility with
    democracy, 6, 276–81; as foreign
    enterprise, 231–32; in liberal

privately owned enterprise (*cont.*)
theory, 60–61; as national
champion, 233–35; privileged
position of owners, 130, 152
privatization, 6, 11; in Austria, 11, 171,
196–99; in Britain, 11, 150, 153–
54, 160, 266; in Italy, 203n, 208–9
Prodi, R., 28n, 31n, 41n, 49n, 78n,
209n, 268n
Proporz, 117n, 171, 188, 191, 193,
200–201, 210. *See also* Austria
Pryke, R., 79n, 155n, 159–60n, 164n,
166n, 167n, 253n
Przeworski, A., 7n, 13n, 29n, 42–44,
45n, 46n, 47n, 48n, 49n, 50n, 57n,
86n, 109n, 113n
public enterprise. *See* state-owned
enterprise
Putnam, R., 93n

Rae, D., 67n
Raiffa, H., 30n
Reconstruction Finance Corporation, 40
Redwood, J., 6n, 73n, 76n, 150n,
154–55n, 156n, 157n, 164n
Regini, M., 206n, 207n, 214n, 222n
Rehn, G., 212–13n, 214n, 219n
Reich, R., 138–39n
Riker, W., 139n
Rivlin, A., 212n, 271n
Rockman, B., 93n
Rogowski, R., 250n
Rohatyn, F., 3n
Roll, E., 160n, 166n
Ross, G., 207n, 209n, 212–13n
Rowley, C., 164n, 167n
Ruth, A., 214n, 217n, 219n

Sabel, C., 92n, 110n, 207n, 216n
Sachs, I., 39n
Salvati, M., 89n, 92–93n, 208n
Sandmo, A., 69n, 71n, 72n, 77n
scale of firms, 64–65, 284
Schiantarelli, F., 204n, 205n, 206n
Schloss, H. H., 31n
Schmidt, E., 107n, 125n, 172n, 192n
Schmitter, P., 5n, 91n, 107n, 150n, 172n,
203n, 207n, 210n, 211n
Schneider, F., 88n
Seidel, H., 177n, 190n
Selvik, A., 108n
Sen, A. K., 67n, 77n
Shafer, M., 228n, 236n, 238n
Shonfield, A., 40n, 52n, 72–73n, 109n,
163n
Short, R. P., 9, 10, 182n
Silberston, A., 159n

Sinn Fein Workers Party, 79n, 89n
Sinowatz, F., 199
Skocpol, T., 39n, 47n
Skouras, A., 153n
Social Democratic Party, 163n
Soskice, D., 92n
Smith, A., 22
state administration, 82, 92–96, 250; in
corporatist–mixed systems, 128–29;
in corporatist–private enterprise
systems, 110–11; in pluralist–mixed
systems, 120–21; in pluralist–
private enterprise systems, 104–6
state enterprise workers: collective
ownership efficacy, 126–28; privileged position, 79–80, 126–30,
238n, 240, 245–50, 276–81. *See also*
Austria; Wellington-Winter
hypothesis
state entrepreneurship, philosophy of,
41
state-owned enterprise: behavior
compared to private enterprise,
11–13; compatibility with
democracy, 5–6, 276–81; financial
performance, 8; foreign public,
230–36; investment and social
welfare, 8–10; in liberal theory,
22–25, 69–71; as national champion
239–41; in radical theory, 27–33
Steel, D., 29n, 48n, 150n, 164n, 165n,
169n
Stefani, G., 31n, 76n, 203n, 205n, 207n,
267n, 269n
Stern, G., 84n
Stoffaes, G., 13n
Suleiman, E., 52n, 93n
Sweden: capital market and mobility,
212, 278; corporatism, 211, 215–23;
nationalized industries (state-owned
enterprises), 213–15; openness of
economy, 269–72; party politics,
217; pension funds, 213, 217n,
218n, 270; state administrators,
217–18; workings of political
economy and social welfare, 211–14,
relative to Austria, 211, 219–21,
270–72, relative to Britain, 151,
211, 214, 219, 222–23, 270–72, relative to Italy, 140–41, 211, 214, 219,
222. *See also* wage earner funds

Taus, J., 201n
Tennessee Valley Authority, 40n
Thatcher administrations, 48, 150–66,
171, 255–57
Theorem of the Second Best, 63n

Theory of the Optimum Regime, 23–27
Thonet, P. J., 65n, 66n
Tilton, T., 32n, 44n, 113n, 217n, 219n
Tinbergen, J., 23–27
Tivey, L., 167n, 169n
Tomandl, T., 172n, 184n, 185n, 187n, 189n
Törnblom, L., 211n, 213n, 215n, 270n
Trade Union Congress (TUC), 149–50, 160n, 222n
Truchil, B., 38
Tulkens, H., 29–30
Tumlir, J., 177n, 204n
Turner, J., 86n
Turner, L., 3n, 143–44n, 152n, 173n, 176n, 183n, 184n

Ulman, L., 92n
ungovernability thesis, 6n
United States: as mixed economy, 14n, 40; political economy compared to that of Austria, 264

Vak, K., 177n
Vallet, C., 78n
Van der Bellen, A., 28n, 76n, 178n, 188n, 190n, 200n, 201n, 261n
Véliz, C., 52n
Vernon, R., 11n, 27n, 236–37n, 238–39n, 246n
Violette, E. M., 40n

von Beyme, K., 146, 150n, 173n, 203n, 211n
Von Furstenberg, G. M., 25n, 27n, 68n, 71n

Wade, R., 206n, 208n, 209n
Wadensjo, E., 217n
wage earner funds, 216, 220–22, 271
Wallerstein, M., 42–44, 45n, 46n, 47n, 49n, 50n, 57n, 62n, 63n, 64n, 67n, 90n, 110n, 228–29n, 234n
Walters, K. D., 6n, 8n, 11n, 29n, 205n, 211n, 230n, 231n, 256n
welfare criteria, 8–14, 137–40
Wellington-Winter hypothesis, 50n, 79, 159n. *See also* state enterprise workers
Wiesenthal, H., 91–92n, 109n
Wilensky, H., 3n, 143–44n, 152n, 173n, 176n, 183n, 184n
Wiles, P., 139n
Willett, T., 181n
Wilson, E., xi
Woolf, S., 205n
Wright, E., 7n, 15n, 279n

Zaller, J., 85n
Zysman, J., 6n, 49n, 52n, 64n, 68n, 87n, 93n, 94n, 102n, 105n, 160–61n, 163n, 167n, 229n

Cornell Studies in Political Economy

EDITED BY PETER J. KATZENSTEIN

Collapse of an Industry: Nuclear Power and the Contradictions of U.S. Policy, by John L. Campbell

Power, Purpose, and Collective Choice: Economic Strategy in Socialist States, edited by Ellen Comisso and Laura D'Andrea Tyson

The Political Economy of the New Asian Industrialism, edited by Frederic C. Deyo

Dislodging Multinationals: India's Strategy in Comparative Perspective, by Dennis J. Encarnation

Democracy and Markets: The Politics of Mixed Economies, by John R. Freeman

The Misunderstood Miracle: Industrial Development and Political Change in Japan, by David Friedman

Politics in Hard Times: Comparative Responses to International Economic Crises, by Peter Gourevitch

Closing the Gold Window: Domestic Politics and the End of Bretton Woods, by Joanne Gowa

The Philippine State and the Marcos Regime: The Politics of Export, by Gary Hawes

Reasons of State: Oil Politics and the Capacities of American Government, by G. John Ikenberry

The State and American Foreign Economic Policy, edited by G. John Ikenberry, David A. Lake, and Michael Mastanduno

Pipeline Politics: The Complex Political Economy of East-West Energy Trade, by Bruce W. Jentleson

The Politics of International Debt, edited by Miles Kahler

Corporatism and Change: Austria, Switzerland, and the Politics of Industry, by Peter J. Katzenstein

Small States in World Markets: Industrial Policy in Europe, by Peter J. Katzenstein

Industry and Politics in West Germany: Toward the Third Republic, edited by Peter J. Katzenstein

The Sovereign Entrepreneur: Oil Policies in Advanced and Less Developed Capitalist Countries, by Merrie Gilbert Klapp

International Regimes, edited by Stephen D. Krasner

Power, Protection, and Free Trade: International Sources of U.S. Commercial Strategy, 1887–1939, by David A. Lake

State Capitalism: Public Enterprise in Canada, by Jeanne Kirk Laux and Maureen Appel Molot

Opening Financial Markets: Banking Politics on the Pacific Rim, by Louis W. Pauly

The Business of the Japanese State: Energy Markets in Comparative and Historical Perspective, by Richard J. Samuels

In the Dominions of Debt: Historical Perspectives on Dependent Development, by Herman M. Schwartz

Europe and the New Technologies, edited by Margaret Sharp

Europe's Industries: Public and Private Strategies for Change, edited by Geoffrey Shepherd, François Duchêne, and Christopher Saunders

Fair Shares: Unions, Pay, and Politics in Sweden and West Germany, by Peter Swenson

National Styles of Regulation: Environmental Policy in Great Britain and the United States, by David Vogel

International Cooperation: Building Regimes for Natural Resources and the Environment, by Oran R. Young

Governments, Markets, and Growth: Financial Systems and the Politics of Industrial Change, by John Zysman

American Industry in International Competition: Government Policies and Corporate Strategies, edited by John Zysman and Laura Tyson

Library of Congress Cataloging-in-Publication Data

Freeman, John R., 1950–
  Democracy and markets : the politics of mixed economies / John R.
Freeman.
      p.   cm. — (Cornell studies in political economy)
  Bibliography :   p.
  Includes index.
  ISBN 0–8014–2326–0 (alk. paper)
  ISBN 0–8014–9601–2 (pbk.: alk. paper)
  1. Comparative economics.   2. Comparative government.
3. Capitalism.   4. Mixed economy.   I. Title   II. Series.
HB90.F73   1989   330—dc19   89–869

Comments —
— Figure typos
p. 184   4T